THIS WAS THE ESSENCE OF THEIR WORK: HOURS OF BOREDOM INTERRUPTED BY SECONDS OF SHEER HEART-STOPPING TERROR

The Emergency cops were getting a bit tired standing around up against the door, their heavy tools in hand, yet the job was suddenly interrupted by what sounded like a *thomp* . . . followed by a high-pitched scream. "Shit, he's killing them!" yelled one of the cops. "Crank up the Hurst tool!" While several officers maneuvered the Hurst tool around the door frame, Police Officer Dan Donnelly began pounding the wall with his sledgehammer, hoping to create a hole large enough to reach in and grab a hostage. The cops didn't know if Miller had shot at them or at his parents. A sense of desperation set in. Gnawing feelings began to creep from the inner stomachs of the E-men up toward their chests and throats. They didn't know what they'd face on the other side of the door. . . .

Chronicling a harrowing year spent closely documenting daily life inside NYPD's Truck-Two, Samuel M. Katz delivers a riveting, moment-by-moment account of this elite, lifesaving squad, and the courageous officers who will be called into action . . .

ANYTIME, ANYWHERE!

Books by Samuel M. Katz

Anytime, Anywhere!
The Night Raiders: Israel's Naval Commandos at War
Fire & Steel
The Elite

Published by POCKET BOOKS

ANYTIME, ANYWHERE!

ON PATROL WITH THE NYPD'S EMERGENCY SERVICE UNIT

SAMUEL M. KATZ

POCKET BOOKS
New York London Toronto Sydney Tokyo Singapore

An *Original* Publication of POCKET BOOKS

POCKET BOOKS, a division of Simon & Schuster Inc.
1230 Avenue of the Americas, New York, NY 10020

ISBN: 0-671-00342-9

First Pocket Books printing December 1997

10 9 8 7 6 5 4 3 2

POCKET and colophon are registered trademarks of Simon & Schuster Inc.

Cover photos courtesy of the author.
Unless otherwise indicated, all insert photos are courtesy of the author's collection.

Printed in the U.S.A.

This book is dedicated to the loving memory of

Police Officer Joseph P. McCormack, #27434
Emergency Service Squad No. 2

and

Police Officer James P. McKenny, #26734
Emergency Service Squad No. 2

We are all diminished by their loss.

To Uncle Everetts + Aunt Pat

Love, Jackie's "AICA ICON"

Acknowledgments

•

"Highway One Sergeant to Central, K. I am ninety-eight from the fifty-three pin on the Harlem River Drive and 155. Please thank responding Emergency Service personnel, as always, for their assistance and backup . . ."

There are very few police departments like the New York City Police Department, and very few specialized units like the NYPD's Emergency Service Unit (ESU). A 400-man, and -woman, force, ESU is one of the only police tactical units in the United States that does both SWAT and emergency rescue jobs. It is certainly the largest unit of its kind anywhere, and the world's most experienced. ESU cops are jacks of all trades and have been known to be in the middle of the East River one moment searching for a drowning victim and, with their automatic weapons at the ready, kicking down the door of a crack den along with narcotics detectives an hour later. Their tasks run full circle in the 360 degrees of life and death in a city where everything and anything has been known to happen. This book is a small glimpse into the life and times of one Emergency Service Unit truck, or squad, in New York City over the course of about one year. This book is a serious look at the life-and-death situations that these super-cops must face on a daily basis, and the routine interrupted by the few moments of sheer terror and exhilaration that these officers encounter while on patrol. This book is also a lighthearted look at police work and at the heart and soul of a small part of that greater society known as the New York City Police Department.

Yet this book is a lot more than one particular ESU squad under the microscope, and it is more than a look at a unit, a department, and a city. This book is a story about individuals. It is a look at brave cops who, for no extra pay and very little orchestrated recognition, perform the impossible on a daily basis—both in the course of their duties as police officers and as lifesavers, rescuing anyone and everyone in distress that they can get to in time, no matter if they are trapped in the twisted remnants of a car or standing precariously over a ledge looking to take the plunge into the suicidal mess of a city sidewalk. On a personal note, however, this book is a testament to the career of one man, Lt. Bob Sobocienski. In his twenty-eight years on the job with the NYPD, from walking a foot post in Harlem's notorious 3–2 Precinct to being the man in charge of the counter-sniper detail during "UN 50," Bob Sobocienski has done his job in the only way he knew how—professionally, successfully, and with his warm, and now trademark, smile. New York City has had only a few men like Bob Sobocienski protecting its citizens from crime and harm, and it was a safer place to be while he was on patrol and on the job.

In the four years that I have known "Lieutenant Sobo," as he is known to about half the NYPD, I was lucky enough to make a terrific friend, and fortunate enough to learn from the very best this city has produced. Beyond being one of the most decorated officers in the NYPD's history, Sobo was a true Harlem cop. A street cop who relied on his instincts, his sense of duty, and a tireless dedication to the job. There is a difference between a Harlem cop and one who serves elsewhere in the city. It is something in their faces, in the glare in their eye, the confidence in their step, and their very sarcastic view of life. "You don't become a good cop working in a slow house," reflected one decorated cop now serving as an ESU lieutenant. "It is in the ghetto, in a shitty precinct, where the empty data banks in a young rookie's head are quickly filled with knowledge, experience, guts, and street smarts." There is a term for cops who are energetic and dedicated to the job. They are known as *workers*. Harlem cops are workers—plain and simple.

If there ever was a worker in the NYPD, Lieutenant Sobocienski was it. I met Lieutenant Sobocienski while I was writing my first book on ESU, called *NYPD: On the Streets with the Elite Emergency Service Unit,* and watching him in action was an awe-inspiring display of a great cop at work. Although during some of his tours on patrol, he was a citywide supervisor, responsible for ESU jobs from the southernmost tip of Brooklyn to the northernmost stretch of the Bronx, Lieutenant Sobo's favorite stomping grounds were the streets of Harlem and Manhattan North. He knew each and every street like the back of his hand, he could glance into an alleyway and determine if it was good or being used for narcotics sales, and would cruise in his unmarked Chevy Caprice searching for a job, looking to help with an arrest or assist the beat cops in the course of their duty. More often than not, he would find himself leaping from his car, Glock in hand, to assist members of the department in arresting drug dealers, robbers, and murderers.

Although he was a member of a citywide unit, Harlem and Manhattan North was still pumping through Lieutenant Sobo's veins, as it was his first tour on patrol in 1969. It is where he enjoyed working the most, and where he had many of his biggest jobs. It is often said of the Emergency Service Unit that "when a citizen needs help, he calls a cop; when a cop needs help, he calls ESU." In his years in ESU, Lt. Bob Sobocienski was a lifesaving and reassuring "911" to a good many cops—from plainclothes cops in the Street Crime Unit to the chief of the department. On many big jobs, "the really big jobs," NYPD Chief of Department Louis R.

Anemone (himself a legendary Harlem cop) would always reach the scene, walk past a small army of deputy chiefs, inspectors, and captains who had gathered to brief him, but always head straight for Lieutenant Sobocienski. "Bobby, what do we have here?" Chief Anemone would often ask, knowing that on any big job, there wasn't a cop he'd rather have running things than Lieutenant Sobo.

But just as a police officer becomes a true street cop by working in a busy house, in ESU you become a good E-man by working in a busy truck, and Two-Truck is the unit's busiest squad. The officers there are all Harlem cops in their hearts and souls. It doesn't matter if they have been in the department for a dozen years or if they are former housing and transit cops, they are all workers. And they are all terrific E-men and -women.

As the fortunate—and grateful—soul that Lt. Bob Sobocienski took under his wing, I found that Harlem, Manhattan North, and Two-Truck became my favored stomping grounds. With Lieutenant Sobocienski as my rabbi (the departmental slang for "guardian angel") and the cops of Two-Truck serving as my tutors, I was privileged to learn about the NYPD and the Emergency Service Unit from the inside. It was a fascinating place to visit, to observe, and to learn. I knew that I wanted to write more about these incredible cops. The adrenaline of Manhattan North was infectious; a unique part of the city, from 59th Street in the heart of Midtown to the Bronx frontier, it encompassed the richest parts of the city and the poorest Two-Truck is responsible for everything from the most glamorous zip codes on the island of Manhattan to areas where people live in abandoned buildings. This place had it all, and I knew that if I would be lucky enough to write another book on the unit, this was the truck I'd want to focus on.

It goes without saying that this book never would have been possible without the friendship, support, guidance, tutelage, intervention, and interest of Lt. Bob Sobocienski. Meeting him turned out to be one of the luckiest things ever to happen to me, and becoming his close friend and eager student has developed into one of my life's happiest turn of events.

Before he retired, Lieutenant Sobocienski saw to it that I was well taken care of in the unit, and, as always, Lieutenant Sobo performed above and beyond the call of duty. He put me in the hands of some of the most decorated and dedicated cops, bosses, and E-men, who not only have gone on to serve as true inspirations but have also become close friends. There are literally hundreds of cops who deserve a heartfelt thanks for their assistance, enthusiasm, and outright help in writing this book. They are too numerous to mention here, and they might not want a public acknowledgment. Yet I am sure that they know who they are, they all know how grateful I am to them, and, most importantly, they know how much I care for them all. I was in awe watching them in action and listening to their tales, and I am forever grateful to them for their friendship. And these cops aren't solely from Truck-Two in Harlem. In working with the unit, I have come across ESU cops in the Bronx, Brooklyn, Queens, and Staten Island who are nothing but spectacular in the execution of their duties, their dedication to the job, most of all, their desire to make a difference. These cops have climbed the outer walls of Grand Central Station to talk down jumpers, and they have risked their lives in unforgiving currents to pull in drowning victims. They have lifted cranes off trapped citizens, and they have wandered into the gauntlet of incoming bullets. These remarkable police officers have made news, and they have made history. These super-cops are underpaid, underappreciated, and under-celebrated, yet they continue to perform an impossible mission on a daily basis with the utmost professionalism, with infrangible guts and determined skill, without the glory these heroes truly deserve. I am incredibly honored that they have included me in their unique world and made me part of their special family. They have taught me, looked after me, and made me feel as if I, too, wore the ESU cap on the job. My affection for them is clear and evident in the following pages of this book. They are truly a unit second to none.

Stay safe, guys—you are all the best!

I would like to offer a very special word of thanks to Inspector John Harkins, the commander of ESU, for his support and kindness. I would like to thank former Deputy Commissioner for Public Information Tom Kelly for authorizing the book (twice) and offer my most sincere gratitude to the current (at the time of this writing) DCPI Marilyn Mode for authorizing this book and making it all possible. I would also like to thank Detective J. Martinez for being *the* contact who made sure that all the paperwork concerning this request was processed expeditiously, righteously, and properly.

I would also like to offer a special word of thanks to S.V., D.P.D., J.G., V.T.M., and R.P. for getting me from Point A to Point B so often and so happily. I am forever grateful to you for all your kindness and help. I would also like to thank Joe Kuedlhaus (ESS-3-Retired) and the survivors of the shield.

A very warm thanks must go to my agent, Al Zuckerman. Al's belief in me and this project helped me through the rough spots and raised me toward another level of writing. Words cannot express my thanks to him. I would also like to offer my gratitude to my editor, Tris Coburn. A true professional and a good friend, Tris labored long and hard for this book—from its inception to the chaos induced by having to read through the first (and subsequent) drafts of the manuscript. This book never would have been possible without him, and I am forever grateful for his support and the opportunity.

Finally, I would like to offer a loving word of thanks to my wife, Sigi, for patiently and understandably enduring my long nights out, at all hours, in some of the oddest places of the city, realizing that this book was not an easy one to assemble and write, and understanding that an author, under the gun of a deadline, was not always the easiest person to live with. As always, Sigi was sweet, supportive, and an often needed crutch to lean on.

Samuel M. Katz
New York City, March 1997

Author's Note on Cop Talk, Cop Comedy, and Cop Anonymity

"Do you speak English?" the E-cop asked the cab driver he pulled over for failing to give the right of way to a responding police vehicle with its lights flashing and siren on.

"What does it say on my truck?" the cop continues to ask. "What does P-O-L-I-C-E spell? What does E-M-E-R-G-E-N-C-Y spell?"

By its very mandate, the New York City Police Department is meant to protect and to serve the citizens of the five boroughs no matter who the mayor is, what party he is from, or which political bosses are in charge of the city council. The NYPD is meant to be an apolitical department, but nothing in the City of New York is that simple or that clean and dry. Politicians often use the police department and impressive crime statistics as an electioneering prop, much as they use the photo op of kissing a cute baby, as a backdrop to get votes. Cops are often a politician's best friend, and politicians often refer to the department as a sacred entity of virtue and sacrifice. Once the shit hits the fan, however, and a scapegoat is needed for political expediency, the department and the careers and lives of good cops are often hung out to dry with unforgiving abandon. While the practice is not fair, it comes part and parcel with the job description.

The department, too, is far from immune from the

trappings of politics. Like any large bureaucracy, the NYPD is a highly political organization where hooks, connections, and political clout can mean the difference between being a gold shield detective or an E-man in ESU, or walking a foot post along a deserted rail yard in Staten Island. Often, it isn't what you know that propels you ahead, but whom you know. And, of course, you are propelled even further when others know exactly whom you know. A powerful hook is worn on a uniform in much the same way as a shield and decorations. It has been that way in the NYPD, in one form or another, ever since the 1840s, when commissioners had the power personally to appoint all members to the force, and it continues to this day. The currency of politics is as much a part of the department and the bureaucracy that interconnects City Hall and One Police Plaza as anywhere else in a pulsating metropolis built atop a mosaic of different races, creeds, religions, and individual sensitivities. Surviving in the political maze is a thriving facet of the currency that is the NYPD society—it has always been like that and probably always will be.

Against the backdrop of this political minefield that is New York City and its police department is the fact that this is also the media capital of the world. With its four major daily newspapers and ten television stations broadcasting news at least three times a day, the city is a camera lens and a writer's pad constantly in search of a story. The city, as a result, is a fifth-estate feeding frenzy that is competitive, cruel, and, often, satisfied with hysteria-inducing headlines and sound bites over truth and justice. As a result of this vibrant electricity that permeates City Hall, the police department, and every other facet of public life, virtually every public statement made by a public servant (notably an NYPD public servant), from a patrolman being interviewed by New York One to a chief commenting to a reporter "off the record," even a benign off-the-cuff remark, has the potential of erupting into a fireball of political controversy that could eventually reach to the pinnacles of power in

One Police Plaza or even City Hall. As a result, each cop will think a few dozen times before he or she will open his or her mouth and talk freely outside the safe confines of a patrol car. Any statement, even an innocent reflection, could come back to haunt a cop at a later date in his or her career, and go as far as even squashing a highly promising future in the department. That self-imposed gag order, a survival reflex, is an understandable additional veil of armor that cops wear alongside their guts and bulletproof vests each turn out for a tour of duty. One thing cops are not, especially in New York City, is PC—politically correct. Cops are often loud and boisterous in their opinions, and their language is truly unique. It is profane, prophetic, and pointed, and it often hits home with the painful reverberations of truth and candor. Their terminology, responses, and cadence are meant as a pure sarcastic reflection of the life and death that surround their everyday lives on the job.

The cops' wall of silent armor is really a pity, though. Cops are terrific observers of the human condition—even in a city as complex as New York, and in a department as large, diverse, and politically entrenched as the NYPD. They see humanity at its best and at its worst, and they are social workers, psychologists, and social critics as astute as can be found in an Ivy League think tank. I truly believe that you can learn more about life, love, liberty, and laughter by spending eight hours in a police car than you can after spending eight years in a graduate school classroom.

The cops I talked with while assembling material for this book truly educated me with their views, their knowledge, and their language. They had me sitting down many times, my mouth open in awe and disbelief, as they explained, in sentences spoken with the rigidity of a police report and the language of a teamster, about shoot-outs, perp searches, and rescues where seconds were the deciding factor between life and death. These same cops, in describing other jobs, often forced me to grasp at the inner reaches of my internal stamina to keep from keeling over in laughter. Cops have to be, by the very nature of the job, great comedians; they are Rhodes scholars in the often cruel but always "right on the mark" honesty of that social affliction known as NYPD humor. There are many officers in ESU, and a few in Two-Truck, who could literally make a million dollars working a stand-up comedy routine. Humor, however, isn't a personality trait on the job; it is a survival mechanism. Their uniform might attempt to shield them from the elements, and their Kevlar PBA vest might be useful in protecting their vital organs from certain types of bullets, but cops see too much shit not to be affected somehow. As a result, as an extra layer of protection to their outer skeletons, cops tend to laugh at misery with vengeance rather than cry at the inhumanity and cruelty. It is better to stand over a murdered drug dealer, his body riddled with bullets, and say, "Having a bad morning, are we, fella?" than for cops to allow their psyches to be overcome by the blood-soaked, stench-of-a-rotting-corpse landscape that they'll have to wash off their boots once they return to quarters. A cop's sense of humor isn't kind, nor is it anywhere near being politically correct. Anyone can become a target, and everyone is the brunt of someone's biting wit or tirade. The more sensitive the target, the more cruel the barrage. It is the kind of biting humor that, if taken out of context, could cut a blossoming career short and get an officer in trouble with everyone from the NAACP to B'nai B'rith to the Hindu League of America to the Sons of Italy. When in the safety of their natural surroundings, cops are brutally honest. If they hate anything, they despise bullshit. The bullshit police and the cruel humor are especially cruel inside the confines of an ESU squad, where the cops not only work together but live together as well.

In sharing about themselves and many of their jobs, the cops I talked to for this book treated me as one of their own and often held back little while I talked to them in quarters. In order to maintain the careers and camouflage the identities of the some of the department's most insightful social and political critics, as well as some of the department's funniest and most sarcastic SOBs, I have taken the liberty of adding an additional officer to the Truck-Two roster who will be known as "Officer Anonymous." Officer Anonymous is both male and female, black and white, Jewish and Gentile, E-man and regular cop on patrol. Officer Anonymous speaks Spanish and is also old school Irish, brogue and all. Officer Anonymous is the true soul of a cop and his or her well-protected mouthpiece, an anonymous reflection of the honesty of a cop, a cop's humor-filled means of coping with the difficult, the desperate, the terrifying, and the heart-wrenching. Officer Anonymous speaks for none of the cops featured here and for all of them. Officer Anonymous is their silent soul.

ANYTIME, ANYWHERE!

Introduction: The NYPD's Ballistic Backup

•

"ESU-4 to Central, K"

"Go ahead, ESU-4."

"Central, this is ESU-4. For the past twenty-eight years, it has been my good fortune to serve the people of the City of New York as a member of the New York City Police Department. The greatest police department in the world. During the past seven years, I have had the honor of working with all of you while being assigned as citywide supervisor with the Emergency Service Unit. These are distinctions which I shall forever be proud of. As I finish my final tour of duty with the department, I would like to say thank you to all of my brother and sister officers. It has been a pleasure working alongside you through the years. I commend you for your dedication to duty and applaud your professionalism.

"Thank you for your suggestions, and always making me look good on the big one.

"Thanks for taking care of me during these years and for protecting my family—our family. We all will always be family.

"Let it be known there will never come a day in my life that I will not think of all of you with pride.

In closing, I'd like to say God bless the New York City Police Department, God bless the job, and God bless and protect each one of you forever.
"Central, this is ESU-4. End of career!"
—Lt. Robert Sobocienski, June 28, 1996

A cop lives by the encyclopedic knowledge of police work that comes only with his experience, the proximity of his partner, and the sharpness of his instincts. Instincts, to a cop, are like having a second gun, a second vest, and nine lives. If your gut tells you not to go into an alley until your partner has called in a ten-thirteen, the radio code for "officer needing assistance," then you'll probably be back on duty the next shift, instead of being readied for a wake. If your instincts tell you a scene is wrong, a face looks guilty, or a trigger needs to be depressed, it is a personal call that must be taken. And when you've been a decorated cop for twenty-eight years and are one day before retiring, if instinct tells you not to come to work on your last day, you wake up late, kiss the wife, and be grateful that you didn't suit up that one final time. Cops survive by their instincts.

June 29, 1996, was supposed to be Lt. Bob Sobocienski's last day of work—for months, he knew that it would be the last day of a brilliant twenty-eight-year career on the job as one of the most decorated cops in the history of the New York City Police Department. Being a cop was all Bob Sobocienski knew how to do—his veins bled NYPD blue from the day he was eighteen. In his professional career, he never had to ask the boss for a raise and never had to look for work. Bob Sobocienski was simply a cop, and with twenty-eight years on the job, he was one of the most experienced and trusted bosses in the Emergency Service Unit. As his mind debated the merits of retirement over staying on the job throughout the months of May and June, he continued being a cop as if retirement were the last thing on the horizon and as if he'd be suiting up for another twenty-eight years. With only a few weeks to go until he'd be tending to his small farm and enjoying not having to drive an hour to get to work every day, he would still race out of his red unmarked Chevy Caprice supervisor's car at the sight of trouble or danger.

But as his final day of being on the job neared, the realization that he'd need to start saying his good-byes soon dawned upon him and gained a sense of urgency. In twenty-eight years, you make a lot of friends and work with a lot of people whose faces you trust, whose sense of humor keeps you laughing on the floor for hours, and who you'd want to be behind you while chasing a gunman through the darkened halls of a Harlem tenement. Yet, in twenty-eight years on the job, you also develop a sixth sense concerning danger and concerning a situation not being exactly right. You need courage to be a cop, but courage without instinct ends up getting someone killed. Instinct helps you survive. You are usually born brave, but instincts are taught. Lieutenant Sobocienski was taught to survive as a young patrolman in Harlem's notorious 3–2 Precinct, as an anticrime officer in the 3–2, and later as a plainclothes member of the 3–2 Precinct's Special Narcotics Enforcement Unit. Instinct had helped Lieutenant Sobocienski earn an astounding chest full of medals and citations, and it had helped him, as a boss, lead squads of E-men in some dangerous jobs, on some precarious "hits," in some of the nastiest bits of real estate New York City has ever known.

Instinct, however, told Lieutenant Sobocienski that he should take off on his last day of work—that he should end his career on a Friday and not the Saturday's "four-by" (the department's term for the 4:00 P.M. to midnight shift). Instinct had served Bob Sobocienski and the city well for twenty-eight years. It wouldn't let him down now, either. June 29, 1996, was a good day to stay at home.

It was a bright and sunny afternoon in Harlem, and both Police Officers Dan Donnelly and John D'Allara arrived for work early at the Emergency Service Unit

Truck-Two's quarters on 126th Street and Old Broadway, "in the good part of Harlem." Saturday nights were usually busy, but there was a relaxed atmosphere that night. The temperatures had reached the mid-eighties, the citywide Special Operations Division (SOD) radio was quiet, and the mood in quarters, and their Third Squad, was a surprisingly happy one. Sgt. Juan Garcia, the squad supervisor, was drinking a cup of coffee and attending to some paperwork, while Police Officer Steve Vales, one of the squad's senior members, was taking care of the log book and the Two-Truck mascot, a nine-year-old boxer named Mojo.

"What we doing tonight?" Donnelly asked, checking the roll call to see what his assignment for the night was.

"You and D'Allara are flying to Three-Truck," Sergeant Garcia advised. "There is some big hit in the Bronx somewhere, and they need you guys to cover."

"Ten-four, Sarge," Officer D'Allara responded. "You guys will do anything to get rid of us."

Although both Donnelly and D'Allara were veteran Harlem cops, both had started their careers in law enforcement in the treacherous confines of the Bronx, D'Allara as a cop in the 4-6 Pct. and the Bronx Task Force and Donnelly as a beat cop in "Fort Apache," the notorious 4–1 Precinct in the South Bronx. Donnelly's dad, in fact, had served as a fireman in Engine Company 82, a unit that, when the Bronx burned in the late seventies, was the busiest firehouse in the world.

Although both cops would have preferred to stay in Harlem, it was too nice an afternoon to bitch and moan. The Third Squad in Three-Truck were all good cops and a friendly group of guys, and, what's more, they were known throughout the division for cooking the best dinners in all of Emergency Service.

For Lt. Richard Greene, one of the Emergency Service Unit's premier tactical officers, the sunshine and refreshing summer's breeze were doing little to remove the inner gnawing of a cop's instinct telling him some nasty shit was about to come down. The hit in the Bronx was his baby, and it had all the signs of a miscarriage. Even though he had been coordinating the operation with the Bronx narcotics task force and the Drug Enforcement Administration for several weeks, Greene was experienced enough, smart enough, and tactically proficient enough to know that this night was going to be a hairy one. It was going to be a night of the "Oh shits!"

The DEA was after the "Power Rule," a notoriously violent drug gang that made its mark ripping off narcotics and cash from other groups, often at the barrel of a gun. The DEA wanted to snare the gang into a sting operation, where they'd be able to steal a large supply of cocaine and cash ostensibly from a rival drug organization. The drug gang, a mixed cast of Hispanics and blacks, was known to favor heavy firepower. The festivities were to come down inside a warehouse in the Bronx Terminal Market, a squalored piece of commercial real estate that handled much of the city's produce. Situated in the shadows of Yankee Stadium, the Terminal Market overlooked the Harlem River and Manhattan to the west and the Grand Concourse, a primary artery in the Bronx, to the west.

The Emergency Service Unit's Apprehension Team One, an eight-man force permanently on call for serving tactical warrants led by Sgt. Tommy Urban, was to provide heavy firepower backup for the joint NYPD-DEA operation. But even the eight men assigned to Sergeant Urban's team, with their Heckler and Koch MP-5 9mm submachine guns and Ruger Mini-14 5.56mm assault rifles, needed additional firepower. The perps were shooters and not the type to be cuffed without a struggle. Lieutenant Greene summoned four extra bodies for the hit—Al Powell and Larry Serras from Seven-Truck and Jim Malley and Richie Winwood of Three-Truck. Something big was brewing in the Bronx, and ESU wanted to be ready.

The prehit tactical briefing was held at the old 4-4 Precinct station house on the Major Deegan Expressway just before the turnoff ramp to the George Washington

Bridge. Usually, the mood at the tac meeting is one of smiles and schmoozing. The ESU cops seek out past acquaintances working in the precinct, and the chance to mill about and talk always brings about that great NYPD talent known as bullshitting. This time, however, there was little socializing to be done. The Bronx narcotics detectives, dressed in plainclothes adorned by gold shields and Kevlar body armor vests, were serious and deadpan. The federal narcotics agents, always distanced and professional, were aloof and anxious. The mood did not breed an enormous sense of confidence among the ESU cops, nor did the operational plan. To snare the drug gang off guard, the narcotics detectives and DEA agents would mill about the hangarlike warehouse until the bad guys arrived, and the ESU cops would lie in wait inside a graffiti-covered meatpacking truck used by the DEA for covert surveillance and stakeout operations, waiting for the bust to go down and their services to be needed.

In the parking lot of the old 4–4 station house, now home to the NYPD's Bronx task force, the Emergency Service Unit officers went tactical. They put on their heavy Kevlar tactical vests and Fritz helmets, readied the diversionary devices, and locked and loaded their weapons. Without the banter and joking that usually preceded a hit, the cops entered the rear of the truck and ventured south for the ten-minute drive into the market. For the duration of the sting, until they were to burst through the rear door and assist in the apprehension of the perps, the cops were to remain absolutely silent in the rear of the truck—silence not being one of the stronger talents of a New York City police officer. Inside the meat truck, the officers sat in pitch darkness and absolute silence, their only visual link to the outside world being a small peephole where the cops had placed the optic-fiber lens of a peep camera

"It was uncomfortable as hell inside the truck," one of the cops remembered, "and we were all broiling in our PBA vests, tactical vests, and helmets. To break the tension, the cops began to joke that their peeking through the peephole reminded them of a *Little Rascals* episode. Which one is Spanky? Who is Alfalfa? Who is Porky? We all began to joke. Lieutenant Greene naturally volunteered himself as Buckwheat."

But the jokes and the smiles were brave efforts to mask some very true anxieties. Lieutenant Greene sat stoically in silence with a radio earpiece in his left ear as he monitored the DEA frequency. When the perps arrived, stoic silence turned somber. It was showtime.

Eight perps arrived in four separate cars, and, as one of the cops recalls, "they must have just come from a christening, a wedding, or a bar-mitzvah, because they were dressed in their Sunday best—dark suits, white shirts, and patent leather shoes." The cops clutched their Mini-14s and MP-5s ever so tightly, awaiting the moment when the truck doors would swing open and they'd burst into action. The cops carrying the twelve-pound Body Bunker shields wiped the sweat off their hands as they readied their shields and Glock pistols for action, and the cops carrying the Ithaca 37 12-gauge shotguns tightened their grip around the wooden pump bars to the point where they were just about ready to pull the trigger in the split-second they'd need to.

Inside the truck, seconds felt like hours. That tense feeling of impending terror, the true essence of police work, began to fill the mind of each of the cops, and the heavy sounds of hearts thumped to an uncontrollable cadence of heavy vests restricting frightened chests from expanding.

Lieutenant Greene, known throughout the division as a boisterous and lead-from-example officer of unquestioned courage who was taken aback by very little, was equally anxious. "I have a bad feeling about this one, guys," he said in a low voice inside the truck. "Please be careful."

Yet before the DEA could summon Lieutenant Greene and his cops for the takedown, shots rang out. The first crack of gunfire resonated throughout the market like a grenade inside a crowded elevator. A collective "Fuck" was sounded, as were the sounds of ten pairs of boots racing out the rear door of a saunalike truck. Whenever shots are fired in a small area where there are lots of cops, the first order of the day is chaos. The emergency cops' first priority in such a situation is to secure the lot and sort everything out later. As several cops swung out of the truck to the left, their automatic weapons and shotguns in hand, another line moved out to the right. Had the perps been of a logical mindset (then, though, they wouldn't be perps), the entire bust would have gone down easy. In fact, two cars full of perps were taken down without as much as a "Put your hands up, motherfucker!" being uttered by the federal agents and NYPD cops. But two cars loaded with bad guys were determined not to be taken into custody, and they felt that, man for man, they could outdrive and outshoot the cops.

Firing wildly through the opened windows of the Chevy sedan, the perps swung around inside the market in a wild example of high-speed driving. Bullets were flying everywhere. Several rounds, fired by the perps, missed the cops and flew right into the open window of a truck's cab, where its driver was receiving oral favors from a fifteen-dollar-a-trick crack whore. Officer Richie Winwood, peering through the sights of his MP-5, saw that he didn't have a clear shot at the perps as they began their mad escape from the police trap; his big fear was that a round would hit someone in the background or even strike a fellow cop. Instinctively, and without any tactical justification behind it, Winwood removed a diversionary device from his front pouch, pulled the pin, and, with the accuracy and devastating speed of a Tom Seaver fastball, hurled the device at the fleeing car. Not only did the device make it to the car, but it flew in through the open window and hit the driver square in the head. Seconds later, the device, now on the driver's leg, exploded in a blinding flash and a deafening bang. Stunned and burned severely, the driver continued to burn rubber out of the Terminal Market with a small convoy of police vehicles in hot pursuit. The toss was a million-to-one shot that still has cops talking, but it worked.

The Emergency Service cops of Lieutenant Greene and Sergeant Urban grabbed a police van and followed the chaos with lights and sirens ablaze and their weapons reloaded with fresh clips of ammunition.

Officers Donnelly and D'Allara, on patrol in an REP, were in the confines of 4–1 Precinct in the south Bronx, when the ten-thirteen ("officer needing assistance") came over the SOD frequency. "Oh fucking shit," was Donnelly's response as he flashed his lights and sirens and floored his truck's gas pedal en route to the shoot-out. Unlocking the 12-gauge Ithaca shotgun and making sure that there was one round in the chamber, he raced the REP through the Bronx along with dozens of other ESU vehicles from Three-Truck in the central Bronx and from Four-Truck in the northwest Bronx. Back at Two-Truck's quarters in Harlem, Sergeant Garcia and Steve Vales did not need to wait and hear a confirmation of the job before racing down the stairs into their big response truck. They knew from the voices of the officers putting the job over that this was the real McCoy. By the time the job was confirmed and the ESU city-north supervisor was directed toward the Bronx, Garcia and Vales were racing uptown, toward the 145th Street Bridge and across the Harlem River.

The suspects were desperate to evade the enclosing net of blocked streets and responding patrol cars, and they raced through the crowded avenues of the Bronx as if they were on a speed track. To keep the pursuing cops at bay, they fired wild bursts of 9mm ammunition from the two Mac-10 submachine guns through the shot-out rear window of their Chevy. Bullets were flying like mad, pedestrians jumped into parked cars to avoid getting struck, and a sense that this job could go from bad to worse suddenly overtook many senior NYPD commanders rushing to the scene.

For the responding Emergency Service Units, tracking the job, let alone responding to it, was a mystery wrapped in confusion. The perps were swerving and turning around in their mad dash to escape the Bronx, and the dispatchers updating the developing chase were having a hard time pinpointing exactly where the pursuit had been and where it was going. Officers Donnelly and D'Allara, fearing that they might pull up on the perps, decided that in a bad-case scenario, they were simply going to ram the hell out of the fleeing felons. "Our truck is bigger than your car," was the reasoning inside the REP. Instead, it was the perps, under fire from several responding marked and unmarked cars, who rammed their speeding Chevy into a row of parked cars on East 172nd Street and Fulton Avenue in the Tremont section of the Bronx. As the cop cars moved in for the arrest, the perps were determined to go out in a blaze of gunfire and glory. The cops were only too happy to oblige. In the words of Two-Truck supervisor Sgt. Juan Garcia, "When cops face off against bad guys, the bad guys will always lose!" Such was the case in Tremont. One perp, his body left lifeless on the dirty pavement of a Bronx street corner after being peppered by police bullets, lay near the Chevy, a Mac-10 near his fingers, while the second perp, the driver, was left with scorched trousers from the detonated diversionary device and chunks of brain matter splattered throughout the car.

The perps were none too happy that warm afternoon in the Bronx, though the feds were grateful that they had the ESU backup, and the patrol units were smiling that all they had to do was rope off the area and keep the press at arm's length. For the Emergency Service Unit officers involved in the chaos, from the officers in the apprehension team to those coming in from Harlem to intercept the bad guys, they were just happy that no cops were hurt. In their heavy vests, their MP-5s hanging off their shoulders in tattered slings, the ESU cops stood around and engaged in the required postjob schmoozing right where the heart-pumping events had terrified their souls only seconds earlier. Louis R. Anemone, the NYPD's four-star chief of department, arrived at the scene and was amazed by the ballistic trail of spent shells and bullet holes left by the perps. New York City might have had a rough reputation, but it rarely hosted Hollywood-like shoot-outs and car chases. Even by New York City and NYPD standards, this was something new.

After he met with media and the assembly of chiefs, inspectors, DIs, and captain, Chief Anemone returned to the ESU cops to do a bit of schmoozing himself. He found the E-men in a good mood. They had done good, and they had done their job. They had provided ballistic backup to the men and women on patrol, and no cops had been injured or worse. The bad guys had challenged ESU, and they had lost. It was, in the department vernacular, a "good job."

Once again, ESU had been there to back up their fellow officers, and once again, instinct had been correct for Lt. Bob Sobocienski. In police work, especially the work of an E-cop, there are always two rules of surviving the streets—you never know when the big job will come down and you must always follow your gut instincts.

1

From Pelham Parkway to Pitkin Avenue, from Queens Boulevard to 152 and B'way: The World of the New York City Police Department's Emergency Service Unit and Truck-Two

●

"There are two things that these guys can't handle," a duty captain told his sergeant after watching the men and women of the Emergency Service Unit end a barricaded perp job, "the impossible and the extra-terrestrial!"

There is an old saying in the NYPD: "When a citizen needs help, he calls a cop. When a cop needs help, he calls Emergency Service." The men and women of ESU are without question *the* elite unit of the New York City Police Department. As one female ESU supervisor once said, "They are the boys with the big toys!" In essence, though, the ESU is New York City's thin blue line of last resort—from air crashes to armed terrorists, from ten-thirteens to barricaded psychos holding their families hostage. "If ESU can't handle it," one patrol captain once remarked, "then this city is in very deep shit." Over the years, ESU cops have been known as supercops: they are SWAT operators capable of meeting and overcoming virtually any and all tactical situations, they are emergency medical technicians who can administer treatment and lifesaving procedures to the victims of any and all disasters, and they are heavy-tool craftsmen who can rescue trapped victims from overturned vehicles or from blown-up buildings with uncanny speed and remarkable resourcefulness. Being that thin blue line of last resort is an awesome responsibility and one the department and the unit do not take lightly.

Officers on patrol, detectives in the middle of their investigations, and supervisors on the beat may have different tasks and stake their claim to different beats in the city, but these brothers and sisters in blue know one simple fact of survival on the streets they safeguard that is reassuring if not confidence-building: whenever they need it, whenever the shit hits the fan, they will be backed up by a 400-man unit of E-men—the NYPD's Emergency Service Unit. The ESU traces its creation to 1925 and the formation of a reserve force of officers who could be called on to perform "extraordinary" rescue assignments. Many of these volunteers were also part-time carpenters, welders, riggers, and electricians, and the trucks they rode, modified firetrucks, soon carried larger and more specified emergency equipment. Years later, lifesaving gear was added to the trucks, and the cops were sent to emergency medical training. These officers could do anything and everything, and they prided themselves on being able to rescue any officer or civilian no matter what the situation—from a worker dangling off the Brooklyn Bridge to a man trapped inside an elevator.

The unit was also among the nation's first mobile tactical response forces with what was once called the department's Firearms Battalion (as a force of officers armed with the old reliable Thompson submachine gun, the unit was also known by the nickname "Machine Gun

Squad") and was the city's first defense against riot situations and large-scale political insurrections. Racing about the city in old police trucks reminiscent of Keystone Kops days, the unit was the city's final line in the sand—from mobsters armed with dynamite to pirates who used to work the waterways of the Hudson River. During the Second World War, it has been rumored, the unit stationed officers atop city bridges armed with elephant guns and binoculars to search for Italian and German midget subs attempting to enter New York City harbors. In the years to follow, the unit eventually developed into a force called the Mobile Security Unit (MSU), which would be tasked with responding to emergency situations such as wrecks and disasters but also with meeting dangerous tactical situations that the precinct officers were too lightly armed to meet. Its personnel were drawn from the range and equipped with suburban vehicles loaded with weapons. In the late 1960s, the unit included the legendary Stakeout Unit, a force of NYPD firearms instructors and officers who were concentrated into one effective squad tasked with combating a rash of murders and robberies, mainly liquor stores; many law enforcement experts agree that ESU's Stakeout Unit was one of the most effective special teams in American police history. The unit's counterterrorist tactical role, especially involving hostage rescue, developed in the early 1970s, specifically following the 1972 Munich Olympics massacre. At the time, few police forces possessed a special tactics and weapons unit that could deal with a hostage crisis, and few police forces knew how to deal with the rising tide of criminals armed with heavier firepower than the cops on the beat. Virtually every police force in the world created a special hostage-rescue force following Munich, and virtually every police force in the United States created a SWAT unit. New York City already possessed such a unit, but it needed to be expanded.

ESU has always prided itself on the fact that it is one of the only tactical police units in the world that also handles rescue work and emergency medical treatment. In fact, ESU handles just about every type of job imaginable—from EDPs (emotional disturbed persons) to dangerous animals, from building collapses to plane crashes, from pin jobs and car crashes to scuba work. It is the multifaceted character that, many feel, makes this unit unique in the world—a distinction that highlights not only their talents but also their overall approach to both tactical and emergency rescue work. ESU is the only emergency rescue unit to go from slicing its way through the mangled debris of a car wreck in order to extricate a wounded motorist to racing, moments later, to a hit against a fortified crack house. They are the only tactical unit in the world to be tossing in diversionary devices inside the apartment of a man wanted on a homicide warrant and then rushing to a Harlem subway station to provide oxygen and medical care to passengers overcome by a pepper mace bomb set off by kids out for kicks. "We treat tactical operations with precision, care, and skill," boasts an ESU officer from One-Truck, "and rescue work with the speed and determination of tactical assignments." There is no major emergency—criminal or accidental—in this city that escapes the attention and the desperately needed services of the ESU.

Currently, ESU's order of battle consists of 400 officers (including bosses)—a small force considering the fact that with 38,000 men in uniform, the NYPD is the largest municipal police force in the United States and the second largest in the world (next to the Tokyo police). It is, next to helicopter pilots in the Aviation Unit, one of the most prestigious jobs in the NYPD and one of the most difficult units to get into. While many cops join the NYPD solely to wear the ESU cap one day, by the time many cops make it through the academy and end up on patrol in a precinct, they realize that there is no cooler or more exciting place to be than ESU. On big jobs, from the World Trade Center bombing to a plane crash, they are always the most important cops on the scene. They drive the big trucks, have the big tools, and on big jobs actually tell bosses what to do and where to go. According to one precinct cop working the 19th Precinct in Manhattan's ultra-chic Upper East Side, "My first big job, a hostage case, was unbelievable. Here come these guys, with their heavy firepower and tools, and they handle the job as if it were routine and ordinary. What's more, while all of us beat cops were outside maintaining a perimeter and tucking in our jackets for the bosses, and saluting the chiefs and inspectors who came to the scene, those chiefs and inspectors were simply walking up to the emergency cops, patting them on the back, and then talking to them on a first-name basis. In a department like this, that is a unit with power and respect."

When cops get out of the academy and are about to receive their commands, most hope and pray that they'll be posted to what is known as an "active" precinct. A rookie can learn a lifetime's worth of police experience and skills by working a few years in a precinct like Harlem's 3–2, the precinct with the most cops killed in the department's history, and the notorious 7–5 in Brooklyn. Working the streets of these patches of urban crime and violence, reacting to crimes of untold brutality and randomness in places where hopes and dreams are no longer the currency of day-to-day life, hones the skills of officers to the point where they can pick a perp out of a crowd of dozens *before* knowing what crime has been committed. Many of the rookies who are fortunate to be thrown into the fire from day one on the job eventually end up as detectives and sergeants—where they have an opportunity to teach a new class of green rookies what life on the streets is all about. Others will serve and protect and, in five years, volunteer into the department's elite unit.

Getting into ESU was once considered as hard as hitting the lottery—currently, there are more than 1,500 police officers, male and female, throughout the NYPD on a waiting list even to be considered for the unit, let alone be interviewed, tested, and trained. In order even to be considered for a spot in an ESU training class, an officer must have at least five years on the job and possess an exceptional service record. It helps if the officer volunteering is a veteran of one of the busier precincts in the city. Part of the ESU requirement is that the cop be a worker, someone who'd rather rappel down the side of a building than sit in a patrol car and sip coffee, and in busy precincts a cop can't help but be a worker. Also, it is extremely helpful if he or she also possesses a useful skill, such as being an electrician, carpenter, diver, or former serviceman; many of the cops who end up volunteering for ESU are already trained, somewhat, in the art of rescue as volunteer firemen in their hometowns on Long Island or upstate in Westchester, Putnam, Rockland, or Orange counties. The skills that many applicants list on their forms when volunteering are incredibly diverse—some worked in construction before entering the academy, some were plumbers, others drove heavy rigs, and some were carpenters; some were even cooks. The purpose of the additional skill is simple: ESU work involves heavy machinery and being able to improvise. It helps to have been in construction, which demonstrates that the officer has a tolerance for heights—he might be atop a bridge, after all, trying to talk down a jumper. The ESU officer needs to be a worker who is able to use his hands and tools to achieve and to improvise, and not to be intimidated by getting dirty, getting wet, or getting his hands near tons of heavy equipment. "Let's face it," claims one ESU officer with ten years in emergency and a world of experience notched on his utility belt, "there is a special characteristic that is required to be an E-man. It isn't as much one's skill in hitting a target with his service weapon, and it isn't being able to work a saw, or a spreader, or a Hurst tool. It is a characteristic that says we are able to use our hands, our tools and our minds to always improvise. It is a characteristic there isn't anything that we cannot do, because we can do everything!"

The final hurdle before a cop can be accepted into

ESU is recommendation from a commanding officer and, of course, a nudge or push from someone in the unit. It always helps to have a "rabbi" in the unit, an officer or boss who can recommend and lobby for you. It is even better if that ESU hopeful has a hook, or someone with a high-rank connection in the department, who can make a phone call and guarantee an interview; it is better still to have what is known as a "crane," or a very powerful hook, to make that phone call. A rabbi, a hook, and a crane are important, but all they do is get someone's foot in the door. The litmus test that will determine if the cop sitting before a review board of lieutenants will end up going back to his precinct or to Floyd Bennet Field for some training consists of an intense psychological and oral exam and a grueling interview. The reasoning behind the psychological exam is simple: ESU isn't for everyone, and just because a cop has passed the academy and is on the job doesn't mean he or she is mentally right for this job. When dealing with some of the jobs that ESU handles, from jumpers to protecting dignitaries, a cop must have a firm psychological foundation to be able to function and, more importantly, make the other cops in his truck confident to work with him. The oral exam is of equal importance. One of the E-cop's most important tasks is to assess a situation and coherently and accurately articulate it to his own supervisors and bosses ranging from a duty captain to the chief of department. Relaying an ongoing job in a nutshell, void of emotion and fear, is no simple task—especially when the job involves the lives of innocent civilians and the cops on the scene.

The now legendary ESU interview is the final hurdle for a cop to pass before actually being assigned to ESU training, and some cops hoping to volunteer into the ranks of ESU can wait as long as ten yeas before they are called in to the Special Operations Division headquarters for that once-in-a-career chance. In the interview, the bosses try to razzle and frazzle eager hopefuls with questions meant to agitate them and make them uneasy. As ESU cops live and work in relatively close quarters and must be able to function as an interwoven team where getting the job done is more important than an individual's sensitivities, the interviewers hope to expose any cop who might think that anyone who disagrees with him is wrong. ESU does not look for people who know it all or, worse, think they know it all. A volunteer may be a military veteran, from a special forces unit, and know how to fire his Heckler and Koch MP-5 with stunning accuracy, but in ESU he will relearn his skills to adapt to how the unit operates. ESU doesn't want ready-made robots in the unit. They want cops who can think and, more importantly, cops who are willing to learn.

The actual ESU training class, called the Specialized Training School (STS), lasts sixteen weeks, and, beyond the heavy tactical instruction that the officers receive, the curriculum consists of the following courses:

- Bridge and building rescue techniques (including talking down a jumper and pulling one in).
- Vehicle and train accidents and building collapse extrication.
- Rigging and line techniques.
- Welding and burning.
- First aid as first responders.
- The operation of power rescue tools.
- Elevator and escalator emergencies and rescues (helpful when a frightened child in a housing project is trapped atop an elevator, thirteen stories high, after "elevator surfing" for kicks).
- Animal control systems (in New York City, a potpourri of "animal jobs" from breaking up the Super Bowl of cockfights in the Bronx to trapping wild raccoons in Brooklyn).
- Water rescue techniques.
- Helicopter rescue, rappel, and medevac.
- Recognition of bombs and improvised explosive devices.

- Transportation of bombs and explosive devices.
- Recognition and rescue relative to hazardous material (hazmat).
- Operation of specialized vehicles.
- Dignitary protection and escorts.
- Specialized police apprehension and hostage-rescue tactics.
- The handing of emotionally disturbed persons, more commonly known as EDPs (not to be confused with the majority of New Yorkers, however!).
- Use of chemical agents.
- Use of self-contained breathing apparatus.
- Use of auxiliary electrical generators and lighting equipment.
- Handling of electrical and gas emergencies.
- Aircraft emergencies (such as the USAir crashes at LaGuardia and the crash of TWA Flight 800).
- Forcible entry techniques.
- Hazardous materials.
- Department of Corrections procedures.
- Crime scene investigations.
- High-rise structure rescues.
- Torch and welding procedures.

Other specialized training includes a one-week emergency psychological technician certification course; a two-week special weapons certification course; a three-day remote tactics (robotics) course; a one-day nonlethal weapons course (Taser gun, pepper mace, and water cannon); a two-week scuba certification course known as PADI (Professional Association of Diving Instructors) including basic and advanced certification, dry suit, and search-and-recovery special certification; and a three-week emergency medical technician (EMT) certification course.

Each phase of the STS must be passed by an ESU hopeful in order to earn a spot on the unit roster, and the intensity of the study is competitive and harsh. Upon completion of the STS requirements, each ESU officer is assigned to work with a senior member of the unit for a three-month on-the-job probationary period of training and evaluation. Each ESU officer, whether he is fresh out of STS or an experienced E-man in the Bronx with more than fifteen years on the job, must undergo a variety of refresher and advanced training courses annually. Even though they might do this type of work on a day-in, day-out basis on the streets of the city, the refresher courses ensure that they do it right. These courses include:

- Three one-day special weapons classes.
- One five-day specialized training course covering rescue techniques and tactics.
- One seven-day course every three years to maintain EMT certification.
- Three five-day courses on advanced tactics and techniques.
- Weekly in-house documentation "trio" training conducted by ESU supervisors.
- Advanced hazmat instruction.
- Regular drills relative to high-rise fire rescue, ship and plane disasters (as well as hijackings) and large-scale ESU responses.
- One-day nonlethal weapons and tactics refreshers.
- Six scuba dives per year.

At the end of the grueling course, when the future emergency cops have learned everything from how to shut off a Con Ed electrical power substation to how to "properly" toss in a diversionary device on a warrant, the new member of the NYPD's Emergency Service finally gets to wear the ESU baseball cap and dark blue fatigues. Once in the unit, most cops are there to stay. "This is the greatest place, in the greatest job, in the most interesting city in the world," one ESU cop working Queens once said. "Even the lure of promotion and more money are poor arguments against leaving the unit and possibly never returning." In one instance, a respected veteran of the unit passed the sergeant's test and was promoted out of the unit to work in a precinct in northern Manhattan (NYPD policy is that once a cop is promoted, he is transferred to a different command). After a few days with his sergeant's stripes and away from his truck and his squad, the newly promoted sergeant turned down his promotion and considerable raise in pay and returned to the unit he loved so dearly.

Once on the streets, the cops of ESU have so many patrol and response tasks and responsibilities that, on paper at least, appear so overwhelming that one would think a force of at least 3,000 cops would be needed just to do the job adequately. The job on the streets make the description on paper look clinical and orderly. It is anything but. According to the official NYPD guidelines, ESU's job assignment is as follows:

- **Routine patrol function**—(a) a patrol omnipresence; (b) summons issuance and arrests; (c) assist precincts in CPOP (Community Policing Program) efforts; (d) response to priority assignments and crimes in progress.
- **Warrants, search and arrest**—(a) assist in search for evidence and armed perpetrators; (b) apprehend violent felons; (c) assist in tactical planning or raid; (d) provide specialized weapons and heavy vests; (e) assist in search, removal of walls, flooring, and structural modifications, especially narcotics cases; (f) provide entry into premises through battering rams, forced entry tools, secure doors, animal control (pit bulls, Dobermans, etc.); (g) provide special equipment, entry tools, Hurst tools, hand tools, lighting.
- **Searches**—(a) crime scene searches, evidence searches (weapons and materials) and collection of same, difficult search areas, elevator shafts, duct work, venting systems, construction sited,

sewers, manholes, street excavation, safeguarding crime scene, perimeter security and police lines; (b) perpetrator searches, provide heavy weapons and vests, secure perimeter, tactics for systematic/safe search, provide specialized equipment and expertise; (c) missing person searches, lost children and adults, special equipment and lighting and difficult search areas; (d) entry areas, access to rooftops and entry holes in floors walls and other locations.

- **Emotionally disturbed persons (EDPs)**—respond to all EDP runs, mental health removal orders, suicide attempts/jumpers, specialized equipment (Kevlar gloves, EDP bar), nonlethal weaponry (Taser, Nova, water cannon), restraining devices (Mesh blanket, Velcro straps), assist EMS in preparation for transport, develop tactical plans for approaching and restraining person with minimal injury to all involved; ESU officers are also trained in bridge and building rescue techniques and suicide prevention dialogue, and trained in robotics and erecting a net and air bags.
- **Barricaded perpetrator/hostages**—establish and secure inner perimeter, develop tactical plans, provide specialized weapons and heavy vests, assist hostage negotiation team, recovery of hostages, apprehension of hostage takers, provide specialized equipment, bomb blankets, monitoring equipment, surveillance positions, observation teams, special weapons teams, and emergency rescue vehicles (ERVs).
- **Crime-in-progress responses**—police officer shot, robbery in progress, shots fired, bank alarms/holdups.
- **Other emergencies**—water/ice rescues, disasters, sniper situation, riots/crowd control.
- **Dignitary protection**—the ESU is also the department's primary force in providing dignitary

protection and VIP security—a monstrous task in a city as large and diverse as New York City; this includes visits from presidents, national political leaders, foreign heads of state, religious leaders, and other dignitaries who require special security details and consideration; as New York City is a truly an international city and headquarters of the United Nations and various international financial institutions, these details are carried out virtually all year round; in performing these duties, ESU interacts and operates with state and federal agencies, such as the U.S. Secret Service, the FBI, State Department Diplomatic Security, the New York State Police, and foreign security agencies; ESU supervisors and offices work together with representatives to develop and formulate escape and rescue routes; in their dignitary protection role, ESU utilizes all its vehicles and equipment, including a counterassault team vehicle (or CAT car) to follow motorcades and observation teams and countersniper marksman; ESU also provides additional security assistance in bomb sweeps and motorcade security, a precarious undertaking on New York's gridlock-plagued streets; ESU officers provide additional tactical security to sensitive convoys heading through New York City, such as escorting dangerous felons heading upstate to prison and large shipments of narcotics being ferried out of the city to be destroyed upstate.

- **Explosive devices/bomb scares**—ESU is also responsible for assisting the NYPD Bomb Squad in the event a suspicious package or device is located; ESU units secure a safe perimeter and follow the ICE doctrine (isolate, contain, and evacuate); ESU officers assist in the search for any reported device and then assist the Bomb Squad in its removal in either the bomb truck or a total containment vessel (TCV).

ESU units do not work out of precincts, but rather their workstations and operating bases are known as "trucks." Although ESU cops will hate the analogy, a truck resembles a firehouse more than the typical NYPD precinct. In a truck, the E-cops truly live, work, and depend on one another. For their routine (if there is anything routine about the work they do) duties, ESU squads deploy two types of vehicles, mini-command and mobile rescue platforms. The smaller ESU vehicle is the REP, or radio emergency patrol, a cabin of emergency gear loaded on four six-wheel ambulance chassis. The patrol cars that most precinct cops ride around in are known as RMPs for radio mobile patrol. Battered-looking Chevy Caprices or Ford Crown Victorias, in dark red or blue schemes, with flashing grill lights and red flashing lights attached to the roofs, are known as unmarked vehicles. Each ESU truck usually maintains three REPs, and two are usually on patrol through the truck's area of responsibility. They are known as the "Adam," "Boy," and "Charley" cars; on rare occasions, during times of heightened terrorist awareness, there might be a "David" car, as well. By performing roving patrols, REPs are in an excellent position to respond to jobs requiring ESU expertise, such as pin jobs and tactical support for precinct officers responding to confirmed reports of shots fired or robbery in progress. The REP carries much of the unit's emergency rescue equipment and protective body armor, though the heaviest bit of firepower carried is the Ithaca 37 12-gauge shotgun. The equipment carried in an REP includes:

- **General equipment**—two high-intensity portable lights, two gas masks, two sound barriers, two goggles, jumper cables, slim Jim, two heavy vests, two construction helmets, two ballistic helmets, two ballistic shields, ballistic blanket, battering ram, two shotguns and ammunition, two batons, two hand lights, hazmat book, rescue harness, Larakus belts with carabiners, webbing, and binoculars.

- **Nonlethal weaponry/EDP equipment**—Tasers and darts, Nova stun device and pole, water cannon, shepherd's crook, Kevlar gloves, chemical mace, pepper gas, EDP bar, mesh restraining blanket, Velcro restraining straps, fifteen-inch chain handcuffs, and plastic shield.
- **Hurst tools**—gas motor with jaws, cutters, chains, gas can aviation tips, ram, twenty-six-inch hose.
- **Pneumatic tools**—pneumatic saw kit, paratech air guns.
- **Air bags**—air bags in three sizes, air bag bottles, air bag regulators, train kit, assorted chocks, cribbing.
- **Gas-powered chain saw**—Sthil chain saw with tool kit, spare chain, fuel.
- **Scuba gear**—two Viking dry suits, two open-cell thermal underwear, two AGA masks with regulators, two scuba tanks and backpack, two sets of fins, gloves, knives, compass, two weight belts, two BCD vests, two sets of rescue line, two underwater lights, two 150-foot polyprop lines.
- **Tools and other equipment**—bolt cutters large and small, wire cutters, ring cutter, lock buster, sledge hammer, Haligan tool, ax, bow saw, come-along tool, small Haligan, tool box, hack saw, pry bar, gas key, crow bar, J hook, assorted small tools, lock cylinder tool, two J chains, chain with hooks, radiac kit, Kelly tool, lanterns, dosimeters, isolation kit, flares, circle cord, reflective tape, oil.
- **First aid kit**—resuscitator, two oxygen tanks, demand valve, suction, assistant masks, cervical collars, KED extrication, spare oxygen bottles, body bag, DB-45, sterile water, OB kit, burn kit, stokes basket, scoop stretcher, folding stretcher, backboard long and short, blankets, assorted

splints, disposable body bags, canvas body bags, DB-45 deodorizer.

- **Other equipment**—two Scott packs, two one-hour bottles, B suit, rubber gloves, electrical gloves, magnet, elevator and electronic kit, two waders, exposure suit, fifty-foot line and life ring, Kapock vests, work line assorted, life line, dog noose, animal control kit, hot stick, gas masks, goggles and work gloves, reflective tape, sound barriers, sixteen-foot extension ladder.
- **Fire extinguishers**—one water, one dry chemical, and one carbon dioxide.
- **Vehicle stabilization equipment**—four six-by-six hardwood chocks, four three-by-three chocks, assorted wedges, chocks, shoring and cribbing.

The larger of the two vehicles is the "truck," a hulking $250,000 vehicle ($1,000,000 when fully equipped) the size of a garbage truck, usually dispatched to large-scale jobs and as backup for the REPs. If the equipment carried inside the REP can be considered mind-boggling, then the multitude of rescue and tactical gear on the truck would appear to be enough to equip a small police force. The truck's equipment inventory consists of the following:

- **Gas-powered chain saws**—Sthil chain saw with tool kit, spare chain, fuel, K-1200 saw with wood blades, steel blades, masonry blades, tool kit, and fuel.
- **Electric power tools**—reciprocating saw, circular saw, high-torque drill, all with spare blades and bits all sizes.
- **Radiac equipment**—two Geiger counters, four docemeters, twenty film badges.
- **Electrical and lighting equipment**—four 100-foot electrical reels, four 1,000-watt portable lights, two 500-watt portable lights, two 1,000-watt light towers, two 4,000-watt light towers, assorted

adapters and plugs, two multiport junction boxes.

- **Hand tools**—forty-piece tool box, two sets bolt cutters large and small, sledge hammers (five pound and ten pound), Haligan tools large and small, two pike-head axes, two flat-head axes, three bow saws (small, medium, large), carpenter saws, pry bars (twelve-inch, eighteen-inch, twenty-four-inch), lock buster (duck bill), hydraulic bolt butters, "rabbit tool," various gas and utility shutoff keys, shovels (trench, spade, flat), various hydrant wrenches, lock puller, K tool kit, Kelly tool, grading hooks, hot stick, assorted spikes and nails, rakes and brooms, twenty-four-foot extension ladder, pike polls, twelve-foot closet ladder, portable vise, winch (come-along), assorted hand tools.
- **Truck-mounted equipment**—five-ton winch, air compressor, twenty-four-kw generator, light towers, PA radio system, spot and flood lights.
- **Cutting torches**—one Caldo torch with rods, one oxyacetylene backpack, assorted tips, ten-foot hoses.
- **First aid equipment**—major trauma kit, backboards, cervical collars, resuscitator, spare oxygen bottles, KEDs, blankets, assorted splints, burn kit, stokes basket, scoop stretcher.
- **Pneumatic tools**—pneumatic saw kit (wizard), paratech air gun, pneumatic jacking bags five-sized, control kit, pneumatic air chisel.
- **Hydraulic tools**—Porto-power kit ten-ton, Hurst tools, Hurst 5000 gas motor, Hurst electric motor, Hurst 150 cutters, Hurst model 32-B, Hurst model 26 champ, Hurst model 16 ram, Hurst model 30 ram.
- **Specialized equipment**—metal detector, train kit, two ten-ton jacks, hydraulic bolt cutters, electric jack hammer, line gun, Porta-lights (hand lights).
- **Heavy weapons and ammunition**—Ithaca 37

pump-action 12-gauge shotgun, Heckler and Koch MP-5 9mm submachine gun, Ruger Mini-14 5.56mm assault rifles, Glock and Beretta 9mm semi-automatic pistol, Federal 37mm tear gas projectile gun.

- **Tactical equipment**—six ballistic helmets, six ballistic vests, one body bunker ballistic shield, two ballistic barrier blankets, one forced-entry door ram, six MSA gas masks with filters, one Kwik-View mirror, one spotting scope.
- **Rope**—two 200-foot half-inch life line, one 220-foot ⅝-inch life line, 100-foot ⅝-inch work line, 100-foot half-inch work line, 100-foot ⅜-inch work line, 500-foot quarter-inch ploypropcord, four Morrisey life belts, two rescue harnesses.
- **Hazmat kit.**
- **SCBA equipment**—two SCBA Scott packs in case, six spare sixty-minute bottles, six spare thirty-minute bottles.
- **Hydraulic tools**—Hurst hydraulic manual pump, post support plate, two chains with clevis hooks, two clevis links, clevis pins, assorted tips, fuel, oil, two spare sixteen-foot hoses.
- **Vehicle stabilization equipment**—six six-by-six hardwood chocks, six four-by-four hardwood chocks, assorted wedges, chocks, shoring, and cribbing.
- **Fire-extinguishing equipment**—two pressurized water extinguishers, dry chemical extinguisher, two carbon dioxide extinguishers, two fifty-foot rolls, one half-inch fire hose with attached nozzles.
- **Elevator and electrical equipment**—elevator and electric kit.
- **Nonlethal weaponry/EDP**—Taser and darts, Nova stun device and pole, water cannon, shepherd's crook, Kevlar stainless steel gloves, chemical Mace, pepper gas, EDP bar, mesh restraining

blanket, Velcro restraining straps, fifteen-inch chain handcuffs, plastic shield.

- **Water rescue equipment**—six kapok vests, two ring buoys with eighty feet of rope, two shepherd's hooks, exposure suits, two sets waders, four-man inflatable raft (AVON) with oars, one four-horsepower outboard engine.
- **Scuba gear**—two Viking dry suits, two open-cell thermal underwear, two AGA masks with regulators, four eighty-cubic-foot scuba tanks, two BCD vests, two sets fins, gloves, knives, compass, four Darrel-Allen underwater lights, two sets of 150-foot water rescue lines, two sets of weight belts.
- **Animal control equipment**—two dog nooses, animal control kit.
- **Other equipment**—assorted rigging equipment, block and tackle.

Other vehicles in the ESU fleet include two bomb trucks, two total containment vessels, trucks for three remote mobile investigators, four mobile light generators (MLGs), two construction accident response vehicles (CARV truck); three jumper response vehicle (air bags), a hazardous material decontamination trailer and tender, generator trucks, photo observation vehicle, temporary headquarters vehicle, two snowmobiles and ten jet skis. Among the more specialized ESU vehicles are two M75 APCs known as ERVs (emergency rescue vehicles), which are used primarily to evacuate a wounded officer or civilian in an area under fire, and two Peacekeeper armored cars for special tactical deployment and emergency rescue assignments where cops or civilians are under fire and pinned down.

There are few departments, let alone specialized units, in the world of policing that have the equipment, the vehicular support, and the exotic tools that ESU brings to bear on the streets of the city. Yet, considering the amount of work that ESU gets and the number of jobs that the unit gets called to throughout the city, the equipment isn't lavish or extravagant. It is just enough to make sure that ESU gets its job done. New York City can be a truly wild place.

To many, New York is one of the cities that should just be unpoliceable. While one mayor has described the city as a gorgeous mosaic of neighborhoods, races, and cultures, New York is more like the melting pot it has always used as its calling card—a sizzling cauldron of dangerous gases and fumes, where the lid can blow off the pot at any moment. There are neighborhoods in New York that look like the poshest areas of London or Paris, and there are neighborhoods and areas that make Third World malaria farms look like luxury palaces. The mix, the tumult, and the varying sights and sounds are supposed to be part of New York's charm. Add to the mix the fact that besides being a mosaic ("looking more like an aftereffect of a weak stomach after a full night's drinking rather than a work of art by one of the great French masters," a Bronx detective once said), New York is also a magnet. A powerful magnet. Every nut, psycho, and fanatic with an agenda and poor personal hygiene is attracted to the five boroughs—its pace, its zaniness, and its virtual anonymity. A lot of these international loonies are harmless—a lot aren't. New York also attracts the criminal element from virtually every corner of the world: big and burly gangsters from the former Soviet Union, Fukanese extortionists from the People's Republic of China, Israeli guns for hire, Mexican murderers, Dominican drug traffickers, and even Pakistani pickpockets. As one sergeant in Manhattan once commented, "The engraving on the Statue of Liberty should be modified to read, 'Give us your tired, your poor, your criminally insane'!" From the World Trade Center bombing to the Empire State Building massacre, from a Taiwanese fusillade on Queens Boulevard to Nigerian carjackers on the Upper East Side, that amendment to New York's historic welcome is not all that inappropriate.

Anytime, Anywhere!

The NYPD doesn't look at the city like a mosaic, a melting pot, or a magnet. To the NYPD, the Big Apple is divided into borough commands, divisions, and, of course, the venerable precincts. Run out of "One PP" (One Police Plaza), a red block of a building in lower Manhattan sometimes referred to as the "Puzzle Palace," the precincts are the life blood of the department—the epicenter of NYPD life. Precincts are as diverse as the city itself and can range from a quiet location in Queens, such as the 104 covering a large stretch of residential neighborhoods, to the middle of Manhattan, such as the Midtown South precinct, the busiest precinct in the world. Precincts are bastions and bedlam centers. They are the epicenter of a neighborhood and the symbol of its sense of security. They are always active. Walk into a precinct, *anywhere* in the city, at *any time,* and the activity is mind-boggling. If one happens to stroll into the 3–4 Precinct in Washington Heights, one of the major narcotics trafficking centers in New York City, the desk sergeant will be on the phone while a detective is taking into evidence a sawed-off shotgun seized during the case of a perp somewhere near Riverside Drive. Suspects are brought, in cuffs, before the front desk, and holding cells fill up to capacity before the wagon arrives and the suspects are taken to central booking and arraignment before a judge. Three times a day, at 8:00 A.M., 4:00 P.M., and midnight, roll call is read and a new shift sent out on patrol. Some precincts, like the 5th in Chinatown, attract officers from specific ethnic groups who speak the native language and understand the local customs. Other precincts, like the 6–7 in Crown Heights, Brooklyn, are so diverse and so flooded with always-changing cultural groups that a precinct officer would have to be a Spanish-speaking Hasidic Jew born in Kingston, Jamaica, just to fit in.

New York City has been described as many things, and it is everything and more. A melting pot and the Big Apple, the city is, in essence, a tinderbox of millions and multitudes, ethnic diversity and aggression, an international financial and entertainment capital. Today, more than ten million people call New York home, and an additional three million come into the city each day from the outer suburbs. Geographically, the city is divided into five boroughs. The Bronx is the northernmost borough, bordering Westchester County to the north and separated from Queens courtesy of the East River and Long Island Sound and from Manhattan courtesy of the Harlem River. Brooklyn, once called the fourth largest city in the United States, is connected to Queens, the largest borough in size and population. Queens reaches from the skyline of Manhattan along the banks of the East River to the Atlantic Ocean in the Rockaways to the border with Nassau County and Long Island to its easternmost reaches. Both the city's major airports, LaGuardia Airport in Astoria and John F. Kennedy International Airport in Jamaica, are in Queens, as is Riker's Island, a Department of Corrections facility housing 16,000 prisoners at the entrance to the main runway at LaGuardia in Flushing Bay. Manhattan is, of course, the most glamorous, most famous, most exciting borough. It is home to Wall Street and Broadway, Fifth Avenue and Greenwich Village; it is Chinatown and Central Park, City Hall and Grand Central Station. Yet Manhattan is also the heroin supermarkets of Alphabet City, the Lower East Side, Harlem and Hell's Kitchen, and the cocaine center of Washington Heights. Manhattan is crowded, overpriced, overdeveloped, and a microcosm of the entire city, the entire nation, and the entire world, for that matter.

In terms of the geography of the New York City Police Department and its Emergency Service Unit, New York is divided into ten very unique, very diverse, very competitive slices. ESU's headquarters, once centrally located on a small edge of Flushing Meadows Park next to Shea Stadium and two of the city's primary highways, is now at Floyd Bennet Field, on a desolate stretch of airstrip attached to a federal park at the southern end of Brooklyn. In terms of having the "office" respond to jobs in most locations in the city, the Field (as Floyd Bennet is commonly known) is as far off the beaten path as can be found. With traffic on the Belt Parkway reduced to a permanent crawl and all the subsequent interlinking roadways always mired by construction, decay, and too many damn cars, it can literally take an hour to get from the Field to a job in Manhattan or the Bronx. The location, also home to the NYPD's Aviation Unit and its fleet of helicopters, is not one of the most beloved spots on the ESU atlas, but it is the unit's nerve center, where the bosses sit and turn out, where decisions are made and contingencies planned for. In terms of special operations in the NYPD, Floyd Bennet Field is its Pentagon. Since ESU is headquartered in Brooklyn, the Borough of Kings is the ideal spot to begin a tour of ESU.

Brooklyn possesses three trucks, or squads. Six-Truck, covering Brooklyn South, is one of the most diverse trucks in the unit, tasked with an area from the Brooklyn Bridge and Brooklyn Navy Yards to the old boardwalk at Coney Island all the way to Bensonhurst and Canarsie, Redhook, and Flatbush. Based next to the 6–8 Precinct in Bay Ridge, Six-Truck is a potpourri of everything Brooklyn, and everything New York. Six-Truck can be summoned to a water job near Park Slope amid the view of the Verrazano and the lower Manhattan skyline and called to Redhook and the infamous Redhook Projects, a congested area with the notorious distinction of being the most dangerous, with the most homicides per square inch, in the entire United States. Six-Truck also covers Brighton Beach, the now notorious "Little Odessa," where the Russian Mafia has set up shop and is involved in anything and everything illegal—from hiding gas tax revenue to heroin smuggling—and a whole slew of neighborhoods where Jamaican, African, Yiddish, and Spanish dialects are all heard. Seven-Truck, situated right behind the notorious 7–5 Precinct in East New York, is responsible for southeastern Brooklyn and the neighborhoods of East New York, Flatlands, Canarsie,

Cypress Hill, and East Flatbush. They are in an area where they can back up both Six-Truck and Eight-Truck in Brooklyn, as well as Nine-Truck in Queens South. And, finally, in Brooklyn there is Eight-Truck, among the busiest trucks in the city—especially in terms of tactical work. Situated behind the 9–0 precinct near the elevated Broadway subway line, Eight-Truck is in the middle of some of the worst neighborhoods in Brooklyn. Its area of responsibility stretches from the Queens border to the East River where the Williamsburg and Brooklyn bridges cross into Manhattan. It is involved in more gun runs, perp searches, and hits than any other truck in Brooklyn.

The one ESU squad in Staten Island, known locally as HESSI (Highway Emergency Squad Staten Island), is referred to as Five-Truck, and although they are not the busiest squad in the division, they are by no stretch of the imagination bored. With more than its share of EDPs, housing projects, and barricaded perps, not to mention miles of highway (and New Jersey drivers), Five-Truck can be a hectic place to work.

Queens, the city's most populous borough and one of its most diverse, with three million residents who speak 100 languages and follow every conceivable religion and way of life known to man, is home to two ESU trucks. Nine-Truck, located behind the 1–13 Precinct in Jamaica, is responsible for the southern half of the borough. Queens South reaches from the Nassau County border to the Brooklyn line, from the southern half of the Queens shore along the East River to the Van Wyck Expressway and Hillside Avenue. Because of Kennedy Airport, southern Queens has always been among the borough's most criminally active. Convicted mobster John Gotti operated out of the Italian enclave of Ozone Park, hijacking freight from the airport to the Rockaways, which, once a subway-ride-away beach resort, is now a crime-infested series of shacks and projects that is, according to one NYPD detective, "the rectum of the world." Ten-Truck, responsible for Queens North, is perhaps the only police facility in the five boroughs with a No Parking sign stenciled on its garage doors in Korean; but, based behind the 109 Precinct in the heart of Flushing, why would it have a parking sign in English? Queens North is the home of a million languages and the home of Ten-Truck. Situated behind the 109 Precinct on Union Street on the border of Chinatown and Koreatown, Ten-Truck's personnel are among the most experienced rescue officers in the city as the unit covers three of the city's busiest bridges, near three of its busiest highways (in an area with the city's, and possibly the globe's, worst drivers).

In the Bronx, ESU fields Three-Truck, which covers the southeastern portion of the Bronx, including the now infamous and notorious 4–1 Precinct, once known as Fort Apache. Positioned amid a criss-cross of networking roadways, Three-Truck is a busy rescue outfit called to countless pin jobs on the major arteries, such as the Cross-Bronx Expressway and the Hutchinson River Parkway, and is also called to countless EDP jobs as a result of being situated in the area of Bronx Psychiatric Hospital. Four-Truck, known in the ESU vernacular as "Ice Station Zebra" for being located in one of the northernmost edges of the city near the exclusive domain of Riverdale, covers some of the more desperate stretches of the Bronx, such as Marble Hill, University Heights, and East Tremont. Because one of the ESU's three air bag trucks is based at Four-Truck, the unit responds to a great many jumper jobs in the Bronx, Manhattan, and even Queens.

When most people think of New York City, the one image that immediately enters their minds is the awe-inspiring skyline of Empire Manhattan marked by such landmarks as the United Nations, the Empire State Building, and the twin towers of the World Trade Center. Manhattan is considered by many to be the epicenter of the world, the global mecca for art, communications, power, and finance. It is also naturally the heart that pumps the blood of the city. Several million people live on the island of Manhattan, from homeless skels to ambassadors, and millions more come every morning to be on time for their nine-to-five jobs. There are tens of thousands of businesses in the city, Wall Street, the seats of city government, Broadway, the United Nations, consulates and national offices, banks and world-renowned medical facilities. Manhattan has it all.

In terms of police work in New York, for cops on patrol and for ESU, in many ways Manhattan is it.

ESU maintains two trucks in Manhattan, and it divides the island in half, in a one-two punch that patrols, secures, and saves many a day. One-Truck, situated on East 21st Street next door to the 13th Precinct, is responsible for the lower half of Manhattan—from 59th Street, river to river, all the way to the very bottom tip of the island at Wall Street and Battery Park. Known as the Hollywood Truck because it was once the subject of a very colorful, and very bad, TV show called True Blue and because it usually attracts journalists and news crews from all over the world, One-Truck is responsible for the hustle and bustle of Wall Street and the World Trade Center, the congestion and clamor of Chinatown and Little Italy, the trendy streets of Soho, and the bizarre realm of Greenwich Village. One-Truck covers midtown with offices and tourist sites, and areas like the East Village and the Lower East Side with their narcotics supermarkets, squatter-filled warehouses, and teaming housing projects. Because of its proximity to the federal courthouses at Foley Square, One-Truck gets a lot of security work for sensitive trials and arraignments (terrorists, bombers, notorious drug dealers) and a lot of VIP and dignitary protection work safeguarding important guests speaking at the United Nations (inside One-Truck's area of responsibility) or staying at the luxurious hotels in the city—most of which are also in One-Truck's half of the island.

There are, though, two separate Manhattans. The southern half of the island is where people come to work, to play, to sightsee, and to be part of the scene.

The northern half of the island is, however, where the action is. The northern half of the island is the domain of Truck-Two.

Known as the "Jewel of Harlem," Truck-Two is responsible for the northern half of Manhattan, from the border at 59th Street north to the Bronx border along the Harlem River Drive and Inwood. Truck-Two encompasses some of the most diverse socioeconomic groups in the city, where, sometimes, a single street separates those who pay $4,000 a month for rent and those who are on public assistance squeezing out a meager existence. Northern Manhattan is truly a dichotomy. At the border at 59th Street, both One-Truck and Two-Truck share an area of midtown Manhattan that can best be described by one word: *posh.* All along 59th Street, from the Queensborough Bridge at the East River to the multi-million-dollar yuppified area currently planned for construction along the Hudson River to the west, the color of 59th Street is green. On the east side, from 59th Street to 96th Street, from the East River to Central Park, is the Upper East Side. Under the watchful eyes of the NYPD's 19th Precinct, the Upper East Side is a conglomerate of tree-lined streets with million-dollar brownstones, multi-million-dollar apartments on Fifth and Park avenues, and stores and bars on Madison and Lexington Avenues so swank that one needn't even think of entering to buy something unless they can produce an American Express platinum card for inspection. The city's Who's Who lives on the Upper East Side, from Mayor Rudolph Giuliani and Police Commissioner Howard Safir, to diplomats, dukes and duchesses, playboys (and some bunnies), high rollers, and captains of industry.

On the west side of Central Park, from 59th Street to 96th Street, from the museum-lined swank of Central Park West to the Hudson River, the 2–0 Precinct is responsible for law and order. A bit less posh than the East Side, the Upper West Side is no less glitzy. Seemingly with a restaurant for every apartment and home to many of the city's artistic elite, the Upper West Side is also a network of brownstones, apartments, businesses, thoroughfares, and theaters. It is on the Upper West Side where many opera stars and classical musicians live, and where John Lennon was assassinated.

If 59th Street can be described as posh, 96th Street is nothing else than the border. From river to river, 96th Street in many ways separates the haves from the have nots in a way that the Berlin Wall used to separate the free from the Communists and the way the Green Line in Beirut once separated Christians and Muslims. On the east side, 96th Street takes on a true frontierlike appearance. On the south side of the street, *still in the confines of the 19th Precinct,* apartments fetch up to $3,000 a month in rent, many resident have blood bluer than the clear skies on a crisp winter's day, and the average medium income is well into the six figures. Across 96th Street, however, to the north, the skyline develops into housing projects and graffiti, the elevated train tracks, and vandalized cars. North of the border is the barrio, the mean streets of Spanish Harlem, and the confines of the 2–3 Precinct. The difference between the areas covered by the 19th and 2–3 precincts is blatant and obvious, tragic and poignant.

On the West Side, the confines of the 2–4 Precinct from 86th Street to 110th Street assume a very liberal, very bourgeois atmosphere. It is the land of *Seinfeld,* the upper echelon and upward mobility. It is where the police are viewed as an intrusion and a nuisance, where a cop, stopping off to pick up Chinese food, will literally be lambasted by a diner: "Are you on duty? My tax dollars aren't being wasted while you stuff your face with Chow Fun, are they?" The 2–4 Precinct is a transitional precinct. In its confines, low-income housing first becomes apparent. The maroon red-brick blocks of long rectangular housing projects join brownstones and high-rises in the area's skyline, as both high-income and low-income meet in an invisible border area leading into Harlem. Next to restaurants where Perrier is a staple, bargain basement stores, OTBs, and Kentucky Fried Chicken places dot Broadway and Amsterdam Avenue.

Still on the West Side, the 2–6 Precinct is lovingly (and not so lovingly) referred to as the "Hole in the Doughnut." Encompassing 110th Street and Cathedral Parkway to its southernmost boundaries to 133rd Street, 141st Street at Edgecome, and east to Morningside Avenue, the 2–6 includes Columbia University, Barnard College, the Jewish Theological Seminary, and St. Luke's Hospital. "The 2–6," according to one officer, "is the good part of Harlem." Yet the 2–6 Precinct, on 126th Street between Amsterdam Avenue and Old Broadway, is also a busy house with more than its share of homicides, robberies, rapes, assaults, and drug sales.

Northward, from river to river as the island of Manhattan narrows and constricts, from 120th Street toward 155th Street, is the legendary neighborhood known as Harlem. Harlem, the mecca for African-American culture, is where some of the greatest jazz musicians once played at the Cotton Club and where many of the world's greatest rhythm and blues bands have played at the legendary Apollo Theater. Harlem is 125th Street, a vital artery of commercial and cultural life that runs from the Henry Hudson Parkway and Twelfth Avenue on the West Side through Adam Clayton Powell and Lenox avenues at its center, to the East River and the entrance to the Triborough Bridge at the east. Harlem is covered by three precincts—three very busy precincts. In the center of Harlem, snuggled between the 2–6 Precinct to the west and Spanish Harlem's 2–5 Precinct to the east, is the notorious 2–8. Four blocks long and seventeen blocks wide, the 2–8, some twenty-odd years ago, was one of the most dangerous stretches of the planet—next to Beirut, the Mekong Delta, and the streets of Belfast. In the day of the Black Panthers and the Black Liberation Army, cops were routinely targeted for assassination, and a night rarely passed when the 2–8 wasn't engulfed by gunfire, death, and destruction. The precinct still remains a battlefield bearing the scars of its earlier days. South of the 2–8 Precinct is the 2–5, covering much of Spanish Harlem, and to the north is the 3–2, which encompasses Harlem from West 127th Street all the way west to Edgecome Avenue and east toward the Harlem River and the four bridges that cross into the Bronx. "A shithole" is how one Harlem cop describes the 3–2, and more cops have been killed in the 3–2 than in any other precinct in the city. Finally, on the West Side, is the 3–0 Precinct, which covers 133th Street to 155th Street, Edgecome Avenue to the Hudson River.

Completing the portrait of Manhattan North is Washington Heights. Covered by the notorious 3–3 and 3–4 precincts, from 155th Street north toward the Bronx, Washington Heights was once an enclave for German Jews fleeing Hitler, though it has become the largest concentration of Dominican life outside the Caribbean. Because of thriving Dominican drug gangs, and because the George Washington Bridge and the Cross-Bronx Expressway run through it, Washington Heights has become a major conduit for narcotics suppliers bringing drugs into the city and selling them to all points beyond. In the NYPD guidebook of dangerous precincts, the 3–3 and the 3–4 usually run neck-and-neck for that ever-elusive title of most notorious.

"In many ways, we are lucky," claims a Two-Truck cop returning from a patrol in his REP. "There is no other truck in the unit that covers a stretch of the city so diverse, so interesting, and so busy." Yet posh doesn't mean immune from crime and mayhem, and poor doesn't necessarily mean bad. This dichotomy of terrain makes for one of the most interesting, diverse, unique, and sometime heart-stopping areas to work in American law enforcement. Truck-Two covers one of the most densely populated stretches of earth, next to Calcutta and poorer parts of Shanghai perhaps. One would think it would take three times the number of emergency cops to handle the jobs they get called to. But ESU is that kind of unit, and Two-Truck that type of squad. It is a busy truck, one whose officers would rather be out on the street, working and getting their hands dirty, than doing anything else. And in the ESU world, in these diverse and unique areas, are parks, housing projects, hospitals, universities, and two of the city's busiest roadways—the Henry Hudson Parkway along the Hudson River on the West Side, and the Harlem River Drive and FDR Drive along the eastern portion.

In 1996, the thirty cops assigned to Emergency Service Squad Two in Manhattan North performed the following:

- Aided cases (ranging from administering oxygen to removing DOAs): 381 jobs.
- Accident (nonvehicular, ranging from trains to construction): 921 jobs.
- Accidents (vehicular): 951 jobs.
- Suicides and jumpers: 244 jobs.
- Aided other cops (from lockouts to 10–13s, from providing lighting to the truly bizarre details): 3,015 jobs.
- Tactical assignments (hits, barricaded perps, etc.): 433 jobs.
- Bomb jobs: 260 jobs.
- Miscellaneous: 667 jobs.
- Emotionally disturbed persons: 4,397 jobs.

The way 1997 looks as of this writing, 1996 will go down in Two-Truck's operational book as an easy year!

Two-Truck is one hell of a place.

Because of the sheer volume of their work, because of the fact that some of the best cops in the division work out of the "Cotton Club," as Two-Truck is sometimes known, and because of the incredibly dangerous and diverse terrain they cover, the men and women of Two-Truck are truly unique. Yet, while this book might cover the diverse duty and some of the quirkier aspects of the life and times of one particular truck in one particular part of the city, no squad can operate by itself. The trucks interact and overlap, support and carry the burden. They are ten separate and equal pieces of the complex puzzle known as the NYPD's Emergency Service Unit.

Emergency Adam-Two, Truck-Two, you are being requested in the confines of the . . .

2

The Essence of ESU: REPs on Patrol

Just another typical, atypical four-to-twelve in Manhattan North. Just more of the chaos. Police Officers Steve Vales and Dan Donnelly, returning to Harlem after a perp search in the 3–4 Precinct, respond to a stuck occupied elevator on 133rd Street between Broadway and Riverside Drive. The site is in the midst of the mother of all block parties. The human wave is so dense, the cops are forced to park their REP on Broadway and walk through the crowd, carrying their elevator rescue gear the length of the block. For the two Harlem cops, the scene is one of dizziness and sensory bombardment. The pulsating Latin rhythms coming from loudspeakers the size of Volkswagens penetrate ear drums and shake ribs and bones to the core. The residents of the block, some stoned, some drunk, and others fornicating on the street to the cadence of the music, party in a hypnotic frenzy. Old men, beer bottles nestled in their toothless mouths, sit on stoops and talk about happier times, while babies, wandering on the street barefoot and in dirty diapers, search for their intoxicated parents. Inside the building with the stuck elevator, a strong smell of marijuana pervades the hallway, and undelivered court notices and crack vials litter the entrance. On the third floor, about twenty firemen attempt to rip open the door and pull up the people trapped in the elevator, while Vales and Donnelly, one floor below, use a long stick to dislodge the blocked mechanism and bring the people out to safety. One of those trapped is beyond inebriation in both the legal and the moral sense; another rescued victim, wearing a black bra and a Dominican flag tattoo over her bouncing left breast, emerges from her trap happy as a clam and begins dancing wildly. An EMS worker stands with his mouth open in awe. Back up 133rd Street, toward the REP, Vales and Donnelly once again wade through the human sea of gyration and deafening noise, to return to their search for jobs in Manhattan North.

"You look like you've been in the twilight zone," an EMS worker tells the cops.

"Twilight zone, naaaah!" one of the cops responds. "We're on patrol!"

Police statisticians, the pencil pushers at One PP who analyze crime figures (how many old ladies are mugged on the streets, how many livery cab drivers are found in their vehicles with a .38 slug behind the ear, and so on), embrace the arrival of winter with a false sense of back-slapping pride usually claimed by those who are applauded for tasks they had no role in seeing through to fruition. After all, perpetrators are like bears. They hibernate in the cold and come out to play—to rob, harm, kill, and offend—when the warmth of spring makes lurking in an alleyway part of the occupation as opposed to an occupational hazard. It is too hard to stand on a street corner and sell crack when the wind chill can cut through a body almost as hard as a Teflon-coated 9mm bullet. It's dangerous snatching purses when you could slip on the ice and end up recuperating on the Island (Riker's, that is). Police statisticians love the winter, especially if it's a cold and nasty one. They can attend the now infamous compstat meetings, the weekly grilling sessions with commissioners, deputy commissioners, chiefs, deputy chiefs, inspectors and captains, with the gleam of brilliance in their eyes, present sparkling crime stats showing how safe the city actually is.

The world of Police Pollyanna exists only at One PP, of course. In the precincts, where the pulse of the city is taken on a minute-by-minute basis, beat cops walk the city's frigid and threatening streets in uniforms that neither keep out the cold or keep in body heat. Plainclothes cops still have to ride around with windows open so that they can watch for crimes in progress, and they often have to chase perpetrators on foot over mountains of snow and thick and treacherous sheets of sidewalk ice. Armani-clad detectives, too, the department's gold-shielded golden boys, still must pound the shoe leather while canvassing a crime scene for witnesses, even if that shoe leather, $250-a-pair Bally grooved shoe leather, is forced to step in frigid puddles of ice-floating brown and gray slush. Even undercover narcs, a separate breed of creature in the department, suffer in the frigid cold. Crack heads tend to migrate inside during the bitter cold, requiring the narcs to leave the false safety of an outdoor buy-and-bust operation indoors where they are beyond the protective eyes of their surveillance teams. In the ice cold of winter, undercover narcs have no choice but to venture into dangerous locations alone, where all they have for safety are the loose-fitting rags of their costumes (crack heads aren't known for wearing L. L. Bean sweaters and long johns) and .38 Smith and Wesson snub-noses worn on their ankles or in special holsters that straddle their inner thighs.

And, inevitably, in the upside-down world of emergency service, winter means work. Lots of it.

If "average" crime tends to drop during the finger-numbing cold, spectacular crimes, the ones motivated by passion, insanity, or sheer bad luck, rise through the statisticians' charts, graphs, and neat audiovisual presentations like a shotgun blast through the roof when the mercury dips below 32 degrees. While Harlem and Washington Heights don't own any exclusivity on spectacular crimes or disasters in the winter, it's in the snow-frosted confines of Harlem and Manhattan North that, to borrow a popular phrase, "shit happens." Buildings, after all, don't collapse on picturesque spring mornings, they crumble at the first heavy snowfall, and Harlem and

Washington Heights are filled with buildings in borderline collapse. EDPs, the politically correct title for psychos, just happen to find an ice-covered night the right time to hold a neighbor hostage, take the family's .308 rifle for a walk, or ponder a jump from the upper roadway of the George Washington Bridge. It is, of course, only in the winter, when a lethal sheet of black ice coats the West Side Highway or the Harlem River Drive, that a motorist decides it would be a prudent move to floor the gas pedal and make good time and then smash into a divider or barrier when they discover that their traction, or ability to brake, has disappeared.

Patrol is the essence of what ESU squads do in New York City. Each truck has two, sometimes three, REPs out on patrol in one portion of a borough at any given time so that an experienced, well-trained pair of officers can respond, in a matter of moments, to any type of developing situation—with both their tactical firepower and their first-responder expertise. A man is run over by a subway train and Adam-Two is there. Shots are fired, and Adam-Two and the Boy car are there. A big job comes over, and Truck-Two is there along with the REPs and responding personnel from other trucks in the city backing up their fellow E-cops. The purpose of patrol is for the emergency cops to fulfill their routine police duties and to be in a position close to a developing job as it comes over. Usually, in American law enforcement, specialized units are responders. They wait at their home base, they train, they maintain equipment, and they wait for a call-out and the big job. ESU, of course, is different. In regular SWAT units, where cops sit around at quarters or train, while waiting for the big job to summon them to suit up and grab the MP-5s from their lockers, the officers develop into specialists. In regular rescue units, emergency personnel sit around waiting for a car wreck, a medical emergency, or a natural disaster to summon them into the fray. ESU does not want its cops to be standby specialists who emerge from their barracks only when the shit hits the fan. Because of their patrol functions and their attendance to rescue work and other nontactical assignments, ESU cops get very little "pure" tactical training. They don't spend one day a week on the range or two days a month assaulting a TAC house. Instead, they perfect and hone their police skills on the street, where there are no do-overs or second chances. It is on patrol that the E-cops keep their instincts fresh, which is as important in tactical work and a cop's survival on the streets as a Kevlar vest and a full clip of ammo in one's MP-5.

On Columbus Avenue in the heart of the Upper West Side one crisp winter's evening, Police Officer John Politoski and Detective Mike Corr were patrolling the streets of northern Manhattan, in one of the ritziest and highest-rent portions of the city, when they pulled up to an intersection and a red light. The two cops, gazing through their open windows, were trying to decide where to stop off for a quick bite and were talking about the gamut of geopolitical events, from "golf is not a stupid sport" to who were better warriors, the Zulus or the Vikings. Suddenly, a male in his early thirties wearing a sports coat and a cap, standing by the curb waiting to cross the street, reached into his coat pocket, his right arm sliding toward his left chest area. Instinctively, immediately, and *simultaneously,* the two veteran cops abandoned their discussion, moved their heads in a leftward motion, unfastened their black leather holsters, and, removed their Glock 9mms. The male, oblivious to what was transpiring around him, removed a pack of Kool cigarettes from his pocket, lit up a smoke, and never realized how dangerous it could be for a perp to make a suspicious move near a police car. "I need some Spanish coffee," Politoski told Corr in sigh of relief. "It's my treat!"

"When we have our cops on patrol, they are out there, close to the precinct cars and citizens and able to respond in a heartbeat and a flash to any developing emergency," claims an ESU officer, "whether it's an old lady stuck on a street corner or precinct cops suddenly under fire after they walked into a 10–30 [a robbery] of a bodega. When we respond, we come with speed, with tools, and, most importantly, with knowledge."

For ESU, being on patrol is much more than simply a cost-effective means for the department to have additional personnel riding around, stopping bad guys, and writing summonses. It is while on patrol that the E-cops are summoned to jobs. Sometimes jobs come over the air just as the REP is in front of a particular location, and sometimes even an REP is the first unit on the scene. In northern Manhattan, for example, where Two-Truck units routinely criss-cross some of the most crime-ridden streets in New York City, the sight of the REP slowly moving about the side streets of Harlem and Washington Heights reassures the law-abiding citizens that the department's finest unit is on patrol ready to respond the moment 911 is dialed.

In the ESU, there are cops who are remarkable with an MP-5 or a Ruger Mini-14 in their hands. They carry their weapons with dexterity and grace, and not only is their firearms accuracy dead-center, but their trigger temperaments are cautious and their instincts right on target. There are also cops who are rescue aficionados, who can pull up on a pin job and have the Hurst tool and its generator out of the REP in a matter of seconds. As amazed EMS technicians and fire personnel watch in awe, still trying to figure out where the intake nozzle and power lines go on their Jaws of Life, the E-cops have already inserted hardened backboards inside mangled vehicles and have enabled the expedient and medically safe extrication of the victims to awaiting ambulances. Most of the cops, however, not only shine while on patrol, they excel out on the street. Those who love every aspect of the job, from the boring to the ballistic, from the routine to the rescue, are known as workers.

Workers are generally the cops who care little about promotion or politics. They don't care if they'll be helping an old lady into her apartment or rappelling down the brick facade of a housing project ready to crash through a window with Glock automatic in hand. It is the job itself, the rush of adrenaline and the attention to detail, that is everything to them. Workers are usually highly decorated cops even before joining ESU, and they would rather talk about what gauge of rope is better to pull a fat man's bloated corpse out of the water than which team beat the point spread or who scored high on the sergeant's test.

ESU Truck Two has all types of cops in its ranks, but mainly it has workers—the truck is just too busy to pull the load of a cop who isn't doing his share. And in Two-Truck, there are few workers like Police Officer Seth Gahr. Like many in Two-Truck, Seth is a Harlem cop—it is in his blood and in his instincts. He is as much a part of the geographic landscape as are the Abyssinian Baptist Church and the Apollo Theater. "He exited the police academy on 20th Street and took a one-way ticket uptown," as one cop has commented on Seth. He spent nearly five years in the 3–2, one of the busiest precincts in Harlem and the city, working one of the city's busiest houses in both uniform and plainclothes.

There are very few things that could take Seth away from Harlem, one being the United States Army. Seth is a soldier—it is in his blood and in his heart. He is the only cop in ESU, and perhaps the department, who survived the grueling hell of the U.S. Army's ultra-torture known as Ranger School. While he was a young MP lieutenant in Germany, his efforts in securing a U.S. military facility were so good that German Red Army Faction terrorists, in documents seized by police, recommended against attacking a base guarded by Seth's team because the security was just that tight. Perhaps he was also a cop at heart, too, because Lieutenant Gahr left the glamour and beer of Germany to take the NYPD test in his native New York. Like the good soldier and cop that he is, Police Officer Gahr was later removed from the garden spot of the world, Manhattan, U.S.A., for all of seven months for service in the Persian Gulf with the massive American buildup of Operation Desert

Shield. During Operation Desert Storm, the actual war, and after, he processed thousands of Iraqi POWs. A man determined not to get hurt and not to risk his future on the job, especially with an application in for the Emergency Service Unit, Seth Gahr was awarded the Army Bronze Star for valor.

How many American soldiers who served in the Persian Gulf can claim to have gone from a place like Harlem to the rectum of the world (the Kuwaiti-Iraqi frontier) and then back to Harlem? After his months in the no-alcohol, no-women, no-nothing confines of Saudi and Kuwait, Seth came home to the sunny shores of Harlem, U.S.A., glad to be back. When he returned to the 3–2 tanner and leaner than when he had left, he wasn't congratulated for his courage or saluted for his sacrifice. Instead, he encountered "emotional" observations such as, "Seth, why do Iraqi men have mustaches. Give up? So that they can look like their mothers!" "Hey, Seth, is it illegal to fuck a camel?" "Hey, Seth, even the mutts missed you while you were away!" Welcome home, indeed.

By outside appearances, Seth Gahr looks nothing like an ESU cop. He isn't large, nor is he boisterous. His face is not adorned with a bushy mustache, nor does he sport a shamrock tattoo on his forearm, biceps, or thighs. In fact, it has been observed that when he's wearing his spectacles, Police Officer Seth Gahr looks like a professor in a 1920s Berlin University philosophy class. Among many E-cops, Seth Gahr is the enigma of the squad. Quiet, unassuming, and the brunt of more ribbing from his squad members than he deserves, he is a quiet professional who, for the lack of a better phrase, lives for the job—not police work per se but emergency service. "In the dictionary, under the word *E-cop,*" claims a former ESU supervisor, "is a picture of Seth Gahr."

In the truck's second squad, Seth is what's known as a centerpiece, beloved for his unique personality and distinctive New York accent laced with the Southern drawl of a U.S. Army sergeant, as much as he is for his courage on the streets. They just accept him for what he is—a damn good cop.

Seth is an integral cog in the machine that makes the entire apparatus work smoothly. Every day of his weekly tour, he comes from Brooklyn into Harlem and the zig-zag hop to quarters at 126th Street for five shifts' worth of police work. The cops (and bosses) from the adjacent 2-6 Precinct tend to take any and all available parking spots, and Two-Truck personnel must double-, triple-, or even quadruple-park around quarters, making the narrow confines of 126th Street almost impassable, or they might search for a spot near the corner bodega, where a ten-dollar food stamp and a smile get you a quart of malt liquor and a vial of rock cocaine and where a small army of junkies and mental patients call home. Seth tries to get to work early each day, something that the others in the truck find somewhat amusing. After he checks out what happened on the previous shift ("He did what with the Hurst tool on whose car, when?"), he checks in with the supervisors for any word on special assignments (hits, escorts, security details) and then proceeds to the sink, where he attempts to make a pot of coffee from a gush of brown tap water not suitable for human consumption. The remote control in the kitchen is seized and a cup of coffee consumed. Semi-dressed, he emerges from the locker room to check in with the truck supervisor and to fasten his utility belt and holster in a sweeping move of fastening clips and tightened loops that he has done so many times before, the motions now appear effortless. Every item on the belt is checked and double-checked—from the canister of pepper spray to his mini-Mag light. Seth tightens the leather holster for his Glock Model 19 9mm pistol firmly around his right thigh and positions it just right so that he can clutch it, in an instant, should the need arise. "Preparation is everything," he often likes to say. "Preparing your gear and preparing your mind is one extra coat of armor against the scumbags out there."

Seth likes to explain his preparation as an inherited

trait from his military service and parachute training when attention to detail is the difference between a peaceful leap from an aircraft at 1,200 feet to splatting on North Carolina grass, dead on impact. Others in the squad, however, look at Gahr's preparations with more ominous tones. Seth is what the department refers to as a magnet, an individual who attracts jobs. The big jobs. "I don't know," claimed Lt. Bob Sobocienski, the City North supervisor responsible for Two-Truck, "but Seth is always stepping in shit! Whenever there is a big job, whenever the media is around and the area crowded with bosses, Seth is either the first one through a door, the first one to pounce on the perp, or the one, as has happened before, who ends up having to shoot the perp." In a span of less than twenty-four hours last winter, Gahr was the first EMT at the home of former mayor Abe Beame when he suffered a mild heart attack, he rescued a family of four from the flaming ball of what was once a Chevy station wagon, and he saved the lives of two squad mates, Detective Henry Medina and Police Officer Jim McVey (now a pilot with the NYPD's Aviation Unit), when he shot and killed an EDP who had charged the E-cops with a chain saw in one hand and a sword in the other.

In the second squad, where most of the cops are decorated veterans of the mean streets of the city, the cops tend to work well with one another, each appreciating the other's gifts, talents, expertise, and temperaments. Yet if there are two cops who truly work well side-by-side in an REP, while on patrol and out on the big job, they are Seth Gahr and Henry Medina. Medina is one of the senior men in the truck, and in the division as well. His eyes have seen more life-on-the-line moments and more heart-racing instances than most of the other cops in emergency combined, yet for someone who can be considered an old-timer, Medina brings with him a fresh, energetic, and highly positive attitude to work each tour. He is not a case of burnout, grumpy in his golden years of emergency work, like so many other veterans. Medina is one of the most good-natured cops in the division, who is always smiling (whether he is listening to one of his fellow cops tell a joke or he is the brunt of the joke, usually something to do with Puerto Ricans and rice and beans), always happy to be at work, and always ready to offer a word of advice to a newcomer to the unit. He is a stoic figure of experience and knowledge in the truck whom his squad mates appreciate when out on patrol. Knowing every bit of the terrain he covers, Medina is a leader in a squad of workers and skilled emergency cops who make Two-Truck one of the division's best. "There are many great cops in the unit," claims one former ESU lieutenant, "but Henry is the one I'd want next to me on the big job."

Detective Medina is, though, a calming effect on the squad. When he works with Seth in Manhattan North, they offset each other remarkably well. They provide each other with checks and balances, two experienced viewpoints of the dangers of emergency work, and they get along in a unique, quite remarkable manner. On patrol, few do it like the team of Medina and Gahr.

The winter's chill that gripped Manhattan North in the weeks before Christmas was deceiving—it was comfortable for a moment, and then, in an instant, once the wind whipped up off the Hudson River, it cut through a cop's bones and the regulation blue tunic like a cold blade through paper. As the day tours were ending and the evening tours coming into work, 2–6 Precinct cops from both shifts were meeting outside and talking about the football games, the disappointing Giants and the miserable Jets, as well as other bits of gossip. "Cops," according to one Jewish sergeant working Harlem, "are terrible yentas." At quarters as well, gossip was the conventional currency of the day. For Sergeant Spratt's second squad, this was day four of a five-day stretch that had been both busy and quiet, tumultuous and mundane. There was, however, a feeling that there would be work tonight. It was too quiet. Harlem is never that quiet.

The tour, with Detective Medina and Officer Gahr in the Adam car, had begun quietly enough, with the citywide SOD frequency assigning only a handful of jobs involving elevators and aided cases, and all those were in Brooklyn. The sunset had bathed the Manhattanville Houses across the street in a beautiful orange glow, and the cascading rays of light from the setting sun were immersing the nearby elevated lines of the Number One and Nine trains, causing the uptown clanking of a local train heading to the Bronx to fly by in a stream of white light. As the two cops completed placing their gear inside the REP, a call came over for a gun run at St. Nicholas Terrace and Jackie Robinson Park, where cops from the 3–0 had chased a perp with a gun inside an apartment building. In a flash, the Adam car raced toward the 3–0, its lights flashing and siren blaring, Medina behind the wheel and Gahr maintaining constant radio communication with both the division and SOD dispatchers. The REP reached the location two minutes after receiving the call and found four 3–0 sector cars blocking traffic. The cops, their service weapons in their hands just in case, were busy scanning the nearby park for anyone who resembled the suspect. Nobody was found. "It's a ninety-Z," the 3–0 sergeant told the E-cops. "Sorry to have troubled you."

The streets of Harlem were filled with holiday shoppers spending their cash on new toys, new coats, and anything else that would fit under the tree. On Frederick Douglass Boulevard and 145th Street, as the REP stopped for a red light, the SOD radio came over with a job.

"Emergency Adam-Two, K?" the dispatcher announced. "In the confines of the 3–0 you are requested at West 145th for a gain entry."

"Ten-four, Central." Gahr looked at his partner and said, "Henry, that's right here, man." Gahr returned to the central dispatch. "Adam-Two responding. We are eighty-four at the scene!"

Medina flashed the emergency lights, but before he

sounded the siren to cut across traffic, his eyes began to bulge and his mouth opened slowly and widely. "What the . . . ?" In front of West 145th were three 3–0 Precinct sector cars and a four-by-four belonging to Chief of Department Louis R. Anemone. Gain-entry jobs are as routine in the ESU vernacular as they come, and four-star chiefs rarely make it a point to pound on a sledge and join the E-men on the entry, but chief Anemone is a hands-on commander who likes to be out on the street and on patrol, whether it be weekday, weekend, or holiday.

The job at West 145th Street was fairly routine but laced with possible danger. A woman had returned home from some Christmas shopping and found her door battered to the point where she couldn't get inside. Making matters worse, she had heard sounds coming from behind the door, making her feel there might be burglars inside.

Suddenly, this became a perp job, and Officer Gahr raced downstairs to the REP to grab his ballistic body bunker. If you are going to make a tactical entry, the reasoning goes, be prepared. A sledgehammer and a halligan tool were brought up just in case, but both Medina and Gahr felt that an old ESU door knock would do the trick just fine, the ESU door knock being a powerful kick to the frame with the might of a cop's boot. Both cops removed their Glock 9mms from their holsters, and Gahr placed his body and body bunker in the forcible entry position that would enable him to make a quick entry once his partner's leg dislodged the door from whatever was keeping it shut. "You ready, Henry?" Seth asked, his twelve-pound bunker hoisted against the door.

"*Police, get down now!*" the two cops shouted at the top of their lungs as they made entry, searching each room carefully and methodically to ensure that the perp wasn't hiding under a bed, in a closet, or under a pile of laundry. The bedroom window was opened, though, and it was likely that whoever had been inside was long gone.

Before the tools could be returned to the REP and the two E-cops resumed their patrol and got comfortable, another call came over concerning an EDP and possible jumper in the confines of the 2–8 Precinct, at 121st Street off Lenox Avenue. The building, a 100-year-old architectural wonder that looked as if it could be a set for some Transylvanian horror flick, was temporary housing for several street people in rooms converted into single-room occupancies. The premises looked neat and well kept, though the smell of marijuana and the mumbling of people who were definitely mental patients upstairs raised flags inside the minds of two E-cops. With the report of a jumper, the first thing Medina and Gahr did was to check the roof, but there was nobody standing by the ledge waiting to jump. As the truck responded, with Officers Ann-Margaret Lyons and Kevin Flanagan, the ESU and responding precinct cops began to interview the residents to find out, in the words of the 2–8 sergeant, "what the fuck was going on."

Inside a top-floor apartment, a young white male with dreadlocks, a cigarette in his mouth and one nestled between his fingers, began to yell at the E-cops, promising to "have their jobs" since his mother was a former city commissioner. As the EDP ranted and raved, Gahr and Medina moved in around the subject, just in case he made a sudden and violent move. "I don't care who your mother is or what she was the commissioner of, just tell me when's the last time you were in the hospital," Gahr said, "and have you been taking your medication?" Without force, without restraints, and without such tools as a Y-bar or a Taser, the EDP was politely persuaded to be handcuffed and transported by ambulance to Bellevue.

EDPs are a true challenge. They can run the gamut from a man wearing nothing but a suit made out of newspapers, talking to himself out of the corner of his mouth, to a man in a business suit carrying a copy of the *Wall Street Journal* who also happens to be rubbing excrement on himself. While many living outside the New York metropolitan area might very well consider most New Yorkers to be insane, the true emotionally challenged, those who post a threat to themselves or their fellow New Yorkers, are the domain of ESU. Over the course of a typical patrol tour, an ESU truck will receive dozens of jobs in regard to "unconfirmed EDPs" in the confines of one precinct or another. This means that someone has dialed 911, complained that a neighbor is nuts, and the citywide SOD dispatcher is awaiting confirmation from a responding precinct car before ESU is officially summoned. Most unconfirmed EDPs are unfounded runs—a man yells at his wife, and the 911 call so exaggerates the situation that the precinct thinks the man is holding his wife hostage; a woman sings the tune from *That Girl* to herself on the subway, and a transit official calls 911 complaining of a woman talking to herself. In 1996, ESU handled more than 40,000 EDP calls.

"Every time we get a call, we have one name in the back of our minds," claims Officer Anonymous, "and that name is Eleanor Bumpers." On October 29, 1984, officers from Three-Truck in the Bronx responded to a call for an EDP inside a project. The housing cops had gone to the location to serve an eviction notice and were confronted by a very large woman with a long history of mental problems threatening to kill them. According to one former ESU cop, in the past, in a different department and in a different ESU, E-cops used to determine the veracity of an EDP job with what used to be known very unofficially as the litmus test. If the individual was faking a spasm of mental illness or going through the "crazy routine" for attention, the sight of a cop cradling an Ithaca 37 12-gauge shotgun was usually enough to dissuade even the greatest feigner of mental illness that the time to behave was now. If that didn't work, then the sound of a round being pumped into the 12-gauge shotgun was usually enough to bring most people back to their senses in a hurry. If the shotgun was ignored, then the EDP was genuine, and the shotgun might possibly be a wise tool to employ. In the 1980s, when psychos were smoking their brains on PCP, cops often needed shotguns (and sometimes they could have used tanks) to subdue nut jobs who felt little pain and were bent on hurting themselves and scores of others.

Eleanor Bumpers did not need the litmus test, though the shotgun was used for the cops' self-preservation. The sixty-six-year-old grandmother was a 300-pound hulk of a woman with a lengthy psychiatric history. When the officers attempted to enter her apartment, she proclaimed that she would kill anyone who tried to evict her. As the officers slowly moved into the apartment, she lunged at them with a ten-inch kitchen knife. Fearing for his life and the life of his partner, E-cop Stephen Sullivan fired twice, killing the woman in an explosive fury. When the dust cleared, chaos had gripped the city. Bumpers was black, and African-American leaders urged retribution against the white cops. Police Commissioner Ben Ward, the city's first African-American PC, stood by while public outcry led to the E-cop's indictment. The politics of race in the city, exacerbated by weak-willed politicians and bile-spewing rabble-rousers, helped plant the seeds for Sullivan getting charged with second-degree manslaughter. Although charges eventually would be dropped after witnesses' testimony vindicated the cop as having acted in self-defense, the Bumpers incident became a turning point that the city, and ESU, would never forget.

The NYPD realized that new regulations and nonlethal means needed to be found to handle EDPs, and they also realized that ESU was the sole unit in the department, let alone the entire city, that was willing to handle EDPs. Much research was pursued into nonlethal equipment, and material eventually adopted for ESU service included a Taser electronic dart gun, a device that propels two barbed darts connected to a twelve-foot wire that produces an electronic pulse to temporarily immobilize an EDP; a pole-mounted NOVA XR500 stun device; a five-foot-high Plexiglas shield; two half-gallon water cannons (to shoot water, propelled by 100 pounds of air pressure) to distract and disorient an EDP; Kevlar stainless steel gloves to protect the officer from an EDP carrying a knife; chemical Mace and pepper spray; an EDP bar, an ingeniously designed restraining bar manufactured by the ESU training unit; and the Arwen Model 37 which fires rubber projectiles. In addition to these devices, ESU also deploys a wide variety of restraining equipment designed to transport individuals safely to a medical facility. These include Velcro restraining straps designed to immobilize the person but still permit medical evaluation and treatment. ESU officers also designed and constructed a unique mesh blanket for use with persons believed to be suffering from or exhibiting signs of cocaine psychosis. Known as the "nut bag," the device is meant to keep the EDP restrained, calm, and alive until he or she can be transported to a hospital emergency room for additional evaluation.

EDPs, to play on a quote by a former mayor of New York, are the true mosaic that is New York City. EDPs are white, black, Jewish, Muslim, Catholic, Hispanic, men, and women. They are the unemployed and unemployable, the educated and the aristocratic, the filthy and the habitually tidy. EDPs are the one aspect of ESU work that can be found in literally every part of the city and any time of day. In Manhattan North, for example, EDPs can be psychotic blue-blooded guests at swank Central Park hotels who run naked through the lobby while holding razors to their wrists, or an EDP could be a mother of twelve on welfare, so despondent over the loss of a loved one that she attempts to kill herself by swallowing a fistful of Drano. EDPs are found in precinct holding cells, and they are found on subway platforms. Some are found in hospital emergency rooms and rehabilitation clinics.

On Thursday, December 19, 1996, witnesses said, James Aaron Rowe, a well-dressed thirty-nine-year-old man, calmly walked into New York Hospital on Manhattan's posh Upper East Side and, armed with a straight razor and mental callings for revenge, took the elevator to the seventh floor in search of the doctor he believed had negligently treated his daughter. Rowe had spent nine years in prison for attacking a nurse attending to his late daughter, who had been treated in New York Hospital for leukemia, and nine years was a long time for the juices of retribution to stew in the dark recesses of a mind. On the seventh floor, Rowe began slashing and hacking away at doctors and nurses, seriously wounding several.

Even though New York Hospital is on 68th Street and York Avenue, Two-Truck units were in the process of completing a hit when the job came over, and the call was given to One-Truck and Sgt. Dominick Amendolare's squad, who raced uptown. By the time the job was confirmed, though, and it came over as an EDP holding hostages, Two-Truck units were at the 2–5 Precinct for a TAC meeting prior to a hit, and both the Adam and Boy cars, as well as the truck, raced over to the East Side. From the blood and horror on the seventh floor, it was evident to all responding ESU personnel that this was no ordinary psycho. This guy was on a mission.

ESU's primary task in such cases is to isolate the EDP, contain him or her, and then use nonlethal tools to neutralize and take the individual into custody; lethal force, still an option, is to be used only when all that stands in the way of a cop or a citizen getting killed turns out to be an NYPD-issue 9mm Glock or Ithaca 37 shotgun. Rowe, though, did not want a confrontation with the cops, especially since the E-cops, in their Kevlar vests and carrying shotguns, were offering him little slack or room to maneuver. E-cops carrying water cannons and canisters of pepper spray followed his every twist and turn, and Police Officer Roger Mack from One-Truck followed the EDP through the sights of his 12-gauge Ithaca—just in case. Rowe tried at first to hide behind a nurse's station, and then he retreated to a nurse's bathroom, where he ventured to attempt suicide by slashing his own throat. Officer Dan Donnelly, carrying the heavy-duty pepper spray canisters, popped open the bathroom door and zapped Rowe with a powerful beam of the debilitating mist. "This stuff is effective," claimed Donnelly after the job, "because he went down like a sack of shit after I peppered him."

Handling EDPs, along with gun runs and tactical work to back up the precinct cops, is one aspect of patrol that helps to hone the specialized skills of all the ESU cops and it is one of the reasons "workers," the cops who enjoy being busy, like to be in either the Adam or Boy car and out on patrol. Patrol keeps them busy, it keeps them alert, and it gets them ready.

Watching Officer Gahr patrol in the REP is like observing a highly trained operator, a well-honed commando, plying his trade deep behind enemy lines. At each corner, at each intersection, he sounds out the street number and the cross street as a mental reference—just in case the shit goes down and bullets fly, he'll remember where he is in the midst of chaos and terror. Back in Washington Heights, as the REP slowly twists and turns through the narrow streets of the 3–3 Precinct, up and down the blocks separating Broadway and Amsterdam, where young Dominican males, carrying cell phones and probably guns, stand posts in front of brownstones turned into narcotics supermarkets, the two cops patrol in a deliberate, almost machinelike manner. Detective Medina drives slowly through these darkened streets, the streetlights shot out by the drug sellers to make IDs by the "5–0," as the police are known, more difficult. It was on one of these streets that, in 1991, a 3–4 Precinct plainclothes anticrime cop killed a notorious cocaine distributor in a gun battle, resulting in a week of rioting and chaos that made the streets of Upper Manhattan look more like Watts in Los Angeles after the Rodney King verdict was announced. On one of these streets, too, a young housing cop was killed when a Dominican mope tossed a bucket of spackling off a rooftop that landed on the poor patrolman's skull, killing the rookie officer. Seth Gahr was one of the first

E-cops responding to that ten-thirteen. He worked tirelessly on the rookie cop in a desperate attempt to save his life. Gahr knows the danger that lurks behind every parked car and inside the darkened vestibule of every building on the streets of Washington Heights, where on patrol nothing is ever to be taken for granted.

As the two cops patrolled Washington Heights, in their slow and methodical zigzag of streets and avenues, the typical banter of patrol car bullshit grew in its variety and oddity. The conversation included weight training to weapons cleaning, where to go for a meal, the importance of a woman's posterior in the Puerto Rican community. Yet before the discussion could escalate (or denigrate) any further, a job was coming over concerning a shooting and a homicide at First Avenue and 109th Street. "Emergency Service Adam-Two," Officer Gahr instructed the divisional dispatcher on the REPs radio. "Show us responding to the 2–3 in regard to the shooting." In a matter of seconds, the REP was zooming down the Harlem River Drive into the FDR Drive, toward exit fifteen and a chaotic scene of spent shells and bloodshed in front of the East River projects. A supermarket security guard had been shot dead in an apparent robbery, and the perps had fled on foot toward Second Avenue. "What d'ya need, Cap?" Detective Medina asked the duty captain as he offered ESU's assistance. "We'll check the garbage and the sewers for any tossed weapons or possible shell casings." For the next half hour, the two E-cops did what E-cops always do best—they got dirty by crawling inside garbage and under cars and lying down over sewer gratings.

No weapons or additional rounds were found, though.

There is never a known, a given, once the REP is out on patrol. The same night, as Officer Gahr and Detective Medina were out on a gain entry, an EDP, a reported pin, a homicide, and a barricaded perp, something truly tragic would happen. In a section of Washington Heights, where a Con Ed transformer had blown, a row of apartment buildings were without heat or light. Because each ESU truck is also a mobile power station, Truck-Two tandems were offered the golden chance of earning some extra overtime by using the truck and several REPs as a mobile generator position; whoever wanted to stay around for the fun and games of setting up lights was welcome. At around 4:00 A.M., after Detective Medina and his overtime partner, Officer Kevin Flanagan, were wrapping things up, a horrific ten-thirteen came over the air from the confines of the 5–0 Precinct in the Bronx. Police Officer Neil Forster, directing traffic following an accident on the southbound Major Deegan Expressway, was suddenly, without warning, slammed against his sector car by an allegedly drunk driver. Compounding the tragedy was the fact that the other driver, James Kalenderian, was an off-duty officer who worked at the 4–4 Precinct in the Bronx. Kalendarian's station wagon had slammed so hard into the officer that Forster was thrown 100 feet into the air.

A ten-thirteen with an officer down is the worst type of call cops on patrol can receive, and both Detective Medina and Officer Flanagan raced to the 5–0 Precinct in their REP the moment it came over the citywide SOD radio. Blood was everywhere, and the damage to Officer Forster's body was massive. Responding ESU officers tried their best to keep the young cop alive until an ambulance and a police escort could rush him to an emergency room.

The accident and the fact that a cop was now a perpetrator in the maiming of a fellow officer had, no pun intended, a sobering effect on all involved. That a cop was responsible caused anger, embarrassment, and pity, all at the same time. Cops rarely realize that even though they chase people with guns for a living, one of the most dangerous elements of their job is just driving around in their patrol cars and trucks. The streets of New York are very dangerous.

Flanagan and Medina, the image of a shattered fellow cop still vividly imprinted in their minds, drove slowly down the Cross-Bronx Expressway toward the George

Washington Bridge and the Henry Hudson Parkway for the trip back to quarters. The Henry Hudson is itself one of the most dangerous stretches of roadway in the city—especially when the weather hovers near the freezing mark and a thin, deceiving, and lethal sheet of black ice covers the asphalt. As the REP headed back, carefully avoiding pockets of noticeable ice, it came across a stretch of the thin black slippery stuff that it could not avoid. The REP banked off a divider into a barrier and then flipped and rolled. The E-cops, used to responding to pin jobs, now found themselves tossed out of the REP's cabin, badly bruised and seriously hurt. The REP was seriously damaged, looking as if some giant had simply squashed it without mercy.

"You know what happened to you?" one of the nurses asked Medina in the emergency room, hoping that he was alert and responsive.

"Yeah," Henry replied with a smile. "Some big guy rolled over on me!"

For weeks, the damaged REP remained outside quarters awaiting a tow to its final trip to the junkyard, serving as a reminder to all the cops in Two-Truck: you never know what's gonna be out there and if, and when, you'll make it back to quarters and in what condition.

A few weeks later, back out on patrol in the Boy car on another cold night, Seth was working the stretches of Upper Manhattan with Ann-Margaret Lyons. A former transit rescue cop, Lyons is also what is known as a worker—an E-cop with great skill and energy. Seth works well with Ann-Margaret, and even though he must tone down some of his four-letter views of the inhabitants he passes by (especially large barking dogs), they make a good team.

The Boy car was summoned to secure a premise near 125th Street, a bodega selling such healthy fare as malt liquor, rolling paper, and expired milk. The owners, Middle Eastern entrepreneurs, had violated several court orders, including fire safety code violations and the sale of drug paraphernalia, and they were locked up by the precinct. But when the cops took them to the station, they couldn't figure out how to close the store up. ESU was summoned in what the unit calls a secure-premise job.

Inside the store, as the two E-cops searched for the electrical system that would lower the metal gates, Officer Lyons came across some photos, apparently of the owners, and apparently when they were soldiers in the Iraqi army. Knowing that Seth had been an MP and had handled thousands of Iraqi POWs in Desert Storm, Ann-Margaret thought that maybe he would recognize someone from his fun and games in the Gulf War—after all, don't all cops remember the faces of the perps they lock up? "Look like anyone you remember?" Ann-Margaret asked, smiling with a sarcastic grin as she awaited her partner's answer. "No, Ann," Seth replied. "None of these guys looks familiar."

On patrol, especially in Harlem, anything can and does truly happen. Patrol is hours of routine and boredom interrupted by seconds, minutes, and sometimes an hour of absolute terror. The unknown is a lure to many cops, a great mystery that makes coming to work every day a new and exciting experience. Many sergeants, though, because their role in the squad is to be in the truck with the chauffeur, often miss the interesting hours of patrolling the city. Occasionally, when sergeants are assigned as ESU citysouth or citynorth supervisors, they enjoy the freedom and mobility of being on patrol in their marked and unmarked cars. Or, when the big truck is out of service and the squad is forced to deploy from REPs, the sergeants often will make the most of the opportunity to sit inside the maneuverable confines of the smaller ESU truck and work the streets of the city.

On one eight-to-four, on a warm summer's day, Sgt. Juan Garcia and Police Officer Dan Donnelly were patrolling in their REP, returning from Washington Heights and a gun run, and from the La Famiglia Pizzeria with lunch. As they headed down Amsterdam Avenue, they came across a young kid on a bike, flagging down the REP and seeking ESU's help. "Excuse me opficas, mira mira, theah id dis hopeless man beating some fool updide da head and he gonna kill dis hopeless person!"

"Whaaaaaat?" the two cops said to each other, trying to figure out what the kid was talking about.

"Din ya hear was I say? Dere id dis hopeless man gonna whip somebody's ass, right dere on the tsoop."

"Emergency Truck-Two to Central, K. We are going to respond to the corner of 133 and Amsterdam, possible dispute. Please notify division and have them send a sector car forthwith."

Two men had been fighting over a woman, though by the time Garcia and Donnelly managed to ascertain what was going on, by the time everyone stopped yelling, shouting, cursing, and spitting, nearly 100 people had assembled on the corner, some threatening to throw rocks and bottles at the cops. In Manhattan North, where a routine argument can result in a full-scale riot, no job is ever to be handled lightly. "You could hit a thousand drug locations on warrants, and nothing will ever happen to you," claims a Two-Truck veteran, "but let your guard down for one fucking second on patrol, and you end up a dead cop!"

The scene had become ugly, but the two E-cops helped to talk down the emotion, alleviate the hysteria, until reinforcements from the precinct could race to the scene.

On one four-to-twelve in the summer, for example, Dan Donnelly and Steve Vales were riding through the northern half of Manhattan Island, responding to a call about a pit bull by City University. The dog had thigh muscles bitten away (apparently the loser of a pit bull fight staged by local drug dealers). There were also a few stuck elevators, a gun run in Washington Heights on Overlook Terrace, a domestic dispute with EDP potential in the 2–3, and a routine patrol of the Central Park area. It was, after all, summer, and New York's most beautiful and glamorous would be out in the park in their latest designer spandex.

The two had stopped back at quarters for their meal, they had rechecked the transmission on the REP, and, as darkness engulfed the city, they resumed their patrolling duties in Harlem. The citywide SOD radio was relatively quiet—very quiet for Manhattan North. Then, suddenly, after the crack of a 9mm fired indiscriminately into a crowd of kids playing in a park, Adam-Two was summoned to the corner of Fifth Avenue and 135th Street in the 2–5 Precinct, in front of the Abraham Lincoln projects, to help homicide detectives search for spent rounds and evidence. The shooter, a black male in his early twenties, had fired without letup into a crowd by the corner park, leaving one dead and three seriously wounded. An angry crowd had assembled, and the E-cops were needed as much for their flashlights and extendable Porta-lights on their REP as for the shotgun carried in their vehicle's cabin. Some of the victims' friends were vowing to skin the shooter alive. They had assembled outside the yellow tape of the crime scene, and the potential for large-scale violence was growing by the second. Both E-cops, veterans of jobs near housing projects, immediately focused their vision upward, toward the windows and the roof, looking to avoid the skull-crashing impact of any incoming "airmail."

As they headed back to quarters, close to the end of tour, they came across a raging fire in the 2–8 that was driving the precinct cops mad and then were suddenly summoned to a gun run in the 3–2. With the grace of a veteran Indy 500 driver, Vales maneuvered the REP through the maze of livery cabs and cars, racing to be first on the scene to back up the cops on patrol. Donnelly had unlocked the shotgun and was about to race out of the REP when the cops emerged out of the alley of an abandoned building with the perp already in cuffs. Patrol is always a mystery—the cops never know when the job will involve shots fired or whether the perp will be secure and in custody by the time they reach the scene.

Anything can happen on patrol. On one eight-to-four, as Officers John Politoski and Dan Donnelly were returning to quarters for lunch, the REP pulled up to 125th Street and Amsterdam Avenue and to a red light. The two were hungry, and they had been busy all day darting rabid pit bulls and removing aided cases from the remnants of their former vehicles. At the intersection, only a block from quarters, where they were already tasting the Chinese food they had brought back with them and nestled securely over the dashboard, Politoski gazed out the passenger window to see a cloud of billowing smoke coming from the Grant Houses at 55 LaSalle Street, between 123rd and 125th. He opened his mouth wide with disbelief and simply yelled, "Holy shit!"

"Adam-Two, K," Politoski radioed in. "We have a pickup of fifty-nine [NYPD term for a fire]. Get FD here forthwith!"

The two cops decided that they couldn't wait for New York's bravest to make an appearance at the inferno—the time to act was now. They pulled their REP to the entrance at 55 LaSalle and noticed people streaming out of the building like cockroaches, a cloud of thick black smoke racing from the top floors. In a furious race against time, Politoski and Donnelly removed their Scott pack breathing gear from the REP's hold, as well as their forcible entry tools. It was a smoldering chaos.

Some local pyromaniac had taken it upon himself to bring a mattress to one of the project's poorly lit stairwells and light it up like a Roman candle. The "high-quality nonflammable paint" that the city had painted the stairwells with was engulfed like dry wood on a barbecue, and a fireball raced up to the sixteenth floor. On the twentieth floor, some of the residents, smelling smoke, opened their front doors and the door to the stairwell, creating a massive backdraft effect which engulfed much of the building in a sea of deadly fire. By the time Politoski and Donnelly made it to the top floors, in search of victims and 2–6 Precinct cops who had courageously raced into the inferno to help rescue people, visibility was reduced to zero. The heat was mighty and unforgiving, and some of the elderly residents of the sprawling housing project were collapsing in the hallway. Both E-cops removed their Scott pack face pieces to give the precious air to the aided cases, and they evacuated nearly eighty people from the fourth to the fifteenth floors, including the five 2–6 cops who had ventured inside. The situation had gotten so bad that Politoski summoned the Four-Truck air bag, as he feared people would begin jumping out of their windows, and he ordered an NYPD chopper to the roof to assist in the evacuation of those trapped by the smoke and fire.

Ten minutes later, the Fire Department arrived. Instead of thanking the two E-cops, now covered in a thick coat of black soot, for helping out with the fire, one of the chiefs said, "If you want to do our job so badly, why don't you take the test?" Not wanting a confrontation and almost overcome by the smoke and exhaustion and depletion of adrenaline, Politoski simply said, "If you guys would get here on time, then I wouldn't have to do your job for you in the first place!"

As the two E-cops cleaned themselves off, attempting to recover from the smoke and the aching muscles, they looked at each other with smiles of approval. Courage, compassion, and the sense of duty are things that each cop brings to work every start of tour, but the dangers of running into a blazing fire are something that all E-cops are well aware of. On January 5, 1987, Police Officer Frank La Sala, a mainstay at One-Truck, was in quarters when a fire raced through a building adjacent to the 13th Precinct at 222 East 21st Street. Grabbing a small air pack, La Sala raced into the burning building, where his efforts helped save the lives of more than a dozen people. He became trapped on a staircase engulfed by fire and flame, however, and collapsed. Firefighters found him unconscious and burned over fifty-five percent of his body. He died days later.

A visiting British police constable once called New York "the most bizarre city on the face of the earth." His comment, the conclusion after a visit to the Midtown South precinct, was a tame reflection of the comings and goings inside a busy precinct. He never made it to an ESU truck.

On patrol, while responding to the ostensibly routine, ESU units are often summoned to jobs that few people outside the job would ever believe were genuine but happen on a fairly regular basis. Because they have the tools, because they have the expertise, and because they have the reputation for never turning down a job, no matter how distasteful, dirty, or dangerous, cops throughout the city have come to rely upon ESU to handle the jobs that they cannot or are not willing to do. That reputation has spread to the medical community and the ranks of EMS, as well. It results in jobs that E-cops rarely tell anyone about, since nobody would ever believe it anyway.

ESU could also be called the "Dirty Harry squad." They get called to every bizarre, filthy, and tasteless job that cops usually encounter but don't have the stomach or equipment to solve. From kids with their hands stuck in meat grinders to men with handcuffs on their testicles, anything that can evoke a cry or a chuckle usually ends up on Two-Truck's run sheet. Because of the diverse territory they patrol, because of the range of social, religious, and sexual deviancy they encounter, the cops of Two-Truck have seen it all, removed it all, and, with a big "thank God" for their work gloves, touched it all.

Because of the very bizarre nature of some of the calls, and because the precinct cops on the scene aren't always forthcoming with a great deal of information when calling ESU (because they are either aghast with horror or on the floor laughing), the cops responding never really know what they are about to encounter.

Some of the jobs are just stupid. "Emergency Boy-Two," the dispatcher will summon. "Report of a woman in the water at a house on Amsterdam Avenue." Silence overtakes the two cops inside the cluttered confines of the REP. They look at each other and say, "Amsterdam doesn't overlook the river, does it?" More silence. Yet, before they can get back on the air and request additional information, the radio becomes a frenzy of activity. "Central, this is Scuba Launch 32. We are responding to Amsterdam." "Central, this is Harbor Charley. Show us responding." "Central, this is Aviation Air-Sea Rescue. We are on our way!" More silence inside the confines of the REP, as the deeply analytical minds both cops are trying to exert to their maximum potential are pressed into a peculiar state of puzzlement. "Central, this is Emergency Boy-Two. Can you please ten-five the job and see if a sector car is eighty-four and have them update us?" Another few minutes of silence, and then, "Boy-Two, K. The woman is reported to be four hundred pounds and stuck in a bathtub. Do you copy?" As the two cops spend the next five minutes cursing out the dispatcher, all seaborne rescue units inform the embarrassed dispatcher that they will not be responding to the Amsterdam Avenue address. "No shit, Central," replies one of the cops in the REP, mimicking talking on the radio. "No fucking shit!"

When dealing with New York's tales of the extraordinary and the wacky, one can hardly blame the dispatcher for not getting the job right. When one hears a precinct cop report a job with the words *woman* and *water,* one does not think of a fat slob who, when combined with water, has created a powerful industrial-strength vacuum that even the mightiest of cops (let alone ESU cops) would have trouble dislodging. No matter how distasteful the job might be, especially after a large plate of rice and beans from the Floridita on 125th and Broadway, extricating the sea of blubber from her porcelain prison is part of the job and part of that honored distinction that makes an E-cop.

Each cop in Two-Truck, each cop in the division, for that matter, has his or her own library of bizarre jobs. They are comical and unreal escapes from the routine of regular patrol and regular emergency work.

At 4:30 P.M. on one four-to-twelve, Police Officers Dan Donnelly and Richie Miller were still in quarters when the phone rang. The emergency room surgeon at St. Luke's Hospital, a few blocks away on Amsterdam Avenue, had gotten Two-Truck's number from somewhere and needed the E-cops to respond to his operating room for "a very delicate matter." All the doctor would say on the phone was that it involved "the removal of a ring."

When Donnelly and Miller arrived at St. Luke's, they found the patient, a Hispanic male in his mid-forties who spoke not a word of English, lying on a crash cart writhing in pain. Without uttering a word about what was the medical emergency requiring ESU's attention, the attending doctor lifted the poor soul's gown and revealed a gold high-school ring stuck on the infected, discolored, and obviously about-to-fall-off penis. The ring had been placed halfway down the shaft and had become stuck. Either the ring or the penis had to come off. "Can you help us?" the doctor asked, realizing that this was not a case for a scalpel, forceps, and plenty of sponges. "We'll do our best," was the cop's sole reply.

Dan Donnelly is many things—he is a good cop, a volunteer fireman and EMT for nine years, an experienced and hardworking E-cop. He is also at times a cantankerous soul who is probably the last human being on earth anyone would want operating on him—especially when it involved something as important as one's penis. Yet, with the seriousness of a surgeon and the mind of a mechanic rather than a cop, Officer Donnelly sized up the situation. "Hey, Doc," Donnelly replied. "We have a Dremmell tool, a little wizzer saw that can engrave things. That just might work."

Donnelly and Miller suited up and scrubbed, and while the nurses injected a generous dose of Novocain into the man's penis, an ESU operation was about to commence. One nurse joked, "This is something I am sure you'll never see on the show *ER*." Another nurse, displaying a look that bordered laughter and nausea, held the penis straight up while Officer Miller stuck a forceps underneath the ring—to prevent the man from receiving a Dremmel amputation, something hard was needed under the metal in case the saw cut clean through. As Officer Donnelly plugged in the Dremmel, causing it to hiss and grind loudly, the doctor began spraying the penis and the ring with saline solution in the attempt to keep the metal, and the member, cool. The moment the Dremmel's blade hit the ring, though, sparks began to fly, and the deafening clanking of metal cutting metal began to make everyone in the operating room a tad nervous. Cutting gently and slowly, Donnelly wedged the blade of his portable saw until he could see the spinning blade cutting through the ring and finally slicing the band in half. The operation took all of five minutes. The sigh of relief lasted much longer.

"Gee, honey, what did you do at work today?" a thoughtful wife or girlfriend of a Two-Truck cop might ask upon her man's return after a nine-hour shift. "Oh, nothing, sweetie. We had a gun run, and I removed a man's engorged schlong from a high school ring. That's it."

Other rescues are not as bloody or as desperate but bizarre nonetheless.

During the midnight hours, ESU units throughout the city get lots of calls for "gain entries." As in the infamous TV commercial, "I've fallen and I can't get up" really happens. Mostly, when ESU is summoned to gain entry into an apartment, it is because the person inside is injured and can't make it to the front door to open the array of locks that most New Yorkers have decorating their doorways. Sometimes, though, the person in need of help is simply glued to a keyboard.

On the night of January 20, 1997, a middle-aged woman, a screenwriter living on East 68th Street, managed to lock herself inside her bedroom and was unable to open the door. Nervous about being trapped inside the small room, she opened her window and began yelling for help, but it was 1:00 A.M., and the only people walking the streets were not the type you'd want to call out to for assistance. She had no phone with her, but she did have her laptop computer and a phone jack. What did she do? Simple. She went on-line, over the Internet, and entered Prodigy chat rooms searching for someone not interested in talking about sex or threesomes who could call 911 in New York City for her. Her search took two hours.

At 3:00 A.M., Adam-Two, with Police Officers Ronnie Bauman and Vinny Martinez, received a gain-entry call in the 19th Precinct. They managed to burst through the door and rescue the harried woman. For Martinez, a computer wiz, the ordeal was a comical turn from the pin jobs and gun runs that usually happen in Harlem once the clock strikes twelve. He actually made history. It was the first Internet rescue on the NYPD's books.

On patrol, ESU units also get summoned to their fair share of "animal conditions." In New York City, and especially Manhattan North, that could mean Police Officers John D'Allara and Ray Nalpant darting a herd of rabid pit bulls at a drug location in the 2–8, or Police Officer Kevin Reynolds coaxing down a raccoon from some scaffolding outside a church on West 95th Street. Officers have handled squirrels, pigeons, hawks, eagles, snakes, lizards, monkeys, alligators, and even bears. On one job, Police Officers John Politoski and Eddie Reyes were called to a woman's apartment in regard to a "wild rat" running around the bathroom. The two arrived with an animal control kit and a dart gun, but the rat was an elusive SOB, and the cops had to break through part of a wall in order finally to get in position to dart the damn thing. That would have been all well and good were it not for the fact that the rat job was filmed by a TV crew from the show *Cops.* Although a highly decorated cop, one of the most popular and capable cops to ever serve in ESU, and now a sergeant, it took Politoski "forever" to live the incident down.

One day, Two-Truck units were summoned to Fort Tryon Park, in Washington Heights overlooking the Henry Hudson Parkway and the Hudson River, for what the SOD dispatcher was describing as "a boat atop a hill."

"Ten-four, Central," the Adam car responded. "We'll take that job." Yet, for both Vinny Martinez and Eddie Reyes, it suddenly dawned on them that there was no water in Fort Tryon Park, just trees.

"Ten-five the job, Central?" Officer Martinez asked. "Please respond to Fort Tryon Park for a boat on a hill."

As the REP reached the center of the park, they came across a half dozen chickens and a goat, not a boat, "a billy the fucking nanny goat." Several Santeria worshippers had decided to have a festival, and some of the local four-legged creatures decided to go berserk and try to escape rather than be sacrificed in an orgy of blood and incense. So, what started as a boat job ended up being a lasso job, as the E-cops chased scores of goats and chickens through the park with animal control kits, ropes, and other exotic bits of gear for the next thirty minutes. It looked like a buffalo hunt from the Wild West, as some of the cops chased the animals with .22-caliber animal control dart rifles while chicken feathers and goat shit were flying everywhere. Lt. Bob Sobocienski, the city north supervisor known throughout the division for his fondness for open-air barbecues, rubbed his hands together in delight as he checked back with the dispatcher concerning the goat job.

"Central, this is U-4. Is that a *confirmed* goat in Fort Tryon Park? Show me responding forthwith!"

Primarily, though, patrol is designed to have the ESU in position, somewhere in a sector, when precinct cops need backup. On one midnight tour, as the Adam car was completing its Bronx border to 59th Street patrol, Police Officers Vinny Martinez and Ronnie Bauman came across a wild call for a ten-thirteen at the foot of the Queensborough Bridge. Two rookies in the 19th Precinct, fresh out of the academy, had come across two men with guns in a stolen sedan. Shots had rung out, and the terror-filled call of cops being fired at went out over the divisional airwaves. With Martinez driving and Bauman grabbing the Ithaca, the REP cornered the stolen car and forced it to stop at the entrance to the bridge, with the lights of Long Island City in the background. They ordered the perps out one by one with the loudspeaker ("LA style"), until each was lying face-down, legs and hands spread. Martinez speed-cuffed the pair, while Bauman covered his every move with the barrel of the trusted shotgun. By the time the two rookies, their faces white and haunted from the experience of having bullets fired at them, made it to the bridge, the perps were in cuffs and the Two-Truck cops were enjoying the view of Sutton Place and the East Side skyline of Manhattan.

One early spring day in the Big Apple, Police Officers Vinny Martinez and his partner, Ronnie Bauman, found themselves working a circular corridor of precincts and commands as part of the Northern Manhattan Initiative. Although these two denizens of the midnight tour are used to fulfilling their E-cop functions from 59th Street to the borders with Queens and the Bronx, their duties with the initiative had them confined to one precinct, in support of counternarcotics operations and to be there in case a warrant went bad and additional hands were needed. Yet it was a "slow" night for the truck, *only* having a dozen perp searches and gun runs, a few vehicular accidents, and several aided and elevator jobs.

Martinez had wanted to grab a few moments from the tour to race into a church and go to confession so that he could fulfill the obligations of serving as godfather at his nephew's christening the next day, but the constant racing around from job to job would not permit meeting a religious obligation that night. "Hey, don't make a face," Bauman told his always hyper partner. "I'll bless you if it makes you any happier."

As the two continued their harried tour from one call to another, they were, miraculously, dispatched to a church on the corner of St. Nicholas Avenue and 174th Street in the 3–4 Precinct for a stuck occupied elevator. A group of youths were working in the church facility when they got stuck in a service elevator. The priest had called the job in, and Martinez wasted no time in seeking his moment of religious comfort at the same time as he and his partner jostled their elevator pole through the metal workings of the lift in order to free the soon-to-be-claustrophobic misguided youth of the city.

"Father, do you have a minute?" Martinez asked respectfully, taking off his hat and gloves while talking to the man of God. "I am to be my nephew's godfather tomorrow at his christening, and I wanted to trouble you for . . ."

"Confession?" the priest completed the question. "You guys do a really fabulous job, a difficult job, and you get little respect for what you do. You want to be absolved? Say one 'Our Father' and three 'Hail Marys'!"

"I guess I'm absolved, then?" Martinez asked gently.

"God forgives you, my son. Amen!"

From the deadly to the divine, anything and everything will happen to ESU on patrol.

3

October 1995: The Visit of the Pope, the Departure of Santa Claus, 152 World Leaders, and a Psycho in Bayside

"The world will be watching you."—NYPD Chief of Department Louis R. Anemone, in videotape training tool issued to the 38,000 cops in the city prior to the pope's visit and the UN 50 celebrations

"Nineteen ninety-five has been 'the year of the police' in New York City. It happens to be our 150th anniversary, but you didn't spend the year looking back on our past accomplishments. You spent it establishing a new benchmark for police performance. In 1995, the NYPD proved itself to be the most vital, innovative, effective, and forward-thinking police department in the nation, if not the world. The papal visit and the UN's fiftieth anniversary showcased your skills. You rose to an enormous challenge, and you made it look easy. It was a textbook demonstration in how to manage large crowds and maintain blanket security."—Former Police Commissioner William J. Bratton, in the September/October issue of the NYPD magazine, Spring 3100

As a Housing cop, Ralph Pascullo knew the importance of rooftops. Purse-snatchers sifted through their stolen merchandise on rooftops, junkies used rooftops as high-altitude shooting galleries, and rapists and perverts often dragged their victims up toward the high-floor terror of the rooftops. Housing cops inspected rooftops alone, never truly knowing what they'd find or who they'd confront. It was dirty and dangerous duty. If you controlled the rooftop, after all, you controlled the tower, and if you controlled the tower, you controlled the entire project. On November 18, 1973, a young and wide-eyed Ralph Pascullo entered the New York City Housing Police Academy as a new recruit to the city's least heralded law enforcement agency. With 252 public housing projects in New York City, with their 600,000 legal low-income residents, more people lived in subsidized housing in New York City than lived in most major cities around the world. Many of the residents were hard-working, and many were not. Crime was rampant in the projects, from murders to rapes, savage beatings to incest. A project had everything. Even though the Housing Police, with its nearly 2,000 officers, was, before it merged with the NYPD, the seventh largest police department in the United States, it was light-years behind virtually every other agency in terms of everything from procedure to very basic equipment such as radios and squad cars. The projects were overcrowded, riddled with crimes and criminals, and home to just about every crime imaginable. In Housing, if you weren't a good cop, you weren't anything at all.

Ralph Pascullo had the great fortune of being an energetic soul whose police skills were molded by a formidable "rabbi," the legendary Capt. John Filan, who showed him the ropes and taught him the zealous skills of policing. Pascullo would follow in his rabbi's footsteps, and the two would make hundreds of collars in the process—nabbing robbery suspects and a father-and-son rape team, caught red-handed, as the father proudly wanted to teach his boy what it was to be a man. The first housing cop to routinely carry an NYPD radio in the notorious 7–3 and 7–5 precincts of East New York, Brooklyn, Pascullo worked his way up the ranks and through a chestful of medals to become one of the most decorated cops in that department's history, During his career in the Housing Police, he held coveted positions in various investigative and narcotics units, including serving as a lieutenant in the notorious Fort Greene Section of Brooklyn. His last assignment, prior to the merger, was a the commanding officer of the Housing Emergency Rescue Unit. Often, as a young cop on patrol, he would stand on rooftops, gaze out over the skyline, and wonder where his job would take him. As fate would have it, his career would travel full circle, and the job would take him once again to rooftops, though these wouldn't overlook slums and wouldn't involve walking through the waste left behind by heroin addicts who used rooftops to shoot up and then as convenient toilets. These rooftops were atop the United Nations, the Plaza Hotel, and the U.S. Federal Courthouse. Fate would take Capt. Ralph Pascullo into the vanguard of the world's most audacious dignitary protection detail, in the ranks of the New York City Police Department and a center spot in its flagship unit and chosen as the unit's first Archangel "Package" commander.

In the spring of 1994, there had been talk of Pope John Paul II coming to visit New York for a week. Because of his importance, because of the world climate in terrorism, and because there had already been one attempt on his life, a tremendous security package was scheduled around the Holy Father. One of ESU's primary duties is VIP and dignitary protection. ESU cops are the NYPD's heavy-weapons specialists, the only force in New York capable of coping with terrorist attack, and because they have the machinery and the vehicles to counter most threats, every dignitary visiting the city worthy of an assassin's bullet or a terrorist's TNT has come under the watchful and muzzle-flash security of the NYPD's Emergency Service Unit. In most cities, where there aren't many VIP visits, protective work is infrequent. In New York City, though, viewed by many (especially heads of state) as the true capital of the world, security details are so frequent and high profile that ESU has become, perhaps, the worlds's premier dignitary protection unit.

The pope, though, was a different type of "package," as protective details are known. He wasn't the type of world leader who used his visit to the Big Apple for meetings, a speech here and there, and dinner and a Broadway show. The pope wasn't likely to stay in his hotel suite for the duration of the visit, either. Although slowed down in recent years, John Paul II was an energetic figure who, borrowing from American political practices, enjoyed pressing the flesh. He'd be traveling frequently, he had planned a mass in Shea Stadium, and he certainly would visit St. Patrick's Cathedral on Fifth Avenue. For any would-be assassin, John Paul II would be an accessible target, providing numerous opportunities in numerous parts of the city. For ESU and the rest of the NYPD, John Paul II was a package to be protected at all costs.

News of the pope's planned visit reached the desk of Inspector John P. Harkins, ESU's commanding officer, at a time when ESU was busier than ever. The NYPD in 1994, under the dream crime-fighting tandem of Mayor Rudolph Giuliani and Police Commissioner William Bratton, was involved in nothing less than a war to reclaim the streets of the city from the criminal element. The NYPD would adopt a proactive method of policing, rely on computerized information for plotting crime trends and anticrime strategies, and tackle quality-of-life crimes like never before. ESU, as the tactical spearhead of the department, was involved in the dangerous works of warrants and dynamic entries, serving narcotics and homicide warrants on crack dens and heroin labs, weapons stashes, and killer cribs. Together with precinct bosses finally unleashed to do their job, ESU helped the department clean up the city one block and precinct at a time. The results were staggering, as crime dropped by leaps and bounds. The might of the NYPD was reinforced by the merger between the regular NYPD and the two other city agencies that maintained law enforcement in the five boroughs, the Housing Police and the Transit Police. The ranks of the NYPD swelled to 38,000.

Even before the departments formally merged into one happy family, the Housing Police Emergency Rescue Unit already had been serving on loan with ESU. The housing cops were, on the whole, dedicated, hardworking, and eager to join such an esteemed unit as ESU. Having worked the projects, known as the shittiest precinct in the city next to Riker's Island, many of the newcomers to ESU were thrilled for the chance to do some of the more exciting tactical aspects of the job, such as VIP details. When the merger became formal and the Transit Police Emergency Unit was made into ESU, the city's tactical spearhead boasted nearly 400 cops.

Overseeing the merger into his unit and the increasing number of warrants ESU was carrying out, Inspector Harkins had little time to think of such a large-scale operation as a papal visit. When poor health caused John Paul II to delay visit, Catholics in New York were saddened, but many in the NYPD were relieved. That relief would be short-lived. John Paul II rescheduled his visit for the fall of 1995—October, to be exact. It was going to be a busy month. In late October, the United Nations would celebrate its fiftieth anniversary in Midtown Manhattan. "UN 50," as the week became known, wasn't going to be just a large-scale gathering of world leaders, it was going to be the mother of all gatherings. In fact, with more than 150 world leaders scheduled to attend, from President Bill Clinton to Cuba's Fidel Castro, UN 50 promised to be the largest single gathering of world leaders anywhere at any time in world history.

Throughout the late spring and summer of 1995, for a full six months, in fact, the NYPD geared for what promised to be the largest spotlight ever shone on a municipal police department. Although federal agencies, from the Secret Service to the State Department's Diplomatic Security Service, would be participating in the security blanket, this would be the NYPD's moment to shine. From the office of Chief of Department Louis Anemone to the desk of Inspector Thomas J. Mullen, the CO of the Operations Division, from the offices of the Intelligence Division to Inspector Harkins's supervisory roundtable at ESU, the NYPD plotted, planned, and prayed.

Taking one job at a time, Inspector Harkins, together with his captain and lieutenants, realized one thing: to strike out at the city, and possibly the country as well, a terrorist didn't have to assassinate the pope to acquire the global media spotlight. Perpetrating some kind of act of terrorism, from satchel charge of explosives to a sarin gas attack, to coincide with the papal visit would have devastating effects on the city and the prestige of the department. Harkins engineered an ESU top-secret deliberate disaster plan known as "Operation Archangel." The premise of Archangel was simple. While ESU assets were busy protecting the primary package, a separate force, consisting of dozens of cops and several vehicles crammed with equipment, would be on standby status at strategic points throughout the city, ready to respond at a moment's notice to any developing contingency. "When one fuckup could lead to an international incident," one ESU cop instrumental in the Archangel planning commented, "then being cautious was definitely the smart path to take."

Operation Archangel's objectives were simple: to effect a rapid and disciplined response to the site of a deliberate disaster (NYPD terminology for a terrorist attack) or other appropriate incident; quickly to establish specialized emergency operations including the creation of conditions providing for the maximum security and safety of all rescue personnel; to be prepared to address simultaneously an additional incident occurring at the same, or a different, location; to respond to predetermined checkpoints in order to prevent escapes and apprehend suspects; and to maintain adequate emergency service coverage for the remainder of the city. Although the exact makeup of Archangel packages are classified, they were specifically on alert to deal with car bombs or biological or chemical devices.

Operation Archangel was a masterstroke of preventive security. The beauty of the Archangel makeup was flexibility. Although policy dictated each Archangel response in terms of vehicles and deployment, the lieutenants or sergeants who commanded them were permitted to alter plans and deployments as they saw fit. The Archangel setups, with their many ESU vehicles ready in various locations, were also high-profile calling cards to anyone scouting NYPD preparedness and resolve. "Fuck with this city," an E-cop boasted, "and look at what you'll be up against!"

As the summer drifted into memory and the first hint of fall approached, ESU began to intensify its dignitary protection readiness. To all in ESU, from Inspector Harkins to the newest E-cop in the unit, it was clear that October would not be business as usual. There would be no trucks, no routine shifts, and few squads operating as they had grown accustomed to. For a unit long known to be stingy when it came to overtime, October was going to mean double shifts. For many of the cops who lived on the eastern stretches of Long Island or upstate, some forty to sixty miles away (or, as one cop would comment, "so far upstate that their kids go to school in Montreal"), the papal visit meant that quarters would also become a home away from home. It would be a time like no other in ESU history.

For the department, the oncoming security operations were harder to prepare for. The NYPD, in its proud 150-year history, has come across some of the cruelest, craftiest, and most cunning criminals ever to steal a car or kill a stranger, but international terrorists and hit men were perps of a completely different sort. Cops might have the sixth sense and instinct to see who in a crowd of the faithful coming to hear mass at Central Park might be a pickpocket or a mugger. But they weren't trained for the killer who had more than ten kilograms of Semtex strapped to his inner thighs and was ready to incinerate himself and scores of others. In terms of the terrorist's favorite tool of the last few years, the car bomb, most cops only knew that if a car was parked illegally or the meter had run out, it was to be ticketed or towed. Distinguishing a Volkswagen crammed with nails and C–4 from one simply parked illegally was something new to most cops. Nobody knows what terrorists look like, after all; they could be male, female, young, or old. This was something quite new to the NYPD.

Even though much of the heavy-weapons firepower brought to bear would be the domain of the federal agencies involved and ESU, it was the beat cops, the precinct cops, and the other units on patrol who would be the eyes and ears of the specialists. They would be out in force, mingling with crowds and providing that all-important first layer of security. "Patrol cops," according to a detective in the Intelligence Division, "were the department's first line of defense in any protective security package."

In the videotape training tool distributed to every precinct in the city, Lieutenant Sobocienski gave a candid suggestion to the cops who would be watching: "During this time of heightened awareness, just remain alert, and keep your eyes and your ears open. Be nosy. Anyone who acts suspicious is worth looking at and checking out. Don't let anything go that looks strange. Sometimes you feel the hairs on the back of your head standing up, something's telling you that something's wrong. React to it. Please just don't let it go by!"

Sobocienski ended his message with the following: "There are a lot of people out there looking to embarrass America. I just don't want to see anybody get hurt!"

The catchphrase for the NYPD's campaign of diligence and protection was "Security with a Smile!" If the visit went by without incident, there would be smiles throughout One Police Plaza. Police, though, aren't paid to be optimists or to rest on their laurels. Cops on the job a long time recall with great fondness the pope's first visit to New York back in 1979. During that visit, he traveled down First Avenue in a limousine waving to jubilant crowds. This time, though, nothing would be left to chance. "The world has changed a lot since 1979," Chief of Department Louis Anemone was quoted as saying.

ESU's diligence would have mattered little were it not for the intelligence gathered and disseminated by the Secret Service and the true unsung heroes in the security detail, the NYPD's Intelligence Division. Although rarely talked about in the press, "Intel" monitored threats, worked closely with federal and international agencies, and routinely met and coordinated strategies and procedure with ESU bosses. Wearing their traditional suits and ties, Intel officers routinely followed leads on psychos who might present a threat to the Holy Father. Each time a dignitary visited New York, the Intelligence Division put together a threat analysis of the principal to see how dangerous the visit would be and what assets the city needed to put into place to provide the required security. This time, there would be 152 threat-analysis studies conducted—from the pope to the leader of Liechtenstein.

In New York, where nothing ever goes easy, law enforcement was on a heightened terrorism alert in early October, and for good reason. On October 2, 1995, less than forty-eight hours before the pope's scheduled arrival in the Big Apple, ESU was busy securing another detail, though clearly a package of a different nature from the pope or the international dignitaries. Sheikh Omar Abdel-Rahman, the fiery blind Muslim leader who was the spiritual mastermind behind the World Trade Center bombing and a plot to blow up much of New York City, was found guilty in federal court of seditious conspiracy in plans to conduct a holy war of urban terrorism against the United States. Ten of his cohorts also were convicted of various charges. The guilty verdict was little surprise, but it came at a bad time. Muslim fundamentalists in Egypt and Iran denounced the verdict and vowed revenge. Would that revenge come in the form of an attempt against the pope's life? The timing made ESU bosses anxious. As a precaution, Abdel-Rahman, whom the E-cops nicknamed Santa Claus, was immediately flown out of New York once the verdict was read. "If ever there was justification in the Archangel concept," an E-cop commented, "it was Santa Claus and his band of merry followers." That view was correct. In their campaign to topple the secular government of Egyptian president Hosni Mubarak, Rahman's followers have killed more than 1,075 people. In New York, they succeeded in targeting a key landmark for demolition and killed six people in the process. They were a group with fanatical fire, murderous intent, and explosive execution.

On the night of October 4, 1995, Pope John Paul II landed in New York after his arrival in Newark, New Jersey, and an evening prayer service at the Sacred Heart Cathedral. He was flown in, on a U.S. Marine Corps helicopter usually used by American presidents, to the South Street heliport in Lower Manhattan, where a serious motorcade was waiting. The pontiff was greeted by Mayor Giuliani, Cardinal John O'Connor, Police Commissioner Bratton, Chief of Department Anemone, and scores of other clerics, police brass, and political heavyweights. He was rushed to the Vatican residence at East 73rd Street just off Central Park and Fifth Avenue, where his entrance to the building was shielding by a large white tent, meant to dissuade any sniper in the area eager to take a shot at the pontiff.

The moment John Paul II arrived in New York, a simple message went out over the SOD radio: "The package has arrived!"

Part of the ESU way of securing VIP packages is to have a CAT (or counterattack team) car follow the motorcade and escort for a split-second tactical response. A van capable of seating several E-cops in heavy vests, helmets, and weaponry, the CAT car was an essential element of the motorcade that provided a heavy-weapons counterassault team should there be an attempt to either assassinate or kidnap the pope. CAT car work is difficult. The cops sit in the darkened van, understanding what's transpiring around them solely by radio communication. "If we get called to action," an E-cop reflected, "it'll probably be after we feel the heat from the explosion and hear the pounding succession of automatic fire." At Camp Smith, near Peekskill in upstate New York, ESU units routinely train in deploying from a CAT car in a motorcade. The training is long, arduous, and meant to simulate the various scenarios that could result when the E-cops swing open the van's rear door and race out with weapons ablaze. Training is one thing. The shit hitting the fan on the streets of Manhattan is something completely different. It's something that every E-cop hopes will never happen but realizes that he or she must be ready for.

NYPD and ESU escorts, such as the one that met the pope at the heliport, also consist of highway unit radio cars (whose mission is to ram any potential vehicular threat), police motorcycles, an REP, and, just in case, an ambulance. For good measure, heavily armed Secret Service agents in several vehicles led and supported the convoy. Observers and countersnipers were positioned at key elevated positions along the route, and NYPD choppers, with video-reliance systems, piped in the goings-on to a command post at One Police Plaza.

The pope's arrival in the Big Apple was met with joy and jubilation. For the NYPD and ESU, though, the mood was tense yet confident, proactive and professional. As Secret Service special agent in charge Brian Gimlett reflected, "In our business, failure is not an option."

During the pope's visit, there would be six locations in New York where security commands would be deployed in force: the Vatican residence on East 73rd Street off Fifth Avenue, the United Nations, the Vatican mission on West 38th Street, Aqueduct Raceway, Central Park, and St. Patrick's Cathedral. The true burden went to the patrol lieutenants who would be commanding sites where the pope would be staying, visiting, and praying. Each location had its fair share of observers and countersnipers with their Remington M–24 7.62mm rifles, as well as E-cops who stood at the ready, their heavy vests and helmets on their hands cradling their Ruger Mini-14 5.56mm assault rifles and Heckler and Koch MP–5 9mm submachine guns. Besides the Archangel packages and the regular ESU REPs on patrol, Peacekeeper armored cars, four-by-four wonders in extricating personnel under fire, would also be available. It was to be a massive show of force and a high-speed tactical response to any and all contingencies.

At the Vatican residence, the security detail was at its heaviest. Jersey barricades and roadblocks prevented any vehicular traffic from even thinking about coming to within one block of the building. Sharpshooters and observers ringed the rooftops, and CAT car teams stood at the ready twenty-four hours a day, poised to respond to the slightest hint of attack. ESU cops and bosses were positioned inside the residence, as well, all in heavy vests and helmets, with their weapons locked and loaded. Stairwell duty is one of the most difficult jobs for an E-cop. It is lonely, boring, and very hot under the heavy pounds of Kevlar. Residents of the Upper East Side block also were placed under the full security ring. Anyone delivering packages had to be searched and frisked and their credentials reaffirmed; all packages, whether shipments from Victoria's Secret or pints of moo-shu beef from the nearby Chinese take-away, were fluorscoped. Residents of the building were searched on their way home and told not to go near their windows. ESU and Secret Service sharpshooters were on rooftops monitoring nearby windows, roofs, and tree lines.

One of the security nightmares involving the pope was

his mass at Aqueduct Raceway, in the confines of the 106 Precinct in southern Queens, on Friday, October 6. An open-air mass at Aqueduct, with tens of thousands of worshippers in attendance, might seem like a day of spiritual reinforcement to most, but it was a security headache of untold proportions for ESU. For fear that someone had planted a bomb at the racetrack or in one of the pavilions, the entire raceway was swept, re-checked, swept again, and double-checked by the Secret Service, U.S. Army specialists, the NYPD Bomb Squad, an ESU. Lt. Bob Sobocienski's countersnipers, men with eagle eyes and well-disciplined trigger fingers plus the patience of prophets, positioned themselves atop roof girders where they had a constant view of the entire crowd. Everyone coming to Aqueduct would be searched by cops and then fluorscoped by passing through a magnetometer. No large packages would be permitted, and only those who had received tickets from their parishes were allowed entry. Hundreds of ESU cops, patrolmen, and plainclothes officers also would mingle among the faithful. "I got there at 4:00 A.M.," Lieutenant Sobocienski reflected, "and I remember thinking as to what an awesome task this was going to be, plus how important it was that nothing go wrong. I remember it was a gorgeous sunny day. Something out of the ordinary. And as the crowds gathered and the pope began, you felt a real electricity in the air. It was so powerful you could almost touch it. I don't care how religious a cop was that day, I don't think that there's a man or woman in the unit that will ever forget that day."

Yet of all the papal events, the celebration of mass on the Great Lawn at Central Park would prove to be the department's greatest security challenge.

In one of his early comedic offerings, Eddie Murphy, in reviewing current events back in 1981, posed the following question to his audience: "What kind of person would shoot the pope? I guess somebody wanted to get into hell and didn't want to stand on line." The NYPD's Intelligence Division had learned of several individuals who had made threats against the life of the pontiff. Some of the threats were unfounded, some simple cranks, and others much harder to check out. Making matters worse, on the morning of the mass, there were reports of a man wearing camouflage fatigues who was carrying a bag believed to be holding a rifle. The "Oh shits" had come to a holy gathering.

For all papal events, guests allowed to get close to areas where the pope would be needed specially coded tickets and badges that indicated to security units, both federal and NYPD, that the person was, for lack of a better word, kosher. For Central Park, 120,000 tickets had been issued for "seating," but how do cops seek out the nonkosher individuals in a crowd that by conservative estimates was expected to exceed 200,000 people? It was destined to be the NYPD's finest moment.

To provide security, from routine patrol to tactical response units, the NYPD dispatched thousands of cops to work the mass at Central Park. Cops were pulled out of every precinct in the city for patrol duty in what planners hoped would be a show of force the likes of which the city had never seen before. Only days earlier, on October 1, the NYPD had abandoned its light blue shirts (what cops used to call the "Maytag repairman look") and returned to its traditional solid navy blue uniform. The cops assembled at Central Park, standing tall in their new uniforms, created a sea of blue that stretched from Central Park West to Fifth Avenue, from the Midtown approach to the park to 86th Street and the Metropolitan Museum of Art. NYPD choppers hovered overhead, checking out every roof, water tower, and treetop.

Crowds began to filter into Central Park at 5:00 A.M., and everyone was given what cops like to call the onceover. Anyone who looked suspicious was talked to and searched. ESU cops, in radio communication with observers, countersnipers, and Archangel supervisors, walked through the area just to make sure that everything was in place. For Lt. Bob Sobocienski, the event gave him the opportunity to work hand-in-hand with Capt. Lewis Manetta, his former partner and close friend from the early 1970s. The two had telepathic communication with each other and had made hundreds of collars together, both in uniform and in one of the city's first plainclothes anticrime units. Manetta and Sobocienski were known throughout the department as "Bulldog and the Jackrabbit." As commander of the 3–3 Precinct in Washington Heights, Manetta had the opportunity to work closely with his former partner in the confines of Manhattan North. They were a team to be reckoned with.

As part of the massive security detail, Manetta and Sobocienski were working together supervising their cops in the field. As the mass commenced, both men, their minds working in the same crisp telepathic partnership that had made them legends years ago, came across a person in the park who, Sobocienski remembers, "had that *Taxi Driver* look." Manetta worked his way to the front, to be in position to grab the potential threat from behind, while Sobocienski walked slowly toward the individual to start talking. From the outset, Sobocienski had the impression that this guy was wrong. Being courteous, not confrontational, Sobocienski began to do what he likes to term "the old schmoozarooni" with the subject as he innocuously patted the individual down to make sure that he wasn't carrying a gun or an explosive device. "It was, after all, security with a smile," Sobocienski recalled, but his partner wasn't smiling. As Sobocienski went through his good cop routine, Manetta stood at the ready, along with several uniformed officers just in case the situation became ugly. The subject was gingerly, and quietly, removed from the crowd and investigated by precinct cops. With "that" situation under control, Sobocienski returned to the Great Leader and the job at hand.

In Central Park, a Two-Truck tandem of observers, Detective Henry Medina and Police Officer Pete Tetukevich, climbed atop a sound tower to set up a long-range pair of binoculars and a long-range rifle to scan the crowd for the mysterious man in the cammies who was making everyone so nervous. They found nothing out of the ordinary.

Gatherings weren't the only security headache. Every time John Paul II traveled from Point A to Point B, a massive package, ranging from CAT cars to sharpshooters, helicopters to Secret Service agents, followed his every move. The city came to a halt every time the pope moved, and the potential for a madman's bullet the moment the pontiff was in the glass-encased Popemobile was very real. One such motorcade, albeit a brief one, illustrates the security concerns that came with the pope traveling. On Saturday, October 7, the pope conducted services at St. Patrick's Cathedral on Fifth Avenue between 50th and 51st Streets. Following the services, he was to travel to the Vatican mission to the United Nations on 38th Street off Madison Avenue for a luncheon with religious figures and local and state politicians. Point A to Point B was all of twelve blocks.

Protecting a motorcade traveling down an avenue surrounded by high-rises and office buildings, down what could be called a sniper alley, was precarious. A gunman could be situated behind any one of the thousands of windows along the route, lurking and waiting for that one moment to get off his shot. The NYPD simply shut Madison Avenue to vehicular traffic. The four northbound lanes from 36th Street to 53rd Street were sealed shut and police barricades set up along the sidewalks to contain the onlookers. Hundreds of uniformed police officers, their watchful eyes scanning the crowds that were gathering and always checking in with their supervisors about anyone appearing suspicious. Motorcycle cops went back and forth along the route, checking every pothole and manhole cover, and highway cars checked the avenue on dry runs and fly-through.

At St. Patrick's Cathedral, Sgt. Marty Garvey of the countersniper team acted as the man on the ground, relaying any useful intelligence to his observers and shooters on the surrounding rooftops. At 38th Street, Bob

Sobocienski, Mike Libretto and Richie Greene, lieutenants known as the "Three Amigos," were in position awaiting the pope's arrival. On rooftops, E-cops trained their scopes on nearby windows that were ajar, while on the ground, veteran E-men like Sgt. John Boesch of Nine-Truck in Queens South, readied CAT cars and REPs for any contingency. When word was received that the pope had left St. Patrick's, the entire security package went into high gear. Helicopters hovered overhead, and motorcycle cops positioned themselves for any possible call to open a street in case the pontiff was under attack and needed to be rushed to an evasive route. Inspectors and other bosses rallied their cops to check windows and make sure nothing appeared suspicious. Even members of the press, including reporters who had been working the TV beat in the city for thirty years and whose faces were recognizable landmarks on the city scene, needed special papal credentials, color-coded for a day, and even then they were cordoned off to a remote area by Secret Service agents.

The motorcade moved slowly down Madison Avenue, allowing crowds to catch a glimpse of the Holy Father, standing upright in the Popemobile, a white armored car with a bulletproof glass enclosure. A motorcade of Secret Service sedans and Chevy Suburban follow cars preceded the Popemobile, flanked by NYPD motorcycle units and highway cars. Following the pope's procession was a CAT car, an REP, and an ambulance—just in case. Until the pope was safely inside the building, adrenaline flowed powerfully, and the hearts of the cops providing the security raced a mile a minute. Cops feel a sense of dedication to a "package" that transcends the job. Safeguarding a figure like the pope is a sacroscanct mission.

Throughout his five days in New York City, the Holy Father endeared himself to millions of New Yorkers and the men and women of the NYPD who helped safeguard his pilgrimage. John Paul II understood the tireless effort of the cops dedicated to his safety, and he was adamant about rewarding the gesture. In the United Nations, for example, upon catching a glimpse of countersniper team commander Lt. Bob Sobocienski, he gave the honored lieutenant a set of rosary beads. "Excuse me, your holiness," Lieutenant Sobocienski said in true Sobo fashion, "but I was wondering if I could have one for my mother-in-law as well, as she hasn't been well of late." Sobocienski was the kind of ESU boss few could refuse, from the E-cops in the trucks to the bosses at Floyd Bennet Field, and Pope John Paul II was another who was captivated by his honesty and charm. His candor, openness, and humility impressed the pontiff. The Holy Father, gazing at the embroidered nametag on Sobocienski's navy blue tunic, smiled and simply said, "Ah, Sobocienski, you truly are Polish!"

At the residence, a member of the pope's staff came to the E-cops manning their watch and asked if there was anything the cops would want the pope to bless for them. "It was a truly moving experience for us," Capt. Ralph Pascullo recalled. He remembers placing rosary beads and photos of his kids on the silver platter the Vatican staff member was passing around to the cops. Officer Vinny Martinez placed his white metal badge on the platter, and other cops placed rosary beads, religious medals, and photos of their wives and kids. Police work, especially high-risk jobs like dignitary protection, is often thankless. The reward the E-cops received from John Paul II will never be forgotten.

There are few cops in ESU who will ever forget the pope's visit, from those who protected him in his residence to those who guarded him at Aqueduct Racetrack, Central Park, and the Papal mission on 38th Street.

The departure of John Paul II brought mixed emotions to many of the cops in ESU. Virtually every E-cop, whether Catholic, Jew, Protestant, or atheist, was touched in one way or another by the pope's presence. Yet the end of the pope detail marked what many in ESU called "the dry run." It was a demonstration that ESU could protect one of the world's most beloved, and targeted, individuals. Whoever might have been out there, possibly gunning for the Holy Father, never made it past the ESU veil of blue armor. Now, in a matter of days, ESU and the NYPD would have to replicate its efforts 150-fold, spread throughout the Midtown cluster of Manhattan, and cover transition between a massive security package surrounding one man and an equal effort that would have to be divided 152 different ways. In two weeks, every world leader from President Clinton to the rulers of the Central African Republic would reach the boundaries of the five boroughs. If there were nuts and professionals out to kill the pope, imagine what would be out there in the streets of Manhattan looking to harm President Clinton, British Prime Minister John Major, Israeli Prime Minister Yitzhak Rabin, Jordan's King Hussein, PLO Chairman Yasir Arafat, Cuban Premier Fidel Castro, Indian Prime Minister P. V. Rao, Pakistani Prime Minister Benazir Bhutto, Croatian President Fanjo Tudjman, and Bosnian President Alija Izetbegovic. For each and every one of the 152 leaders who would assemble, there was at least one group who would want to assassinate him or her. No politician lived in an enemy-free society. What better place to knock off a world leader than in New York? What better way to embarrass the United States of America?

"We were lucky that we had the pope's visit only a short time before the UN 50 celebrations," Lieutenant Sobocienski remembers. "It gave us the means to fine-tune our security plans and preparations."

There was, however, something else to fine-tune. Before the celebrations commenced, the Saudi Arabian mission to the United Nations reported the theft of an armored limousine with bulletproof windows. Limousines with diplomatic plates were rarely stolen from well-guarded underground garages by ghetto kids out for a joy ride. Armored cars were stolen for bank heists or something far more sinister. With 152 world leaders about to land on the shores of the city, the prospect was chilling. In CAT cars, E-cops routinely trained in responding to a threat on a motorcade; highway cars, the true mobile battering ran in any convoy, were tasked with running into any car that proved to be a threat. But an armored car was something that even ESU couldn't stop—especially if that car was crammed with a ton of explosives and racing toward a target in a suicidal gesture like the one that had obliterated the U.S. Marine Corps barracks in Beirut. ESU commanders also recalled the plot by "Santa Claus and his crew of holy warriors" to blow up landmarks throughout the city employing car bombs. Targets included the Diamond District (on 47th Street between Fifth and Sixth avenues), the Lincoln Tunnel connecting Lower Manhattan with New Jersey, and, ominously, the United Nations. Raising additional red flags was the fact that the plot also included the assassination of Egyptian President Hosni Mubarak, a scheduled participant at UN 50. As fate would have it, he was one of the only world leaders who felt safer at home, behind the four walls of the Presidential Palace in Cairo, than in the Presidential Suite at the Plaza.

Still, ESU commanders did not want their officers and snipers to be faced with the scenario of a limousine charging through the barricades of a cordoned-off street and then realizing, far too late, that their heavy weapons weren't doing a thing other than bouncing bullets off the car.

Capt. Curt Wargo, ESU's executive officer and an E-cop for nearly thirty years (including being both cop and sergeant at Two-Truck), contacted one of the more energetic and tactically oriented E-cops in Harlem, as well as one of the more mechanically proficient, Police Officer Pete Tetukevich, for help. "The call came in on a Thursday," Tetukevich recalls. "We were doing a four-to-twelve, and eighty hours later, on Monday, the first prototype was operational." What Tetukevich and Wargo devised was a mobile car-stopping device that was completely portable and could stop a speeding armored car. The device was simple—a portable speed bump with a built-in air bag that, on command, would inflate and raise a metal plate that would enter the car's undercarriage, damaging its radiator support and drive train as well as jamming the front wheels. Such devices existed in embassies and consular parking garages throughout the world, but they were built into the foundation of the building and were not portable in the rear bed of a pickup truck. The device, which became known in the department as the Tetukevich/Wargo tool, was to operate in conjunction with other roadblock methods, but it was a barrier of last resort in case the "Oh shits" happened in a big way outside a major UN 50 function.

No matter how talented E-cops might be, no matter how proficient they were with their Glock Model 19 9mm service weapons, Ruger Mini-14 5.56mm assault rifles, or MP–5s, ESU and the NYPD was outnumbered in providing security to the world leaders gathering for UN 50. After all, each world leader, from President Clinton to the premier of Micronesia, received a motorcade and escort from Kennedy Airport in southern Queens. The Van Wyck Expressway, a parking lot on bad days, was closed for much of the first few days as the world leaders arrived literally one after the other. In Manhattan, anyone who thought of parking a car on a Midtown street was in for a rude surprise. Streets were closed sometimes, cordoned off to parked cars (as well as mailboxes, garbage cans, and newspaper vending machines) at others. When President George Bush came to New York years before, reporters termed the traffic nightmare caused by his motorcade "Bushlock." "UN-lock" was like nothing the city had ever seen before. In the span of twenty-four hours, there would be 150 automobile motorcades racing the world leaders to and from their hotels and other various meetings, dinners, and gatherings. Some motorcades consisted of as many as thirty vehicles, while some were no more than a limousine, a Secret Service escort, and two NYPD motorcycles. Each time a motorcade passed, though, streets needed to be closed off and traffic halted.

To help provide the required manpower, the NYPD and local federal offices received massive assistance from every federal law enforcement office in the United States and beyond; in fact, one deputy U.S. Marshal commented, "From Virginia to the Virgin Islands, Des Moines to Denver, anyone not working on a specific case or detail was rushed to New York City." Field offices throughout the country sent agents to the Big Apple from the DEA, the Marshals Service, the Bureau of Alcohol Tobacco and Firearms, the Customs Service, State Department Diplomatic Security, Immigration and Naturalization Service, and even IRS criminal investigators who normally audit the business records of organized-crime figures. A lot of the agents, never having been to New York, were just as amazed by the local sights and sounds as by the job at hand. "This place sure is big," Capt. Ralph Pascullo recalled one federal agent saying. "These building sure are tall!" he heard another one say out loud with a heavy Southern drawl, apparently more interested in the fifty-story skyscrapers than the details being presented at a TAC meeting.

Although never confirmed, there were reports that the massive security umbrella was also augmented by elements of the U.S. military, most notably personnel from the "North Carolina Rifle Club"(the slang title for the operators of the Army's elite Delta Force) and underwater operators from the "Little Creek Scuba Club" (the slang title for the navy's SEAL Team Six); black and olive-drab cigarette speedboats, the kind used solely by James Bond or covert forces, were seen on call in the murky waters of the East River near the United Nations. Several military choppers resembling the MH-60 Pave Hawks used by both the U.S. Army's 160th Special Operations Regiment (Airborne) and the U.S. Air Force's Special Operations Squadrons were seen on several occasions hovering over the city.

UN 50 would prove to the NYPD and ESU just how easy the pope's visit had been. In a part of New York no larger than ten blocks by twenty blocks, there were

152 world leaders, 152 separate motorcades, 152 separate dinner plans, 152 spouses going shopping, 152 separate meetings, and 152 migraine headaches. "Forget about us and our heavy-weapons response, forget about the snipers and the CAT car and the Archangel setups," an E-cop commented following those exhaustive days. "Imagine the mind-boggling work that traffic cops must perform just to make sure that two motorcades don't end up smacking into each other, and our guys don't end up looking like the Keystone Kops." In fact, ten years earlier, during the UN's fortieth anniversary, traffic planning for the ninety motorcades had been poor. Motorcades routinely converged, sometimes from two countries that didn't get along, and although arguments among nations were common, fist-waving exercises in profanity, with two converging security packages, blocked city traffic sometimes for as far as fifty blocks.

Of all the locations to safeguard during the week of meetings and celebrations, the single most vulnerable target was, of course, the United Nations headquarters. Standing alone on the shores of the East River between 42nd and 45th Streets, the United Nations was visible from a large stretch of Queens and Brooklyn, from the tip of Roosevelt Island under the 59th Street Queensborough Bridge to the industrial sections of Long Island City and Greenpoint. The General Assembly building, in fact, overlooked the waterway and the Queens skyline. What worried police planners was the fact that when all 152 world leaders gathered in one central location, one nut or one determined team of professionals with a .50-caliber sniper rifle or an RPG could kill scores of kings, prime ministers, presidents, and premiers. There had never been such a gathering in one city before, let alone in one small location. This was, as one E-cop joked, "the mother of all headaches."

When the world leaders met, for both the General Assembly addresses and the obligatory "all the leaders of the world standing together" photo op, police and federal officials simply held their breath. NYPD Harbor

Unit vessels and Scuba launches were moored off the East River, guarding against frogmen. ESU officers were on Roosevelt Island to be in tactical position in case there were any attempts to launch a sea strike at the facility. Archangel packages were in Manhattan and Queens, and a ring of Secret Service and ESU snipers were on rooftops in a horseshoe ring of 7.62mm and .308 protection around the building.

There were a few false alarms, including fallen bricks exposing pipes (mistaken to be devices) on the outer facade of the UN General Assembly building, and one true moment of heart-racing terror.

As the world leaders met, talked, and exchanged speeches and niceties, ESU observers atop the building noticed something truly bizarre: a man flying a motorized hang-glider southbound down the East River, on a path toward the United Nations. In the past, most notably in Israel, terrorists had used hang-gliders to murderous effect. Was this guy a nut, strapped with explosives or armed with a sniper rifle or silenced .45 automatic? At the first sighting of the unidentified flying object, the entire NYPD and federal apparatus went into full gear. Harbor units fired up their engines and readied their on-board Mini-14 5.56mm rifles, NYPD Aviation choppers scrambled and rushed to the area, and scores of snipers peered through their sights and began to caress trigger housings. As the individual neared, the trigger fingers began to become sweaty, and the art of controlled breathing, a must for a sniper, was practiced. The Secret Service snipers were ready to fire, but the NYPD sharpshooters were ordered to wait. As the flier unveiled a banner in support of Greenpeace, an NYPD Bell 412 hovered above him and, in a down draft, forced him to land the craft on Roosevelt Island. "That guy just doesn't have a clue as to how close he actually came to being splattered all over the East River," an ESU sniper commented. "His life was literally seconds away from a quick and ballistic termination."

If the United Nations building itself was a nightmare

to secure, Cuba's Fidel Castro was a pain in the ass to protect. The Cuban president, snubbed by Mayor Giuliani and the American delegation, ended up traveling to the Abyssinian Baptist Church on 138th Street and Lenox to speak to scores of supporters. Most world leaders didn't include the land north of 96th Street on their itineraries, but Castro was definitely a bird of a different feather. He did what he wanted, when he wanted, the security package be damned. On another night, he decided to invite his entire entourage to a meal at Jimmy's Bar and Grill, a noted establishment in the Bronx on Fordham Avenue near Yankee Stadium. The decision to go to Jimmy's was immediate, without allowing much lead time for the snipers, an Archangel setup, or Secret Service walk-through of the area. Castro's evening was fun, but it came very close to being his last.

Like the Greenpeace protester flying high above the East River, Castro never realized how close he came to getting killed. Although never publicized before, ESU sources say federal and local authorities came across two plots to assassinate Castro in New York. The first hit man, seeing that the package around the Cuban leader was virtually hermetic, abandoned all plans—he simply couldn't get near enough. The second gunman, who made it close enough to Castro near Jimmy's Bar and Grill to pull the trigger, realized that he could have killed the dictator but would have been taken out in the process, and decided that the exchange wouldn't be a fair one.

The pressure and the potential for a deadly screw-up were enormous. The work was exhausting. Every cop in ESU worked a double shift. If the E-cop wasn't patrolling a stretch of the territory his truck covered, then he was on a rooftop somewhere, inside a Peacekeeper, or inside a CAT car. During the week of events, meetings, conferences, and galas, quarters at Two-Truck, as well as the other trucks in the city, resembled a military barracks. Cops slept in rotating shifts, snoring in brief intervals, while their fellow cops, out on patrol, routinely came and went as the jobs were called in. "It was impossible to sleep in quarters, with the TV on in one room, the radio chattering away in another, and the loud beeping noise of the garage door opening and closing all the time," remembers a cop in Two-Truck still tired from that week in October, but working a seventeen-hour day and then some made driving home foolish. Underwear, socks, and laundry were hung out to dry on impromptu clotheslines set up within the caverns of the locker room, and cops shaved, showered in sinks, and fell asleep in the always bustling bathrooms. There was always a cop on the phone, talking to his wife or finding out how school was from a young child wondering when Daddy would be coming home. The lucky cops were those who lived in the Bronx, Queens, or Brooklyn, who could race home for a quick three hours of sleep in comfortable sheets beside someone they didn't have to sit next to for a tour in the close confines of an REP. Lt. Bob Sobocienski, who lived out in Suffolk County, stayed at his mother's home in Astoria during the pope's visit and the UN 50 celebrations. "I would get home at ten at night and wake up at two," Sobocienski fondly remembers, "and no matter what the time, my mother would insist on waking up as well and cooking me breakfast. I'll never forget that!"

Police work is a mind-boggling exercise in finding out that shit happens. For nearly six months, the NYPD, the Secret Service, and ESU prepared for contingencies ranging from Abu Nidal and his hooded gunmen attacking the United Nations to some local terrorist group, perhaps a right-wing militia, detonating a truck bomb in downtown Manhattan. ESU and the Secret Service trained, with exhaustive detail, on the abandoned runways at Floyd Bennet Field in Brooklyn to perfect their skills in maneuvering high-priority motorcades out of harm's way in the event of an attack. Nobody prepared for a scenario in which a homicidal EDP, armed with a Ruger Mini–14 and magazines full of shiny 5.56mm ammunition, would decide to wage war against the City of New York in an explosive display of murderous rage.

Saturday, October 21, 1995, was just such a typical "you never know what's going to happen until the shit goes down" day in the life of ESU's Truck-Two. Police Officers Vinny Martinez and Ronnie Bauman, steady partners on the midnight and working their first shift of the night, safeguarding the dignitaries was demanding work. Inside quarters, they sat with their combat gear on the truck, their German-made MP-5 9mm submachine guns and Ruger Mini-14 5.56mm assault rifles cleaned, checked, locked, and loaded. For Martinez, dignitary work as all new and exiting. As a former cop in the Housing Police Emergency Rescue Unit, his specialty was rescuing kids from stuck elevators and ending barricaded situations involving crack-addicted mothers and their families. Boris Yelstin, after all, had never visited the General Grant Houses in Harlem. Dignitary work was new to his partner, as well. When the Transit Police merged with the NYPD, his unit merged with ESU. Bauman was another transfer. Highly decorated and the survivor of a hellacious shoot-out in Manhattan while serving in the Transit Police Emergency Rescue Unit, Bauman was a worker, a courageous officer, and one other cops always knew would be there for them when things turned dangerous. VIP work was also something new for Officer Bauman—after all, how many dignitaries took the subway?

Both officers were veterans of the streets and subways, but they were also quick learners in the geopolitical magnitude of their current assignment. And they were more than cognizant of the risks involved. A holy warrior could drive a U-Haul truck through the front of a building and blow himself, and everyone else around, away in a thunderous blast. A suicide team of terrorists could race into the hotel where Yitzhak Rabin was staying, overcome the NYPD, Secret Service, and Israeli contingent, and assassinate the Israeli leader in a hail of gunfire. Or a professional hit man, armed with a Browning and a silencer, who was able to squeeze off just one shot, could attempt to assassinate one of the leaders from the embattled Balkans. However it could go down, both cops wanted it to happen overseas—far from their city and far from their watch.

Capt. Dan Connolly was also new to ESU, having just been promoted and transferred over from the Harbor Unit. A former jumper with the 82nd Airborne Division, Connolly was a respected and highly decorated cop, what the department terms a "Harlem cop." He grew up in the NYPD in what was at the time the world's most dangerous precinct—Harlem's 2–8. Covering a small stretch of landlocked terrain, the 2–8 was four blocks wide and seventeen blocks long, and there wasn't a night in the early 1970s when the sound of automatic gunfire was not heard cascading through the air. It was the nerve center for the Black Panthers and the Black Liberation Army, and cops were routinely marked for assassination in the confines of the long, narrow precinct. In the 2–8, cops didn't measure their length of service by the time on the job; they counted time by the number of firefights they participated in.

As midnight approached, Captain Connolly found himself in Midtown Manhattan, checking in with his crews on security details and hoping that the night would pass quietly. The SOD radio, ESU's frequency, was buzzing with jobs, though. There was an unconfirmed EDP in Brooklyn's 6–9 Precinct, a reported floater in the East River, and a vehicular accident near Kennedy Airport requiring ESU attention. Harlem, Midtown, and Downtown, however, were quiet. There were no barricaded perps, no gun runs, not even a stuck elevator. Most importantly, there were no reports of terrorists. Officers Martinez and Bauman relished the quiet. They were trying to get down from the adrenaline high from the security detail they had participated in only hours earlier.

At 2:31 A.M., quiet turned to panic. A routine call of jobs on the SOD frequency was suddenly interrupted by a screaming officer from the 1–11 Precinct in Bayside, Queens, yelling, "Ten-thirteen! Shots fired, officer down!" Ten-Truck units, nearby in Flushing, were the first to respond, as were Officers Scott Kushler and Jay Strauss from Three-Truck in the Bronx. Captain Connolly, already shifting his unmarked patrol car from park to drive, was racing toward the FDR Drive when he informed the SOD dispatcher that he was responding. "What the hell is going on in Bayside?" he thought to himself as he raced through the deserted bridge toll plaza and Grand Central Parkway heading toward the northeastern corner of Queens. "I hope this isn't a diversion."

Back in Harlem, Officer Martinez looked at his partner and cautiously asked, "Is that confirmed?" There was another call of a ten-thirteen, this time with background noise of automatic weapons fire, was heard. Martinez grabbed the radio, said, "Central, this is Truck-Two. Show us responding with the RMI at the job in the 1–11. Over!"

"Ten-four, Truck-Two."

"Hold on, Ronnie," were the last words heard before the REP flashed its lights, cranked up the siren, and raced back to quarters at eighty-five miles per hour across the Triborough Bridge into Queens, into Bayside, and into a wall of fire.

One Leo Yoelson, a disgruntled worker in his family pizza parlor, had murdered his mother and dog and decided to empty his collection of ammunition onto the service road of the Clearview Expressway. He unloaded more than 100 rounds of ammunition before police arrived. A neighbor, attempting to flee to safety, was shot in the back of the head and killed, and a police officer from the 1–11 Precinct was hit in the ankle and thigh and pinned down in the crossfire by a parked car. ESU faced two dilemmas on this job. First and foremost, they had to rescue the wounded officer. Yoelson was firing military-caliber weapons, ammunition that could slice through the officers' bulletproof vests and body bunkers, but it didn't deflect from the pressing priority of removing the shot officer to safety. Secondly, of course, Yoelson had to be stopped—one way or another.

The wounded officer, screaming in agony and bleeding profusely, had caught the attention of Yoelson, who now tried to zero in on the target in blue. Instinctively, Officers Kushler and Strauss, in an act of great foresight and heroism, came up with a novel idea. They wrapped a ballistic blanket, a bulletproof sheet used for barricaded situations and bombs, around the front of their REP and cut across Yoelson's lawn, racing between the wounded cop and the gunfire. Nearly a dozen E-cops, their Mini-14 assault rifles covering the windows of the Yoelson home, watched in anxious terror, ready to dedicate full auto blasts of fire at Yoelson's window. "If I'd be peering down the sights of a weapon and pulling the trigger," Officer Martinez thought, "I was sure it would be against some Third World yahoos out to disrupt the UN celebrations. Not against some psycho in Queens."

Miraculously, the rescue attempt worked. The Truck-Three REP was driven up to the wounded officer and, under intense fire from Yoelson, managed to pluck the officer to safety. "It was a gutsy move," reflected an E-cop hearing about the job. "Running into a wall of bullets was something worthy of a medal of valor!"

Once the wounded officer was safely evacuated, ESU's order of business was to isolate and contain the suspect until he could be talked out or forced out. Homes along the Clearview Expressway Service Road were quickly evacuated, and the Peacekeeper made its path from Manhattan. As the hostage negotiators, Capt. Ralph Pascullo, and the Two-Truck RMI arrived, Yoelson decided he had had enough. He strapped two assault rifles to his arms, inserted specially modified magazines with twice the load of ammunition, and decided to go out in a blaze of glory. He emerged from the doorway as the negotiator urged him to surrender. Instead, he began firing. The E-cops responded in kind. "He was lit up like a Christmas tree," reflected one of the cops. "There wasn't enough left of him for an autopsy."

For the next twelve hours, Captain Connolly sat in the 1–11 Precinct, waiting to be interviewed by the assistant district attorney in regard to the shooting, while he ordered the responding ESU units *back* to their Archangel positions and their areas of patrol. Some psycho, now demised (in the NYPD vernacular), wasn't going to deplete manpower from the serious task at hand of safeguarding the 152 VIPs in Manhattan.

Almost as quickly as it had begun, the chaos ended, and 152 motorcades brought the who's who of world politics to Queens and Kennedy Airport for the trips back home. Without incident, without any threats materializing, the NYPD had done it. The most complex dignitary security operation in the history of international law enforcement went off without a hitch. From all involved, from Chief of Department Anemone, who operated much like Eisenhower around D-Day as the operation's overall commander, to the E-cops atop roofs and inside CAT cars, the papal visit and UN 50 were the NYPD's finest moments.

Several weeks later, on November 4, 1995, the E-cops in Two-Truck in Harlem were once again back to their normal duties of serving warrants, extricating motorists from overturned and mangled vehicles, and rescuing cops and citizens from harm's way. As a four-to-eight commenced one Saturday afternoon, and the cops suited up, checked their weapons, and hunted down clean cups for a pot of fresh-brewed coffee, a news flash interrupted the college football game on TV. It was a breaking story from Israel, from downtown Tel Aviv, and it was shocking. Yitzhak Rabin had been shot in the back and assassinated following a political rally in the heart of the city. His security detail, their alertness overconfident and lackadaisical, had allowed a lone gunman to get to within inches of the prime minister and unleash several 9mm rounds straight into his back. The assassin, a Jewish zealot, had penetrated the inner sanctum of the prime minister's detail and simply waited for the opportunity to pull the trigger. Israelis were shocked. They thought that if ever one of their leaders would be killed, then it would certainly be an Arab terrorist behind the plot, not one of their own. Leaders in international law enforcement were equally surprised. The Israelis had vaunted themselves as international leaders in protective security. In New York City, in Harlem, the E-cops looked upon the news reports with exhausted reflection. They knew that no package was 100 percent secure. ESU and the NYPD had been diligent. They had also been lucky.

"Thank God it didn't happen here," one of the cops said as he shook his head and recalled those sleepless nights inside a CAT car outside one hotel or another. "Thank God!"

In reflecting on the wild and incredible two weeks in October 1995, perhaps Special Agent Brian Gimlett, the Secret Service's man in New York City, said it best. "I have supervised security efforts around the world and can honestly say that only this city and this police department is capable of hosting events of this magnitude," he was quoted in the NYPD's magazine *Spring 3100*. "Without the dedication and cooperation of every member of the NYPD, this could never have been pulled off."

October 1995 was truly a month unlike any other in the history of New York City. No department, from Tokyo to Topeka, could have carried out the security nightmare that was the visit of Pope John Paul II and the 152 world leaders for UN 50. October 1995 was, without doubt, one of the finest moments in the history of a unit whose legacy and skills are evident in tens of thousands of fine moments.

4

When Seconds Truly Count: Pin Jobs, Emergency Calls, and ESU Rescue Work

"The purpose of our unit is to save lives."
—ESU Lieutenant Bob Sobocienski

To the true E-cop, the one from the old school, there isn't anything as enjoyable as rescue work. Saving lives is part of the E-man repertoire—pure and simple. Tactical work is one thing, and not all ESU cops are tactically gifted, tactically initiated, or even interested in kicking down a door with an MP-5 in hand, but virtually all E-cops will race like the devil to be the first ones on the scene just to be in position to salvage life from the grasp of death. Look at ESU cops after a successful warrant in which they've safely entered a known drug location with heavy weapons in hand, and there is usually very little emotion expressed. It is, after all, business as usual. Look at those same cops, however, after they've pulled up on fifty-three pin, the NYPD term for a car crash with people pinned inside the wreck, and have used their heavy tools to extricate a family of four from the mangled metal wreckage of what was once a minivan, and those same cops are pumped up, elated, and thrilled at the chance to serve in ESU. It is the type of job that is truly dramatic and truly desperate, and the type of flying by the seat of one's pants that demonstrates just how remarkably well the E-cops function while under the pressure of being in a race against time. Rescue work is also the most dangerous type of job for the E-cops. More cops are hurt by falling bricks, jagged pieces of metal, and flying glass on rescue assignments than are shot at or stabbed by perps.

Of all types of rescue that ESU handles, from elevators to train wrecks, the one that truly gets the unit pumped up is the pin job. A car, crunched up from the wicked impact of a crash, has been so badly damaged that the vehicle's occupants are trapped inside the wreckage. One doesn't walk away from a crash involving a pin, and usually the hapless person (or people) trapped inside are suffering from potentially life-threatening injuries resulting from the crash. They could be bleeding, ribs could be piercing lungs or other vital organs, or they could have stopped breathing altogether.

Over the years, Two-Truck has been fortunate to have had its fair share of cops serving in its three squads who not only are rescue-oriented but truly live for the chance to save a life. It will often be joked about these cops that "they should have been firemen," but there is nothing funny about the seconds ticking away on a critically injured person. Police Officer Dan Donnelly is one such cop and a staple of Harlem. Interestingly enough, though, being a cop, let alone an E-man, was never in the forefront of Donnelly's plans. The son of a firefighter, young Dan Donnelly ate, slept, and dreamed of only one thing: being a fireman. His father, a seasoned twenty-eight-year veteran of Engine Company 82 in the South Bronx, was a legend in the FDNY and had spent much of the late 1960s and early 1970s battling blazes in Fort Apache. Most of the people Dan Donnelly saw growing up were firemen. The only stories he heard when growing up were about firefighting, he went to Emerald Society functions, and he had always pictured himself with a taunt line in hand spraying a burning tenement with 5,000 pounds of flame-crushing water. With all his hooks to get into the FDNY, the department just wasn't hiring when he left high school, so he put in for all other civil service tests in the hope that he would have something to fall back on until his slot in the department came up. He took up electrician's work in Westchester and waited for the call. Naturally, as fate would have it, the first agency to call him was the NYPD. In 1987 Dan Donnelly retired his dream of driving in the big red engine for the blue-and-white charm of an NYPD Chevy Caprice. At least he followed part of the family tradition. His first foot post was Fort Apache. Shithole of the world. The South Bronx's 4–1 Precinct.

For nearly five years, Donnelly served as a patrolman in the 4–1, Perp City U.S.A. It was the kind of precinct that made you, broke you, propelled you to a gold shield and lots of citations, or it got you shot in an alleyway and a place in the "box of honor" at an inspector's funeral. For Donnelly, it was bliss, a learning experience the likes of which he could never have imagined. When he was a kid, he heard stories about the South Bronx from his old man, but those were fire stories. Police work, of course, was a different universe from the FDNY, the old FDNY, that is, but Police Officer Donnelly was what the precinct calls "good people." He worked hard; opinionated yet always willing to learn, he showed the courage and the instinct that many old-timers with gold shields and chests full of medals recalled with youthful jealousy. With a lifetime of fascination in anything military, and with a cousin in the U.S. Navy's SEALs, SWAT work was where Donnelly wanted to take his career. Because he had grown up in a firefighter's house, the A-to-Zs of rescue work were also in his blood; having served as a rescue lieutenant on the volunteer fire department in his native Mahopac in Putnam County in upstate New York, he knew the operating manual for the Hurst tool, the legendary Jaws of Life, like the back of his hand. He was a natural for ESU. With a 1,500-name waiting list just to get into the

ESU Special Tactics School, Donnelly's skills were more important to the unit than all the hooks and politically charged phone calls usually required for acceptance into emergency.

Known throughout Manhattan North as the cop with the piercing blue eyes and giant shamrock tattoo on his right forearm and boxing leprechaun on his left forearm, Donnelly is known to be a vocal police presence. Because of his very colorful, though unrepeatable, social commentary while in the interior of an REP, prompting many in the squad to joke that Officer Donnelly's next career stop in the NYPD will be to wear the blue windbreaker of the Community Affairs Unit, yet he is a worker, a body and a pair of hands, who can always be relied upon whether in separating an Upper West Side yuppie from the mangled remnants of a smashed-up Lexus or inside a Washington Heights crack den where a bunker man is needed to be the first through a booby-trapped door.

In Sgt. Juan Garcia's Third Squad, where there are former recon operators from the U.S. Marine Corps like Police Officer Ray Nalpant, robot technicians with RMI expertise like Police Officer John D'Allara, and expert builders and master mechanics like Police Officer Eddie Torres, the favorite type of assignment for the crew always involves rescue work. Police Officer Steve Vales, one of the squad's senior men and most energetic E-cops, is, like Dan Donnelly, a cop who many joke should have been a fireman because of his interest in anything rescue-related. A decorated Harlem cop and mechanical wiz, Vales can repair any vehicle, no matter how battered, vandalized, or charred, and get it running as if it had just come off a Detroit assembly line. Donnelly and Vales work well together. Both cops are magnets. When the shit comes down the pipe and the big bosses are summoned to a job, it is Donnelly and Vales who are usually in the middle of it all. If they didn't always catch the big jobs, they usually went out looking for them.

Three types of calls come through over the SOD

radio: routine, bizarre, and desperate. Routine calls "request" ESU on a job calmly and with little fanfare: "Emergency Service Adam-Ten, in the confines of the 1–12 Precinct getting reports of an unconfirmed EDP." Bizarre calls tend to elicit amused responses for assistance from the police dispatchers and even funnier commentary from the cops inside the REP: "ESU requested in the confines of the 5–0 for a raccoon stuck in an exhaust pipe." Desperate calls are the real thing. They are made with fear and adrenaline and come over the radio with a frantic plea of urgency that sometimes causes cops from distant precincts (and even distant boroughs) to respond for backup. The desperate calls are made only when the shit has truly hit the fan—when shots are fired, buildings explode, and cars and airplanes crash.

The one type of New York City cop considered to be the calmest of all is the highway cop. They like the high-speed danger of chases, lone-cop car stops, and emergency response work; they provide escorts to high-security details and are always among the first units to respond to a ten-thirteen, an officer in need of assistance, anywhere in the city. Police Officer Dave Howly, one of the city's finest highway cops assigned to the Highway One unit in the Bronx, has a legendary reputation among the cops who use the SOD frequency for his calm and cool demeanor under pressure. A kind and jovial cop, Howly not only enjoys the job, he lives for it. He is the kind of cop, in fact, who many E-cops feel would be an ideal fit in ESU. He is hard-working, brave, and friendly, and he doesn't ask, he simply does. In fact, anytime an ESU supervisor finds him on a job, he pulls him to the side and asks, "So, when are you gonna put your papers in and come over here and join us?"

Highway cops are usually busy on Christmas Eve. The city's arteries are clogged with holiday traffic headed toward Grandma's and Uncle Bill's, and drunken accidents result in more than their fair share of AI, or accident investigations, work. Because traffic is so dense on

Christmas Eve, there are usually few pin jobs to report; after all, it's hard to get to the required velocity to cause a wreck resulting in a pin when traffic is moving along at a snail's pace. This Christmas Eve, however, would be different. This time, Highway 104 was a far cry from his usual calm and cool demeanor.

"Central, this is Highway 104. Get ESU over here forthwith. We have a car impaled on a dividing beam dangling off the Bronx River Parkway, northbound, at the Sagamore Street exit. Get them here *now,* or these guys are lost!"

The Bronx River Parkway was the domain of Emergency Service Squad Three, but Three-Truck was understaffed that day, and Adam-Three, with Police Officers Eddie Lutz and Steve Stefanakos patrolling much of the eastern Bronx by themselves, and they were some distance away when the call came over the SOD radio. Responding to the job, they became stuck in the holiday traffic slowed down by the fifty-three and completely boxed in. With Police Officers Donnelly and Vales patrolling Manhattan North in Adam-Two, the two cops knew that, with some inventive driving and some luck, they could make it to the job in time to be the first unit on the scene. By the time Vales was able to report "Adam-Two to Central, K, show us responding," their REP was racing at flight speed east on the Cross-Bronx Expressway to the fifty-three pin with injuries.

Although between them Donnelly and Vales have more than ten years of experience in emergency, they had never seen anything like what they were about to encounter.

A boyfriend and girlfriend, riding in their beat-up station wagon, decided that the ice-slicked pavement of the Bronx River Parkway was just the ideal spot to have a major fight. Yelling turned to screaming, screaming to small slaps. The female, driving, opted to try a tactic that her boyfriend had done countless times before during such arguments—she floored the pedal and exceeded the speed of eighty miles per hour. It was a bad idea.

At the Sagamore Street exit, they swerved around the yellow dividing line separating roadway from departing exit, hit three sets of water-filled barriers, throwing the girlfriend out of the car, and then flew ten feet in the air until the vehicle, and the boyfriend, landed through a piece of steel divider. The divider split in two, with the upper portion piercing the roof and holding the car over a thirty-foot-high embankment; the other piece of divider entered through the dashboard and sliced its way through the boyfriend's foot and calf muscle. The car hung in a suspended animation, and any slight movement could have snapped the beams and forced the car to crash thirty feet below, causing the man's leg to be snapped off from the rest of his body.

When Donnelly and Vales arrived, they knew that minutes were all that they had—if at all. They removed a set of heavy-duty industrial chains from their REP's cabin and hooked them to the Adam-Three car's front bumper as well as to secure the rear axle of the dangling station wagon. Soon, Lutz and Stefanakos arrived at the scene and immediately raced into action. They reversed their REP to create enough tension that would secure the car into a precarious stable position—if they pulled too tight, they not only would have ripped an additional few inches of ligaments and tissue from the boyfriend's leg, but they also might have torn off the axle altogether and initiated the end to what they hoped would be an exciting rescue.

With the car seemingly secured, Vales played the spotter as Donnelly grabbed his DM50 saw and tried to assess the situation. It was bad. Without causing it to tip over, he couldn't get into the car to use any of the heavy equipment to lift the dashboard off the boyfriend's chest and begin work on his left leg, nor could he use his power saw to cut through the beam hooked into the mangled leg—it might have been that the beam was actually holding the car up. As he began to ponder what to do, fire engines, hook-and-ladder vehicles, and fire rescue trucks arrived. "Hey, look at the super-cops over there," one of the firemen yelled. "Ten-to-one odds he fucks the job up and kills the bastard!"

"Stevie," Donnelly whispered, so as not to upset the injured passenger, who already had enough on his mind without worrying about FD-ESU feuding, "get FD away from me." Luckily, an FDNY Rescue Three lieutenant, one who had no time for the regular bullshit that usually followed a roadside rescue when both ESU and FD showed up, ordered his men out of the area and asked if there was anything he could do. "You bet," Vales replied, thankful to have a fireman on his side. "Get a ladder down below, and try and prop up the dangling tires of the car. That'll allow my partner the leverage he needs to get in."

In a good pin job, when pieces of dashboard, steering wheel, or steel have impaled the body of a motorist, the ESU cops like to cut off as little of the impaling objects as possible and allow the surgeons waiting in the ER the opportunity to make a clean and orderly removal. This job gave no such luxury of time or forethought. The boyfriend was going into shock, he was going through spasms of pain and numbness, and he was cold. Vales rushed a blanket to Donnelly, who quickly covered the patient and ordered him to move his toes—"at least it gave him something to do!" "His calf muscle," Donnelly recalls, "looked like a chunk of chopped meat that had been left out in the garbage for a few weeks. It was a wicked sight." Luckily, it appeared, the beam had pressed against a main artery, and bleeding was a small spray of blood and tissue matter; had it been worse, Donnelly might have had to amputate the leg right there and then.

As Donnelly tried to maneuver the collapsed dashboard and cut the beam in order to remove the boyfriend to a waiting ambulance, the car began to teeter and bobble, moving up and down like a see-saw in a children's playground. The car crashing down guaranteed not only the boyfriend's death but Donnelly's, too. He was hanging through the driver's-side window working as hard as he possibly could to extricate enough of the automobile from the passenger so that the beam could safely be cut. Additional chains, meanwhile, were placed around the rear of the car, and firefighters and cops, in a rare act of unity, positioned their bodies on the rear of the station wagon, so that just in case the chains hooked to the REP snapped the axle clean off, the car wouldn't fly down the embankment. The human weight was just the leverage Donnelly needed. He brought the saw down below the gas pedal area and, in a flurry of sparks and screams (the boyfriend thought his leg was being amputated), sawed the beam in two. A Plexiglas backboard was brought in through the driver's-side window, and Donnelly gingerly slid the boyfriend, three feet of beam still stuck in his calf, through the window and out the car. He was immediately rushed to Montefiore Hospital, where surgeons successfully removed the six-inch-wide, three-foot-long beam and saved the boyfriend's life. So, cops would later say, he could walk again and go back to kill his girlfriend for causing the accident in the first place!

Nearly fifty cops had assembled at the job, and all stood in line now to pat Dan Donnelly on the back. In his typical low-key manner, Donnelly removed his black plastic comb from the breast pocket of his tunic jacket and slowly, with his hand trembling, combed his bushy black mustache several dozen times. He had been shaken to the point of such fear only two weeks earlier, when he and his partner, John Politoski, rescued fifteen people from a smoldering stairwell fire in a Harlem housing project.

"Dan, this'll be your second medal in two weeks. All you Irishmen are nuts!"

There are two things that drive E-cops nuts in regard to pin jobs: not getting the job properly dispatched and having to fight with another city agency over a job. Many times on patrol, an unintelligible voice will come over the SOD radio dispatching ESU to one job or another.

"What was that?" the cops will often comment inside the REP, unsure where they were dispatched to or, in fact, who was dispatched. "Was that Adam-Two?" one of the cops will ask. "Naaah," the partner will reply. "I think I heard Adam-Seven." Once in quarters on a slow day, when six cops were sitting around the table at quarters eating their lunch, a job came over the air requesting an ESU unit to a job on some unrecognizable street. "Was that Two?" "No, it was Ten, I think." Finally, each cop threw a dollar on the table and called out the number of the truck he thought got the job. With six bucks on the table, the winner was the E-cop with the finely tuned ears who guessed Adam-Four.

Getting dispatched improperly, incorrectly, and not on time is no laughing matter, though. As victims lose blood and go into shock, seconds count.

Seconds also count because ESU now finds itself forced into competition with another city agency in the business of rescue. "Saving lives, even in New York City," a former E-cop once commented, "is not always cut and dry." In most cities around the country, and around the world, for that matter, vehicle extrications are the domain of local city and county fire departments. In New York City, though, for seventy years, the ESU has been responsible for all rescue work. ESU has become experienced at it, expert at it. The unit lives and breathes for the opportunity to pull people from twisting wrecks—pure and simple. But the FDNY was offered rescue work in the late 1960s, as much of the older buildings in the city burned to the ground, and in the 1970s and 1980s, but they refused the assignment, citing an overburdening workload. Today, as the city's fire codes have made buildings more fireproof than ever, the Fire Department of New York has found rescue work to be a job-security alternative that will keep them busy and help keep firehouses open.

The rivalry that has developed between the FDNY and ESU over rescue work has escalated and intensified over the last few years. The Fire Department, which usually responds to a pin job with more than twenty firemen, has employed a strategy of surrounding the vehicle and refusing to let the E-cops do what they do best, often with little regard for the poor person trapped inside a car with a steering column poking a hole through his chest. On various jobs, all described in written reports by ESU officers, firemen have threatened cops with axes and halogen tools, firemen have spit on the backs of cops busy in the extrication of trapped motorists, and they have even assaulted E-cops. Cops who have locked up firemen as a result of the petty silliness have been warned by "upstairs" that locking up anyone from FDNY will not be permitted. The situation has grown to such disdain that many in ESU simply shake their heads in disbelief at how the silliness has escalated and can only wonder as to where it might lead.

Cops who are workers in ESU often will monitor two radios in their REPs when out on patrol—the citywide SOD frequency and divisional radios, which cover zones and clusters of precinct radio traffic. Cops who are true rescue-minded monitor three, listening in on an FD frequency as well. Sometimes, especially at quarters, three radios blaring at once, combined with the chatter from someone on the phone and the sounds emanating from two TVs, bring a sense of chaos to the room full of cops, but well-honed ears can decipher the important from the clatter; they can pick out an emergency call with fine-tuned ears. Sgt. Juan Garcia's Third Squad is definitely one of the more rescue-oriented in ESU, and at any given time in quarters, there are always three radios heard in quarters; sometimes an additional radio is brought along in the REP. Sometimes, in those rare instances of luck, monitoring additional radio traffic is an instrumental tool in saving lives.

On one fairly average eight-to-four, when it had been pretty quiet uptown, almost too quiet, the units on patrol and those in the truck had returned to quarters to grab a quick lunch. The FD frequency was quiet, as was the

SOD radio. Sgt. Juan Garcia, though, was in the back room going over some paperwork and listening to division radio frequencies, monitoring the jobs in the precincts Two-Truck covered. For some reason, Garcia's intuition told him to monitor the division frequency that covers the 19th Precinct, the 2–0, the 2–4, and Central Park. On division, though, there was a ten-thirty of a business in the 2–4 and an unconfirmed EDP in the 2–0. Relatively routine stuff. Good intuition in police work is usually worth its weight in a chestful of medals, and Garcia's intuition was right on the mark. As the squad scarfed down Chinese food and pizza, a frantic ten-thirteen came over on division. "Get ESU here forthwith," the 19th Precinct cop screamed over the airwaves. "I have a confirmed lady under a car, and she's going out of the picture." All the cops eating their lunch saw was Garcia running out like a cruise missile.

"There's a confirmed pin in the 19th at Eighty-two and Park. Let's move it!"

"Eighty-two and where?" one of the cops said as he raced downstairs toward his waiting REP and the race to the scene of the accident at 82nd Street and Park Avenue. The Adam car with Officers Dan Donnelly and Eddie "Tool Time" Vasquez (flying in from Three-Truck), the Boy car with Police Officers Eddie Torres and Joe Ocasio, and the truck with Sgt. Juan Garcia and Steve Vales sped out of quarters in a flash of blue and white. Listening to divisional radio had been a godsend—the job came over the SOD radio several minutes later, just as the ESU units were pulling up on the scene.

What had happened on 82nd and Park was, tragically, so common in New York City that it has become an accepted part of the landscape. "More accidents are caused by cab drivers in the city," claims a highway cop, "than by booze, faulty brakes, and running red lights." Cab drivers, many from countries where until recently the only mode of transportation was a donkey or a camel, have turned the streets into a Dodge City of flying Caprices. To get a fare, cabbies will race through red lights, switch lanes haphazardly, and follow their own individual rules of the road. The cops call them flying carpets, because the actual cab is not even hugging the road with its four wheels but literally flying through the air.

Elizabeth Staten, a thirty-six-year-old innocent pedestrian on the sidewalks of the Upper East Side, was minding her own business as she stood on Park Avenue at the median on 82nd Street. Suddenly, without warning, a cab tried to cut across two lanes of traffic and ended up clipping a van, actually a private ambulance, causing the vehicle to race up along the median and pin the poor woman between the pavement and the van's front axle. A woman standing next to Staten was blown sixty feet away from the scene by the impact of the collision.

When a person is pinned under a vehicle, the usual procedure is for the E-cops to prop up an inflatable air bag underneath the car or truck, place some wooden cribbing underneath the air bag as it inflates, and repeat the process of inflating the air bag slightly and increasing the cribbing until enough of a safety gap has been produced to pull the victim to safety. This pin was different. Because Staten was pinned directly under the van, in a most inconvenient spot beneath the axle, there was no safe place to insert the flat air bags under—having them inflate improperly would simply crush her. As the E-cops maneuvered their tools and equipment into position for the rescue, one of the paramedics from nearby Lennox Hill Hospital who had rushed to the scene grabbed the woman's arm and declared, "I just lost the pulse." The E-cops were no longer faced with choices. They were fighting the clock, and every second counted.

"Fuck this, the air bags aren't going to work," Donnelly told his partner as he grabbed the Hurst tool spreaders and, going against the usual practice, inserted his hydraulically powered Jaws of Life underneath the axle, in a two-inch-wide pocket where the woman wasn't pinned, and slowly began to lift the van off the crushed woman. Every few inches or so, Officer Vasquez placed the small wooden blocks up against the axle, creating the required cribbing to keep the van elevated should the hydraulic tool fail for whatever reason. The seventy-pound Hurst tool has saved thousands of lives throughout the world, and it saved one more on Park Avenue. When the weight of the axle was no longer crushing the woman, paramedics pulled her out and began to administer immediate CPR. She was rushed to Lennox Hill Hospital while the E-cops simply wiped the sweat off their brows and gazed at the cab driver as he was questioned by police.

Miracles do happen—even in New York City. The quick thinking of the Two-Truck E-cops shaved seconds off what could have been a precarious and lengthy extrication. Two-Truck's Third Squad gets a lot of kidding from other squads and trucks in ESU about its knack for getting in the paper or on the news as a result of a spectacular rescue. Another truck had even printed a phony menu, in which each cop in the squad was represented as a hero sandwich, which was photocopied and distributed throughout the division. This act of heroism added one more sandwich to the menu. The next day, the family of Elizabeth Staten requested a face-to-face meeting with the men who had saved her life. It was an emotional gathering in the lobby at Lennox Hill Hospital, where tears were shed and hugs of gratitude offered. Although the cops got brief play on TV as a result of their actions, the personal thanks of a family glad that their daughter, wife, and sister was alive were far more important than any ten-second recognition by the media.

Cops feel a certain sense of responsibility for the people whose lives they save, and the cops of Two-Truck kept a close eye on Staten's progress, which has been nothing short of miraculous. Although doctors at Lennox Hill initially issued a limited prognosis, at this writing she is in the final stages of rehabilitation and expected to recover fully.

"These guys will do anything to save lives," one of

the Lennox Hill paramedics said upon seeing the E-cops after the accident. "They are just incredible."

"If I had a dollar for every pin I've worked that a cabbie caused," a cop on the Upper West Side once said, "I'd be Donald Fucking Trump! These cabbies are a menace." On most fifty-threes on the streets of Manhattan, the cops racing to the rescue will always speculate on whether one of New York's Yellow Cabs was involved. Most of the time they are right.

One warm summer Sunday on the Upper West Side was typical for yellow menace. It was muggy in Manhattan, but not the typical humid fare that grips the streets of the city and makes for difficult breathing. Manhattan was packed with shoppers, hungry souls standing on line outside Zabar's, and thousands of people strolling up and down the avenues and boulevards in search of a bargain, a meal, or a good time. It was also one of those Sundays when there was very little police work—especially for ESU and Truck-Two. As Adam-Two, with Police Officers Dan Donnelly and Steve Vales, ventured around Harlem and the eastern reaches of Central Park, a possible fifty-three pin with injuries came over the SOD radio in the confines of the 2–0 Precinct at Broadway and 77th Street. "FD will be all over it," Donnelly commented as the REP raced south on the Henry Hudson Parkway heading downtown. "Who gives a shit?" Vales replied. "Bet ya we'll be the first unit on the scene."

By the time the REP made it from Harlem, nearly sixty blocks away, they found the streets in utter chaos. Three seriously wounded passengers sat motionless inside a Chevy sedan, hit by a Yellow Cab and forced to swerve wildly into the curb. The doors of the Chevy had been smashed by the impact, and the only way to extricate the victims was by using the Hurst tool to gain access to the people trapped inside and then using the hydraulically powered clippers to cut the roof off and pull the people out on backboards. One of the victims was bleeding profusely. The passenger in the front seat had lost consciousness.

Usually, on a pin job in which both ESU and FD arrive at the same time, the chances for a confrontation are ripe. This time, though, the firemen faced a small problem in getting their Hurst tool to operate, and it was all ESU's show. With Dan Donnelly operating the tool and Steve Vales cranking up the machine, the two managed to spread and cut the obstructing bits of steel and glass and help EMS workers rush the victims to the hospital.

One of the fire chiefs at the scene, who lives next door to a senior ESU captain upstate, turned to the E-cops, smiled, and said, "Job well done. I wish that it could always be this smooth between us, and I know that the problem isn't really with you guys." The two E-cops accepted the gracious words from the FD boss, smiled, and returned to the task of folding their power lines and returning their gear to the rear cabin of the REPs. No matter how hard the Hurst tool was worked, it needed to be in position and ready to go the next time a pin came over the air.

If a cop has been in emergency long enough, he will build a thick outer skin to shield his psyche from the heartbreaking sight of a family of four perishing in an accident. Yet, no matter how hard-skinned an E-cop is, no matter how ornery and cantankerous a soul he has become, there are some jobs that end when the bodies are loaded onto an ambulance and the cop turns around the corner of his vehicle and finishes a good cry. One such case was the March 1996 accident on the Cross-Bronx Expressway in which ESU units from Manhattan and the Bronx responded to what was first reported to be a pin but then turned out to be an overturned Jeep in which a beautiful ten-year-old girl was crushed to death. The sight of the lifeless body was rough enough for the cops—many had kids of their own, and they could not imagine the tragedy befalling them—but the sound of her parents crying was enough to penetrate even the most resistant mental armor. "There wasn't a dry eye among any one of us in uniform after that job," one of the Two-Truck cops said. "I cried like a baby when I got home."

Some pins, though, are absolutely hilarious. On one midnight tour, Police Officers Ronnie Bauman and Vinny Martinez were patrolling the stretches of the Upper West Side at 110th and Riverside when the call came over division radio concerning a carjacking and subsequent high-speed chase in the 2–0. Racing toward the pursuit, in the flash of the REP full-speed potential, the two E-cops readied their shotguns and sidearms just in case the chase turned into a shoot-out. Bullets flying, it would turn out, would be the least of the perp's worries. He turned into a pin—literally. At 75th Street and Riverside, the carjacker attempted to bail out of his stolen Toyota, but, never having graduating from stunt driver's college, he was a bit new to the explosive and dangerous task, and he screwed up. As he opened the front door and readied himself to jump out, he got part of his body twisted in the seat belt, and when he jumped out, only half of him went out the door. When his car hit a row of parked cars, the impact jostled and turned him to the point where his body was dangling outside and his head was stuck between the driver's side door and another car.

The cops responding, their hearts pumping like nuclear-powered engines, couldn't help but laugh at the sight before them. "What a fucking stupid mope," one of the cops said. "Let's call *Candid Camera,* because nobody will believe us on this one." No matter how funny, this was a pin, and Martinez and Bauman removed the Hurst tool from the rear bin of the REP and proceeded gently to create a gap between the door and the car so that the perp could be cuffed and sent to the precinct for a nice long headache in the holding cell.

"He must have been retarded," an old Irish lieutenant commented to the E-cops.

"No, he's not retarded," Martinez replied. "He's just special."

Sometimes rescue work is preventive and more dangerous than responding to an actual rescue assignment.

On March 6, 1997, New York City endured one of the most tragic occurrences in its recent history when sixty-mile-per-hour wind gusts blew through the northeastern United States, centering around New York State. In New York City alone, more than 100 trees were blown down. In Laurelton, Queens, a sixty-foot maple tree was toppled by a wind gust and crushed a van taking small children to parochial school. Four children, all girls, were crushed to death in the heartbreaking tragedy, and four more were wounded. ESU crews from Nine-Truck and Ten-Truck worked at a fever pitch to extricate the victims, but the girls were killed instantly by the unforgiving might of the crushing tree. Cops, seasoned veterans of the street, openly wept and called home on any phone they could find, just to hear the voices of their kids for one brief second.

In Manhattan, the wind was particularly merciless on high-rises—from the Battery to Bradhurst Avenue. Screens were blown off thirty-fifth-floor apartment windows and tossed through city streets like incoming missiles. Launched TV antennas rained destruction and near death on cars and storefronts, and flying garbage cans broke more than a few windows. In Harlem, an abandoned tenement on Bradhurst Avenue and 145th Street, in the 3–2 Precinct, simply collapsed under the impact of the winds, spreading bricks and debris for blocks.

For the Second Squad on the four-by, as the four-to-twelve shift is known, it was crystal clear that this was going to be one of those days; as they suited up and drank their coffee, they heard tales from the work at Bradhurst, and they had seen the news reports of the girls killed in Queens. Rescue work doesn't necessarily have to be reactionary. If a life can be spared through deterrent action, it is treated with the same seriousness and speed as a job involving a trapped motorist.

With Sgt. Jimmy Spratt off in Queens in charge of A team #2, Detective Henry Medina assumed command of the truck and was the officer in charge. Calm, cool, collected, and owning a wealth of emergency experience, there was little that fazed Henry. But the winds and the tragedy in Queens were a blinding light in every emergency cop's mind, and anything that could be done to prevent such a tragedy *had* to be done. When a call came over regarding a dangerous condition of sheet metal dangling off a roof in Washington Heights, Medina and truck chauffeur Police Office Seth Gahr raced "Big Blue" to 178th Street. When they arrived at the scene, the sense of urgency to the call was more than apparent. A twelve-foot-by-four-foot chunk of roof sheeting was swinging dangerously back and forth at the mercy of the howling winds. The gusts had ripped the piece of metal off its mark, and it was dangling precariously in the whipping winds. If it would have become dislodged in one violent burst of wind, it would certainly have flown for several blocks in a high-velocity orgy of destruction, acting as a guillotine to anything in its path.

At first, Medina and Gahr tried to lasso the dangling sheet of metal from an apartment window, but the wind was too blustery. Roping it off temporarily, they raced to the roof, where the two tied in and then proceeded to the ledge. "Any cop who goes to the ledge of a five-story building on a day with seventy-mile-an-hour winds is a hero in my book," a Manhattan Task Force sergeant said to himself as he watched the harrowing display from the street below. Up on the roof, the work was incredibly difficult. Faces turned from flesh tones to a wind-scarred blush of red. Fingers, even under the protective sheathing of work gloves, turned red and frostbitten and painful. With Detective Medina lying on the ledge and Officer Gahr holding on to him for dear life, the metal sheet was finally grabbed, cut, and brought down safely without incident.

* * *

Anytime, Anywhere!

One of the most difficult aspects of rescue work involves calls for assistance underground, in the tunnels and stations of New York City's subway system. Most rescue work underground isn't really rescue work at all but body part recovery. When human beings meet several hundred tons of steel traveling at fifty-plus miles per hour, the results are usually less than picturesque. Sometimes a person being struck by a train is accidental. You're running late for an appointment, you're waiting for a northbound train at Grand Central, a moment's lapse in concentration, you lean over to see if the train is coming, and then *bam*! It's arrived, and you've lost a head. Sometimes some of the city's more vile and cowardly criminals think of the speeding subway cars as a convenient weapon for a homicide. All it takes is a push and a shove, and some poor commuter ends up under the train. And sometimes one finds oneself under a train because of an accident. A slip of the foot, a slippery tile, and all of a sudden a limb or a head is severed by the force of the oncoming train.

For E-cops, subway jobs are always dirty business. They are usually messy, bloody, and dangerous. Transit officials don't always turn off the power when they are supposed to, and being electrocuted by the 600 volts of juice in the third rail is not in the top ten of ways a cop should die. "Coming onto a train job," an E-cop once reflected, "where a limb is cut off here, a shoulder is cut off here, and the head has just roasted against the third rail, is not the most pleasant of things to witness—especially after a large helping of shrimp lo mein from the Broadway Cottage." Yet one of the most bizarre and most heart-wrenching cases for a subway rescue involves what ESU cops refer to as a "space case," when a person falls into the path of an incoming train yet is trapped, literally pinned, between the platform's edge and the car. The force of the moving train will turn and twist the person like a soft piece of dough and usually wedge the victim until he or she is stuck.

E-cops who are rescue-oriented like to call victims

they treat patients—they are like combat medics, and their objective is to save lives no matter who or what the circumstances. In space cases, though, victims are known as goners. There is nothing medically that can be done for the victim of a space case. The twisting of the bodies through the gap of the train and the platform edge has severed their spinal cord and completely mangled their insides. In fact, that they are pinned is all that keeps their insides from flowing out. It is the only thing that keeps them alive—albeit temporarily. The moment E-cops on the tracks place an air bag between the train and the platform and separate the two, the victim will die instantly. In fact, two E-cops usually place a body bag underneath the victim in order to collect the guts that drop out once the bag is inflated. For professionals dedicated to the preservation of human life, space cases are among the most difficult jobs an E-cop could have. "How do you look at a person you know is going to die soon and tell him it's gonna be fine?" an E-cop reflected. The E-cops who respond to space cases never let the victims know the true score. In some cases, cell phones are brought to the trapped persons so that they can call their husbands or wives and tell them they'll be "late for dinner." In some cases, a priest is rushed to the scene. It is never an easy task to tell the victim, "Just close your eyes, and it'll all be OK," but the cops have to, even though they know that the moment a gap is produced by the inflating hiss of the expanding air bag, the space case becomes a morgue case.

Besides rescues on the city's roadways and underground, ESU is also one of the city's primary agencies involved in waterborne rescues—from boaters in distress to drowning victims in swimming pools. Water rescues are another ESU specialty, and Two-Truck's territorial domain is one of few areas of New York City policing completely surrounded by water—with the Harlem and East rivers to the northeast, and the Hudson River to the west. As a result, in terms of water rescues, Two-

Truck is among the busiest in the division. Some water rescues are fairly simple and involve nothing more than the E-cops tossing out a rescue line to someone who has fallen into the river. Other rescues involve people who haven't come up for air after jumping off one of the bridges connecting the Bronx to Manhattan. Each REP and the big truck carry wet suits, oxygen tanks, and inflatable raft, and an outboard motor.

When the call comes over concerning a person in the water, the E-cops race to the river's edge with furious speed and determination—every second that a victim is underwater, after all, is a second when the brain is not getting oxygen. On some cases, the cops will venture into water that is frigid and unforgiving. The Hudson River is a mighty waterway, and currents and undercurrents can be merciless. Other bodies of water in New York, next to sewage treatment facilities, can be equally dangerous. Even calm waters can be lethal.

In June 1996, Sgt. Jimmy Spratt's Second Squad responded to a call of a woman drowning in the reservoir in Central Park. The reservoir, a body of water that most visitors to the park usually jog around, isn't deep, at only about twenty feet, but it can be dark and treacherous. A female in her mid-forties had wandered into the reservoir in an apparent attempt to commit suicide, but a jogger with a cellular phone had called it in. After pulling up at the scene, Police Officers Pete Tetukevich and Seth Gahr, in the Adam car, raced into the water, uniforms and all, to swim to the hapless women. As the two intrepid cops swam through the chilly waters, Sergeant Spratt and Officer Paddy McGee followed close behind on the inflatable raft. As the two cops moved in, clutching to the ropes on the side of the raft, Gahr dove in after the woman, but the search was difficult and exhausting. Seconds before both victim and cops might have gone under completely, they were pulled to safety.

To make future rescues easier and faster, squads will routinely train on waterways, such as the East River or a Central Park skating rink, in perfecting their rescue techniques.

Some water rescues are truly remarkable and demonstrate the versatile ability of the E-cops. They illustrate their skills, their dedication, and the "let's rescue them no matter what" attitude that most E-cops bring with them to the job each and every tour. One such illustration came on Tuesday, April 15, 1997, when a corporate helicopter with four people aboard crashed into the East River off the 60th Street Metroport seconds after takeoff. Two pilots and two passengers were on board when the chopper went down just north of the 59th Street Bridge. Sgt. Kenny Bowen's First Squad was working the streets of Manhattan North that four-to-twelve, and they raced to the scene with pedals to the metal, knowing that a person underwater has only about four minutes before he or she starts to suffer irreversible brain damage. At the scene, Sergeant Bowen's team was joined by units from One-Truck in Lower Manhattan and Ten-Truck in Queens North. They were also joined by an NYPD Aviation Unit Bell-412 air-sea rescue chopper and its two veteran divers, Police Officers John Drzal and Eric Tollesfen, who had been scrambled out of Floyd Bennet Field at the southern tip of Brooklyn the moment the call came over the air.

The chopper, a twin-engine BK 117 built by the German-Japanese firm of MBB-Kawasaki, had crashed thirty seconds after takeoff when the tail rotor came off, and it had plunged into the depths of the East River to a resting spot thirty-five feet below. The currents in the East River have been described by some veteran NYPD divers as hellacious, and they were certainly kicking up wildly that afternoon. "I was sure these guys were dead," claimed an eye-witness who was walking her dog when the chopper went down, "and I am sure it was only the quick thinking and the courageous effort of those cops that saved those poor people."

* * *

Anytime, Anywhere!

On a cool and wet morning in the northern corner of Manhattan, the day tour had just started work for the day. The Second Squad, in full force, is in quarters at the crack of dawn, readying their gear and equipment before another eight-to-four. A fresh pot of coffee was placed on the machine, a bowl of bagels prepared, and the cops thought the very first moments of their day tour would allow for the mandatory ingestion of caffeine and pretour chitchat. On the Harlem River Drive, though, on one of the most treacherous pieces of twisting and winding roadway in all of New York City, a deadly accident was about to get the morning off to a bang.

A schoolbus full of yeshiva students was heading north on the rain-slicked roads of the Harlem River Drive and 165th Street when it slid, flew over a highway divider, and crushed the roof of a southbound Dodge Intrepid filled with Korean bank executives, before flipping over again. The bus driver, Mikhail Lieberman, was crushed to death instantly, but the schoolkids, all teenagers, were trapped inside the twisted remnants of the bus. Within moments of the crash, 911 had been notified and the job came over the SOD radio. Two-Truck units, as well as those from Four-Truck in the Bronx, were on the scene in a matter of moments, using their heavy tools and specialized skills to extricate the students safely.

As the squad retrieved its gear, returned the Hurst tools, Stokes baskets, and first aid kits back to inside their REPs, the sight of the blood and destruction was a sobering first act in what would prove to be a busy day at work.

"Hey, Seth," one of the cops coming in for the four-to-twelve asked. "How come I didn't see you on TV at that job on the Hudson and One Sixty-five?"

"Who has time to be on TV and give interviews?" Seth said with a burst of pride. "I was busy saving a life!"

5

Massacre at Freddy's, December 8, 1995

"This is Harlem at its worst. For the first time in my life, I am ashamed to come from here."—A resident of 129th Street off Lenox, interviewed on a local radio show following the massacre at Freddy's Fashion Mart

Harlem has always been the kind of neighborhood that lives and dies with its passion. Years ago, in the 1920s and 1930s, the glory days of Duke Ellington, Cab Calloway, and the Cotton Club, Harlem was a bohemian paradise for jazz, the blues, great dining, and sins of wild assortments. Harlem was vibrant, a cultural and spiritual center for the city's black population. It remains the very center of black life in New York City today, and it will probably retain its title as epicenter for African-American society for generations to come. "Harlem, in its heyday in the time of Prohibition, was like no other place on the planet," claims a New York historian who has studied the decline of one of the city's most famous—and infamous—neighborhoods, "and Prohibition was the curtain call to one of the greatest neighborhoods ever known on the planet." His reflections are accurate. Harlem during Prohibition was a far cry from Harlem in the 1960s, when race riots were common, and Harlem in the 1970s, when heroin killed a generation, and Harlem in the 1980s, when crack cocaine killed the offspring of those left maimed by heroin a decade earlier.

Harlem in the 1990s became a desolate landscape of

hopelessness and despair fueled by crime, narcotics, and violence, yet it also became a neighborhood of hope and promise. Many of the buildings abandoned and destroyed by the years of poverty and neglect were torn down and resurrected as new structures, inhabited by the upwardly mobile and those raising families. Harlem was a renewal of business opportunities, stores, merchants, and Afrocentric dealers who brought, with their hearts and their passion, much of the enthusiasm back to the stretch of land from Columbia University north toward Washington Heights, back to a sense of vibrancy and future.

Harlem, though, has always been a tinderbox—a pocket of political fire-branding that promised either absolute salvation or uncontrolled violence. It was in Harlem, in the Audubon Ballroom, that Malcolm X was assassinated. It was in Harlem, in the late 1960s, that race riots erupted and cops and residents fought each other like cats and dogs in a fight to the death over who ruled the streets. It was in Harlem that a young Muslim minister, Louis Farrakhan, first gained notoriety and infamy, at the mosque on 116th Street and Lenox Avenue, and it was at that mosque in Harlem that two police officers were ambushed and assassinated in 1972. ESU Capt. Dan Connolly, a highly decorated Harlem cop, survived the gunfire of the early seventies as a rookie cop, in a place that was the greatest learning center for a police officer in the history of law enforcement. To Captain Connolly, and anyone else who survived the streets in those days, the 2-8 Precinct was a small strip of land measured by the geography of shooting deaths. Each street had a landmark where someone had been shot, where someone had been killed, and where a cop had been shot, stabbed, or assassinated. "There wasn't a night that went by that you didn't hear gunfire," Connolly reflects today. "The place was like Beirut." To many who survived the period, the shootings and the bombings, Harlem is engraved in their minds like the rhythms of the streets and the terror of back alleyways.

Harlem can be that vibrant. It can be that deadly. It was a place that always had the potential for enveloping everything around it in full conflagration.

Harlem, in the early months of winter of 1995, had been smoldering for quite some time. It was a pressure cooker, and the lid was about to blow. Lines had been drawn in the sand, rhetoric had replaced reason, and racial and economic angers had reached a point of no return, where violence, the type fueled by uncontrolled rage rather than response, was bound to claim lives. "Harlem is on a fuse," police officers serving in the 2-8 Precinct felt, "and it's gonna blow any time now!"

What Fifth Avenue is to Midtown, 125th Street is to Harlem. It is a primary artery of commerce and of urban identity. Harlem might be known for a thousand and one reasons around the world, but it is identifiable by the words *125th Street.* Harlem's past, present, and most certainly its future are all linked to the four lanes of east- and westbound traffic and the shops, stores, government buildings, and theaters that line its spacious walkways and thoroughfares. It runs the entire width of the island of Manhattan, from First Avenue and the end of the Harlem River Drive at the base of the Triborough Bridge in the east, straight through Spanish Harlem and into black Harlem, all the way west toward Amsterdam Avenue, Broadway, and the entrance ramp to the Henry Hudson Parkway. In all, three NYPD precincts protect 125th Street: the 2-5 at its eastern end, the notorius 2-8 in its central and most volatile section and the 2-6 Precinct North of Morningside Avenue. The street is a cross-section of the true mosaic that Harlem promises to be—merchants sell African trinkets all along the main street, shoppers venture uptown from all around Manhattan, and hungry souls from around the five boroughs look for parking on 125th Street as they venture to the world-renowned Sylvia's Soul Food restaurant on 126th. At one end of 125th Street, you have the followers of Muslim minister Louis Farrakhan, members of what many old-timers in the NYPD call the "bow-tie gang," manning stalls and soap boxes exposing their view of the world and the "white devil." At the same time, red double-decker buses, filled to capacity with camera-snapping tourists from Japan and Germany and a hundred other countries, tour the true sights and sounds of New York City.

Yet, according to one African-American leader, the business of 125th is business. He who possessed the economic lifeline of the community, black activists preached, owned the community, and that ownership, many complained, was not African American. Months earlier, the NYPD had taken the initiative and moved scores of illegal merchants who clogged the sidewalks of 125th selling everything that could be bought and sold. The sidewalk vendors paid neither rent nor taxes, and they were taking business away from established merchants and shops that struggled to squeeze out a living on the grand avenue of Harlem.

The removal of the vendors had been a risky political move by Mayor Rudolph Giuliani but a necessary step in restoring the rights of the legitimate merchants of 125th Street. The vendors were offered a new venue at an outdoor mall located at 116th Street on the northeast corner of Lenox, but few were satisfied with the police move or the force they displayed. They felt that the police were dictating how Harlem residents should shop. They were dictating who would make the money on 125th Street. Most importantly, they felt, the cops were protecting the many *white*-owned businesses on the street.

Years ago, in the bustling twenties and thirties, Harlem was a thriving community of nightclubs and jazz, of a black renaissance and scores of Jewish-owned businesses. To this day, all along 125th Street, evidence of this golden mixture are still evident. These store owners were intrinsic elements of the community, stubborn stalwarts who refused to be moved and continued to support, employ, supply, and invest in the bustling community of Harlem. To many in the community, however, the white-owned businesses were a threat and an insult. Harlem was African-American property, pure and simple, and the white faces had no business being in business on 125th Street, or anywhere else in Harlem, for that matter. So-called leaders, bombastic proponents of hate and turmoil, played the race card on 125th Street with the reckless disregard of a man holding a can of gasoline and smoking a cigarette. Men like the Rev. Al Sharpton, who had helped fuel the fires of the notorious Crown Heights race riots in Brooklyn by labeling the Jewish residents "diamond merchants," were also responsible for helping fan the flames of hatred on 125th Street. Sharpton had often referred to the Jewish businessmen as "interlopers." By grandstanding for the media and whipping their loyal flock into a frenzy, these community activists help to lay the kindling for the fires of hate. All that was needed was a spark and a call to arms.

The spark and that racial cauldron of flamable liquid found a home in a most unlikely of settings.

Exacerbating the tinderbox atmosphere was a small tenant-landlord dispute that was being used by militant fringes of the community as a call to arms. The owner of Freddy's Fashion Mart, on 125th Street between Frederick Douglass Boulevard and Adam Clayton Powell Boulevard, a Syrian Jew named Fred Harari decided to expand his discount clothing store and, as a result, not renew the lease of the Record Shack, a music store situated adjacent to his business. The Record Shack had become something of an institution in Harlem, known for its incredible selection of vintage jazz, rhythm and blues, and soul music, and the business's owner, South African-born Sikhulu Shange, was an energetic and beloved merchant on 125th Street. When it appeared that the Record Shack would be gone forever, the Rev. Sharpton and Morris Powell organized protests and picket lines—they turned into demonstrations of hate rather than an effort to preserve a Harlem merchant. According to Deputy Inspector Joyce Stephen, the commanding officer of the 2-8 Precinct, there were reports that the protesters were also shouting anti-Semitic epithets. One protester was even heard chanting, "We're going to come back with twenty niggers and loot and burn the Jew!"

One of the most vocal protesters, seen often at the demonstrations, was an out-of-work fifty-one-year-old named Ronald Smith.

Friday, December 8, 1995, was one of those days that just seemed too beautiful to be happening in New York City. It was brisk, quite cold, but the sun was out in tremendous and awe-inspring force. A bright yellow glow had cast itself over the island of Manhattan, from the Battery at the southern tip of the island to Harlem and Washington Heights to the north. For the Second Squad, starting an eight-to-four shift, this was hoped to be a day tour of peace and quiet. In fact, it was such a nice day that Officer Pete Tetukevich simply declared it "Sunday." The week before had been busy beyond belief—even by Two-Truck standards—and bones were aching and minds were tired. Before heading out on patrol, the officers cooked a hearty egg breakfast, relaxed a bit as they drank their third and fourth cups of coffee, and ventured out in the REPs with their sunglasses on and their Sunday mindsets in place. They began to answer the SOD radio and respond to jobs. Two-Truck veteran Tetukevich and former Transit Police rescuer Ann-Margaret Lyons were in the Adam car, Two-Truck mainstays Henry Medina and Seth Gahr were in the Boy car, and Pete Conlin and Kevil Flanagan were in the truck.

For ESU Capt. Ralph Pascullo, Friday, December 8, didn't feel so much like Sunday; it felt like just another ordinary day on patrol. Back at Queens, where he turned out for his tours on the street, Pascullo had gone over some paperwork, made some calls, and then checked his heavy vest and gear in the trunk of his unmarked car. He headed west on the Grand Central Parkway and a visit to Two-Truck in Harlem. Listening to the jobs coming over the air, Pascullo realized that by the time he made it to 126th Street and quarters, most of the squad would be out, but any excuse to go visit Mojo, the ten-year-old boxer mascot, certainly warranted a trip uptown. Traffic was fairly heavy on the Grand Central Parkway leading past LaGuardia Airport to the Triborough Bridge. The warming sunlight immersed much of the skyline in a golden haze. It was almost too pretty to be New York City.

At 10:15 A.M., apparently fed up with the protests, Ronald Smith set out to settle the matter at Freddy's by himself. Armed with a handgun and a bottle of lighter fluid, he was going to save Harlem's black-owned businesses in a fury of violence. Entering the store at 272 West 125th Street, Smith began yelling wildly, apparently stating, "It's on now," and ordered people out of the store. When 2-8 Precinct cops responded, he fired at the cops, pinning one down, while another raced out to the crowded street to radio in a ten-thirteen, officer needing assistance.

Pete Tetukevich and Ann-Margaret Lyons were cruising nearby in the Adam car when the call came over. Henry Medina and Seth Gahr were also close, patrolling the streets of East Harlem in the Boy car in the confines of the 2-5 Precinct. For the cops of the Second Squad, it had been a busy morning, with barely enough sitting time in the REP for the Sunday breakfasts to be properly digested. Captain Pascullo, across the East River and heading down toward the toll plaza on the bridge, could see the skyline of the northern tier of Manhattan, a skyline laced with housing projects. It was a skyline he was intimately familiar with.

Over division radio, the call came in with desperate pangs of fear. "There is a robbery in progress at 272 West 125th Street. Shots have been fired, and ESU is requested forthwith."

"Shit!" Officer Gahr shouted as Detective Medina floored the gas pedal of the REP and raced toward 125th Street. "What the hell is going on there?" As the REP swerved around the double- and triple-parked cars, Gahr unlocked the 12-gauge Ithaca 37 shotgun, made sure a round was inside, and readied himself for what promised to be a hellacious experience. The Adam car responded, as well as the truck. Sgt. John Lampkin of One-Truck, the city north supervisor that morning, also raced uptown to the ten-thirteen, as did Captain Pascullo, who flashed his lights and siren and raced to the location.

In confirmed shots fired and ten-thirteens, cops live by their instincts, and that instinct is always to respond. Within minutes of the ten-thirteen, sector cars from the 2-8 and 3-2 precincts raced to 125th Street, right across from the Apollo Theater. They were joined by the two REPs and "Big Blue" moments later. ESU's first order of business was to establish a safe perimeter in which they, and only they, would operate. Then, safety coming first, the E-cops suited up in record time, affixing Kevlar protective helmets to their heads and their heavy Kevlar assault vests around their torsos, and getting their heavy firepower from Officers Kevin Flanagan and Pete Conlin in the truck.

"It was a wild scene," Detective Medina recalled. "You couldn't see anything, and you couldn't hear anything, because there was loud music coming from somewhere." All they could hear was a gunshot, and they saw the onset of smoke. A fire had started, and thick glowing clouds of billowing smoke engulfed the storefront.

Instinct again was coming into play. The E-cops wanted to get inside.

Officers Tetukevich and Lyons raced around the back, their heavy weapons in hand, to try to cut off any route of escape for the perp or perps. The tandem of Medina and Gahr, meanwhile, were about the enter the Fashion Mart, but Seth kept holding his partner back, trying to slow him down and slow down the entry until they had a clear picture of exactly what was going on. "You got a wife and baby," Medina recalls his partner telling him as he tugged on the back of his Kevlar vest. "Don't do this to me, Henry!"

"The first instinct that a good cop has on a job when

everything is happening before them is to run in and ask questions later," Lt. Bob Sobocienski once commented, having been through more than his share of jobs when everything was happening. Chaos and confusion are the last things E-cops want when faced with a gunman and arsonist, especially one who has already shown a propensity for aiming his weapon at cops and firing.

Soon after the ten-thirteen came over the air at 272 West 125th Street, the whole world had arrived in Harlem. Hundreds of cops surrounded the block, and dozens of firetrucks and ambulances had converged on 125th. New York's vibrant media had rushed camera crews and reporters to the scene, and NYPD and Channel Four helicopters hovered close above the chaos. Police Commissioner William Bratton arrived, as did scores of first deputy commissioners, chiefs, inspectors, deputy inspectors, and captains. The Peacekeeper, the armored car that made such a high-profile impact during the massive ESU security blanket surrounding the pope's visit and UN 50, was brought to 125th Street, as were the sharpshooters of the countersniper team. Until the smoke and death settled, ESU wasn't taking any chances: The E-cops responding to the scene also had to provide ballistic protection for the firemen attempting to put out the flames.

"If you are gonna peer around the corner, I'll get you a body bunker," a concerned Captain Pascullo offered a fireman, ready to race to the truck and get a shield.

"Naaaah," the fireman replied. "I've already got bunker gear," referring to the pull-up trousers that all firemen wear when fighting flames.

"On big jobs like the mess at Freddy's, one of two things can happen," according to one E-cop. "There can be such a cluster fuck that everyone gets in everyone else's way, and nothing happens other than cops get hurt and the perps get away, or everyone does just what they are supposed to, and the job ends quickly." Outside Freddy's, the E-cops were running the show calmly, methodically, and professionally. Officer Pete Conlin, the

Two-Truck chauffeur, was monitoring his guys as well as acting as liaison between the E-cops and the bosses who were quickly assembling. Nobody really knew what they were up against, and it was still unclear how many gunmen there were or if all the stores were connected by common basements. The chances of a large-scale underground perp search came across everyone's mind. Additional ESU units were summoned from the Bronx, Queens, and the Apprehension Team.

At the rear of the store, Tetukevich and Lyons came across a man escaping through a small hole in the wall behind the compactor room. The man had a hole in his chest, and his T-shirt was covered in thick pumping blood.

"What's happening, guy?" Tetukevich asked as he rushed the wounded man to an awaiting EMS crew.

"There are more people inside," the wounded man uttered. "There are people still inside!" The man, an Irish immigrant and construction worker working next door, was determined not to die in the fire. Even though Ronald Smith swore he'd kill anyone who tried to leave, the feisty son of Ireland thought his odds were better with a bullet in the belly than lungs full of smoke. The construction worker was shot five times. Ironically and miraculously, he was the sole survivor of the massacre.

The news of additional victims propelled ESU to act. Saving hostages from a gunman was never an easy task, but tactically entering a building that was on fire was something completely different. In hostage jobs, when there is a dialogue with the barricaded subject, the negotiators have time to develop a rapport with the subject before deciding if it's a lost case or not. That time gives ESU time to mobilize its assets, prepare a plan of action, and deploy its technical and long-range tools. At Freddy's, there was little time to do anything other than act and act decisively. With their Scott packs on so that the cops could breathe in the smoldering inferno, the E-cops conducted a systematic search of the store. They moved through the location, still smoking and still dripping from the firehoses, covering one another with Ruger Mini-14s and MP-5s. The fire inside Freddy's had been a horrific one. The combination of the accelerant and the synthetic materials had created a dirty, black, and smoke-filled blaze that made visibility minimal and search-and-rescue efforts, let alone a tactical entry, quite difficult. Coats and shirts were melting from the heat; feathers were flying around like airborne snowflakes. The initial search upstairs yielded a horrific find. Next to the entrance of the store, behind a wall where the register was, police found the bodies of three young women, all black or Hispanic; they had died from smoke inhalation. Also upstairs, near the stairway leading to the basement, cops found the smoldering body of Ronald Smith. "He was cooking like a piece of meat on the grill," one of the cops recalled. "He had sprayed lighter fluid on some coats and then caught fire along with the merchandise." When cops turned the dead arsonist over on his back, they discovered that he had been lying atop a pistol.

Downstairs, in a storeroom, the E-cops came across the bodies of four more women, young black and Hispanic girls who appeared as if they had just closed their eyes and were going to sleep but who were dead from smoke inhalation. "I'll never forget that scene in my life," one of the cops reflected, still shaken by the sight. "It was as if they simply folded their bodies in the fetal position, as if they were going to sleep, closed their eyes, and just died."

The job at Freddy's lasted around forty minutes that cold and bright Friday morning. Firefighters were there much of the day extinguishing embers and wooden frames, and homicide detectives and NYPD diplomats from Community Affairs, identifiable in their light blue windbreakers, were seen talking to local religious and community leaders in the attempt to calm down shattered nerves. There was tragic irony to the massacre at Freddy's, in what became known in the local media as "The Killing Store." In his desire to strike out against a white-owned business in the center of Harlem, Ronald Smith had killed seven minority women and himself. The girls killed were all young, all innocent, and all working hard for a meager living.

Many times, during an eight-hour tour at the end of a really hairy job, the very nature of the job doesn't allow for down time. But following a job where seven people and a perp are found dead, where the cops have inhaled smoke and smoldering flesh, and where the rush of adrenaline and terror have left their invisible, though very real, marks, down time is an absolute necessity. For the cops of the First Squad, swinging in for a four-to-twelve, that requirement was more than obvious. The First Squad was one of the more veteran in the unit, and Police Office Eddie O'Neil would usually greet the working squad with bits of sarcastic humor. Following Freddy's, there was really nothing to say. What had happened on 125th Street, what they had witnessed, and what they had gone through were imprinted on their soot-stained faces.

"As long as there is Harlem," one of the truck cops mentioned, readying his gear for the four-to-twelve out on patrol, "there'll always be the big jobs." But Harlem did not own exclusive rights to the horror of senseless massacre. Less than two weeks later, after the blaze at Freddy's Fashion Mart, a young man in the Bronx walked into the Little Chester Shoe Store in the Bronx and opened fire with a pistol. It wasn't clear whether or not the gunman, twenty-two-year-old Michael Vernon, was deranged or bent on robbing the store, but no one can dispute the horror of his actions. Five people were killed and three critically wounded in his spasm of violence.

As far as massacres go in New York City, the killings at Freddy's were among the bloodiest. There was, of course, the infamous March 25, 1990, arson fire at the Happy Lands social club in the Bronx, in which eighty-seven people died. There was the "Palm Sunday Massacre" in Brooklyn, in which ten people, including eight children, were shot execution-style. And there was the "St. Valentine's Day Massacre" on February 14, 1993, in which six people were shot to death on Prospect Avenue in the South Bronx in a drug-related massacre.

But Freddy's was different. It wasn't over guns, and it wasn't a crime of passion or personal revenge against the scorn of an ill-fated romance. It was a tenant-landlord dispute that was permitted to escalate from a simple matter of a lease into an unforgivable bloodbath. One year after the massacre, Al Sharpton helped an elated Sikhulu Shange cut the ribbon for the reopened Record Shack. A store had been saved at the cost of seven young lives. Life is surely cheap on 125th Street, where the business of the day is, after all, just business.

To cops, precincts aren't remembered as much for their people or their landmarks as for their outbreaks of violence and senseless heartbreak. Harlem's 2-8 Precinct is one set of patrol sectors and streets that few in the NYPD could ever forget.

6

The View from Above and Below: Jumpers

"Don't you come near me," the man on the ledge of a fifteen-story building told the Emergency Service cop, who was already roped in and slowly walking toward the edge of the building.

"I am not going anywhere, guy," the cop replied. "Just out here admiring the view of this fair city. Want some company?"

EDP is a benign and politically stomachable term, short for *emotionally disturbed person* or what years ago cops would call "a stark raving fucking psycho." To many, anyone living in New York City can be clinically classified as an EDP. To others, walking around the streets of the city, unbathed, mumbling to oneself, and wearing a toga are signs of being absolutely normal. Some EDPs are quiet and content to be insane in their own little private puzzles, and New York is kind enough to let these free spirits live an unhindered existence. Other EDPs, less the free spirit than the tortured soul, are violent, a threat to themselves and to others, and they end up as a job over SOD radio. That's when ESU comes into action.

The majority of ESU calls involving EDPs are "unconfirmed." Someone calls 911 and says, "My son is nuts. Help!" A precinct car will investigate the complaint and usually find the subject to be a bastard and possibly a perp but not falling under the NYPD definition of an EDP. Other times, however, EDPs are flip-crazy lunatics who not only hope to do harm to themselves, for whatever demented reason their damaged minds offer, but also want to take cops down with them.

One sunny afternoon in the Alfred E. Smith Houses in Lower Manhattan, ESU patrol supervisor Capt. Ralph Pascullo had just finished a close encounter of the third kind with one of New York City's more resourceful and insane. For Captain Pascullo, it was a throwback to his old days in the Housing Police, though this job was like no other that he had encountered in his twenty-plus years of pounding the pavement. One-Truck units were serving a mental hygiene warrant on an individual who, for reasons that would soon become obvious, needed to be committed. The EDP was described as violent and extremely volatile. That was an understatement. In order to guarantee that he would not be taken into custody with the subsequent long-term stay in a mental health facility somewhere upstate, the white male in his thirties had filled his apartment with containers of gasoline, spread out piles of newspapers, and positioned road flares throughout to ignite the inferno. As One-Truck cops gingerly stationed themselves outside the door and responding fire units waited outside ready to respond to the first signs of flames, the cops, the hostage negotiating team, and a team of psychiatrists tried in vain to start a dialogue. There was nothing to say. When ESU officers popped the apartment's peephole in order to insert a pole camera and try to find out what they would be up against inside, the EDP launched a flare through the small opening. The flare, shooting out like a tracer round, bounced off the Kevlar helmet of Sgt. Karl Smith, another former housing emergency cop, and rolled harmlessly in the hallway. But the sparks from the launch had started a blaze, and the apartment was completely engulfed in seconds. With little recourse, the officers forced the door open, made a tactical entry, and subdued the EDP while firefighters waged a ferocious fight of their own not only to stop the fire but also to keep the canisters of gasoline that had yet to ignite from exploding.

It was an ugly job, a dangerous job, and a good job—none of the One-Truck officers was hurt. The thick black smoke had turned white faces black and uniforms sooty, and lungs were scorched with the biting taste of burnt gasoline. As the cops assembled outside, in the fresh air kicking up from the East River, the discussion centered on just what a dangerous piece of work EDPs actually are. Most of the cops had gone up against drug dealers, murderers, and violent scumbags looking for a fight, but this job had disaster written all over it. Just as the smell of fire and smoke was removing itself from Captain Pascullo's nostrils and he had a chance to share a word about the job with the city north supervisor, Lt. Bob Sobocienski, another EDP job came over the air. "What? Everyone's going nuts today?" Sobocienski asked as he quickly headed toward his Chevy Caprice. Seconds later, with sirens howling and emergency lights flashing, both Captain Pascullo and Lieutenant Sobocienski were racing northbound toward Harlem and another close encounter with insanity.

On this lovely day in New York City, when the sun was shining and the birds singing, a Hispanic male in his mid-forties, despondent over some tragedies in his life and the sudden onslaught of voices in his head, thought it a wise idea to climb onto the roof of the Jefferson Houses at 115th Street and Second Avenue in Spanish Harlem, grab a can of Laser beer (a sixpack at $1.99), smoke some cigarettes, and think about falling from the good graces of the sky to a most unsanitary demise. Cops on bike patrol from the 2-3 Precinct were the first ones on the scene, and they confirmed the job as a genuine jumper. The four-to-twelve shift had begun for the Second Squad in ESU Truck-Two, and its units were on patrol. Detective Henry Medina and Officer Ann-Margaret Lyons were in the Adam car, Officers Seth Gahr and Paddy McGee in the Boy car. Back at quarters, squad commander Sgt. James Spratt and chauffeur Officer Pete Tetukevich were monitoring the SOD radio in search of the "big job." It came over just after 4:00 P.M. A jumper was, is, and always will be a big job in the ESU playbook.

Both the Adam and Boy cars responded with lights and sirens and the pedal to the metal, as did the truck. ESU units were on the scene, atop the roof, less than five minutes after the job came over the air. The air bag truck, coming from Four-Truck's quarters in the Bronx, was also en route.

When handling jumpers, ESU has several golden rules. First and foremost is the concept of safety. The officers must tie themselves in with ropes, so that when they go out at treacherous heights to try to make a grab on a jumper, they won't end up blood-and-flesh pancakes on some stretch of scorched sidewalk. Second, the first officers on the scene commence a dialogue, while others carefully position themselves so that if and when a grab is attempted, they can rush in and pull in both cop and EDP. Finally, dialogue must be attempted and maintained until the air bag can deploy. According to its official specifications, the air bag can safely cushion the fall of a jumper from heights of up to eight stories. As this particular EDP was fifteen flights up, the dialogue would have to be good. There could be no mistakes.

Detective Medina immediately attempted a dialogue with the jumper, who seemed a bit inebriated, even by Spanish Harlem standards, and who was swaying in the crisp winds. When talking to jumpers and attempting to get in close, the emphasis is on the slow and the deliberate. An E-cop cannot just race toward a ledge and make a grab; the jumper will probably be through the roof of someone's new car by the time the cop reaches the railing. And any sudden movement, even a quick hand gesture, might just take that jumper by surprise so that he loses his balance and ends up taking the plunge regardless. "With jumpers," Detective Medina would reflect, "it's a slow dance. You take one step backward, two steps forward, until you inch your way within range."

The rest of the squad had arrived, and they were all being tied in securely by Tetukevich, as Captain Pascullo and Lieutenant Sobocienski were arriving from another nut job all the way downtown.

As Medina talked to the poor soul, hearing about the loss of the jumper's son and the voices that were making noise inside his head, Ann-Margaret Lyons looped in from the right awaiting a signal from her partner, or a slip of the jumper, to race into action. As a former rescue member of the Transit Police Department's emergency rescue squad, Lyons had spent much of her rescue career pulling dead bodies from underneath subway cars.

Luckily for the jumper, a man identified only as Rolando, Detective Henry Medina was one of the most experienced cops in ESU, and he had been on his fair share of jumper jobs. First, he handed Rolando a cigarette—this created a rapport and got Medina a few inches closer. Then he did something that even the bosses on the rooftop cannot forget.

"Hey, man," Medina told the jumper. "It's really hot, and I'm thirsty out here talking. Can I have a sip of your beer?"

"Sure, man," the jumper uttered. "Here."

Whether or not Medina is a Laser beer consumer, and whether or not he was really hot and thirsty, taking a sip was an act above and beyond the call of duty. Most of the beer was gone, and all that remained was the backwash of saliva and spit-back beer. Nevertheless, as his comrades and bosses cringed, Medina continued to inch forward. As he hoped to make a grab, Rolando closed his eyes as if to say he had made peace with his maker, dropped his head back, and spread his arms as if he were on a diving board somewhere, ready to put on a display for the Olympic judges.

"C'mon, Rolando," Medina pleaded. "Be careful. Why don't you come in?"

It was that simple and that terrifying. A man was

standing on the edge of a ledge, with only a few inches of concrete support for his toes, and the trust of a cop who had offered him a cigarette and shared a beer was enough to end the insanity of suicide.

"OK, man, sure!" Rolando replied, and he allowed the emergency cops to pull him in without a struggle. As onlookers applauded from the street below and the bosses and cops hugged Medina with an appreciative gesture of respect and affection, Rolando was rushed by cops and EMS to a nice warm bed in a rubber room somewhere.

New York City offers the suicidal a virtual smorgasbord of outs. If you are so inclined to terminate your own existence, you can jump in front of a speeding subway train, or you can walk along subway tracks and touch the third rail for a once-in-a-lifetime jolt of thousands of volts of electricity. The city is surrounded by water, so a late-night dive in the East River or the Hudson River can be a one-way trip to being washed up miles away later—if the drowning or exposure doesn't kill you, the polluted water certainly will. Some even take a ride in a Yellow Cab where some friendly soul from another land can play pinball against other cars, other pedestrians, and even, in some cases, buildings.

New York is the land of the massive structure, from the World Trade Center to the Empire State Building, from the Verrazano Narrows Bridge to a housing project. In a city known for its nosebleed buildings, leaping to one's death has become a favorite means of buying the farm. There is nothing as fatal as standing on the rooftop of a twenty-story housing project, outside the fenced-in ledge, and leaping to one's splat of a demise. Concrete does not make a soft cushion for a smooth landing, and the results are certainly final, if not absolutely grotesque and messy. New emergency cops usually will be taken to a sloppy burger joint following their first "fallen jumper" and the chunks of its messy aftermath. The kind and compassionate seasoned veteran tasked with teaching a rookie E-man the ropes will almost certainly order that fresh-eyed rookie a hamburger, almost raw, with all the trimmings. If the cop can hold in his lunch long enough to puke at home, or on the Saw Mill River Parkway heading north to the suburbs, then he's proven to his squad that he is an E-man in the making.

For the ESU cop, jumpers are a great challenge. There are never truly proper means for dealing with someone atop a ledge, and never truly wrong means—the only thing the cops can do is tie into a secure posting and make sure that if the EDP decides to leap, he won't take anyone with him. Saving a life is paramount, of course, and nothing is as important in police work as ending the tour and coming home to your family. Jumpers are life-and-death litmus tests of an E-man's skills, his psychoanalytical approach, his determination, and even the strength of his stomach. For a new E-man, successfully handling a jumper is an important step to being accepted into the squad. Talking a woman off a bridge or a man off a roof can endear a rookie in the hearts and eyes of his colleagues like few other jobs. Being able to stomach the effects of not getting there in time is just as important.

Case in point. On a cool winter's afternoon, Christmas Eve 1995, Police Officer Vinny Martinez and his partner, Police Officer Eddie Reyes, had just completed patrolling a sizable stretch of black and Spanish Harlem and had picked up a pizza pie to take back to quarters with them. Even though the cop's law that "the radio calls you to action the moment your fork touches the plate" is always in effect, the two officers had hoped for a few minutes in quarters for a meal, a soda, and some time to unwind. With the steaming-hot pie sitting on the REP's dashboard, a call came over the SOD frequency. "In the confines of the 3-4 Precinct, a confirmed jumper, on the ledge, on 183rd Street, on the thirty-fifth floor. Adam-Two responding?" With the smells of the pie engulfing the REP's cabin and two stomachs growling for chow, the REP raced up Broadway, hugging the narrow passageway between the sea of last-minute Christmas shoppers and livery cabs double- and triple-parked, in what was literally a race against time. The Boy car and the truck were responding as well, as was the Four-Truck air bag. The air bag would have little effect on someone cascading to earth from the thirty-fifth floor. At best, the woman would look at the inflated device below her, look at the cops and their sincere smiles and promises, and come in from the ledge. In the worst-case scenario, the woman would hit the air bag and it would "limit" the scattering of her debris to a reasonably controlled area.

This was one of Officer Vinny "Termite" Martinez's first jumper jobs in ESU. He had been on call for several jumpers while in the Housing Police emergency unit, but this was a whole new ballgame. Adrenaline takes over the body's natural sense of fear and foreboding. The urge to succeed engulfs the senses and permeates tunnel vision and purpose. As Officer John Politoski, the Two-Truck chauffeur, supervised from the street below, the tandem of Martinez and Reyes raced upstairs to the roof. Reyes, the experienced ropeman, immediately tied Martinez onto the roof landing staircase, ensuring that if the jumper was determined to leap off the roof this blustery morning, her tumble to flesh-flattening sidewalk below would be a solo gig. Opening the landing door gingerly, Martinez took one look at the attractive black women in her mid-thirties, pretty well dressed for the circumstances. Sometimes, in cases of male cops and female jumpers, the woman will think the officer to be sincere, calming, and even handsome. Other times, though, the police officer could be a Chippendale dancer and the jumper will not budge. Although being short makes him a target for some cruel humor in the squad (he is often called a "fucking midget"), Vinny's size also makes him unassuming and unthreatening. Yet, looking at the jumper, Martinez realized he was in trouble. She was looking at him, but right through him. He could have been the pope, Jesus, or even Elvis, it wouldn't have mattered any. She had the look of the next level in her. The ESU cop with an apprehensive smile was just a piece of her landscape now.

Cop instinct is very important in scenarios such as this. Cops' eyes can also see into the next level. It is a gift that many get the moment they hit the street. They know when someone is strapped (carrying a gun), when someone isn't straightforward, and by looking into the eyes of an EDP jumper, they know when someone is about to jump. Martinez, in remembering what he had been taught in STS about "taking the territory away from the jumper," attempted to inch his way closer toward the woman on the ledge. Seeing through the officer's plan, she said, in a reserved monotone, voice, "Take one step toward me, and I am gone." It was a challenge with room for negotiations, and Martinez was in bad bargaining position. Since he was standing more than thirty feet from the jumper, it would be very difficult to inch his way toward her without the loss of territory between them becoming apparent. As the precinct sergeant stepped back, making the roof ready for the E-cop to commence his routine, the woman simply turned her back, coiled her legs like a cat waiting to spring into action, and jumped. Martinez, the moment her back was turned, began a mad dash toward the ledge hoping to grab her, but he was too far away. The jumper was down.

"The one thing that I shouldn't have done," Martinez would later reflect with a straight stare, "was stand at the ledge and watch her land. When she leaped there were a few moments of silence followed by what sounded like a 12-gauge shotgun blast going off in my ear." The noise was the skull and bones hitting the asphalt; the wet splash that followed made everyone's queasy stomach move upward all the more quickly. Bits and pieces of the woman were everywhere. Even with an eight-foot landing, a twenty-foot sidewalk, and the ESU vehicles double-, triple-, and even quadruple-parked, bits and pieces of her hit the truck's windshield and the roof of the REP. It was not an endearing sight.

Martinez and Reyes exchanged few words on the way down; they barely made eye contact. Martinez was pissed. Truly angry. "You don't care about the mess on the sidewalk and the work it involves," an experienced E-man in the Bronx would comment. "You are about the fact that for whatever reason, even if it was beyond your control, you lost one." Martinez was met by the squad and by Capt. Ralph Pascullo, his former CO in the housing unit.

"How you doing, Vinny?" Pascullo asked as he wrapped his forearm around the cop's shoulder. "Wanna go to the hospital? Need a drink? Need anything?"

"No, no, no," was Martinez's reply as he stared through Pascullo, much in the same way as the jumper had stared through him, in his attempt to allow his tunnel vision to dissipate.

"Hey, guys." Captain Pascullo looked at the rest of the squad reloading their rope equipment back onto the trucks. "Want to get her off the street?"

"No," Martinez said. "I'll do it." The gruesome task was attended to quickly and without the urge to heave the bile in his stomach onto the pavement in Upper Manhattan.

No matter how white in the face and about to throw his empty guts up Martinez was, E-men cannot allow a fellow cop to be affected by the gore around him. It is cruel, it is insensitive, and it is funny. While the citizens on the street corner looking at the cops' attempt to make light of the tragedy can think of them as heartless souls, that humor and that irreverence are the only way the police officers can return to their houses later in the day and remain sane.

So, without waiting for too much time to go by, the gallows humor began. "Hey, John," someone in the Boy car asked. "What was her score?"

Score? Back at the truck, John Politoski removed index cards from the truck and issued an Olympic score of 6.5 for the dive. "What she lacked in style she more than made up for on impact!" If scooping up what had been a woman moments before hadn't been bad enough, the squad had some additional bad news for Martinez. They wanted him to eat the pizza, now cold, that was waiting on the REP's dashboard. The cops weren't concerned for Martinez's appetite or nutritional requirements. They wanted to see if he was going to hurl up a sea of bile and pizza. As he munched on the cold slices, the cops began to comment on how the cheese looked a lot like the brains, and so on. It went on for only a few minutes, though to the new member of Truck-Two, it felt like hours. Martinez is a highly decorated cop who has in his eight-year career made hundreds of gun collars and survived hellacious shoot-outs with bad guys. But it took all of his internal stamina and concentration to survive that pizza and not empty his insides on the sidewalk.

Police Officer John D'Allara, one of the senior men in the truck, recalls a similar experience. On one of his first jumper jobs, on a jumper that jumped, the new member of the squad was asked to place the body pieces in the body bag. Easier said than done. The woman had fallen from a tenth-floor roof into an alley below. She had hit a fence, and her body was cut in more than two dozen chunks spread out over a fifty-foot field of damage. Although D'Allara was armed with a master's degree and a sense of humor that could make even the dead roll over and grab their guts laughing, the sights and smells were sickening. Cleaning up the body, however, would be the simple task. His partner took him right to some greasy spoon where even the cops were afraid to eat. "Lunch is on me, kid," the veteran E-man said with a smile. Indeed, it was. D'Allara was treated to a hamburger deluxe, consisting of a beef patty that was barely cooked and still simmering in blood.

Realizing that losing a jumper was rough, D'Allara now attempted to reach out to Martinez in his own special way. "Hey, Vinny," D'Allara said. "You can't talk to jumpers anymore on school nights." A former teacher, D'Allara had been working with Martinez a few weeks earlier when the young cop was forced to mace an EDP swinging a large crucifix at him. "Didn't I tell you you aren't allowed to mace EDPs on a school night?" D'Allara had said then. Outside on the blood-soaked sidewalk in Upper Manhattan, that humor seemed apropos.

Every cop in the division has a similar tale to tell. Nobody's first jumper was ever an easy one. Of course, jumpers are not supposed to jump once ESU is on the scene, but many times the call comes over after the unfortunate soul has already taken the plunge. When there is report of a "jumper down," cops respond by laughing about it, trying to maintain their sanity against the inescapable mess of tragedy. On one job, on a chilly spring night, Two-Truck units were alerted by division radio of a jumper in the confines of the 2-3 Precinct. Within seconds, the truck was responding from quarters, the Adam car was en route from its patrol sector near the Willes Avenue Bridge, and the Boy car was acknowledging its response as its officers finished up a stuck unoccupied elevator job. Yet, before the responding emergency units made it to the job, division was reporting that the jumper was down. ESU is not required on jumpers down, as the precinct cops are more than able to clean up the mess. Soon, though, precinct cops were making falling-down noises; someone even went so far as to yell "Timber!"

Cops can truly laugh at anything.

Jumpers come completely by surprise, and nobody is ever prepared or in the mood for them. There are days, of course, when the weather is bad, the roads are iced over, and it is just a matter of time before the dispatcher calls over a fifty-three pin. When it is very hot outside and the evening comes on a weekend after the residents of Harlem have been enjoying the local vintages and herbal offerings, gun runs are bound to come over the air. But there is no specific time, weather, season, hour, climatic, or zodiacal situation that propels people to jump. They are always unexpected.

Friday the 13th usually brings out the worst in people—as do full moons, vampire bats, and so on. New York City is simply that kind of place. But a Friday the 13th combined with the volatile nature of the holiday season was a precarious mixture. It had actually been a slow eight-to-four on a gloomy-looking December 13, 1996, for Sgt. James Spratt's Second Squad. There were a few gain-entry jobs, a few reported pins that turned out to be simple crash-ups along the roadways, and the usual sights and sounds of patrol. Officer Pete Tetukevich was the chauffeur that cloud-covered day, and Officers Seth Gahr and Paddy McGee were in the Adam car. Friday was their first day back to work, usually a day when kinks were ironed out of bodies away from an REP for a forty-eight-hour stretch, and when instincts and reflexes were slower than in the middle of the week. Reflexes, however, are funny. A mind and body can appear sluggish, almost lackadaisical, until that one moment when the brain is forced to make a split-second decision to act, and the electrons the mind sends out to the rest of the anatomy cause adrenaline to be pumped, muscles to tense, and feet to floor a gas pedal.

At 3:00 P.M., with about a half hour remaining in their shift, Gahr and McGee found themselves heading back to Manhattan from the Bronx, where they were involved in a pin job along the Cross-Bronx Expressway leading to the George Washington Bridge. As they observed the holiday traffic heading in the other direction, the SOD frequency came over with a startling call. "Adam-Two, Truck-Two, in the confines of the 2-0 Precinct, getting reports of a confirmed jumper, over the ledge of a balcony on West End Avenue."

"Truck-Two responding," replied Spratt as he and Tetukevich raced down the stairs into the truck for the ride downtown toward West End Avenue.

"Adam-Two responding," Gahr returned with a serious tone in his voice. "Please have the first units on the scene advise when they are eighty-four."

"Truck-Four air bag on the air, K?" the dispatcher pronounced.

"Ten-four, Central," was the reply. "We are responding to West End Avenue. Expecting a twenty-minute ETA, but will advise en route."

Jumpers are a funny breed of suicides. They often choose the public forum of standing on a rooftop or a ledge just so that they can be saved. It is a desperate last plea for help and salvation that a call to Suicide Anonymous just wouldn't provide. It is their last minutes, possibly, to be noticed and to receive salvation. To a soul who feels that all hope is lost and there isn't a human being on the planet interested in his or her existence, the sight of responding emergency vehicles is a litmus test of compassion; the sight of the ESU cops tying in and heading out on a ledge are the positive results of a litmus test that a tortured mind needs to be able to have the courage not to jump. Other times, however, jumpers are angry. They jump because they want their last moments of life to terrify and to disgust. Many times, if they can, they will jump and try to take a cop (or cops) down with them. Murder-suicide—it's a classic New York City combination.

The ESU cops responding to a confirmed jumper never know what to expect. On November 24, 1996, units from Three-Truck in the Bronx were called to respond to a reported "jumper down." It was a project, one of the shittier projects in the city, and it was early. Expecting to find a suicidal male on the ground below, they uncovered a horrifying sight. Chicqua Roveal mother of three, had tossed herself and her seven-year-old twins off the fourteenth-story roof of the project on East 229th Street in the Bronx. The mother and one of her twins died at the scene; the other twin and a two-year-old toddler miraculously survived the plunge. "Always expect the unexpected," one of the Four-Truck cops said later. "Always be prepared for that curve ball to throw you for a loop."

There were no curve balls on West End Avenue,

though. Just a well-dressed man in his late twenties, who had decided that Friday, December 13, 1996, was a good day to die a really messy death. Despondent over a matter at work involving his boss and some of his coworkers, the stock analyst had simply put on his winter coat, had placed one leg over the railing outside his immaculate apartment and was standing on a ledge barely large enough to hold a pigeon, let alone a six-foot male with size thirteen shoes. Cops from the 2-0 Precinct had managed to gain entry into the apartment with the help of the superintendent, but nobody wanted to move in to make a grab until ESU arrived. With lights and sirens ablaze, the truck made it to the job less than six minutes after being called. The Adam car made it in ten minutes. Officers Dan Donnelly and John D'Allara of the Third Squad, which was coming in for the change of tours, suited up quickly and grabbed an available REP. Jumpers are involved jobs that sometimes can require a small army of E-men. The more, in this case, the merrier.

From twenty-one floors up, the view of West End Avenue can be enriching and nose-bloodying. With the Hudson River on one side and the skyline of Midtown Manhattan gleaming through in all its glory, the wonder of the natural and man-made landscape is awe-inspiring. Yet, when looking straight down into an alleyway filled with garbage and pigeon shit, the elevation is not very inspiring. It was not a glamorous place to end up in (especially in about a thousand small pieces).

Police Officer Pete Tetukevich is one of the more enigmatic members of the truck. A member of the ESU countersniper team, an expert tactical officer, and one of the more experienced E-men in the truck, "Tetuk" is the type of cop a boss can rely on, with eyes closed, not only to get the job done but to get it done well. Yet he also enjoys playing around with cops in the unit and in his squad, and he often enjoys playing the part of someone a bit "out of it" when in reality he has the situation well under control. "If you ever would want an E-man on the front line to talk down a jumper," one of his truck mates once said, "then Pete is your man!" And, in true Tetukevich form, he took front and center stage of the opportunity to save a man who thought that the essence of life was no longer worth the effort. As Officer McGee roped everyone in and secured them, Tetuk simply squatted in a semi-comfortable position and began to do what many E-men do best: talk.

In trying to talk down a jumper, a tactic commonly employed is the "hey, pal, so you think that you have a fucked-up life, well, wait till I tell you my story" approach. It works. Misery loves company, and someone who feels his life has just lost all purpose will suddenly find a moment of relief and gladness knowing that some poor slob of a civil servant is suffering more than him. The tactic is designed to build rapport, to establish a dialogue of communication, and to build on a relationship that will see the jumper admit to his mistaken path and come in off the ledge. If a jumper thinks he has found a sympathetic soul only yards away, one who understands his pain and abandonment, he might reconsider the situation and come in from his nosebleed perch. This works best with sober jumpers, of course, those not drinking a sixpack of Laser beer.

The conversation lasted more than thirty minutes, before Tetuk felt tired and called in Sergeant Spratt. Spratt, who served in ESU both as a cop and now as a truck supervisor, had worked a few good jumper jobs in his career, and he handled this one with calm and cool, but he wasn't making much headway, either. Seth Gahr, "the Major," also tried his hand for a while, but the officer who is usually right at home calming down the psychologically challenged of Manhattan North wasn't making any progress. This was Pete Tetukevich's show, and time was running out.

In dealing with jumpers, there are three rules of thumb that ESU generally goes by. First, if the person had wanted to jump, he would not have waited for ESU to arrive and try to talk him down. Second, usually those who are out on a ledge or on a balcony are there, and not splattered on the ground, because they have failed to muster the courage needed to take the plunge; when the jumper begins to take his eye off the cop and then scan the surrounding view, it is usually a sign that there is a strong internal debate inside his head about when and if he can actually leap off his perch. Third, no matter what direction the talks go in, the E-cops *always* try to move into position so that they can have one cop to the jumper's left and one to the jumper's right and then, when a grab is made, box him or her off. Making that tactic difficult on West End Avenue was the fact that the jumper had decorated his terrace with white lawn furniture, and it was hard for the cops to get close to the railing and into position. The only cop who was close was Tetukevich. This was his show.

On a perfect day in a perfect world, the only factor that would have played into the rescue would have been the rapport between cop and jumper. But this was far from a perfect world and far too cold and windy to be a perfect day. The E-cops were fighting a battle against time and the elements. The temperature was in the twenties, the wind was kicking up with a wicked bite, and the cops were more concerned that the jumper would be blown off the terrace than that he would leap of his own accord.

Meanwhile, the jumper's boss and several coworkers arrived at the building to try to help, but Sergeant Spratt didn't think it wise to include them in the mix. "The guy was on the ledge because of a work-related problem," Spratt would later say. "I thought the farther away we could keep his possible reason for jumping, the better."

Pete Tetukevich continued his rhythm of reason and sympathy. To remove the terrain from the jumper, Tetukevich would claim he had a pain in his knee, stand up for a second and then squat down again, several inches closer to the jumper. Finally, only inches from the railing, Tetukevich claimed he was tired, his joints aching, and he asked permission to lean against the terrace. This was the break. There was no sign, no pronouncement, only an experienced E-man reading the mind of a man determined to die that afternoon. Placing his left arm behind his back, as if to attend to a scratch, Tetukevich beckoned his comrades with a small gesture of waving fingers. The cops standing poised like a coiled spring knew that this was the cue to move in and make the grab. They rushed the jumper in one desperate attempt to save his life. At that point, the cops realized just how very much he had wanted to die. He fought like the devil and was successful in evading a pair of handcuffs connected to a strong rope line that one of the cops was trying to bring up to his wrist. "He was kicking and screaming and yelling, and he wanted to die," claimed Spratt. "All we could do was pin him against the railing and hope that we'd have more of a will to save him than he had a will to commit suicide."

As the struggle continued twenty-five floors above West End Avenue, the emergency cops were getting hit and shuffled by the determined man. He had decided to jump and wasn't about to let five Harlem cops interfere with his destiny. Seconds before the man would have come out of his winter coat and plunged the length of the building toward a dismemberment that would surely have been remembered by Upper West Side residents for years, Dan Donnelly leaped into action. Climbing over Officer Gahr's back, with his body almost completely over the balcony's railing, he managed to extend his forearm over the railing and grab the jumper by the rear belt loops on his trousers. Heaving with all the might his adrenaline and desperation could bring to bear, Donnelly, along with the others, managed to hoist the jumper over the railing and safely into custody. Amid the precinct cops and the EMS paramedics watching the drama unfold before them, the suicidal male was subdued, handcuffed, and taken to St. Luke's Hospital for psychiatric observation.

With little fanfare and little celebration, the E-men returned to Harlem. For some, the adventure on West End Avenue had been a great culmination of a day's work. For the others, it was an exciting beginning to a Friday's four-to-twelve shift.

The grab, the actual act of lunging at a jumper with incredible though fleeting strength, holding on for dear life, and then bringing him or her in to safety, is one of the most exhilarating and terrifying acts an emergency cop can manage. Saving one's first jumper is a piece of time that no cop in ESU ever forgets. Grabs are among the many aspects of the job where there is no right and no wrong. There is no manual instructing a cop on when to make the grab. It is all instinct, pure and simple. An E-cop could pull a jumper in from the roof of an office building and be heckled and criticized by his fellow cops for acting too impulsively. On the other hand, a cop can sit and wait too long and then have to explain his lack of aggressive gumption.

On one job, following reports of a jumper on the 59th Street Bridge, Sgt. Juan Garcia and "Termite" Martinez were searching the Queens-bound lower roadway when they came upon a teenager wearing a heavy-duty backpack, walking across the bridge in the pedestrian span. "Hey, guy!" Martinez shouted. "See anything suspicious?" With that cue, the teenager simply climbed over the guard rail and dangled precariously by the traction of his tiptoes and the strength of his grip. "I guess this is a confirmed job," Garcia said with a sarcastic swipe. Soon, units from One-Truck and Ten-Truck responded. Aviation units responded overhead, as did Harbor Charley and a scuba launch.

Martinez could tell right away that the kid did not want to jump. He didn't have that blank, sterile stare, nor was he argumentative and looking to take someone with him. He just wanted attention. His girlfriend had dumped him, and he was adamant about getting some press coverage so that he could win back the love of his life. Martinez realized that the kid wasn't going to hold on for very long as he pushed on and off the railing and mimicked playing the piano with his fingers and fist, and whether he wanted to die or not, unless he was brought in, he was about to land head-first in the filthy waters of the East River.

Standing three feet from the youth, Martinez awaited that split-second when the kid's eyes would look somewhere else, at someone else, and he could make the lunge without pushing him over the edge. His knuckles raw with anticipation, Martinez reached over the metal fence and yanked the teenager in with a merciless pull. The kid was denied his fifteen seconds of fame, and Martinez was denied watching another jumper take the plunge. This one was a job that ended well.

There are certain jumpers, persons in absolute agony, whom the cops cannot help but garnish sympathy for—like the man on the terrace, twenty-one stories up, on West End Avenue. A soul in pain is almost as gaping a wound as a 9mm hole in a chest or a broken limb, and, trained to save lives, the emergency cops naturally try to provide relief and comfort whenever they can. Other jumpers, though, attract little sympathy. They are miserable pains in the ass, and become less a pleasant memory than an annoying remembrance. Jack Petelui was one such hemorrhoid.

For the "Third Herd," Sgt. Juan Garcia's Third Squad, the fog and poor weather of Sunday morning, January 5, 1997, had failed to yield the volume of rescue work the officers truly enjoy. Miraculously, there were no pin jobs, and the SOD radio was conspicuously quiet. Even the division radios were semi-silent. The only jobs of the day were an animal condition on 127th and Madison Avenue, where a pit bull in an abandoned brownstone needed to be removed, and a gain entry for a woman in the Abraham Lincoln Houses on Madison Avenue and 132nd Street, whose boyfriend had kicked in her door so severely that she could not get out of her apartment; of course, she needed to get out of her apartment, with her four pet cats, pet squirrel, and parrot who spoke Hebrew. Sundays can bring either absolute routine and boredom to a squad or moments of heart-pumping terror. The routine usually lasts for the endurance of a tour. The terror strikes at the moment when it is least expected and least convenient.

At around 3:00 P.M., as the squad was completing its paperwork and about to remove its gear from the Adam and Boy cars, most of Sgt. James Spratt's Second Squad were making their way into the TV room for the obligatory hello, the required cup of coffee, and the always-welcome bullshit session with the cops of the day tour. It was warm for January, the mercury almost hitting sixty degrees, and when it warms up crime usually increases, as well, but the SOD radio was quiet. As the squad room filled with the cops of both shifts and the talk went from the equipment that needed maintenance to the football playoff later in the afternoon, the calm was suddenly shattered by a call over the SOD radio that caused everyone in quarters to perk up their ears, raise their eyes upward, and slowly begin to stand up, put down their cups of coffee, and begin making the trip downstairs to the REPs and truck: "Emergency Service Adam-Two, Boy-Two, and Truck-Two, in the confines of the 20th Precinct, on Broadway between 73rd and 74th streets, getting reports of a jumper, he is reported to be half-naked and has climbed the outside of the building. Do you copy, K?" Much of the radio traffic that comes over a citywide frequency is uncomfirmed—unconfirmed reports of shots fired, uncomfirmed and anonymous reports via 911 of a cop needing assistance. But once a call comes through and the dispatcher gives it over as "now getting numerous calls to 911," that makes it a bit more legitimate than other calls and causes the officers to take it far more seriously. The cops began racing toward their vehicles, and the members of Sergeant Spratt's crew, still off the clock, raced to get dressed and equipped and head on down to the job in any vehicles that they could find.

By the time the engines were fired up in the garage, lights and sirens sounded, and the departure made from

126th Street, precinct units were confirming the job. It was a jumper, an EDP. The airbag at Four-Trucks quarters in the Riverdale section of the Bronx was summoned as well.

The race to 73rd and Broadway, to the landmark Ansonia Hotel, where the EDP had climbed the facade in a green tank top and soiled white underwear, took all of six minutes. Adam-Two, with Officer John D'Allara and newcomer from scuba, Officer Ray Nalpant, arrived first. D'Allara, one of the more experienced E-men in the truck, quickly assessed the situation, reported back to the truck and the Boy car, and instructed the precinct cars on the ground what to do—mainly to clear the crowds and prepare a path for the remaining ESU vehicles en route, especially the air bag coming from the Bronx. Boy-Two, with former transit rescue cop Joe Ocasio and Officer Dan Donnelly, arrived next. By the time the truck, with Police Officer Eddie Torres as chauffeur, Sgt. Juan Garcia, and the Second Squad's Seth Gahr hitching a ride in the rear, reached the corner of Broadway and 74th Street, a monstrous clusterfuck had assembled in the usually quiet bliss of an Upper West Side Sunday afternoon. A Fire Department battalion chief had brought up a hook and ladder near the jumper and wanted to know what he could do to help save the jumper. "You want to help, Chief," one of the cops said, "move your fire truck out of the way!!!" Ambulances had assembled on Broadway, as had patrol cars, Hatzolah volunteer ambulances, and several news vans from the local TV networks. A crowd of people had also assembled below, and taxis, realizing that Broadway was now shut for them, began crossing police barricades and nearly killing half a dozen people making U-turns and detours. "Jumpers usually bring about chaos and stupidity," one officer would comment, "but on Broadway, the job becomes a fucking zoo!"

"I hope he jumps," an old lady walking a Schnauzer and smoking a More cigarette told one of the newsmen,

Commander of the NYPD's Special Operations Division, Assistant-Chief William Morange shares a laugh with Police Officer Steve Vales (middle) and Sergeant Juan Garcia (left) in front of quarters at Two-Truck. *(© Samuel M. Katz)*

Deputy Inspector Robert Giannelli, commanding officer of the NYPD's Emergency Service Unit. *(© Samuel M. Katz)*

During a protective security detail, ESU Captain Ralph Pascullo scans the view of potential threats in Queens with the United Nations in the background. *(© Samuel M. Katz)*

ESU Lieutenant Bob Sobocienski shakes the hand of President Bill Clinton during a presidential visit to New York City, June 1996. *(Courtesy of Bob Sobocienski)*

ESU Captain Dan Connolly monitors the City-Wide SOD (Special Operations Division) frequency on the corner of 116th Street and Lenox Avenue in Harlem. *(© Samuel M. Katz)*

Lieutenant Richard Greene, A-Team commander, peers through the sights of his Glock 9mm. *(© Samuel M. Katz)*

During a visit to New York City by Israeli Prime Minister Benjamin Netanyahu, Lieutenant Mike Libretto, commander of the ESU counter-sniper team, observes suspicious activity on the street below while one of the ESU snipers peers through the sights of his M-24 7.62mm sniper rifle.

Prior to a tactical assignment, Sergeant Juan Garcia, Two-Truck's Third Squad supervisor, shares a joke with Police Officer Manny Hernandez (sitting inside the peace-keeper armored car) of Three-Truck. *(© Samuel M. Katz)*

Police Officer Pete Tetukevich, ESS-2, peers through the sights of his M-24 sniper rifle as his partner, Police Officer Ann-Margaret Lyons, acts as observer. *(© Samuel M. Katz)*

January 5, 1997—"jumper job." On the corner of Broadway and West 74th Street, Jack Petelui, a forty-three-year-old male, climbs up the exterior of a New York landmark in his underwear. *(© Samuel M. Katz)*

Minutes later, Petelui climbs an outer gargoyle and jumps as E-cops try to reel him in. He was saved by the Four-Truck airbag rushed in from the Bronx by Sergeant John Coughlin's Third Squad. *(© Samuel M. Katz)*

During emergency rescue training on the Roosevelt Island tramway, Police Officers John D'Allara (left) and Eddie Torres look down from *atop* the tram, 300 feet above the East River. *(© Samuel M. Katz)*

On a frigid night, Police Officer Vinny Martinez, Two-Truck, looks at the aftermath of a fiery crash on the West Side Highway. *(© Samuel M. Katz)*

During a "hit" on a cra house in Harlem's 2-6 Precinct, Lieutenant Delia Mannix (third from left, below) and Sergeant Juan Garcia (left, top of stairs) coordinate the E-cops rushing in with heavy weapons and tools. *(© Samuel M. Katz)*

During a perp search in the 2-3 Precinct in Spanish Harlem, Captain Ralph Pascullo confers with Two-Truck officers John D'Allara (with shotgun) and Steve Vales after three homicide suspects barricaded themselves inside an apartment.

After Two-Truck Police Officer Ann-Margaret Lyons (lower right) talked down a jumper from the George Washington Bridge, those involved in the rescue smile for a well-deserved photo: (top row, left to right) Police Officers Seth Gahr and Kevin Reynolds, Captain Ralph Pascullo, Detective Henry Medina; (bottom row, left to right) Police Officer Pete Tetukevich, Sergeant Jimmy Spratt, Lyons. *(© Samuel M. Katz)*

The midnight crew at Two-Truck enjoys a laugh in quarters: (left to right) Police Officer Tony Barlow, Captain Ralph Pascullo, Police Officers Steve Vales, Ronnie Bauman, and Vinny Martinez, and Lieutenant Owen McCaffrey. *(© Samuel M. Katz)*

During an A-Team hit on a Brooklyn drug location, A-Team Training Officer Jack Griffith covers Sergeant Jimmy Spratt with his Mini-14.

Police Officer Seth Gahr cradles his Ithaca-37 12-gauge shotgun. *(© Samuel M. Katz)*

Police Officer Dan Donnelly places the water-swollen corpse of a "floater," found at West 96th Street and the Hudson River, into a Stokes basket. *(© Samuel M. Katz)*

In the top photo, Police Officers Dan Donnelly (right) and Steve Vales use their Hurst tools to extricate victims following a serious accident at 1st Avenue and 125th Street. Photo below shows Police Officer John Politoski comforting the driver. *(© Samuel M. Katz)*

During a barricaded-perp job in the 2-5, Police Officers Steve Vales (left) and Dan Donnelly (middle) confer with Sergeant Juan Garcia (right).

Police Officer John D'Allara, Two-Truck, readies his RMI (remote mobile investigator) at the onset of a hostage job in Harlem. *(© Samuel M. Katz)*

hoping perhaps to get on TV. "I love it when their heads hit the curb!"

The legendary Ansonia Hotel was a building on Broadway that had been home to Babe Ruth, Enrico Caruso, and Igor Stravinsky. Yet, on this warm Sunday morning in January, it belonged to one Jack Petelui, a forty-three-year-old hunk of man who had decided that it was time to die. A native of Staten Island, Petelui was having a cup of coffee in the Patisserie Margot coffee shop down on the street when it suddenly dawned on him that it would be a smart thing to remove his shirt and pants and scale the imposing stone facade of the building. A former construction worker, Petelui was used to scaling structures, and he climbed up the Ansonia quickly and quite impressively. At a third-floor landing, he stopped and began to yell at the crowds assembling below. The ESU cops responding raced through the side entrance of the Ansonia and ran up the three flights of stairs toward an apartment shared by two very startled gentlemen. "We need to go through your window," Sergeant Garcia informed the two men who were worried perhaps that the police racing into their apartment were on a raid.

At the ledge, the E-men found Petelui taunting them and the crowds below with drunken tirades and four-letter barrages. A precinct cop on the ledge, together with a paramedic from EMS and a psychiatrist, all looked at one another and in the common language of the profession simply said, "What a fucking schmuck!" As Officers Donnelly, D'Allara, Nalpant, and Gahr began to confront Petelui with a wall of blue, Joe Ocasio and Sergeant Garcia quickly secured everyone in with a rope and rocco belt, so if the "schmuck" decided to jump, he wouldn't be yanking anyone else with him.

"Why you doing this?" Donnelly asked, slowly moving closer to Petelui with small footsteps.

"Don't move any closer you cocksucker," Petelui replied. "One more step, and I'll jump."

John D'Allara began to talk to Petelui, but it wasn't

working, either. "I'm not talking to you, motherfucker!" Petelui yelled at the bewildered officer. "You look too much like that actor James Woods." Seth Gahr made his attempt to reach a common ground with Petelui, but Seth's unique mannerisms were too upbeat and off-center for the man who was telling the officers that God told him to jump.

The conversation lasted more than an hour, although there wasn't much talking. The cops attempted to inch closer, and Petelui warned them that if they took one step closer, he'd jump. At three stories high, this was an ideal job for the air bag, but traffic from Riverdale in the Bronx was fierce, and the cops from Four-Truck were having a slow go of it reaching the Ansonia Hotel. The cops on the ledge were trying to buy time, to keep Petelui stable and talking until the air bag could be deployed. Then, in the bad-case scenario, if he jumped, his thirty-foot fall would be cushioned. If he was talked in, then all the theatrics would have been a successful psychological victory for the cops. Whatever the scenario, and no matter how nasty he was, saving his life was of paramount importance.

Sgt. John Coughlin, a former Marine, is known throughout ESU as a bear of a man with unquestioned strength, and as a cop and a boss with a heart of gold. The Four-Truck supervisor and former sergeant in the housing emergency rescue unit is also a history buff with an uncanny knowledge of local landmarks. Sergeant Coughlin must have been interested in the Ansonia Hotel and its rich history, but he had little time to absorb the sights and think of the hotel's more glamorous past. Looking up at Petelui dangling off the ledge, his underwear flashing a crowd of hundreds, and hearing the Two-Truck cops struggling to keep the EDP from jumping, all Coughlin could think of was getting the air bag inflated as quickly as possible, so that the spectacle could end. As a group of women in the crowd formed a circle and began to pray for Petelui, Police Officers Regina McGee, whose brother works in Two-Truck's Second

Squad, Bobby Steinman, and Steve Lanoce hooked up the inflatable bag to its air pump and watched thousands of pounds of air inflate the air bag in a matter of minutes. The air bag is eighteen feet by eighteen feet, more than enough space of inflated cushion to catch Petelui if he fell to earth and ensure that, if anything, the fall wouldn't kill him.

Forty feet above the filthy Broadway pavement, the negotiations were not going well. The cops had acquiesced to one of Petelui's demands by getting him a cup of water. They had hoped that when he went to grab, the chance to pull him in off the ledge would be at hand. But as the cops moved forward with the plastic cup, Petelui moved back, diminishing any hope for a quick end to the ordeal. Then, without a hint to why or where, Petelui began to climb the outer facade of the building, using a gargoyle as a stepping stone. "He's gonna slip," one of the cops said, knowing that a man in his underwear and no shoes was not in building-climbing form. His premonition was correct. Petelui attempted to evade an E-cop's forearm connected to a pair of handcuffs as he climbed about ten feet higher toward the next floor. Suddenly, and as the crowds shrilled in horror, Petelui fell. There was the cry of the crowd, followed by the swoosh of a fat body hitting an inflated air bag, and then thunderous applause.

There is one remarkable thing about the E-men, and not only in Two-Truck, worthy of mention here. The society of a squad can be called many things, but it is a pressure cooker where egos and personalities (and sensitivities) are often bounced around with no prisoners taken. Work is not always a happy place, and because of the close proximity of the working conditions and the often split-second decisions that need to be taken, tempers tend to flare up at times. When lives are on the line, whether it is an officer putting over ten-thirteen or an EDP threatening suicide, personalities and sensitivities are forgotten, and the unit follows a choreography where everyone knows what he or she needs to do and how to go about doing it. The cops run like clockwork. They move about like a well-oiled machine, and their adrenaline and experience assume an auto-pilot mode where others might allow fear, trepidation, and emotion to take over. "There are professionals, and there are professionals," a 2-0 Precinct sergeant said as he observed Sergeant Garcia's squad break into action. "And these guys are fucking unbelievable!"

The job was receiving national attention. The following morning, it was the topic of discussion and humor on Howard Stern's radio show, although the "King of All Media" seemed more interested in the fact that the jumper was wearing underwear (soiled or clean?) than in the efforts of the ESU.

No matter what any ESU cop will say when asked what type of jobs he or she enjoys most, virtually no one will go out on a limb (no pun intended) and claim that standing on a rooftop somewhere in the middle of winter earns a special smile. Most will claim that they like either the tactical work or rescue jobs. Yet a jumper always does something to an E-man, always propels an unflinching and pedal-to-the metal response. There is just something about the desperation of an embattled soul or twisted mind being one footstep away from a most gruesome death.

On a chilly February afternoon, just after 3:00, the tours were about to change at quarters. The Adam car was returning from a job in the 19th Precinct, the Boy car was coming back from a job in Washington Heights, and the truck was returning from an evidence search in the South Bronx. It had been a busy day, but the SOD radio was busy. In the middle of the dispatcher calling Adam Eight to respond to an unconfirmed pin in the 9-0 Precinct, there was a report of an EDP in the 1-11 Precinct in Bayside and oxygen required in the 5-2 Precinct in Riverdale. Just routine NYC on a Wednesday in winter. Then, of course, routine was shattered by the potentially terrifying: "Emergency Service Adam-Two,

Boy-Two, and Truck-Two, unconfirmed reports of a jumper on the George Washington Bridge. The call came in over 911 and is anonymous and unverified." Before the dispatcher could complete her message, the lights and sirens on three ESU vehicles were ignited, and engines roared to their maximum power as a mini-convoy of blue and white raced up 126th Street toward 12th Avenue and the traffic dodgeball of the Henry Hudson Parkway.

"Emergency Service Truck-Two, K," Sgt. Juan Garcia relayed back to Central. "Port Authority PD has our radios. Confirm the job with them." As the Two-Truck convoy pushed past the 158th Street exit heading north and had the bridge clearly in sight, an NYPD Aviation Unit Bell-412, an air-sea rescue chopper, hovered overhead in search of the person who wished to end his life in the murky strong currents of the Hudson River. A scuba launch was also dispatched to the George Washington Bridge, its divers suited up and ready should the jumper plunge into the river and require an underwater retrieval. Even ESU cops with more than ten years on the job are awestruck by the resources the city sends to save just one life.

There would be no lives saved that day, however. There was no jumper. Like many jobs received over the SOD frequency, it was unfounded. There will always be tomorrow, though.

No matter how many unfounded calls ESU squads take concerning jumpers, cops will race out of quarters, lights and sirens going, hoping to reach a ledge or a perch seconds before some depressed and miserable soul decides to take the unforgiving once-in-a-lifetime plunge. It's simply part of their nature. There could be 1,000 unfounded calls. It's that one real job that makes it all worthwhile.

On a midnight in New York City when wind gusts kicked up to more than seventy miles per hour and anything that wasn't nailed down was flying around the city like an intercontinental ballistic missile, Adam-Two received a job over division in regard to a "possible jumper" on the Manhattan side of the 59th Street Queensborough Bridge. Of all nights to be on the outer railing of a bridge swaying precariously in the wind over the East River, this was definitely not the night that the cops wanted to have to tie themselves in and negotiate with a psycho. Still, however, a jumper was a jumper, and the training in STS did not call for rescues and grabs to be made solely in nice weather. Adam-Two responded from Manhattan, and Adam-Ten came in from the Queens side. Nothing was found. The job was marked a ninety X-ray (meaning unfounded), though there could very well have been a jumper on the outer railings of the bridge that night, and he or she was simply blown into the river.

7

Hits! Two-Truck and Tactical Work

•

"Hey, boss," the veteran Two-Truck cop told his supervisor following a particularly difficult narcotics hit in the 2-8 Precinct. "You just learned the first lesson about being an E-man."

"What's that?" the boss asked, removing his Fritz ballistic helmet so that he could wipe the sweat from his forehead.

"You fucked up on a job and lived to talk about it!"

It was a reminder of the days back in October 1995, when the Emergency Service Unit and the federal agencies worked hand-in-hand on the mother of all protective security details. This time, however, the E-cops and their federal counterparts wouldn't be operating against the plush backdrop of the Plaza Hotel and a gala ball at the World Financial Center. Rather, they'd be in the Bronx, in the "opulence" of the 4-0 Precinct. If the pope's visit and the United Nations gathering was called the mother of all details, this was the mother of all hits! It was called "Operation Triple Play."

On December 17, 1997, more than 600 police officers, detectives, and federal agents swept through the South Bronx in a dawn raid meant to put an end to the drug-selling operations of twelve notorious gangs. More than 200 E-cops, half the unit, were deployed to the South

Bronx, as was the SWAT team belonging to the FBI's New York field office. Initially, the raid was meant to stop *only* three gangs, but, as NYPD Commissioner Howard Safir told reporters, "leg work led investigators to nine more groups."

The gangs, who literally controlled a four-square-block area in the Port Morris and Mott Haven sections, were not the run-of-the-mill mopes selling ten-dollar rocks of crack. They were well entrenched in the neighborhood, operating for more than seven years, and police believed their daily activities sold more than $100,000 worth of crack, cocaine, heroin, and marijuana *every day,* seven days a week—including Christmas, New Year's and Rosh Hashanah. The gangs were also suspected in controlling a very lucrative weapons mart, selling everything from battered .25s to 12-gauge Street-sweepers, though 9mm pistols, from Glocks to Smith and Wessons, were their best sellers. In the drug business, protecting all that worth required "juice," and their juice centered around a propensity for cruelty and violence; in the thirty-eight buildings of the Jose de Diego/Beekman housing projects, residents were literally terrified to walk out of their apartments. Drug gang members were believed responsible for an astounding eighteen homicides and scores of other assaults. "These guys were very bad people," an FBI agent told reporters, "even by drug business standards."

Hitting dozens of apartments was very difficult work—not only with the dangers required in gaining entry to, controlling, and securing so many locations but also with the coordination required among all the various agencies. After all, since many of the locations to be hit were connected with a sophisticated communications network of cellular phones and beepers, the moment the first door was breached, everyone with something to hide in the area was sure to be flushing evidence down the toilet, racing out fire-escape windows, and reaching for Tech-9s and Glocks hidden under mattresses. The moment the first place was hit, the element of surprise would be lost.

Adding to the difficulty in mounting such an operation, the gangs employed a very dedicated staff of lookouts and runners. The moment the "5-0," as cops are known in many neighborhoods, was spotted, the dozens of cell phones and beepers would be dialed. Catching the bad guys off guard is hard enough on hits involving eight cops and five vehicles. Deploying 600 cops in secrecy would prove to be a monumental challenge.

Normally, when ESU tackles a warrant for a precinct or boroughwide command, first dibs on the hit go to the Apprehension Tactical Team, a special on-call force of E-cops whose sole task is warrant work. There are two A teams that usually work on opposite shifts, one permanent, one rotating; on big hits, both teams work side-by-side. This wasn't a big hit, though. Operation Triple Play was humongous. Two teams wouldn't be enough, nor would ten. ESU dispatched 200 E-cops to the Bronx in the predawn hours of December 17, including hand-picked officers known throughout the division for their tactical skills, as well as much of the ESU counter-sniper team.

In charge of the sharpshooters was the countersniper team commander, Lt. Mike Libretto. A veteran street cop, whose first foot post was a lonely stretch of street corner in Harlem's 3-2 Precinct, Libretto is a savvy and professional supervisor who in his career has seen and done it all. A recipient of the NYPD medal of valor during his stint in the notorious 7-5 Precinct in Brooklyn, Lt. Libretto had taken over command of the snipers upon the retirement of Lt. Bob Sobocienski in the summer of 1996. Lt. Libretto was suited for sniper work—he was decisive, charismatic, and, most of all, cognizant of the effects of his work. His first true test as team commander came in July 1996, when Prime Minister Benjamin Netanyahu visited New York City. Netanyahu, a controversial right-wing figure whose policies angered many, both Jew and Arab, was a plush target—especially in the wake of the Rabin assassination. In New York, his itinerary was to be varied and extensive, yet worst of all for his ESU detail was a planned five-block walk from his hotel on Fifth Avenue to a synagogue on East 85th Street for Sabbath services. The stroll would have been a nightmare for most countersniper outfits, but Libretto's team blanketed the area in a near-hermetic mix of observers and shooters.

Here in the Bronx, his leadership skills would come into play once again. Triple Play was a big operation.

Commanders in both the NYPD and the participating federal agencies were naturally concerned about the potential for gunplay. The worst thing that could happen would be for the cops to be under fire and undergunned. With the perps known to enjoy the horrors of gunplay and considered to be ultra-violent, nothing was going to be left to chance or taken for granted.

The first to slink into position under the cover of darkness were the countersnipers. They were to act as high-powered cover for the cops entering the targeted locations. Equipped with cold-weather gear, binoculars, and bottles of water (and empty bottles for urination), the marksmen acted as observers, quietly relaying invaluable intelligence to the cops on the ground and in observation posts and stakeout vehicles spread out along the targeted perimeter. Lying in wait, silently, for five hours in temperatures that routinely dipped below the twenty mark required great tenacity. "Snipers are among the most disciplined type of specialized officer in law enforcement today," claims one tactical commander, "and ESU's sharpshooters are among the world's best."

As much of the city still slept, the 200 ESU cops, ESU bosses, and several hundred more federal tactical officers sat at a predesignated spot in the Bronx for the prehit TAC meeting. Usually, the mood at a TAC meeting is serious but not foreboding. This time, though, there was an electric blanket of anxiety that filled the heart and mind of each and every one of the ESU cops. The federal units, under the guidelines of far more liberal rule-of-engagement restrictions, conferred with their ESU counterparts, "just to make sure that everyone was on the same page." The use of diversionary devices, more commonly known as "flash bangs," was discussed, as were evacuation routes and the predetermined police cars to be used as hospital cars. In the event of an officer being shot, there would be no waiting for an ambulance. Cops would rush the wounded officer to the H car, as the hospital car is known, and speed him to a waiting ER.

The objective of executing warrants, with specialized units like ESU or any other SWAT unit, though, is safety. The cops use overwhelming speed and firepower as deterrents. They move in fast, with force, and with enough firepower to back them up. By the time the perps know what hit them, the bad guys are supposed to be on the floor, their hands cuffed, and the apartment or house they were using as a drug location deemed secure enough to allow detectives and other investigators to get in and do their work safely. A good hit on a location, from entry to the supervisor calling the location safe isn't supposed to take more than a few minutes.

As the first rays of light emerge over the Atlantic coast and begin to touch the Long Island peninsula, the Bronx slowly awakens in a purplish glow. The bad guys, vampires who sleep all day and are up most of the night, are sure to be in the first stages of REM when the operation commences, lying down under the warm covers of slumber as the entry teams and tool men assemble outside their door, ready for their explosive entry. As the cops and federal agents move in on their assigned locations, cops armed with 9mm Glocks and Berettas watch closely for any signs of trouble. Although animal rights activists could never fathom the scenario, one of the cops' primary threats is of the four-legged variety, pit bulls and Rottweilers, some as vicious as the most hardened criminal, whose razor-sharp teeth have been known to gnaw through Kevlar and head straight for the jugulars or, worse, testicles of the ESU cops. Drug dealers, the wonderful humanitarians that they are, protect their locations with twelve-year-olds strapped with Tech-9 automatic weapons, and with herds of pit bulls and Rotties. To make their "puppies," as the cops call them, more vicious and stealthlike, the drug dealers will often surgically remove the dog's voice box. In the darkened stairwell of a dilapidated tenement, illuminated by one flickering twenty-watt bulb, the silent pit bull charging at a cop has the same effect as bombers over Baghdad. To make the dogs even more vicious, they are often fed a steady diet of heroin speedballs and freshly supplied kittens.

Puppies are a big problem on hits. "You'll never ever find PETA [People for the Ethical Treatment of Animals] protesting outside a crack house, complaining that the pusher is inhumane for surgically removing the voice box of a pit bull," an E-cop once commented after having laced a charging pit bull with a 12-gauge round to the head, "but God forbid a cop shoots one of these puppies, splattering his voiceless head clear across a tenement staircase because he lunged, dripping saliva and all at some cop and father of three, and there'll be pasty-face liberals picketing in front of precincts across the city!"

The drug gangs targeted in Operation Triple Play were great animal lovers—pit bulls of every shape, size, and rabid viciousness milled about their apartments and hallways. And it was making the cops anxious. In the police bureaucracy, shooting a dog requires the same paperwork as shooting a human being.

Silently, in more than twelve buildings throughout the 4-0, the cops moved into position. As the countersnipers monitored movement inside the windows, cops outside at observation posts and command centers followed the progression of every unit making entry. At one designated moment the sounds of diversionary devices detonating resonated through the Bronx, as did the sounds of rabbit tools pumping open a gap through metal fire doors and the sounds of sledgehammers being thrust upon locks and deadbolts. There were dozens of shouts of "Police—don't move! Get down!" bellowing through the caverns of brick buildings. It was choreographed chaos with high-speed tactics. Remarkably, it went down without incident. Before the morning was through, fifty-seven people were arrested, and more than 12,000 vials of crack, 891 glassine containers of heroin, eighty-eight tins of cocaine, and nine bags of marijuana were seized.

Hollywood and B-grade TV shows have done a great disservice to the men and women in law enforcement serving in tactical units. When cops move in to a location to serve a warrant, there is none of the cowboylike flying through the window, kicking of doors down by feet wearing loafers, or spraying an apartment with gunfire that most people watch while clutching the remotes on their sofas. Most drug locations, after all, have nice iron bars over their windows, so any attempt to fly through glass would result in the officer getting seriously hurt. "At last look," claimed a SWAT officer in Los Angeles, "most drug dens weren't using balsa wood for doors," so getting inside a location merely by kicking through the front door would result in, at least, that cop snapping several bones in his foot and ankle. "Cops wear heavy boots for a reason," a cop pointed out after a good hit where a door was breached by five minutes of slamming with a battering ram. "You can't kick through steel, fortified wood, or worse wearing Docksiders like Don Johnson in *Miami Vice.*" Finally, the gunfire that Hollywood loves to display on all police tactical entries is rare. When bullets are real, when police inquiries follow every officer involved in a shooting, and when lives are on the line, triggers are only depressed as a final means of a cop's self-preservation. On tactical work, especially hits, gunfire is always a last resort.

And whenever there is anything of last resort in New York City, from warrants to the protective heavy-fire details surrounding dignitaries and VIPs, it is the domain of the ESU. As a boss once commented when watching ESU in action, "If these guys can't handle it, then the city is fucked!"

If there is one thing that ESU does more than any

other police special weapons unit in the world, it is tactical entries. "Hits," as they are known in the ESU vernacular, or high-risk warrants, occur when ESU teams perform a tactical entry into what precincts or commands deem to be "dangerous locations." The dangers, dynamics, determination, and drive that fuel a hit are truly unique. One recent Two-Truck hit in the confines of Harlem's 2-6 Precinct illustrate just how it's done.

It was a cool winter's day in Harlem—a whipping wind from the west, occasional patches of clouds, but otherwise a day marked by brilliant sunshine. For Sgt. Juan Garcia's Third Squad, it had been a quiet morning, in an E-cop's mind far too quiet. There were gun runs in the Bronx, a bomb scare in Brooklyn, and a confirmed EDP in Queens. Yet, in Lower Manhattan, in One-Truck's domain, there were no jobs. Nothing either in Upper Manhattan, not even an unconfirmed EDP. As the Adam car patrolled the precincts north of 59th Street, and Sergeant Garcia talked to Captain Connolly, visiting Two-Truck on his patrol rounds, the phone at quarters rang. It was Manhattan North narcotics. There was a hit scheduled for noon, and Two-Truck was invited.

ESU Apprehension Team One, the nine E-cops permanently assigned to tactical work, would have handled the call were it not for the fact that they had already hit four locations in the first few hours of their tour and were busy on a hit in the Bronx. This hit belonged to Two-Truck, and officers from both Three-Truck and Four-Truck in the Bronx would be summoned there for the afternoon's fun and games.

As the Two-Truck cops readied their gear and prepared to move, the city north supervisor, or ESU Four, arrived at quarters. Lt. Delia Mannix hadn't been in ESU very long, since coming over from the Homeless Outreach Unit, but as a veteran supervisor in some of Harlem's busiest precincts, she had more than her share of experience in tactical work. Often, as the midnight supervisor in the 3-0 or 3-2, Sergeant Mannix would watch as a perp pursuit turned ugly eventually ended up involving ESU. She had seen the E-cops in action gaining entry to apartments filled with perps, guns, and drugs, and she and her cops had been backed up on numerous occasions by the cops from 126th Street coming to the rescue in "Big Blue."

Lieutenant Mannix was a cop's cop, a worker and energetic boss, whom workers enjoyed and slackers tried to avoid. In ESU, she was fortunate not to have a slacker in the bunch. Impressed by the enthusiasm, the tools, and the spirit, Mannix enjoyed her new command and the cops in it. In the past, working in a busy house, she often had called in jobs where ESU came to back up the precinct. Now it would be her turn to back up the cops on patrol, her turn to be the force of last resort.

The hit scheduled was a routine endeavor in the underworld of inner-city drug selling. Manhattan North narcotics was after three males, one believed to be a certifiable EDP, and two females. Their apartment on West 126th Street, only two blocks down from Two-Truck, was supposed to be filled with bags of crack and guns. The crew was known as a violent one. The EDP in the group, rumored to be a pyromaniac in his off hours, on more than one occasion had threatened to blow up the building should the police ever try to gain entry.

At the TAC meeting at the Manhattan North narcotics headquarters in a large brick building overlooking the Harlem River and the picturesque skyline of the South Bronx, the E-cops from the different trucks mingled outside a large office surrounded by file cabinets and six-gallon bottles of mineral water. Most of the detectives and plainclothes officers working in narcotics were dressed like street people—dirty jeans, Starter jackets, T-shirts, Air Jordans, and, for the male officers, ghetto haircuts and four-day stubble. The female officers were dressed either as knockouts or to look like crack whores. Each type of police officer, from detectives to highway, from Bomb Squad to K-9, has a unique angle to his personality, and even though everyone started out in the same academy and wearing the same uniform, they become used to only their kind. It was amusing as the narcotics detectives walked about and looked at the E-cops talking, as if there were something wrong with them, and the E-cops, interrupting their gossip exchange, obliged in kind by commenting on how strange the narcs were.

The TAC meeting, with Sergeant Garcia and Lieutenant Mannix standing next to the lieutenant in charge, was brief and to the point. The lieutenant, wearing a navy blue NYPD windbreaker and a pair of soiled jeans, displayed a map of the location and also distributed photocopy layouts of the small third-floor apartment. The front door entered straight into the living room, which had a small window to the right. To the left, in the living room was a closet (where the perps held cash) and a bathroom. To the right, through a wooden door, was the bedroom. It, too, had one window, though the cops weren't sure if the bad guys had hidden guns or drugs in the wooden floorboards. There was no kitchen in the flat, only a small gas stove where the perps cooked rock cocaine. "It should be routine," the lieutenant added. "We'll have all the windows covered, and ESU will do the rest."

"Any puppies in the apartment?" Lieutenant Mannix asked, wanting to prepare herself and the cops on the hit for any potential confrontation with a four-legged felon.

"Negative," the lieutenant replied. "They have guns but no dogs."

"What about kids?" Police Officer Joe Hernandez of Three-Truck asked. E-cops hate hitting apartments with kids inside. The thought of charging through an apartment where babies might be walking around, innocent to the criminal activity of their parents, sickens most cops, especially those with kids. The last thing on earth that any of the men and women in ESU would want to do is hurt a kid when going in or possibly kick through a door with a small child on the other side. Also, the presence of children dictates tactics. E-cops will not toss in a diversionary device if there are small children around, because the loud noise and blinding flash might harm kids. Kids in an apartment cause cops to be careful. Sometimes, though, being too careful can get someone hurt. Getting the intelligence correct is crucial.

Before the cops leave the meeting, one of the plainclothes officers comments that the perps are believed to have cooked a nice score of crack the night before and that there might be ether in the apartment. Used in the cooking and processing of crack, ether is a highly combustible substance that, when ignited, has powerful explosive qualities. "I guess we won't be tossing in a diversionary device," one of the cops commented, "not unless we want to go back to quarters via airmail."

Outside the TAC meeting, in the hallway, Sergeant Garcia divided his force into teams. Usually, an ESU entry team will consist of a cop with a body bunker and 9mm semiautomatic, an MP-5 man, a cuff man, another MP-5, two tool men carrying halogens, rabbit tools, and sledgehammers, a doorman securing the outer perimeter with a Ruger Mini-14, and the senior supervisors. Garcia, a former Marine, was good at tactical work and always careful—when given the chance, he always liked to have his best cops up front. Police Officer Bobby Steinman of Four-Truck, a seasoned and experienced E-cop, would handle the first bunker and the Glock fitted with a flashlight. Officers Manny Hernandez and Joe Hernandez of Three-Truck among the most experienced tactical officers in the division, would get the MP-5s. So, too, would Officer Dan Donnelly. Officers Joe Ocasio and Jerome Kazlauskus, two of the larger cops in the division, would be responsible for pounding through the door with the entry tools. Finally, Officer Regina McGee would be the cuff person. Officer Steve Vales, the Two-Truck chauffeur would be the E-cops' link outside the targeted location on 126th Street.

Before the E-cops went downstairs to the waiting trucks, to get their tools, their heavy vests, and their weapons, Sergeant Garcia went over some routine basics, some safety bits, and a saying he likes to impart to his cops before a hit. "If the bad guys resist," he said in a low and reassuring voice, "they'll lose." No two hits are ever alike. Sometimes the perps give up without a struggle. Sometimes the perps are listening to music with the volume raised so high that the cops could toss in a thousand diversionary devices into a room, and the bad guys would think of the noise as funky drum work. Cops have hit places where the bad guy was on the toilet, in the shower, or even in the middle of some horizontal hootchy-kootchy with a female (or male) friend. "On one hit," an E-cop recalls, "we came into a bedroom yelling 'Police, get down—don't move!' and we found a rather large Hispanic woman, a phallic object in her hand, intertwined with a male friend in the pretzel position. 'Can I get dressed?' the woman asked us. We all said a very loud 'Yes, ma'am, if you please!' "

Outside the narcotics headquarters, as traffic flowed smoothly southbound on the Harlem River Drive, the E-cops suited up for action. Heavy vests were thrown over uniforms, helmets fastened by taut chin straps, and the heavy weapons brought out, checked, locked, and loaded. Once everyone was ready, once Lieutenant Mannix had coordinated the route with the narcotics lieutenant, the convoy of marked vehicles and Two-Truck's "Big Blue" would head out for the twenty-block ride to the location. For hits carried out by trucks, E-cops ride in the very narrow cavern of supply closets inside the big truck. They must stand, and often there isn't anything to hold on to other than one another when the hulking vehicle swings a wild right turn on street obliterated by potholes. Once they reach the location, the cops will race out the back of the truck and into the target building. The cops who own the warrant, either narcotics or street crime or a precinct anticrime detail, already will have infiltrated personnel into the area to secure back alleyways and get the front door open. Once the convoy nears the target, though, lookouts will be dialing speed numbers and warning their bosses.

The convoy moved slowly through the avenues of Harlem until it reached the corner of Lenox and 126th Street. The convoy turned right and then proceeded slowly westbound until the building was within sight and all that was required was the OK from the plainclothes officers at the scene. The mood inside the truck was quiet. The cops had done this all before, but each hit is different. Each one has the potential for that split-second of gunfire that could change lives forever, or simply end them.

As the tool men stood by the open truck door, clutching their heavy entry devices, Lieutenant Mannix received word that the hit was a go. The truck lit its flashing lights and raced through traffic toward the building. On the street, plainclothes officers, now wearing their identifiable blue windbreakers, covered basement entrances and alleyways with the Glocks. The curious and the frightened, those staring out the window, were ordered to get back inside and shut their blinds. The E-cops poured out of the truck and climbed the eleven stairs to the front entrance of the building. The race up the stairs was quick and organized. Each cop moved hurriedly in formation. Each E-cop knew what to do. They flew up a rickety wooden staircase, applied their entry tools to the wedge separating the door and its frame, and were inside within seconds. "Police, get down!" was shouted with a determined cry as the perps were cuffed and tossed to the floor. The E-cops weren't concerned with evidence or with who these people were. Their sole concern was securing the people inside, and the apartment, so that the narcotics officers could go ahead and do their job without worrying about getting shot. The cops conducted an initial search of the premises once everyone inside was cuffed, to search for a hidden perp. Then they did it again just to be sure. "If I had a dollar for every perp I've found hiding in a closet," a Two-Truck veteran recalls, "I'd retire right now!"

The doorman, guarding the outer perimeter, made sure no one got inside—not even other cops. Mistakes happen, plainclothes detectives walk in, and the potential for a friendly-fire incident can become only too real. The E-cops don't want to shoot a perp, let alone one of their own.

The hit was a success. Inside the location, the narcotics cops found drugs, guns, cash, and perps. Outside, on a street now flooded with police vehicles, the E-cops would de-SWAT, return their heavy equipment, and return to their duties on patrol.

"Good job, guys," Lieutenant Mannix said, proud of her troops. "You guys are the best."

There is always the unknown about a hit—always that gnawing sense of danger that one dumb perp will decide to resist against eight heavily armed men, and all shit will break loose. There is always that element of Murphy's law. One night in the 3-2, Two-Truck was to perform a hit with the Street Crime Unit at a drug location on a crime-ridden block in Harlem. There had been a TAC meeting, the briefing, and the other prehit routines that E-cops go through. As they stood inside the back of their truck, ready to pounce on the location, the Street Crime Unit cops who would facilitate entry to the building noticed the targeted apartment had its front door ajar. Thinking this was too good to be true, they walked in, guns drawn, only to find it empty. The problem was that nobody bothered to tell the E-cops that there were MOSs (members of the service) already inside. As was prearranged, once the cops on the street had managed to secure the building's front door, the hit would commence. "Big Blue" pulled up, the cops flooded out, and they burst through the front door only to find men in plainclothes carrying guns. The possibility for tragedy was real. Luckily, one of the officers recognized several of the cops wearing the color of the day, an armband or shirt of a specific color, changed daily, so that uniformed personnel can recognize their fellow officers on plainclothes assignments.

"It's because of the potential of screwups like this," Sergeant Garcia always likes to point out, "that you have your sharpest people up front with the bunker, so that there can be no mistakes. In what we do, mistakes cost lives."

8

The Mope on a Rope and the Evil Behind Locked Doors: Barricaded Perps

"Hey, Julio," the E-cop shouted against the door, his ballistic body bunker raised high, a Glock 9mm in his right hand, and the sweat streaming from behind the chin straps of the Kevlar Fritz helmet. "We ain't going anywhere, so just come to the door and talk to me!"

"Is Julio known to be a shooter?" the squad sergeant asked the anticrime lieutenant who chased the perpetrator into the apartment following a street-corner robbery.

"Naaah, not that I am aware of. I think he likes knives."

"OK," the E-sergeant replied to his cops. "Let's go in."

The rope securing the door was removed and the rabbit tool's metal teeth inserted between the door and its frame. The pumping sound of air and metal clanking raced throughout the tenement hallway, as did the grinding sound of boots positioning themselves for being launched into the well-choreographed burst through the front door. Once the lock was breached and the door popped, the cops would enter the unknown and the dangerous.

It was one of those four-to-twelves that everyone working in the five boroughs, hoped (actually prayed) would go smoothly and quietly. It was just one of those days.

"Murphy must be a fireman," an emergency cop once said, "because Murphy's law always happens to us!" There is a saying that in Las Vegas people lose their sense of being able to tell time accurately, if at all. For ESU, VIP jobs like that, too. By the time they are over, who can tell when they started, what happened in the middle, and when they really ended? They are red-eye exercises in diligence, ballistic readiness, and exhaustion.

Everyone working on May 7, 1996, knew it was going to be just one of those days. For most of the E-cops working in Manhattan, pin jobs, barricaded perps or EDPs, or even bullshit elevator jobs weren't high on anyone's list of priorities. Terrorism was the order of the day. Earlier in the week, the FBI had advised major Jewish groups to be on a heightened state of alert because of a threat by an Arab terrorist group to embark on a campaign targeting 1,200 Jewish executives and doctors in the United States in retaliation for an Israeli campaign in southern Lebanon weeks earlier. There are lots of threats made against Jewish interests in the United States and New York, by everyone from psychos to organized terrorist factions based overseas, but this one made the hairs on the back of everyone's head stand up. It was one year, almost to the day, since terrorists had parked a truck filled with homemade explosives outside the Alfred Murrah Building in Oklahoma City, resulting in 171 dead and scores more wounded.

Terrorists, when they strike, are prone to search for symbolism in the date or timing of their attacks, and that was what had everyone in the NYPD, the Intelligence Division, and ESU so anxious. ESU was to be involved in a high-risk security detail in Battery Park on May 7, providing an infrangible veil of protection to Jerusalem 3,000, the celebration of the City of David's 3,000th anniversary and a party planned for the very pious location of Battery Park overlooking New Jersey and Staten Island. It was a wild shindig, New York style, meant to be a politically convenient platform for the powers in City Hall and a chance for Israeli officials to shine in front of a rich and influential American audience. They needed to be good salesmen. Weeks earlier, suicide bombings had ripped apart buses in Jerusalem, and scores of civilians had been killed and wounded. Jerusalem was a tricky issue to begin with, and it sparked the worst in people. ESU was out in force to ensure that the blood-scarred landscape of Jerusalem would not replicate itself at the southern tip of Manhattan. It was high-risk and volatile, and with the FBI warning and recent bloodshed in both Oklahoma City and southern Lebanon still fresh in the minds of everyone, as daunting a detail as had been pulled off since UN 50.

For Lt. Bob Sobocienski, the commander of the counter-sniper team, Lt. Richard Greene, in charge of the CAT car, and patrol boss Capt. Dan Connolly, Jerusalem 3,000 was a nail-biting exercise in hoping that an ESU tactical response would not be needed.

Sobocienski and Greene had changed their usual tours to work the security detail in Battery Park overlooking the mighty waters off the southern tip of Manhattan, and they were hoping that the afternoon and evening would proceed quietly, peacefully, and uneventfully. Protective details are among the most difficult of all ESU work, for the repercussions of one small glitch and one small mistake would reach far from the confines of the five boroughs of New York City. There would be diplomats and high-ranking officials attending the banquet from both sides of the Atlantic, and from Albany as well, as New York's Gov. George Pataki also was planning to attend. If a terrorist wanted to show Israeli vulnerability or to embarrass America, this would be as good a time as any. But the federal, NYPD, and ESU ring of protection proved once again to be too successful a gauntlet for anyone even to contemplate an act of violence. It had been a good day's work.

When the party was over and the overtime slips filled out, the supervisors began to de-SWAT themselves and head home for a long night's sleep and tomorrow's tour and regular hours of operation. Yet the adage in police work that "when you least expect it to come down, the shit will definitely fly" was apropos that warm spring evening.

In a world light-years from the crystal champagne glasses and movers and shakers who celebrated the 3,000th birthday of Jerusalem in Manhattan was the 4-3 Precinct in the South Bronx. The only similarities between Jerusalem and the 4-3 Precinct is that they are on opposite ends of the holy spectrum—God apparently shined on Jerusalem and missed the 4-3. The 4-3 is a notorious stretch of crime-ridden real estate in the southeastern corridor of the Bronx and is one of the bastions of the notorious drug gang the Latin Kings. The 4-3 is what is known in NYPD vernacular as a very busy house. A tour doesn't go by without the SOD radio summoning Truck-Three units to the 4-3 at least half a dozen times.

At around 8:00 P.M., the 4-3 was its usual busy self—a mini-universe of kids hanging out in front of overcrowded apartment buildings, drug sales going on outside bodegas, BMWs, their windows tinted almost black and adorned with Dominican and Puerto Rican flags, cruising around the thoroughfares blasting a Latin rhythm at eardrum-shattering decibels. Sometimes even gunfire can't be heard amid the yelling throngs, car stereos, and honking horns. Amid the noise and outdoor activity, a parolee named Paulie had ventured to the home of his former girlfriend, apparently to settle the score of her ending their relationship and finding a new beau. To make his point, Paulie, a Hispanic male in his twenties, came to the woman's apartment armed with a .380 semiautomatic pistol. "Take me back, or I'll kill you," joked one of the cops on the scene. "Gee, what woman could resist that line from a stud just released from the joint?" Yet before the romantic deadlock could turn into gunfire, the girlfriend's sister came home and surprised Paulie to the point where he grabbed his gun and fled through the streets of the Soundview section of the Bronx on his mountain bike.

The two women, frightened and angry, immediately dialed 911, and 4-3 units received the call over division radio to be on the lookout for a Hispanic male fitting Paulie's description. It didn't take an eternity for plain-clothes 4-3 Precinct anticrime cops to locate the suspect. Riding his bike and nervously looking over his shoulder every three seconds, he was easy to spot. Yet he wasn't in the mood to return upstate—if threatening your former girlfriend was a "questionable" (depending on the liberal judge) violation of parole, then carrying a .380 was a guaranteed one-way ticket back upstate. Paulie wasn't going back—not if his trigger finger could help it. He removed the .380 from his pocket and began firing wildly at the anticrime cops. Taking cover and trying to evacuate the crowd of people far from the crossfire, the anticrime cops radioed the job over division and requested a helicopter to secure the rooftops. Additional precinct and anticrime cars rushed to the scene of the confirmed shooting. Cops respond with speed and en masse when one of their own is targeted by gunfire. Outside an apartment building at 1126 Evergreen Avenue, the NYPD was deployed and ready for action. They weren't going anywhere until the shooter was apprehended.

When cops corner a perpetrator in a building or an abandoned warehouse or the desolate domain of a railyard, ESU personnel are summoned to perform what is known as a "perp search." Perp searches can be routine (when the perp sees the large cops in the heavy vests and Heckler and Koch MP-5 come a calling and immediately determines it prudent to surrender) or terrifying (when cops search an abandoned building in poor condition in search of someone known to be armed and known to be a shooter). When the cops corner a suspect in an enclosed location, with nowhere to run but out the front door, that job becomes a "barricaded perp." Again, barricades run the gamut from routine to terrifying. No two jobs are ever the same. This one would be different from any other.

Paulie had not forced his way into someone's apartment to take a family eating their dinner hostage, nor had he raced to the roof in the desire to evade the responding police units. Paulie had entered the building, raced to the basement, and decided that the last place anyone would look for him was the garbage compactor room and the garbage chute. Paulie wanted to climb up the narrow shaft, where he could position his body against the wall and sit on a brick lip meant to anchor the chute door on the second floor when one of the building's tenants was tossing out his garbage, until the cops either didn't find him or got sick and tired of waiting.

A huge ordeal was about to unfold.

When the report of confirmed shots fired came over the SOD radio, ESU in the Bronx, Queens, and Manhattan stopped in their tracks to monitor the job. When the job became a perp search inside 1126 Evergreen Avenue, units began to glide slowly in a direction that would have them in position to reach the Bronx in a matter of minutes. When the job came over as a confirmed barricaded perp, ESU responded in force. "Emergency Service U-4 and U-6," the dispatcher confirmed, "we have a confirmed barricaded perp inside 1126 Evergreen. I show you responding."

"U-4 to Central, K," Sergeant Garcia responded. "Please have the Two-Truck RMI start out for the 4-3." The time was 9:35 P.M.

The RMI is one of those marvelous bits of equipment that specialized units like ESU love to bring to a big job. The remote mobile investigator is a vehicle specifically meant to be brought to barricades, hostage jobs, and barricaded EDPs. Equipped with a robot, a heavy ballistic shield, video and pole cams, porta-lights, throw phones, and other classified bits of equipment, the RMI is a "have hostage job, will travel" package that can be rushed to any part of New York City (or beyond) in a matter of moments. ESU possesses three RMIs—one in Ten-Truck in Queens North, one in Six-Truck in Brooklyn South, and Two-Truck RMI which covers Manhattan and the Bronx. In Two-Truck, the RMI is the domain of Officer John D'Allara, the truck veteran, and robot master. When not on patrol or involved in something else with the squad, D'Allara often will be found in the garage, in the back of the RMI truck, tinkering with the robot, checking the equipment, and making sure that when the big job comes over, the robot and all the other bits of equipment are ready for action.

Deploying the RMI is a sign to everyone in ESU that the job is for real. Initially, when Lieutenant Sobocienski and Lieutenant Greene heard the job come over the radio, they headed slowly in that direction. "I figured that the job would end by the time I reached the Bronx, and then I'd simply head back to Queens and end my tour," Bob Sobocienski recalled, "though once the RMI was summoned and he was confirmed and barricaded, I raced to the 4-3 to lend a hand." So, too, had Lieutenant Greene and the Jerusalem 3,000 CAT car. The 4-3 had become a huge parking lot of responding patrol and ESU vehicles. Contrary to Paulie's desire, the cops weren't going anywhere.

When a perp ends up barricading himself and holding himself hostage, as Paulie did inside the garbage shaft, ESU cops responding to the job are offered the luxury of time and forethought. As opposed to a barricaded job where the perp or EDP is holding innocent hostages and any wrong move by the police could result in the deaths of scores of innocent people, on a job like this the cops are operating in a controlled environment. The only people who could get hurt are the bad guy or the cops—if the bad guy gets hurt, it's of his own accord, and the cops are not about to act impulsively or recklessly and get one of their own shot and killed under any circumstances. This type of job becomes a battle of wits with an endless stopwatch. Time stands still.

When responding to a barricaded perpetrator, ESU's first priority is always cop safety. ESU isn't a force of Rambos eager to go into a location with guns ablaze.

Deadly force, under any circumstances, is always a means of last resort. No matter what the perp has done, whether he has robbed a drug dealer or shot at a fellow officer, the cops always attempt to end a job peacefully. To help make the best intentions a reality, whether the perp obliges or not, the NYPD possesses a small army of professional technicians and negotiators who talk and technically manipulate a situation to the point where the held-up gunman has little recourse other than to surrender. ESU doesn't like to call these units out unless necessary, but the 4-3 would require everything in the NYPD repertoire and then some.

ESU's first course of action in such a job is to secure the area. Until they knew exactly where he was, ESU personnel were kept out of the elevators (since they were opposite the garbage chutes and in the line of fire). Once Paulie was located and isolated, nestled comfortably in the chute on the third floor, ESU cops would try to begin a dialogue, establishing rapport that they hoped would do its magic and persuade the individual to surrender.

If it's a small job, ESU handles it on its own and lets the precinct handle the rest—"We'll get him out, you guys handle the paperwork." When it turns into a small clusterfuck, it becomes a small glimpse into chaos as duty captains, duty inspectors, duty chiefs, and chiefs of detectives are summoned to the scene to ensure that all the Is are dotted and all the Ts crossed. Big jobs have the tendency to snowball and escalate, and everyone wants to be covered and make sure that no move is made without the approval of a boss. For the department, the "big job" can sometimes be a cross of egos and rank, where personalities and sensitive feelings are crushed. In ESU's world, the bosses always spread the work around so that all the supervisors on scene can be responsible.

When an ESU cop or a boss comes to a job, he never says, "What can I do?" to the person in charge. It is always "What d'ya need?"

On this job, Lieutenant Sobocienski was in the basement, Sergeant Garcia and Lieutenant Greene on the third floor, and Captain Connolly, the citywide patrol captain, supervising the entire operation. Cops from three different trucks, two different shifts, and one black-tie affair had all converged on the Bronx. Paulie, however, was comfortable and not going anywhere.

Police Officer John Oliva, usually assigned to Six-Truck in Brooklyn South, was the E-cop who ended up beginning the dialogue with Paulie. "John did a great job," Capt. Dan Connolly remembers, "but this guy just didn't want to go back to prison." When cops talk to a subject barricaded (or about to jump), any bit of background information always helps—who are you? where are you from? what do you think you'll get out of this situation? can all help expedite the end to a long job. In this case, the E-cops at Evergreen Avenue knew very little of Paulie's motivation other than the fact that he had threatened his former girlfriend, he had taken shots at a cop, and he was holding himself hostage. What was infuriating the E-cops on the scene was that every time they felt they had crossed that line of trust and resolve and that Paulie was about to surrender, he changed his mind. This went on for hours, even after TARU and Lt. Huey McGowan's elite Hostage Negotations Team reached the scene sometime around 11:00 P.M. "The suspect is *where?*" the HNT commander asked over their air, not sure he had heard right the first time about the suspect being in a garbage chute.

"The most important thing that we wanted was for him to drop the gun," Lieutenant Sobocienski remembers. "Everything else was secondary. No matter how hard we tried to convince him, even after he dropped a few bullets as a goodwill gesture, I guess, he kept that .380 close to him."

Most challenging to ending the stalemate was the fact that Paulie wanted to dictate how he was going to surrender. No matter what the situation, one constant in barricade jobs is that the police dictate the terms and the means of surrender. When a perpetrator is held up inside an apartment, for example, the E-cops always tie off the door to ensure that the bad guy doesn't suddenly open the door and surprise any of the heavily armed officers on the other side of the door. Whether the suspect is surrendering or about to come out with guns ablaze, surprise in such scenarios is an explosive commodity. More cops have been killed while routinely taking a gun away from a perp than anyone cares to remember, and there wasn't a cop in ESU who hadn't heard a horror story of how cops were senselessly gunned down while attempting to disarm perps seemingly in the process of surrendering. The old-timers all remember the tragic story of Police Officer Ralph Stancci, a cop in Harlem who walked into the Capri Bar on 136th Street and Lenox Avenue to take the surrender of a fifty-year-old male armed with a gun who was holding the patrons hostage. The perp smiled, as if about to give himself up peacefully, until, without warning, he changed his mind and shot Stancci at point-blank range.

If Paulie was going to surrender, he was going to do it on ESU's terms.

To ensure that he didn't fall and kill himself (try explaining that one to the duty captain or to Channel Four), a rope was lowered to him through the shaft and secured around his waist. Porta-lights were positioned in the compactor room and above him, so that ESU cops taking the occasional look-see would always have a clear and illuminating view of Paulie and his newfound residence in the garbage shaft.

For the E-cops, this was not an easy job to stomach. The stench from the garbage room was unbearable. The rotting food, disposed-of diapers, and other miscellaneous odorous offerings were quickly getting to everyone, especially those who had eaten just before the job came over their radio. Some of the cops were already thinking of aggressive steps to end the megillah. "Why don't we toss a diversionary device in the shaft?" one officer offered. "Why don't we hit him with the water cannon?"

One cop suggested zapping him with a burst of pepper spray, but launching the blinding and choking mist into the confined space of the shaft would have made it hard for the ESU cops to do their jobs once he dropped his gun; or, worse, had he started firing through the incinerator door, the cops, too, would have been affected by the harsh effects of the tear spray. Negotiations, for the moment, seemed a tedious, albeit unavoidable, course of action. One cop even suggested tossing a brick at Paulie's head and hand.

According to the NYPD Hostage Negotiations Team handbook, discussions with a barricaded perp should be "positive." The man chosen to try to take Paulie down was Lt. Bob Sobocienski, a supervisor described by all who worked with him as one of the nicest guys ever to wear NYPD blue. For two hours, Sobocienski pleaded with Paulie to end the craziness and to drop the gun, but it was more of the same old shit, different hour. Just when Paulie appeared to agree to toss the gun into a bucket that was lowered to him, he changed his mind and started the process all over again. Sobocienski was being so nice, so understanding, that Captain Connolly started calling him. "Father Robert." Paulie had been despondent, threatening suicide at times, because he'd be going back to prison and his former girlfriend would be taking their child away. "Well," Sobocienski pleaded, "don't you think that staying alive to watch your kid grow up is important?" Paulie was turning out to be a one-way trip to nowhere. Hoping to use the oldest ploy in law enforcement, the proverbial "good cop versus bad cop," Lt. Richard Greene took over the discussions. Greene was not the type of boss who took a lot of shit from anyone, let alone a loser like a perp wedged inside a garbage chute. After a few "motherfuckers" and some other rather less than positive comments, the cops on the scene felt better, but Paulie was still refusing to let go of the gun, still refusing to surrender.

As the hours stretched on well into the night and exhaustion overtook the cops as well as the perp, Paulie tucked his gun inside his waistband and dozed off for a second. The cops decided to take advantage of his brief snooze, and they forcibly yanked the rope snugly hugging his torso. Instead of freeing the gun, as the cops had hoped, Paulie's arm got tangled in the taut bit of rope, and he found himself contorted and sitting, for the first time in the long ordeal, "uncomfortably."

"Bob, Bob, what's going on?" Paulie shouted to Lieutenant Sobocienski, as if the two were old buddies.

"Give up the gun, Paulie. *Now!*"

Having exhausted all possible resources, and with all the bosses having come to the conclusion that Paulie wasn't going to give up and that he was nothing but a liar, it was decided to zap him with a blast from the Taser. It was hoped that biting currents of electricity would jolt the gun free from Paulie's hands and drop harmlessly to the floor of the compactor room. Instead, it got him pissed. Looking to play the victim, Paulie decided to shoot himself. Aiming the weapon at the side of his stomach, in order not to cause too serious a wound, Paulie shot himself. Unfortunately for him, his ballistic expertise was poor. His shot penetrated his stomach, hit a rib, and bounced off his spinal cord. The cringe of debilitating pain finally forced Paulie to drop the gun, and he dropped soon after that. As he was rushed to the hospital, the cops were still in disbelief that the job had ended that way. An hour later, at the 4-3, they were outraged that a valuable piece of information had been kept from them. Paulie's former girlfriend had dumped him, the ex-con, for, of all things, a cop. Detectives believed that Paulie was out to kill the ex-girlfriend and her lover. His anger toward the police explained why he had refused to surrender after so long an ordeal. Perhaps he was still out to kill a cop? Had ESU known this valuable tidbit of information about his hatred of the police they certainly would have handled the job differently.

Looking to find some humor in a job that lasts forever amid the pleasant smells of garbage, Capt. Dan Connolly dubbed Paulie "The Mope on the Rope." The job is now part of ESU folklore.

Not all barricade jobs end like the Mope on a Rope, but they all have that common thread of "once the cops are summoned, they ain't going anywhere until the perp is in cuffs and headed toward central booking." No matter how right-wing or liberal one's view of the criminal justice system might be, one undisputed fact is that most criminals are just not that smart. Not only do they leave telltale bits of evidence that usually result in them getting locked up, but they'll often do foolish things and take themselves hostage.

On one sunny morning in Upper Manhattan, in the "Hole in the Doughnut," a career felon who had posed as a vagrant in an apartment building doorway, walked up to Terence Hart, manager of a Blockbuster Video store on Broadway and 103rd Street, placed the cold-steel barrel of a gun to his back, and announced a robbery. It was every store owner's worst nightmare, but there was a saving grace in the picture. An air-conditioner repairman, sitting in his van and waiting for the store to open so that he could return some tapes, saw the robbery in progress. The repairman, who coincidentally is on the city waiting list to become one of New York's finest, raced to a pay phone and called 911. Minutes later, dozens of sector cars were outside the storefront. The perp suddenly found himself with no place to go but Riker's Island or the morgue.

Immediately, at the thought of hostages being held, the entire world descended on Broadway and 103rd. All Two-Truck units from Sgt. Jimmy Spratt's Second Squad surrounded the store, and bosses including Chief of Department Louis Anemone and city north supervisor Lt. Mike Libretto rushed to the scene. Hundreds of cops from the 2-4 Precinct and other surrounding commands descended upon the storefront in Upper Manhattan as well, including the Hostage Negotiations Team, TARU, and other detectives, bosses, and supervisors eager to take part in the big job. An NYPD chopper flew overhead monitoring developments from 2,000 feet above the skyline of the Upper West Side.

But there would be no hostages to rescue this spring morning. The perp, Alban Johnson of Jamaica, Queens, was not prepared to hold a store full of people hostage, and, even though he was armed with two guns, he was in no position or mood to engage cops armed with MP-5s and Mini-14s. That's why, in fact, he decided to rob the place when it opened; that way, there would be no hostages. But the store manager, Terence Hart, was not about to end up stuck inside the store with a gun aimed at his head for the next twelve hours while the NYPD negotiated a surrender. "Why don't you let me go outside and tell the cops that I accidentally tripped the burglar alarm?" Hart told Johnson. "This way, they'll go away." Johnson agreed, and Hart simply walked out and into the embrace of awaiting cops.

"The doofus is all alone," one of the Two-Truck cops uttered. He was apprehended moments later.

Sometimes the situation isn't so much a case of a barricaded perp, someone looking for a Mexican standoff, but rather a bad guy who knows he's cornered and simply doesn't want to go back to jail.

On a very warm and muggy night in July, the 2-8 Precinct Squad summoned ESU to a shithole of a walkup tenement on Frederick Douglass Boulevard. A young black male in his early twenties had been shot in the inner thigh with a .25-caliber handgun on a staircase leading to the second floor. The bullet pierced his muscle and sliced open his femoral artery, spilling blood in a cruel and unstoppable flow throughout the stairwell and hallway.

Cops believed that the victim's uncle, a seventy-seven-year-old male who lived in the building, was responsible for the shooting, but there was one problem. The suspected shooter wasn't answering his door, even though there was music and the sounds of kitchen utensils clanking about from behind the locked door.

Sergeant Garcia, the city north supervisor for the evening tour, arrived at the scene following a job in the South Bronx, and he found his squad busy suiting up and ready for what the precinct cops feared was going to be a long ordeal. The staircase at the three-story walkup was literally awash in blood; it was dripping off the stairs in a drip-drop rhythm unmistakable in high-crime areas, and it was fresh. The shooting was very recent, and the perp could not have been far away. Officers John Politoski, Dan Donnelly, Joe Ocasio, and Steve Vales quickly grabbed the MP-5s off "Big Blue" and headed upstairs to the apartment where the shooter was believed to be holed up. Politoski quickly roped off the front and rear doors of the apartment, and Vales positioned the body bunker up against the door, calling for anyone inside to come to the door.

"Give it the old ESU door knock," Garcia told Ocasio, who proceeded to pound the steel fire door with the bottom portion of his boot, a pounding so hard that the entire building began to vibrate. "Do it again," Garcia ordered. There was no reply, but there were sounds emanating from behind the barricaded door and the smell of something cooking at high heat on the stove. "Maybe the shooter popped himself?" one of the cops suggested. "Maybe the victim fought back and shot back, and the guy is unconscious."

There was no point in waiting around, and after checking with the duty captain, Sergeant Garcia ordered his men inside. The heavy steel fire door was proving a bitch to pop. The rabbit tool wasn't making any headway, so a sledgehammer was used. The sound of hammer pounding on steel rang out like gunshots, but after Ocasio hit the door a few dozen times, it cracked open, and the cops raced inside. "I love these guys," the duty captain would say. "They have the tools and the muscle."

Inside the two-room apartment, Sergeant Garcia's squad found the suspect passed out on his bed. He was blind stinking drunk and still wearing his Sunday suit as if he'd just come back from church.

Clearly, part of the ESU philosophy in preventing barricaded perp jobs from ever happening is to assist patrol officers, detectives, and plainclothes officers in tactically and forcefully ending pursuits and perp searches before they develop into barricades—cut off the pursuing felon (and alleged felon) before he has a chance to get inside a building, an apartment, or some other small space, either alone or with some hostages. That isn't always possible. Some barricade perp jobs are simply unavoidable. Cops come to investigate a crime, the perp hears them walking up the stairs in a dilapidated tenement, and the perp grabs friends, family, or strangers in any apartment with an open door and hopes that the police will simply go away. Of course, they won't, and the New York City version of a Mexican standoff ensues. Most often, a barricaded perp is able to hear the tumult caused by dozens of cops standing at the ready outside an apartment, guns drawn. The sounds of the arriving emergency personnel do nothing to reinforce a perp's view that the cops will simply go away. ESU cops make a lot of noise when they respond to such a job—when the heavy tools are dropped, they do make an unmistakable bang on the floor; especially the sledgehammers, rabbit tools, and halogen entry tools. Once the door has been secured and roped off, the obligatory ESU door knock, usually strong enough to wake the dead, rock buildings off their foundations, and even get doped-up mopes to get off a couch, are the final ear-splitting indicator to any barricaded perp that the cops are not going anywhere. Precinct cops or detectives usually secure alleyways, rooftops, and windows, and with the door roped off tightly, the only people determining who goes in or out are the cops—and, of course, the perp, should he decide to surrender and end the ordeal quickly and quietly.

Standing in a hallway in some urine-soaked project

floor or in a walkup where the floor is littered with blood (from a past shooting), baby diapers (from a past bowel movement), and condoms (from some past fun), is not one of the most enjoyable things an E-cop can do. The stench, the clusterfuck, the sheer knowledge that hours on patrol are being wasted because some Riker's Island tenant on leave in the real world doesn't want to go back to a life of orange pajamas and baloney sandwiches, don't make moods happy or receptive. There is another aspect to the job that keeps everyone on edge. Something in the perp's mind, some comment made inside that apartment, might result in gunfire and a 9mm ending to what began as a shitty job.

Some days start so busy and psychotic in Manhattan North that the seasoned E-cops can tell that a barricaded job will come over the air before the tour is over. January 4, 1996, was one such day. For Lt. Bob Sobocienski, working the Bronx and Manhattan with a skeleton staff, it was one job after another—from fifty-three pins to EDPs.

The Second Squad was racing about like mad for much of the morning, going from one gun run to another, headed from a reported pin to reports of a cardiac. They had hit virtually every precinct north of 59th Street and had almost been called to three jobs in the Bronx as well. Detective Henry Medina and Police Officer Ann-Margaret Lyons were in the Adam car, Police Officers Seth Gahr and Paddy McGee in the Boy car. From running around to an EDP job in New York Hospital earlier in the day, this was one tour to remember.

Close to noon, the routine argument about where to eat began inside the crowded REP cab—always a critical discussion during a shift. "You want Chinese, Italian, or deli?" Seth asked. "Let's try Mama Joy's?" Driving south down Adam Clayton Powell Jr. Boulevard toward Central Park North, the two observed the civilian and vehicular traffic carefully in search of any jobs before banking a right on Central Park North and then veering north on Morningside Drive. "Check with the truck and see if they want anything." Before Seth could tell the central dispatcher to have the truck go to the frequency reserved for internal (nonofficial) communications, the SOD radio sent a series of five beeps (meaning urgent message) followed by the ominous, "In the confines of the 2-5, ten-thirteen, confirmed shots fired. Officers responding to a ten-thirty of a residence! Boy-Two, over?"

"Shit," Seth uttered as he put his lunch money back in his pocket. "Central, this is Boy-Two, we are responding, K?"

"Adam-Two, ten-four. Truck-Two, do you copy?"

"Central, this is U Four. Have the truck respond forthwith and have the Adam car proceed. K?"

"Negative, K. This is Two-Truck. The truck is out on mechanical. Have Truck-Four respond from the Bronx and meet us at the job!"

"Ten-four, responding forthwith and also receiving additional calls from division for immediate ESU assistance. ESU Truck-Four, do you copy?"

With lights flashing and the siren attempting to cut a path through the Harlem traffic, the Adam car moved from the distinct terrain of black Harlem, across the border of Fifth Avenue, into Spanish Harlem. The response time was impressive. Three minutes, and already the block of 128th Street off Park was congested with dozens of precinct patrol cars, navy blue Chevy Caprices belonging to patrol lieutenants, captains, and commanders, and a small mini-triage center of AMS ambulances, ready to absorb casualties.

What had happened was so typical of the Harlem landscape that it has now become an underground epidemic. Criminals, no longer able to prey on taxpaying citizens as they once did because of the heavy police presence instituted by then-Commissioner Bratton, now tend to prey on one another. The most vulnerable targets in the New World Order of New York City are the richest—mid-level cocaine, crack, and marijuana dealers who are often immersed in tens of thousands of dollars and can't report being ripped off to the police. At 11:40 A.M. on January 4, the nineteen year old owner of a rap sheet that was taller than his six-foot frame, decided to lead a four-man gang bent on ripping off a location where drugs and money were allegedly being stored. The location, an apartment on the ninth floor, was like most apartments in the projects during a winter's day—overheated and engulfed in the deafening sounds of rap music.

According to their plan, the gang was hitting an easy target—they wanted to be in and out with the money in less than a minute. If anyone put up a fight, they'd be dealt with by the 9mms and 12-gauge shotguns brought along for juice and contingency. What the gang didn't take into consideration was the fact that there were good, honest people living in the building, and when they brandished their weapons in the lobby and elevator, neighbors began dialing 911. When they burst into the drug location, weapons in hand, and began making a hell of a noise, heard above even the hypnotic cadence of a Coolio CD, more neighbors began dialing 911. Two precinct cars responded to the calls of a ten-thirty in progress. The officers arrived three minutes later. Guns drawn, the cops banged on the door with their nightsticks and ordered the occupants to open the door immediately. The ringleader, genius criminal that he was, decided to have his gang quickly tie up the occupants and then answer the door while posing as the apartment's tenant. Problem was, of course, that he opened the door while holding his shotgun. A Mexican standoff ensued as officer and perp faced each other in the doorway pointing guns at each other. The perp fired first, his shot missed. The patrolman responded, his weapon's 9mm round splitting into his target's left shoulder and spraying the room with bone and blood. The perp then locked the door and threw a sofa in front of it.

ESU has several ways of dealing with barricaded perps—especially those holding hostages—caught in the middle of a crime. Some perps demand jets and large sums of cash and then surrender an hour later when a negotiator offers them a cheeseburger and a vanilla shake. Those who have committed an act of violence before barricading themselves inside an apartment or storefront usually will hold out for a charge reduction before raising their hands and surrendering. Others opt to kill themselves. Whatever the situation, ESU cops on the scene have a variety of tricks up their sleeves to handle the predicament—from robots that can open doors to handheld video cameras held on sixteen-foot-long poles that can be used to see what's going in a besieged location. ESU handles these incidents slowly and deliberately. After all, the cops aren't going anywhere.

For Capt. John LaRose, the Manhattan North duty captain, barricaded jobs inside housing projects were nothing new. Usually, the cops will chase a suspect through the grounds of a project and up the stairs, with the ordeal eventually ending after the suspect races into an apartment, sometimes even his own, and is then convinced to come out by the responding men and women in blue. This time, however, the perps not only displayed a propensity for violence, but they had taken a shot at the cops. One of the perps was wounded and possibly looking to end it all in a blaze of gunfire. Adding fuel to the fire were the hostages inside, anywhere between five and ten people who were believed to be tied up and used as shields.

Captain LaRose was relieved to see Lt. Bob Sobocienski responding—the two had worked together in the 1-10 Precinct in Queens, and each cop knew how the other worked. "Working a job like this is always hard," claims Sobocienski. "The cops on the scene are pumped and driven by adrenaline, especially if one of their own has been shot at, and the responding emergency service personnel are also racing to the scene, being driven by their hearts beating fast, in order to back up their fellow officers." Working a barricaded job with hostages in a project, however, is no easy task. The floors are usually filled with the curious and those not too sympathetic to the police. The thick walls make radio transmissions to the outside scrambled at best, and as Murphy's law would have it, most jobs are on the top floors on days when the elevators aren't working.

Lieutenant Sobocienski was among the first E-cops on the scene, and he immediately headed upstairs with Captain LaRose and several of the Two-Truck cops. Knowing that more units would be responding, especially Sergeant Coughlin and Four-Truck from the Bronx, Sobocienski told Police Office Seth Gahr to remain down below and act as his liaison with arriving personnel. As Seth looked on, gazing toward the ninth floor of the building, his gloved hand shielding the harsh winter's sun from his eyes, he watched as the officers, shotguns in hand and suited up in ballistic Kevlar assault vests and Kevlar Fritz helmets, awaited the arrival of the truck from the Bronx and its mini-arsenal of MP-5 9mm submachine guns and Mini-14 5.56mm assault rifles. The Two-Truck officers grabbed their bulletproof ballistic body bunkers, too, and readied earplugs, just in case gunfire in the brick caverns of a housing project hallway erupted. Once the truck arrived, most officers exchanged their 12-gauge shotguns for the heavier assault weaponry and joined Sobocienski for the biting urine smells of an elevator ride to the ninth floor. The apartment's door was roped off. Tetukevich placed his body bunker up against the door and Officers Paddy O'Connor and Barry Nagelberg commenced the dialogue. "We know you've been hit," one of the cops yelled through the door, a bunker shielding him from any bursts of gunfire coming through the door. "How 'bout letting everyone go?"

In such jobs, with so many cops assembled around such narrow spaces, the term *clusterfuck* becomes part of the scene. There are captains, lieutenants, E-cops, precinct cops, detectives, and so on. It becomes an unmanageable circus and can sometimes do more damage than good. Captain LaRose ordered the nonessential cops downstairs to secure the outer perimeter just in case the bad guys began tossing guns, drugs, money, or bodies out the window. The E-cops would maintain the inner perimeter. With the forces in position, ready to move in the flash of an eye should the sounds of gunfire be heard, Lieutenant Sobocienski ordered Seth Gahr upstairs. Gahr was one of Lieutenant Sobo's favorites and also one of the best tactical cops in the division. Fearing that a tactical entry might need to be made, Sobocienski wanted his trusted cop right there on the line.

Most cops—all cops, in fact—would have taken the elevator to the ninth floor. Seth, however, being Seth, decided to use the stairs. Placing the flashlight affixed to the barrel of his submachine gun on high-beam, he gingerly walked up nine flights of stairs, carefully turning and twisting his body around the corners of the staircase as if he were back in the Iraqi desert hunting down Republican Guardsmen. Between the fifth and six floors, Seth heard a noise coming from the seventh floor. It couldn't be a cop, and most of the residents had been evacuated from two floors below and above the crime scene. Not wanting to use his radio or attract unwanted attention, he quickly wiped the sweat of his brow, removed the safety from his MP-5, and waited for what could be an encounter with an armed and dangerous perp. His knees tightened, his stomach twisted into a tense coil, and he flickered his finger around the trigger housing, limbering that important extremity ever so agile so that it would respond in a millisecond should it be needed. As the descending footsteps grew louder and the pants and sighs indicated the arrival of a wounded man, Seth aligned his back with the staircase and awaited the encounter. As the subject moved closer, almost to within reach, Seth removed a two-handed grip from his MP-5 and moved the weapon to his right hand; a clenched left fist, adorned in a yellow worker's glove, was wound back and ready to deliver an introductory blow. By the time the perp turned the corner, a powerful punch struck his chest. Seth's left-handed hook knocked the wind out of the nineteen-year-old would-be robber. It also threw him down half a flight of the urine-stained and crack-vial-strewn stairway. Before the perp could open his eyes and assess his predicament, the barrel of a German-made Heckler and Koch MP-5 9mm submachine gun was protruding into his neck. "Don't move, up against the wall!"

Seth removed a 9mm Taurus from the pocket of the person he had just tossed and apprehended—he must have been the lookout, who, when the cops arrived, thought it smart to make his way very slowly down to the street below.

With one perp in custody and the remainder inside the apartment, Officers O'Connor and Nagelberg continued their intensive talks with the injured man and his band of robbers. The pain of the gunshot being almost too much to bear, the leader agreed to surrender. "A story that Sgt. Paul Hargrove [now a supervisor in Ten-Truck in Queens North] once told me stuck in my mind throughout the job," Lieutenant Sobocienski recalled. "It was about a hostage ordeal in a project somewhere in Brooklyn, and when the perp finally decided to give himself up, the surrender didn't go as planned. All of a sudden, when the door was opened, a stream of men, women and children began racing out of the apartment. No one knew who was who or what was what. The last male out was holding a gun,, and it was aimed at the cops. The weapon was raised, shots were fired at the cops, and the perp turned into a statistic and a bullet-ridden corpse." Surrenders need to be controlled, orderly, and almost tedious exercises with one subject after the other brought out, frisked, and secured. Only once the cops know who is who and what is what should cuffs be removed from the innocent and the bad guys begin their long, and probably third, fourth, or fifth, trip through the New York penal system.

One by one, the people inside the apartment were ushered out. Each was tossed, or searched, thoroughly by one of the ESU cops and then handed over to a precinct cop or detective. The process took more than twenty minutes, with the last person out being an almost blind female in her early nineties. It was her apartment, and, allegedly, her nephews were using it to store crack, pot, and cash. She, beaten and frightened, was the true victim of the senseless afternoon's mayhem. Inside the spacious ninth-floor apartment, the cops found blood sprayed everywhere and the place ransacked with the vicious abandon of true psychopaths. "These guys were animals," one cop told another. "This was all senseless."

Outside the building, as the aided cases were rushed to Harlem Hospital and the perps were rushed to the 2-5, Lieutenant Sobocienski conducted his now legendary postjob debriefings as the cops were in the processes of de-SWAT-ing. Sobocienski had nothing but praise for his cops—they had helped bring about a quick and bloodless resolution to what could have been a tragedy. "Seth, once again, stepped in shit," Sobocienski commented, taking note of the fact that every time there is a big job, Seth is right in the middle of the storm. "Seth," Lieutenant Sobo sighed, "we can't take you anywhere."

"Oh, c'mon, Loo," a blushing Seth replied. "Just doing what I do best!"

At around noon on Monday, March 3, 1997, plainclothes narcotics officers in the 3-4 Precinct, the nerve center of the New York city narcotics pipeline, were working buy-and-busts in front of 601 West 190th Street—a shitty block in a real shitty part of the city. The cops, identifiable only by their NYPD swagger, flashed their tin once they participated in a completed drug deal, and then they made their move. But the suspect, a male Hispanic in his early thirties, about five-foot-seven with a dark complexion, produced a gun and immediately launched his Nike Air Jordans and entered the building, disappearing into the maze of darkened hallways, apartments, and garbage shafts. The plainclothes cops and the multitude of patrol personnel rushing in on the ten-thirteen, proceeded with great caution.

The suspect was armed—believed to be holding a 9mm automatic and wearing a yellow shirt and lining to his jacket. The building was surrounded by precinct and Street Crime Unit personnel, and NYPD helicopters hovered above to secure the rooftops.

Two and a half hours later, after suiting up, after removing shotguns, MP-5s, and Ruger Mini-14s from the truck, after entering the building ready for any and all contingencies and searching every floor and every inhabited apartment, they cornered the suspect. Facing the possibility of being lit up like a Christmas tree had he offered any resistance, he surrendered.

No matter how many times they have been arrested or how many times they have been put through the system or spent time in a penitentiary, perps *always* think that they are smarter than the cops. A robber can be caught red-handed, someone's wallet inside his coat and someone's blood on his knife, and he'll deny everything. "The guy gave you his wallet and the blood?" Even when the police catch a burglar trying to crawl out the window of an apartment with the proverbial laundry bag of loot in hand, the bad guy will return inside the location, lock the doors, and logically believe that the cops will not get inside the place, nor will they find him.

On a warm and stormy March Saturday, as the Second Squad patrolled the streets of northern Manhattan on the eight-to-four, the tour was slowly winding down after a considerably grueling shift of pin jobs, elevator jobs, and a few pit bulls that needed to be tranquilized. With Sergeant Spratt away in command of the A Team, Detective Henry Medina assumed the mantle as the squad boss—as the senior man in the truck, there was little in the realm of emergency service work that Detective Medina had not done or seen before. He took his work in stride.

As some of the E-cops were in quarters, looking forward to a soda or a cup of coffee, the call came over the SOD radio in regard to a barricaded perp inside an apartment on Overlook Terrace and 190th Street in Washington Heights. Washington Heights used to be a German-Jewish enclave at the northern tip of Manhattan, and even though Spanish with a Dominican flair is the true language of Broadway north of 155th Street, small pockets of Jewish life still thrive in the area. Overlook Terrace, against the backdrop of Yeshiva University, is one such stretch of territory. The winding tree-lined streets are clean, garbage is not tossed out of living-room windows onto the street below, and graffiti is not part of the landscape. In fact, the small enclave doesn't look as if it really belongs in Washington Heights.

A sector car from the 3-4 Precinct had been on patrol on Overlook Terrace when its officers observed a Hispanic male attempting to make his way onto a fifth-floor fire escape carrying a small bag. "What's wrong with this picture?" one of the cops joked as they responded to the apartment. Soon reinforcements arrived, and both ESU and K-9 were summoned.

When ESU comes on a job like this, it is always impossible to tell exactly what they have until they come upstairs to the apartment and confer with the patrol sergeant or lieutenant. After suiting up and grabbing their MP-5s, the cops made it to the fifth floor, where they found a dozen cops all waiting outside the door, hands caressing their holsters.

"Whatta we got here, Sarge?" Detective Medina asked, hoping to hear that there were no hostages inside.

"Some mutt was seen trying to leave the premises, a sector car came on the scene, and here we are. We have someone on the fire escape, but he can't see anything. Our guys haven't heard anything from inside the apartment, either."

As the 3-4 Precinct duty captain arrived, a veteran of the streets of Manhattan North who had a fond working relationship with ESU, Detective Medina assembled his crew for entry into the apartment. MP-5s were readied, and the rabbit tool and sledgehammer were brought to the front. It was decided to let the K-9 dog go in first, and then, if he failed to make a hit on the suspect, ESU would conduct its search of the premises. As the rabbit tool was inserted into the door wedge, the precinct sergeant said, "I think an old man lives there, but the neighbors don't think he's home."

"Hold up!" Detective Medina said, fearing that the cops would make a routine entry and possibly find some senior citizen with a gun to his head. "Are we sure that there is nobody in there *other* than the perp? Are we absolutely sure?" The consensus was almost 100 percent. The duty captain ordered entry to be made.

With the K-9 German shepherd posed for his scent-inspired search of the location, the E-cops popped the door open. The dog raced in, growling and barking as he searched the premises. His search took all but a few minutes, but it came up negative. Much to the surprise of the E-cops, the dog returned playful, not having hit even as much as food scraps on the table. "I guess it's our turn," Officer Kevin Reynolds commented as he raised his MP-5 into tactical entry position. The cops formed their tactical line, and, with Officer Ann-Margaret Lyons on the bunker, and cops were ready to move in.

"OK, we're going in," Detective Medina instructed the 3-4 sergeant and the duty captain. "Tell your guy on the window that we are not, I repeat *not,* going to chase anyone outside. If someone goes racing out the window, it isn't gonna be any of us!"

The pounding of heavy footsteps and "Police, get your hands up now!" were heard coming from the apartment as the cops, weapons raised and triggers caressed, made their tactical entry into the premises. They had done it a hundred times before, but each entry was different, and each had the potential for gunfire. The six rooms were all secured before being methodically searched, and within minutes Officer Lyons came across the perp, hiding under a pile of laundry in a bedroom closet.

The duty captain had been on many a long job with barricaded perps and EDPs in his time in Harlem's 3-0 and 3-4 precincts, and the smile on his face told of the relief in his heart that ESU had handled the situation so expeditiously and successfully.

"Thanks, Henry," the captain commented as he slapped the E-cop on the back in a show of gratitude and admiration.

"Anytime, boss," Detective Medina replied, "that's what we are here for!"

Sometimes, though, by the time the precinct or anticrime cops have officially labeled a job as a barricade, the perp is long gone. It was 2:00 P.M. on a warm Sunday in April, and the SOD radio has been quiet. In Two-Truck's area, two fly men from Nine-Truck in Queens found themselves patrolling in new territory, on Manhattan's Upper West Side, while in the truck Officers Donnelly and Vales monitored SOD and division radios while fuming over an article in *Firehouse* magazine in which someone from the FDNY was awarded a hundred-dollar grant for "twenty years of puppet shows" while that same "award for valor" went to a volunteer firefighter in Maryland who had died in the line of duty while trying to rescue a woman from an overturned car. Sgt. Juan Garcia, the city north supervisor, returned to the truck following a job in the Bronx and was about to call the desk at Floyd Bennet Field to find out about a morning's exercise in Brooklyn where cops from Trucks Five, Six, Seven, and Eight had scaled the monstrous Verrazano Narrows Bridge, when a job came over SOD. "In the confines of the 4-6, division confirming a barricaded perp on the Grand Concourse and East 179th Street. Truck-Four and Adam-Four responding?"

"Adam-Three to Central, K," Officer Joe Hernandez interrupted. "Show us responding as well."

"U-3 to Central," Capt. Ralph Pascullo informed the SOD dispatcher. "Show me responding to the 4-6."

"U-4 to Central, K. Show me responding to the barricade."

Sgt. Juan Garcia is said to have missed his calling in life as a race car driver, and he has been known to push a Chevy Caprice to its envelope and then some. "When responding to a job with Juan," one boss new to the unit once commented on a learning tour of the north with Sergeant Garcia, "I tend to close my eyes, because what you can't see can't kill you!"

Garcia was at the Grand Concourse in a matter of minutes, arriving at the same time as Captain Pascullo, also a race car driver in a former life, and Officers Manny Hernandez and Joe Hernandez in the Adam-Three REP. Garcia and Manny Hernandez, two former jarheads, are as close as friends can be on the job, and they feel a sense of comfort and security when they work on a job together. The two trust each other with eyes closed and have been on far too many barricaded jobs together to get overly excited. Calm, cool, and restraint were the order of the day. The three suited up outside the location, on a block complete with a halal butcher shop and elderly Puerto Rican males gambling and playing backgammon. They conferred with the Four-Truck chauffeur, ESU veteran Bobby Steinman, as he maintained the perimeter outside on the Grand Concourse.

"Whatta we got, Bobby?" Garcia asked.

"Four-six anticrime was chasing a mutt. I think he was wanted for some robbery, and he was almost naked, into the building, and he pulled some poor woman out of her apartment and locked the door."

By the time Garcia and Pascullo, his muscles still aching from climbing the out cable of the Verrazano Narrows Bridge, made it to the third floor, much of Four-Truck had already roped off the door and were trying to negotiate with the perp. Sgt. John Coughlin, another former jarhead and housing emergency supervisor, was directing the cops while both Manny Hernandez and Joe Hernandez, MP-5s in hand, stood by the doorway. Officer Regina McGee, her body bunker hoisted by her head to shield her from any incoming fire launched through the door, clutched her Glock 9mm, ready for any contingency.

"Hey, Anthony," Officer McGee pleaded with the

perp inside. "We aren't going anywhere, and we won't hurt you. Just open the door and lie on the floor with your hands spread out in front of you."

As Sergeant Garcia looked on, hearing the relaying information from Officer Steinman on the street below, 4-6 detectives began knocking on doors. At first they were looking to see if anyone knew the perp, and then they wanted to find out if there was anyone in the apartment with the perp. A barricaded felon was one thing. A hostage ordeal was something quite different.

Until the E-cops were sure that the perp was alone, they weren't about to make entry, but if there was anyone inside and it was a bad guy, the supervisors on the scene weren't about to let this thing develop into a Cecil B. DeMille, the ESU term for a large production. With Captain Pascullo giving the OK, the metal teeth of the rabbit tool were placed between the frame and the door, and one of the cops began pumping the device with furious energy. Once a gap was produced, one of the officers rolled in a diversionary device that erupted in a deafening blast and a blinding burst of light. Seconds later, with Officer McGee leading the charge behind the safety of her body bunker, the officers entered the apartment and meticulously searched every nook and cranny of the place. Closets were entered, mattresses and box frames overturned, and even the stove searched. Anthony was gone. He had stolen some clothes and jumped out the window.

"It's amazing," one of the E-cops commented. "Here a guy jumps from a third-floor window and doesn't get as much as a scratch. If one of us jumped from a third step, we'd surely break our legs."

Glad that the job turned out to be nothing, the E-cops returned to their REPs on the Grand Concourse and de-SWAT-ed. They had a feeling they'd be called back for Anthony once again in the very near future. They were probably right.

9

The Inner Sanctum: Life and Psychology Inside an ESU Truck

•

A Harlem morning, 7:15. Another eight-to-four is about to begin.

"Good morning, boss," an officer living upstate offers his sergeant.

"You are late, man!" the sergeant, who lives in the Bronx, replies.

"Gee, Sarge," the officer answers back. "Not all of us have the luxury of intermittent gunfire outside our window to wake us up in the morning!"

There is no comment from the sergeant, who, looking at the bulletin board in the kitchen, sees the latest sarcastic offering: a picture of a crying baby with the bold-letter title, "ESU Etiquette Manual."

"This place is a madhouse," one of the cops comments.

"Yeah," another replies as he attempts to juggle a cup of coffee, a bagel, and the weapons log book in his hands. "But it's home!"

Walk into most police precincts in New York City, and the first impression you get is that of chaos. The floors are usually littered with cigarette butts and dirt, the walls are a combination of peeling paint and rusting fixtures, and the fluorescent lights flicker in a wavering cadence that can cause even the strongest-willed human being to lose his mind in an instant. The station is in constant motion, with officers coming in and out of various offices, stairwells, and corners, and sergeants, liieutenants, and the occasional duty captain walking around with handfuls of clipboards and forms, seeking proper signatures and memo initials. The division radio washes the empty reaches of the stationhouse with a never-ending barrage of calls and jobs. Prisoners, in the holding cells behind the sergeant's desk, press their faces against the spit- and semen-stained glass and yell obscenities each time a female officer walks by. A small tape player, on low volume, emits the sounds of the fifties and sixties from a golden oldies FM station. Welcome to Harlem's 2-6 Precinct, located on 126th Street between Amsterdam and Old Broadway.

The TS (telephone service) operator at the desk is fielding phone calls and helping walk-ins, citizens who come into the precinct in search of assistance or a locked-up relative.

"Can I help you?" a young Hispanic officer asks as a toothless male in his fifties walks in, wearing a tattered raincoat and a New York Yankees cap.

"My grandson was arrested, and I want to see him now!"

"How do you know he was arrested sir?" the TS asks, realizing that a missing youth, even in Harlem, doesn't necessarily have to have been arrested.

"Because they said he be picked up by the five-oh [the local slang for the police]."

"You mean the police, don't you? How do you know he was brought to this precinct?"

"What kind of runaround are you giving me? He was arrested on Edgecome and 155th Street. I heard they got him for weed or a gun or some shit like that, and that his monkey ass is here, and I wanna see him!" the grandfather demanded, pounding his fist on the window.

"Sir, first of all, lower your voice. Second of all, 155 and Edge is the 3-2 Precinct, not here, and thirdly, we have no one by that name here this morning. Try the 3-2, and have a nice day."

The grandfather walked out of the precinct cursing to himself and spitting on the sidewalk, calling the cops a bunch of white devils, and cursing his grandson for getting picked up and making him miss the Jerry Springer show. As he walked out of the station, two precinct cops came in clutching a prisoner, a half-naked man mumbling to himself and urinating all over the floor.

Just another day at an NYPD precinct. Whoever said that law enforcement wasn't a glamorous profession surely never visited Harlem!

Just up the block at 126th Street, however, at the home of Two-Truck, the atmosphere is completely different. Although a police facility, it's closed to the public. In fact, it is even closed to most other cops. A truck is in reality a small and isolated world unto itself. It is a base and a bastion. An armory and an escape. "It is," according to one former ESU officer, "like Batman's Bat Cave. It is where all the neat toys and devices are, it is where the Batmobile is maintained, and it is from where Batman deploys, to fight the powers of evil and keep the residents of Gotham safe."

Although ESU cops will hate to admit it, life in a truck is as close to service in a firehouse as one could get. Each truck has its garage for trucks and vehicles, its locker room and weight corner, and an office, kitchen and TV recreation room. A precinct cop could spend an entire eight-and-a-half-hour tour in his patrol car without ever returning to the precinct, while even the ESU entities on patrol, the Adam and Boy cars, will always return to quarters once, twice, or ten times a tour. The truck is a home away from home, a place of safe refuge.

The garage at Two-Truck is typical—parking spots for two REPs on the right and parking for the RMI vehicle and the big truck on the left. The walls, a blinding fluorescent greenish gray weathered to a dull dirt shade over the years by endless clouds of exhaust fumes, resembles a ghetto mechanic shop more than a police facility. Automotive supplies surround the walls and the ceilings, as do rows and rows of lockers. Ropes, industrial wash, and other mechanical bits and pieces are stored neatly in bins and cubicles, and a small repair shop, fitted with enough tools to make the Home Depot jealous, fixes anything from damaged fuel pumps on the Hurst tool to Stokes baskets and pistol grips. Scuba suits, dripping wet from a water rescue job near the sewage treatment plant on the Hudson River, are hung out on laundry lines to dry. The deafening chatter of the SOD radio, pumped in at full volume, resonates in the spacious cavern like a tenor belting out a Verdi classic at the Met.

The main nerve center of the truck is on the second floor, up a poorly lit, narrow staircase. A wall is decorated with memorabilia, some old photos, and a scale model of the old Truck-Two truck, in its now prehistoric green-and-white scheme. The hallway leads to the office and the kitchen. The three truck sergeants, Ken Bowen, Jimmy Spratt, and Juan Garcia, all have their lockers inside the office, and the truck's armory is there as well, well guarded inside a heavily fortified locker in the sergeant's room. The office is a bit more than just a desk and an old Smith-Corona where the runs are typed up, where the sergeants sit and spend time calling Floyd Bennet Field for changes to the roll call or other special assignment details. Two double bunk beds fill in the narrow confines of the room, to accommodate cops working double tours and special assignments such as VIP details. Most importantly, the office is where the supervisors talk to their cops in private—sergeant to cop, man to man and woman. When the door is closed, it means someone is getting yelled at for an infraction or possibly a fuckup while on a job. And when a visiting captain or lieutenant comes to the truck, a closed door means that the sergeant is discussing some problem with the boss and it isn't meant for public circulation. Walls are thin, however, and ears tend to move away from divisional radios and head for the walls the moment the door is slammed shut. Nothing remains secret in a squad, or in the truck, for that matter; "Somebody farts in Four-Truck," claims one Two-Truck cop, "and Floyd Bennet Field has heard of it long before the stench settles in Lower Manhattan."

The kitchen, directly behind the office, is the true social and psychological nerve center of the truck. Equipped with a color TV, a stove, a sink, a refrigerator, a dishwasher, two couches, and an industrial-size coffee machine, the kitchen is where the cops assigned to the truck, the chauffeur and the sergeant, spend much of the tour, and it is where the officers on patrol come back to eat their meals, enjoy a cup of coffee, and do what cops do best—bullshit. There are times when the SOD and divisional radios are so slow, so void of anything more than a report of a bank burglar alarm, that the kitchen is crowded with as many as eight cops. When tours change, and those coming in from the cold and those suiting up are all eager to grab a cup of coffee and catch up on the latest gossip, the kitchen becomes a Grand Central Station of hungry mouths and busy bodies. The typical banter ranges from political to perverse, job-related to just plain nuts. Nothing is taboo, no language or words frowned upon, and no subject avoided. There have been more heart-to-hearts, more "you wanna step outsides?" and more "fuck yous" said in the Two-Truck kitchen than on a picket line at a Teamsters strike.

The kitchen is not for the sensitive—neither is the truck, for that matter. On the main wall in the room, at the very entrance, is a bulletin board ostensibly used for work-related messages from the SOD command, the ESU commander, and the truck lieutenant and supervisors. In reality, the truck bulletin board has become a place where fellow cops in the squad are made fun of, lampooned, and taken to task. God forbid a cop in the unit gets his picture in the paper; immediately, it is drawn upon and vandalized with some very cruel and often very funny cartoons. Once, after the successful rescue of a jumper, a cop with a somewhat large nose who had his picture in the paper found his likeness vandalized with the addition of a beak. A large and hefty cop who bore an unmistakable resemblance to a white-supremacist militia leader, found his likeness spread throughout the division and mercilessly plastered on the bulletin board at quarters. In fact, when making fun of a fellow officer, the bulletin board is a safe, somewhat distanced and anonymous method for hitting below the belt. Nothing is sacred, and the crueler the better. ESU practical jokes are legendary. Once, cops in a truck in Queens imposed a damn good replica of a New York State license plate over the genuine article belonging to Mike McKenna, a six-foot eleven-inch cop with a grand sense of humor and a heart of gold. The fake plate said "ILUVMEN." It took several days and countless advances from affectionate males on the Long Island Expressway before McKenna realized that something wasn't kosher.

It's bad enough that the cops make fun of one another because they are fat, skinny, bald, hairy, ugly, good-looking, tall, short, Jewish, Puerto Rican, Irish, Italian, Polish, or whatever. But the way you speak is attacked (anyone with a speech impediment is ripped to shreds), where you live becomes a matter of scorn, and what you like to do in your off time (the more bizarre the hobby or sport, the more sadistic the jokes) is also subject for discussion and ridicule. Nothing, perhaps with the exception of one's spouse and kids, is taboo. To mimic one of the truck's thinner officers, known by the affectionate nickname "Skelator," the cops in his squad once purchased a balloonlike inflatable skeleton, put an ESU cap on its head, and put it behind the wheel of one of the RMIs parked in quarters. During fast-rope exercises, when it took an officer who stammers a bit longer to get down the rope, the cops immediately responded in kind: "Why did it take him so long to get down? Because it took five minutes for him to say G-g-g-g-g-eronimo!" If a cop is Puerto Rican, he's called Rice and Beans. If the cop is a Jew, he is a matzo eater. And God forbid he has any physical deformity or oddity that paints a large bull's-eye on his back; well, "Welcome to the fucking mosaic!"

If something can be made fun of, it will be made fun of.

Yet the topic open for the most cutting ridicule, the attacks that really hurt, are job-related. If someone does really well on a job, rescues a woman from underneath an overturned van, or saves the life of a jumper, and God forbid it makes the *Daily News* or the *Post,* the jealousy, the callous envy of having someone else bask in the momentary spotlight, results in cops from all three squads making fun, often with little humor and a great deal of insensitivity, of the poor soul of a cop who happened to have been in the right place at the right time. And God forbid one of the cops fucks up on a job; then not only is he the target of numerous cartooned lampoons on the bulletin board, but the word spreads throughout the ten trucks of the unit like a case of crabs in a ten-dollar brothel. You don't need thick skin to be in ESU, you need flesh made out of Kevlar.

All cops operate on their own frequency, and like all units, the cops serving under a specific command develop their own language, idiosyncrasies, habits, mindsets, and personalities. "Look at beat cops," claimed now retired ESU Lt. Bob Sobocienski, attempting to explain how cops who work at various aspects of the job behave. "They talk and act one way, motorcycle cops talk and act another way, highway cops are in a league all their own, detectives in a squad are different from everyone else. E-cops, too, function in their own little universe." In a precinct or a detective squad, for example, many cops work with steady partners. These partners become a central part of their lives, and they spend more time with that other person with a gun sitting next to them inside the patrol car than they do with their spouses and kids. Patrolmen and detectives who are partners often will spend much of their off time with their better halves from work. They go out to eat and go out to bend an elbow together, and they go to each other's home for barbecues and family get-togethers. In emergency, it is very rare that two cops will always work with a steady and permanent partner. In ESU, cops fly from truck to truck, they alternate when they are in the truck, serving as a chauffeur or being sent to one special assignment or another. Unlike a precinct or a detective squad, E-cops in a truck, let alone a squad, will rarely socialize outside the job. They rarely go out to a bar or to a restaurant after work, and on weekends and RDOs (regular days off), the cops try to separate themselves from one another and the job as much as they can. On the job, the cops are a conglomerate of individuals who work together as a team on the same page. Off the job, they tend to go their separate ways.

Perhaps this lack of now-expected cop camaraderie can be explained by the sheer tension and stress involved in emergency work. As in all elite units, life in an ESU truck is a pressure cooker. An air of tension always exists and can explode at any second. To fit in and to survive there is a veil of armor that most cops bring with them to the job—it is a natural byproduct of working in a high-tension place where, chances are, at one point or another in your day you will find yourself knee deep in shit or blood. In most cases, that veil is expressed in being grouchy and miserable. "Hey, how's it going?" one cop will ask another at the change of tour. "Rrrrrrrgghhhhhhhhh," the other cop will respond. "What the fuck do you care?" The cops in a squad or in a truck tend not to want to get too close to one another, and they rarely see one another socially. Many of the cops live upstate, in relative proximity to one another, yet they rarely socialize outside the job. The stereotype of cops going out and sitting in a bar after a shift to drown their sorrows is a Hollywood story-line that doesn't apply to most ESU trucks. Most of the cops, after their eight hours are done, rush home to go to their second jobs or to be with their families. Most just want to get as far from the city as they can.

The cops, in essence, live two completely separate lives—the life at home and that on the job. Because they work rotating shifts, often on weekends, their family lives truly suffer. At home or in their secondary employment, the cops must be able to detach themselves from the dangers of the street, the stress of the job, and the ankle-high bureaucratic bullshit they must step into day after day. It is incredibly difficult to remove oneself from a job as hands-on as a cop—especially one in emergency. E-cops need to be courageous, but they also need to cope with their fears and do so away from the eyes of their fellow officers. To do rescue work, they need to be compassionate and caring, yet to do their law enforcement duties, they need to be impartial and void of direct emotional involvement. It's an incredibly precarious balancing act that only a handful of officers do well and that people outside the job can never truly understand.

The cops function by creating barriers to their personalities that shield them from the insanity and the terror. One chunk of this veil of armor is to argue about everything and everyone at every possible chance. The doctor who said that holding in one's emotions is not a healthy way to fight tension sure had ESU in mind. The truck kitchen looks much more like the floor of the Israeli Knesset or the kitchen of a Greek diner than a police base of operations. Everything that can be argued about is argued about. Obviously, work-related issues are a favored topic of colorful debate. 'He did what with the Hurst tool?" "So what if he has ten years in emergency service, he doesn't know shit!" "Hey, what'd ya do with the DM-50, you fucked up the blade?" "No way I'm flying to Six-Truck again!" "Next time I see a fireman do that, I am hauling his ass to jail!" "He is fucking clueless!" "He thinks he's the senior man in the squad, but he has done zippo in emergency." "He can lick balls!"

"We are the knights of negativity" a cop once said. "We need to bring one another down a peg so we won't take ourselves so seriously."

When the cops run out of work-related topics to argue about, there is always food, women, politics, clothing, cars, what channel to watch in quarters, what to do with

Mojo after he vomits Christmas dinner on the floor, and where to go for a meal. Agreeing to disagree is one of the main things E-cops can all agree to.

Yet perhaps the most important element in the veil of armor that surrounds the sensitivities and soul of each emergency cop is the powerful entity of humor. The cops will—and most certainly do—respond to anything and everything that can evoke a hearty laugh. The most common source of laughter is when cops, bullshitting as always, reminisce about humorous jobs they've endured and survived. "Remember when we had that evidence search on that cold day and the stiff was stuck to the fire escape?" "Remember that five-hundred-pound woman stuck in the bathtub?" "Who smelled worse, the ten dead dogs on Bradhurst or that cab driver we pulled over for running a red light?" "Remember that jumper who took the leap off the building in Midtown and got impaled through his midsection on a flagpole? Remember the cop asking us if we were using new rope, and we said, 'No, that's his intestines'! Remember when the cop threw up?" Even visitors are not immune from the humor. When the commander of the Argentine national counterterrorist team visited Two-Truck during a fact-finding tour of the NYPD, the lieutenant escorting the honored guest to ESU had a tough time finding a cop who spoke Spanish to act as translator. "Hey, Officer Anonymous," he asked. "You speak fluent Spanish, right?" The cop replied, "Sure, boss," as he proceeded to ask the commander for his license and registration in Spanish. On a different visit, when the former commander of the Israeli national police counterterrorist unit visited Two-Truck, that same officer, when showing the various tools in the truck to the impressed visitor and displaying the various saws and blades carried in the REPs and the truck, also said, "In a pinch, we can act as rabbis and perform circumcisions, too!"

Like any precinct divided into shifts and squads, each ESU squad develops an identity and personality all its own that defines not only its ability to work but also how it is known throughout the division. Should some psychologist ever want to examine a closed society made up of thirty individuals with sixty different personalities, then Two-Truck is a good psych-lab. It is a mesh of egos and experience, anger and exhaustion, bravado and burnout. Once, in a discussion about cop shows on TV in the kitchen at Three-Truck in the South Bronx, a former ESU lieutenant commented that of all the shows on television, he thought *Barney Miller* was the most accurate in depicting the life and society that is a police squad. "In that squad," the lieutenant said, "you had a boss, someone who considered himself a philosopher, someone who was slow-witted, someone who was a comedian, someone who stuck to the rules and regulations of the police manual, and someone who put on the impression that he was nuts so that the others would leave him alone."

Each of the three ESU squads has in its ranks the cast and crew from the *Barney Miller* show. Each squad has ten officers (two serving midnights), and each squad has its own collective personality. One squad considers itself the most experienced, the other the most energetic, the other the busiest. While the squads assume an element of the personalities of their sergeants, each tandem is defined by the personalities and quirks of its officers. There is a fair amount of jealousy among the three different squads, but it is usually displayed in practical jokes and snide comments, nothing more. In Two-Truck, the First Squad is the oldest, the Second Squad is considered the busiest, and the Third Squad is usually singled out for unique treatment. Known as the Third Herd and the Three Rs (Ricans, Runts, and Retards), the Third Squad usually ends up in the newspaper for one rescue or another and as a result is the scorn of other squads and trucks. "Jealousy rears its ugly head!" a cop in the Third Squad yells with glee as a cop from another truck says, "You guys made the news again, I see."

Each ESU squad encompasses the gamut of personalities and ethnicity that makes up the NYPD—fourth-generation New York Irish, African-America, Puerto Rican, Polish, German, Italian, Jewish, and so on. Each squad also has its resident moody person or grouch, its resident cynicists, resident philosopher and monitor of current events, its resident gourmet cook and cultural man about town, and, of course, its resident comic. It is a potpourri of every social, religious, and ethnic persuasion unified by the uniform, the job, and the determination of every cop to work and do what he or she gets paid to do.

Each cop also works—and lives—in his or her own little orbit. There are cops who, from the moment they get to work to the moment they return the REP to its parking spot eight hours later, are always out on patrol. Police work to them, forget about being in emergency, is all about patrol. Other cops are mechanics and tinkerers. They will play with the truck and the REP, maintain its engines, replace its fluids, polish the mirrors, check the tools, oil the Hurst tools, and check the tires. Other cops in the truck, weapon cleaning kits in hand, will clean their guns and the squad's MP-5s and Mini-14s and examine catalogs from Heckler and Koch, Ruger, Smith and Wesson, and Glock; these cops are, first and foremost, SWAT officers. Some cops spend any free time in the weight room in the squad's locker room, and others, when assigned to be in the big truck, never move from the chair planted firmly in front of the television set.

To all outside appearance, the men and women in Two-Truck, and ESU in general, are a cantankerous bunch. They are ornery, outspoken, overwhelmed at times, and always opinionated. It isn't that they are a miserable bunch, but beyond the hype of TV and Hollywood, being a cop, especially in New York City, is a really difficult job with pressures that most average citizens can never truly comprehend or even imagine. Besides the dangers that the E-cops face on the streets (getting shot, stabbed, run over, electrocuted; drowning; falling from rooftops; getting bitten by pit bulls, snakes, and rabid bats; inhaling toxic substances, and so on), besides the relatively low pay they receive, and besides the fact that the cop can be legally liable for just about every aspect of the job (cops are among the most sued segments of American society), there is an armor-plated bureaucracy within a department as large and compartmentalized as the NYPD that is simply maddening. Besides having to worry about not getting killed on the streets, not working oneself to death in the second job, and not getting sued, one small fuckup on the job brings the wrath of the NYPD and ESU crashing down like a hammer on a virgin anvil. There are truck disciplines, unit disciplines, division disciplines, departmental trials, internal affairs, loss of pensions, and loss of sometimes much more. Being a cop, whether in an ESU truck or in a precinct is like being a piece of twine pulled against its center at both edges—if the material isn't strong, something is bound to snap. The pressures of the job are enormous. "In my fifteen years on the job, I have never had a partner or a friend die in the line of duty," claims a veteran officer of Two-Truck whose philosophical views of service are respected throughout the division. "Yet six cops I know have committed suicide."

On the street, when they stand outside the apartment of a barricaded perp holding hostages or when they gain entry to an apartment where an elderly female has literally "fallen and can't get up," the cops must act professionally, with courtesy and consideration. But back inside their REPs or inside quarters, the veil comes off, and cops vent—it is how the pressure cooker lets off its steam. They curse (very colorfully), they reflect on their surroundings (with biting candor), and they critique their squad mates and their bosses (with cutting cruelty). Basically, they act like average human beings performing a precarious and dangerous balancing act of pressure, emotions, anxiety, and duty.

Driving down 125th Street, from quarters toward patrolling the confines of Harlem's various precincts, the Adam car comes across a group of kids on the corner of Amsterdam Avenue, beating one another over the head with baseball bats. The REP flashes its lights and sounds its sirens, though the kids continue to beat one another with little regard for the arrival of the police. "This is fucking unbelievable," the recorder tells the driver, and he grabs his nightstick, ready to race out of the REP and make some arrests. "What are we, fucking invisible creatures on another plane of consciousness?"

"It's OK to vent," the driver comments, laughing as he sees responding sector cars arriving from the 2-6 and his partner turning a dark shade of angry red. "Purge your blood vessels, my son, and let the pressure vent."

Three blocks down, still on 125th Street, the recorder sees a man walking a pit bull that is barking up a storm. "Hey!" the cop yells out the window. "Tell that dog to chill out!"

Mostly, when cops vent it is in quarters, and it usually involves an aspect of the job they have all found impossible to deal with—from various bosses to the antics of the Fire Department. One one warm Saturday afternoon, a squad was talking about a certain FDNY supervisor who, over the course of a thirty-year career, has had many unpleasant encounters with virtually every ESU cop working Manhattan. Sgt. Juan Garcia, already in his civvies following an eight-hour tour, rings his negativity bell. "OK, guys," he says as he pounds a cooking pot with a ladle. "You have ten minutes to vent."

Sergeants, in fact, are the great equalizers of a squad. Bringing the insanity, the chaos, the separate personalities, and the bureaucratic necessities of the society that is an ESU truck into line is the job of the supervisors. Each squad has a sergeant who is both boss and shoulder to lean on. The sergeant, for the most part, is the sum of all equations in a truck. He is the final word and the man whose opinions truly count. The sergeants are fixtures and figures of authorities. Yet discipline, for all the chaos and the colorful expression, is based not on intimidation or threats but rather on the realization that in the hierarchy that exists in the department, the sergeant is always right. On the whole, the sergeants make a determined effort to befriend their cops and treat them with dignity, respect, and a fair degree of reserved affection. Virtually every sergeant in emergency was a cop in emergency. They all know the routines and the craziness, what a sergeant expects of his cops when the big job comes down, and what cops, in turn, demand of their boss. "After all," claims one sergeant, "all of us with three stripes started out as lowly rookies. We know what it's like to be cops, and we know it isn't easy."

When an ESU officer scores well on the sergeant's exam and is high enough on the list to make promotion, he is always transferred out of the unit. In the NYPD, a promotion generally means an immediate change of command. Yet even when that former E-man now sergeant is lucky enough, or connected enough, to get back into ESU, he is no longer a white shield (a regular cop). He is a sergeant, a boss, and can no longer be as intimate with the rest of the cops as he was when he was just another worker in the truck. Upon their return to ESU, sergeants are always placed in a truck other than the one in which they served. Of Two-Truck's three sergeants, Kenny Bowen of the First Squad served as a cop in One-Truck, the Second Squad's Jimmy Spratt was a cop in Two-Truck, while Juan Garcia of the Third Squad was a cop in the Bronx's Three-Truck.

Sergeants are loyal to the department, the Special Operations Division, and ESU, but they are ultra-loyal to their truck and their squads. "Don't be ragging on my children," Sgt. Kenny Bowen once told a member of another squad during the discussion of someone's impending retirement. "These boys are my children, and I look after them." Still, the sergeants demand perfection from the cops in their squads. When all goes well and the cops do their jobs with speed, with skill, and with guts, the sergeants will have nothing but praise and accolades for their E-men. If they screw up, do something that endangers the lives of their fellow cops, or bring with them an attitude of "Hey, I don't give a fuck," then the sergeants will be up their behinds like a train through a tunnel. For the most part, the Two-Truck sergeants know their cops, know their capabilities, and know their temperaments. They know who are the stars in the squad, who are the good cops, who are just average, and who on a big job will be told to watch the vehicle outside or be responsible for carrying nothing mightier than some entry tools.

The emergency sergeants look at their E-cops through polarized lenses. The sergeant rarely cares if a cop is tall or short, fat or skinny, Scotch Irish or Jewish. To the sergeant, a cop is defined by his abilities, his attitude, and his enthusiasm. Yet, while sergeants are outnumbered by the cops in their squads by nine to one, in reality it is the sergeant who sets the tone for how a squad will behave and live together.

The cops generally don't care if their sergeants work them ragged and bust their balls. It's part of their charm. "I'd rather have a boss who made sure I was busy than one who didn't give a damn what I did."

Each ESU truck is also assigned an administrative lieutenant who is *supposed* to look out for the bureaucratic aspects of the day-to-day business, as well as truck morale and discipline. The northern trucks (One and Two in Manhattan and Three and Four in the Bronx) have one administrative captain who is *supposed* to tend to matters that the lieutenant is unable to deal with. Yet the true day-to-day running of the truck falls to the squad sergeant—from training to the truck's transmission, from the appearance of his cops to their discipline. What bits of discipline the sergeants don't handle, the cops within the squad tend to, dealing with those who don't fit in through conventional and unconventional means. Sometimes trouble is simply a bad mix of personalities—someone's yin doesn't blend with another one's yang. Usually, those who are problems in a squad are the sensitive ones who cannot take a joke or cannot be critiqued. And once a cop shows the others that something in particular "gets his Irish up," he is marked and targeted with ruthless abandon.

When a squad in Two-Truck works, it is under the

supervision of a city north supervisor, a citywide supervisor, and Ralph Pascullo and Connolly, the two ESU patrol captains. When a boss comes to visit a truck and its squad, it is usually to check up on things and to find out how the cops and their equipment are doing. For many of the bosses, unless they see the cops on the "big job," when there is no time to talk anyway, a visit to the truck is perhaps the only chance to get to talk one-on-one with a squad and its sergeant and find out how morale is doing and whether there are any complaints, problems, or suggestions. Rank, while ultra-important in a precinct or in a squad, has little impact on how cops will talk to their bosses. While a sergeant will always be called "Sarge," a lieutenant always referred to as "Loo," and a captain simply called "Cap," E-cops are not afraid to get a load off their chests when talking to their bosses. There is nothing a boss likes more than to come to a truck, grab a cup of drinkable coffee, catch up on gossip, and listen to complaints from cops who feel they are being underutilized. Cops who bitch and moan because they want more work from the city, more tools, and more opportunities to employ their skills in backing up their fellow officers on jobs, the true workers in the unit, are looked upon by the bosses with great affection. Yet sometimes visiting bosses get an earful of angry complaining concerning harsh working conditions and poor morale.

On one New York night below the freezing mark, an ESU supervisor visited a certain truck to pay a courtesy call and find out what was new. Inside the heated quarters, with the sports channel on cable and a London broil on the grill, the boss had little time to remove his hat and thaw out before a cop, chopping up some onion, began to complain about the unit. "You know, boss, this place sucks, this unit sucks, this jobs sucks . . ." The supervisor, flabbergasted almost beyond the ability to speak, responded, "What the fuck is wrong with you? Here it is, two degrees outside with a minus-thirty wind chill, and you are here toasty and warm cooking some beef and chopping your onions. Imagine if you were out walking a foot post somewhere by the South Street Seaport or by Throg's Neck where the winds off the water would slice through your uniform like that knife of yours through that Bermuda onion. This is *not* such a bad place to work!"

The relationship between boss and E-cop needs to be strong and functional. "On a big job, we need to know that we can rely on one another and work with one another," claims one ESU supervisor. "After all, on a big job, the unit is a line of last resort."

And, in essence, the bosses need the cops' support and advice. A boss might be a new transfer into the unit with little or no experience in emergency, thinking of jobs in terms of how things were done in transit or in a detective squad. All of a sudden, that same boss might now find himself on a real hairy job where people have been shot, and he needs to be able to swallow his pride and the trappings of rank and take the advice of an E-cop who might be nothing more than a white shield but who has more than ten years in emergency to his credit. On one warrant, when a new lieutenant from a detective squad had foolishly walked past a door that had yet to be opened, searched, and secured, one of his cops said with great candor, "You have just learned the first lesson of being an E-man, Loo. You fucked up and lived to try again the next day!"

When asked to describe the place in which he works, one former housing cop, speaking of his home for the last three years in the Emergency Service Unit, said that his work environment can be summed up in the acronym MMM, for "misfits, morons, and malcontents": "Here we are in the greatest department on the planet, working in the greatest unit there is, doing the most incredible type of jobs, from safeguarding a president to pulling a family out of a mangled car, and all you hear when you come in here is complaining, bitching, and moaning. You'd think that people would be happy to be here and you would be content in the fact that they are the cream of the crop, but no . . . this is New York City." That rather gut-wrenching and honest reflection of what he thinks is wrong with the unit is not without merit but certainly has an explanation. As the officers from one squad suit up and ready themselves for an eight-hour tour of the northern tier of the island of Manhattan, the cops in the squad they are replacing are slowly returning, covered in dirt and mess after chasing a perp through the garbage-infested alleyways of St. Nicholas Terrace following reports of shots fired. Many of the officers smell of urine and excrement. Several have sliced open their uniforms, and some are bleeding lightly.

"You know," the same cop said later, "who can blame us for being the MMMs? After all, are we normal? Fuck no. We chase people with guns for a living. We stand on rooftops with psychos, and we crawl under subway trains to remove the headless corpse of a commuter who won't be coming home for dinner. Are we normal? A big fuck no! What normal person would do that? Case closed!"

It's an unseasonably warm winter's day in New York City, and the two squads changing shifts at Two-Truck are both in rotten moods. The squad that just completed a day tour has had a rough one, including a nasty pin and an elongated perp search where the sensitivities and egos of several cops have rubbed the wrong way, causing friction. Some days are good, and some are bad. This one was bad. As the required "four letter word greetings" are exchanged, a cop from the next shift and a boss are having a heart-to-heart in the TV room.

"Look at that," comments one of the cops. "A battle of wits between two unarmed opponents."

"Now, now," a cop in the other squad says. "Have a rough day, did we?"

Before too long, six angry faces depart 126th Street for their pilgrimages to Long Island and upstate happy that the shift is over.

The mood in quarters, with discussion of power tools

and motorcycles, starts off OK but then sours as talk of monetary matters and the cops' lack of a raise for the better part of the decade is bantered about.

"I truly hate this place," one cop says, reflecting that in Nassau and Suffolk counties, rookies on the job only two years make more money than he does.

Before the mood can become truly angry, a call comes over the SOD radio concerning a barricaded EDP in the 2-8. The six cops, in the first minutes of the tour, slam down their coffee mugs and race out the door. They return back to quarters an hour later. The pepper spray launched into the apartment still causes their eyes to tear and simmers in their throats and scorched vocal cords. Their uniforms are filthy from wrestling with the EDP, and the combination of heat, sweat, and hunger is causing most of them to feel weak.

"What were we talking about before the job came over?" one cop asks.

"About how much I hate this fucking job!"

"Well, if you weren't in emergency, what would you want to do?"

"Retire!"

Case closed, indeed!

10

Midnights in Manhattan North: From Monotony to Mayhem, Murder to Martians

•

"How much have you had to drink?" the ESU cop asked the motorist after extricating him from his overturned Chevy on the West Side Highway at 96th Street.

"Drink?" the motorist asked. "I hasn't had enough, but the bar's gotta close at 4:00 A.M. *sharp, so they threw my ass out."*

"Hey, Ronnie," the cop yelled to his partner, who was cordoning off the roadway with flares. "Keep the flares away from his breath, otherwise we'll all blow up!"

Midnight in Harlem. How romantic. As much of the city heads to sleep and much of Manhattan begins to wind down slowly, Upper Manhattan awakens with a burst of life, death, and criminal mischief. If traffic on Broadway, around the hustle and bustle of Times Square and the massive intersection at 42nd Street, lessens to a point where gridlock is no longer the rule of the hour when the clock strikes twelve, Broadway at 142nd Street is so crowded at midnight that it is virtually impossible to walk the sidewalks, and the thoroughfare is bumper-to-bumper with limos, Jeeps, and cars adorned with Dominican flags and gold license plate covers. As the famous

Upper East Side eateries put their last pans of Singapore noodles and corned beef and cabbage on the stove, restaurants in the heart of Dominica East in Washington Heights and Jamaican curry houses in Harlem are just opening. Unlicensed livery cabs and licensed limousines compete for fares with aggressiveness and lawlessness, and drug dealers along the darkened streets between Broadway and Amsterdam approach cars driven by suburban brats from Jersey, eager to cop a bag of crack and then head back to the Garden State over the George Washington Bridge before Mommy and Daddy ever discover that their BMW has been taken from the driveway.

"These people are vampires," claims a 3-0 Precinct sergeant who has worked Manhattan's less glamorous stretches for more than ten years. "They are up all night and sleep until the late afternoon. They operate under their own laws, and they live by their own individual time zones."

Midnight in Manhattan North. One of the most beguiling times in one of the most mysterious bites of the Big Apple. For a cop, it can be both boring beyond being able to stay awake and so terrifying in hails of 9mm and .40-caliber fire that it seems as if the world is coming to an explosive end. No two midnights are ever the same—no two jobs are ever alike. It is the shift when the only rule is that there are no rules of engagement. It is a time of emptiness and madness, a time when a cop must be alert and must perform above and beyond. It is, without doubt, one of the most difficult times to be a police officer, let alone one of New York's finest serving in the Emergency Service Unit in a part of the city where time is measured in crimes committed.

Even though some of the biggest jobs in the city happen between midnight and 8:00 A.M., from shootings to pin jobs, gun runs to EDPs, there isn't an abundance of manpower serving the midnight crew in ESU's ten trucks. In some areas, it's usually just the Adam car and the truck. It's rare for a midnight shift to have a Boy car, and almost unheard of (unless at times of high terrorist awareness) for there to be a Charley car—especially in Harlem. If any truck would get the third patrol car, it is usually in Lower Manhattan or southern Queens. Sometimes, in fact, there is just enough personnel working in an individual squad to man the big truck. As a result of less personnel working, the midnight crews tend to enjoy the reputation of being akin to sheriffs in the Old West, patrolling wide stretches of terrain with little backup. For the most part, the midnight crews enjoy a unique esprit de corps. More than any other shift, the midnight E-men enjoy working as a team. Sometimes teamwork is of paramount importance—they are busier than busy can ever be.

In Two-Truck, the midnight crew resembles the better aspects of the merger that combined the Housing Police, Transit Police, and NYPD into one happy family. Among the better teams working in the division is the tandem of Police Officer Vinny Martinez, a highly decorated alumni of the Housing Police and the Emergency Rescue Unit, and his partner, Police Officer Ronnie Bauman, a former tunnel rat with the TA's emergency squad who is known in the division as a cop's cop. The two work well together, and, like all good cop pairings, they can read each other's mind when the shit hits the fan and lights and sirens are on, relying on each other instinctively rather than based on verbal commands. If one is driving and reports of confirmed shots fired come over the air, there will rarely be any words exchanged. Adrenaline will take over speech, eyes scanning a 180-degree field of view, replacing any hand signals. Holsters will be unfastened, the Ithaca 37 removed from its storage lock, and the REP driven head-on into an ongoing job, with the cops knowing by gut feeling where the other one is positioned, ready for any contingency. Both Martinez and Bauman have been through shoot-outs, and they have survived. Bauman, in fact, during his time as a transit cop, was actually shot in the gut in a wild firefight. Both officers take tactical work seriously, and both are the first out the door responding to pin jobs. They are both "damn good workers."

Police Officers Tony Barlow and Anita Rosato are also partners from some of the less attractive parts of New York City policing. Barlow is a former Housing cop who spent many a night walking up urine-reeking stairwells, and Rosato is a former tunnel rat who worked the lovely-smelling confines of New York subway stations and trains. They, too, have seen and done it all while on the job and are steady partners who work together as a single-minded unit.

Both teams operate on their own frequencies and work very well together. "My partner's loud, and I'm annoying," Martinez comments. "Who the hell else would want to work with any one of us?" They love to work, love to be out on patrol, and love to try to laugh at the sometimes heartbreaking and desperate surroundings they work in. On one detail, against the Latin Kings, a notorious Hispanic drug gang, in the 4-6 Precinct in the wake of the shooting of a police captain and a massive NYPD show of force in the area, both Martinez and Bauman went to Burger King, ordered a Kid's Meal, and received the desired cardboard Burger King crown as a reward. "Latin Kings," the partners joked inside their REP, "meet the Burger Kings."

As much as many cops like to appear aloof and detached from the trappings of emotion, when the foursome work together, the mood in quarters is actually one of togetherness. Videotapes are brought in for mealtime and that "SOD-radio-permitting" break from patrol, and work on the truck, on the equipment, and on anything quarters-related is attended to fairly and quickly. Martinez is usually bouncing around (as one cop says, "He doesn't need coffee to be bouncing off the walls; if we gave him some, we'd have to put a leash on him") and out the door in a second when the big jobs come over the air.

The midnight crew throughout the division is there by choice, but not because they are vampires and must be in bed the moment the first rays of sunlight appear over the Translyvania hills. Cops work the midnight tour because some have family commitments that require their presence at home during the day, others are going to college, and some need a second job because, although City Hall might disagree, cops in New York City are obscenely underpaid and many NYPD families can survive only if the breadwinner brings home a second paycheck. The cops, though, have gotten used to the odd hours. Quarters is like a home away from home. Yet a biological clock is not something to be tampered with, and the cops enjoy the busy nights the most because, as one of the crew stated, "When you are running around like crazy chasing perps and pulling people out of their cars, it's hard to remember just how fucking tired you actually are!"

Patrolling on midnight tours is a unique experience. From 59th Street, river to river, all the way to Washington Heights and the Inwood frontier with the Bronx, Manhattan enjoys a varied and incredibly diverse night life. In the 19th Precinct, for example, the silk-stocking Upper East Side, the upper crust of society is busy munching on lobsters and downing micro-brews. According to one officer—Officer Anonymous, of course—"it's a good place to go on 'special patrol,' especially when all the kids are home from college studying for exams." The 2-0 and 2-4 precincts on the Upper West Side are just as trendy though not as high-nose. Nevertheless, it is a place where restaurants seem never to close, bars and pubs are always full, and everything from aerobics classes to record shops is open twenty-four hours a day. From midnight to 3:30 A.M., if you want anything from bras to bagels, pizzas to Pavarotti, the Upper West Side is the place.

On 96th Street, the invisible border between trendy and the Tech-9, the city is still vibrant and awake at the midnight hour, though patrolling the stretch of the upper northern reaches of the island is a bit more treacherous. On the West Side, in the 2-6 and 3-3 precincts, and in

Spanish Harlem's 2-3 Precinct and Harlem's 2-5, 2-8, 3-0, and 3-2, anything and everything happens, and even the smallest of jobs can erupt into chaos. During the late-night hours, the projects, dozens of which dot the precincts north of 96th Street, are usually very problematic, with drug deals gone sour, EDPs, jumpers, shootings, and robberies. Alcohol and crack make poor side dishes with guns and knives. There is always a sense that danger exists—a sense of lawlessness that naturally follows the clock once it strikes midnight.

Patrolling at midnight is very different from working an eight-to-four or a four-to-twelve. The midnight hours are a perp's best friend. It is when the cover of darkness and solitude make many city streets ripe for crime. It is also the hour when many businesses, following a successful night, are full of cash and void of customers and employees. It is when EDPs, unable to sleep or make love, discover that it is time for a standoff with family and the cops. It is the time when precinct holding cells swell with drunks, drug addicts, and perps, and when the select few behind bars, en route to central booking, decide that the time is ripe to go psycho. After 4:00 A.M., when all bars in the city close, the midnight tour is also the place to be busy, very busy, with pin jobs. Eight beers and a few shots of tequila are the ingredients for a man behind the wheel to end up in a twisted ball of metal and bleeding organs.

Midnights are when, because traffic is usually less, it is actually possible to travel with lights and sirens from the northern tip of Inwood to the Plaza Hotel at 59th Street and make the trek in less than five minutes.

ESU cops throughout the city who work the midnight tour and who work into the latter portions of the four-to-twelve are always a bit more aware in the inner reaches of their sixth sense concerning radio calls for a signal ten-thirteen when it is late and dark. After all, midnights are also when perps get stupid and decide that they can actually shoot-it-out with a police officer and win. Late nights in the city are when police work becomes more dangerous.

Late nights are when the proverbial shit hits the fan!

Had he been in ESU, Police Officer Kevin Gillespie would have been the kind of cop who would have been tagged a "worker." A former Marine, Gulf War veteran, and highly decorated veteran of the Housing Police, Gillespie was a police officer who, although it sounds like a cliché, made a difference. Like many former Housing cops, decorated veterans of America's toughest beat, he volunteered into one of the NYPD's elite squads once the two departments formally merged in 1995 and ended up in one of the most unique police units in the country—the NYPD's Street Crimes Unit. A force under the command of the Special Operations Division, the Street Crimes Unit is a plainclothes strike force that targets high-crime areas with some of the most courageous cops in the department. They wear scruffy clothes, are often as big as a house, and drive around in beat-up unmarked cars that look barely capable of surviving the most meager potholes. In the twenty-five years since the unit was created, becoming one of the first plainclothes patrol units in American law enforcement, cops in SCU have disguised themselves as couples making out on park benches in order to snare rapists and muggers, have worn tight jeans and earrings to pose as homosexuals in Greenwich Village and put an end to a series of gay-bashing attacks, and have masqueraded as winos and junkies (in both physical appearance and the accompanying and unmistakable stench) in antidrug operations. In one of their most celebrated cases, SCU officers arrested a midwestern drug dealer in uptown Manhattan whose car held more than four million dollars' worth of cocaine and heroin. Their main talent, however, is taking guns off the street. The 150 officers of SCU, from 1993 to 1996, have removed more than 2,000 guns from the streets of the city.

Based in Randall's Island, a small dot along the East River underneath the criss-crossing expressways and parkways leading to the Triborough Bridge connecting Queens, Manhattan, and the Bronx, the unit's CO, Deputy Inspector Richard Savage, refers to their base as the "Bat Cave." In reality, that reference isn't such a stretch. Once SCU enters a neighborhood, both perps and the honest citizens attempting to survive in some of the city's worst shitholes realize who owns the neighborhood. In fact, the unit motto is "We own the night."

On March 14, 1996, SCU would have competition for ownership of the city after hours. Four career perps with rap sheets a mile long, with charges and convictions ranging from attempted murder to robbery, what are known as "mutts" in the NYPD vernacular, decided that the unseasonably warm March night was the perfect time to go carjack vehicles and rob bodegas. They were known in the 'hood as the "Park Avenue Boys," and their robberies, shootings, and disregard for human life had left innocent people dead, shot, and robbed of their life savings. In a neighborhood of drug-crazed felons and human cruelty, the Park Avenue Boys enjoyed the reputation of being very dangerous. Their stomping grounds were the drug-ravaged streets of the 4-6 Precinct in the Bronx, in the notorious University Heights section. Fatefully, it was the same area where SCU would be operating.

AT 9:30 P.M., the four carjacked a black BMW sedan at the corner of 178th Street and Arthur Avenue—they all had guns, and they displayed a desire to be pushed into pulling the trigger. High on their conquest, the four robbed a man at gunpoint several blocks later, at 184th Street and the Grand Concourse. Over the SOD frequency, calls were flooding the airwaves concerning the four carjackers and the stolen BMW. As the stolen car proceeded south in search of the next prey, SCU vehicles spotted the vehicle and commenced a loose pursuit—one unmarked Chevy Caprice tagged behind while another raced up ahead, bottlenecking the stolen BMW and cutting off its escape. On a good night, the perps would realize they were in deep shit; they'd throw their guns out the window and hope that their legal aid attorney would get them a good prison job in Sing-Sing or Attica. On a bad night, bullets fly. This would be a very bad night.

When four of New York's frequently incarcerated are surrounded by the cops, a strategy of choice is to split up and book in four different directions. Ricardo Morales, a twenty-three-year-old hood, raced out of the front passenger seat and flew down 183rd Street, where he temporarily evaded police. Jesus Mendez, the driver, bolted across the Grand Concourse in a running gun battle with pursuing SCU and precinct officers; in the melee, before he was apprehended, two bystanders were hit by gunfire and seriously wounded. Angel Diaz, an eleven-time loser, jumped out of the rear passenger seat and confronted Officer Gillespie in a moment of perpetrator machismo. Clutching a 9mm semiautomatic, Diaz shot Gillespie point-blank in the chest and then bled north along the Grand Concourse. As cops rushed to his rescue, the young cop and father of two lay mortally wounded on the cool and heartless asphalt of a Bronx pavement. Two officers from the Transit Bureau, Sgt. Cornelius Douglas and Terence McAllister, riding to work for a midnight, heard the gunshots and swung their vehicle around in a Hollywood U-turn of twisting speed and burning rubber. They exchanged gunfire with Diaz. McAllister was hit in the neck by bullet fragments. Diaz was grazed in the side. Diaz, with a smirk on his face, was taken into custody. In all, more than forty shots were fired in the span of a couple of gut-wrenching minutes.

ESU officers from second squads of Three-Truck, Four-Truck and Two-Truck flooded the area with tactical response and backup. Suited up for action and clutching MP-5s and Mini-14s, Officers Ann-Margaret Lyons, Seth Gahr, Pete Tetukevich, and Henry Medina were patrolling northern Manhattan when the ten-thirteen and reports of officer down came over the air. They were in the Bronx less that five minutes later. Cops will fly through walls to aid a brother or sister in blue, but here all the responding ESU units could do was search for additional perps and assist detectives in gathering evidence. It was a silent and somber crime scene. A cop's worst nightmare.

Kevin Gillespie was rushed to St. Barnabas Hospital, where he died a short while later. The 9mm round that Angel Diaz had fired had penetrated just above the protective area of the bulletproof vest Gillespie wore under his street clothes. The bullet took a downward trajectory and caused massive and irreparable damage to his internal organs. The NYPD had lost one of its finest.

There is a saying in the NYPD that every cop is Irish on the day of his funeral, and the fact that St. Patrick's Day was just around the corner only compounded the sense of loss and outrage among the city's 38,000 cops. In fact, the following day, during the usually merry St. Patrick's Day Parade up fifth Avenue, there were more tears than shamrocks. On one of the department's most joyous days, the NYPD was nursing a bruised and battered heart.

Officer Gillespie was known as a cop's cop—in fact, when actor Harrison Ford wanted to learn what it was like to be a cop for a role in the film *The Devil's Own*, the rugged former Marine was assigned to be his tutor. He was also a family man passionately devoted to his wife and two children. For his cops or his family, there wasn't a thing that Kevin Gillespie wouldn't do. For the city in which he served, he paid the ultimate sacrifice so that others could live.

The four members of the Park Avenue Boys were charged with first-degree murder. Their arrests sparked political debate over the use of New York's recent death penalty statute and the Bronx DA's unwillingness to make the Gillespie killing into a capital case. If there was a bit of solace to the tragedy, it was that the shooter, Angel Diaz, decided to hang himself in his Riker's Island cell rather than stand trial. "How can you compare the life of an animal with the life of a hard-working family man?" a cop uttered to his sergeant in a Manhattan precinct as the headlines about Diaz's suicide made the front page of the news. "This is not an eye for an eye. We were all short-changed."

Gillespie's murder was a reaffirmation of the dangers of the job and the enhanced dangers of working the late hours in a city that, according to the hype, never sleeps. Many of the cops assigned to the midnight tour at Two-Truck had been kept in Manhattan following the shooting; this one belonged to the four-to-twelve, and in the wake of the coldblooded killing of a cop, an NYPD show of force would be desired on the city's mean streets. Yet the midnight crew had gone to Officer Gillespie's funeral—a display of grief attended by nearly 10,000 cops from places as familiar as the Bronx and Brooklyn and as diverse as Yonkers and Yuma; Irish cops from the Garda ventured across the Atlantic to pay their respects to a fallen hero. The cops standing at attention in the Class As, especially those who worked the mean streets of the city, felt anger and helplessness, the need to reach out and the need to exact justice. Going through the motions of laying a cop to rest always leaves a layer of scar tissue in the hearts of fellow officers. It also leaves them with a sense of foreboding and inner apprehension. It makes them think about the ballistic coverage of the vests they wear and the helmets they place over the baseball caps, and it makes them wish that they had spent just another few minutes at the range, honing their skills with their Glock 9mms.

All cops hope that they never experience a night like the one that claimed Kevin Gillespie's life, but life on the streets isn't kind. Five months later, it would be déjà vu all over again.

August 15, 1996, was one of those nights for the midnight crew that was backbreaking, exhausting, and mind-numbing. There was a little bit of everything that night—from EDPs to pin jobs, a few gun runs, stuck occupied elevator rescues, and even an "unconfirmed jumper." At around 4:00 A.M., their blood vessels in need of caffeine and sugar, Officers Martinez and Bauman in Adam-Two returned to quarters, where they hooked up with Barlow and Rosato, who had also just come back from a job. "I hope the radio stays quiet," Martinez told Rosato as he unfastened the Velcro straps of his vest from the sweat-soaked shirt he was wearing. "I need a break." A fresh pot of coffee was put on, some stale M&Ms purchased from the vending machine over the mailboxes, and the remote control clutched so that channels one through seventy-seven could be closely scrutinized.

The 3-3 Precinct was relatively busy that night—more jobs came over in the precinct that night than most major U.S. cities get in a day. For Sgt. Thomas Scollan and Police Officer Francis Lattimer, it was business as usual—another night in one of the most dangerous precincts of New York City. If there isn't a shooting in the congested precinct that covers parts of Harlem and Washington Heights, then it's a robbery or a rape. There is always narcotics dealing. It is always a dangerous beat for the police officers tasked with bringing a semblance of law and order into a section of the city that resembles the Wild West more than it does the western part of Manhattan.

On patrol, the cops follow a lead set forth by former Police Commissioner William Bratton, that going after quality-of-life crimes and petty offenses usually snares career criminals. It was a novel notion. The man urinating in public or jumping the subway turnstile was probably someone who had done far worse things in his life, and he was probably someone with warrants out for more serious crimes committed. Whereas the police once ignored these offenses, precinct holding cells throughout the city were soon swelling with individuals arrested for offenses as minor as public drunkenness and later arrested for murders that had been committed years before. All minor offenses were targeted—from panhandling to running a red light.

At around 5:00 A.M. on Thursday, August 15, 1996, Officer Lattimer and Sergeant Scollan were riding on patrol on Amsterdam Avenue, a street that had never gone to sleep, when they came up behind a white Lincoln Town Car with livery plates traveling north. Livery cabs were the machines that moved people in the ghetto, especially since Yellow Cabs rarely ventured uptown to pick up fares, though the cars were often prey to vicious packs of robbers who showed little hesitation in robbing and murdering a driver, usually an immigrant trying to eke out a meager existence. Being a livery driver in New York City is one of the most dangerous professions in the world. When the Town Car went through a red light at the corner of Amsterdam and 156th Street, the cops had a sixth sense that something was up. They were right. Only minutes before, the current driver had hailed the cab at the corner of 152nd Street and St. Nicholas Place and, a block later, had ordered the real driver, Gilberto Bello, out of the vehicle at gunpoint. The car had yet to be reported stolen when it was spotted. Lights flashing and yelping siren on full blast, the RMP gave chase. A police car in full pursuit on Amsterdam Avenue was a part of the landscape. Few people on the streets paid it any notice.

Attempting to escape the police call to stop and pull over, the driver of the Town Car swung a hard left on 157th Street, heading toward Broadway, but he wasn't interested in getting away. He wanted a showdown. Ditching the car on 157th Street, the driver emerged with a .40-caliber Glock semiautomatic pistol in his hand and moved into a position where he'd be able to catch the cops by surprise. Backtracking behind his car parked on the southeast corner of 157th Street, he waited for the 3-3 RMP to approach. Without warning, the suspect crouched in firing position and released five rounds at the two officers. One bullet found its mark under Officer Lattimer's left eye. The .40 bullet traveled through the nasal cavity and right temporal lobe and exited just in front of the right ear. Lattimer, who had been driving, collapsed when the bullet struck his brain, and his right foot recoiled in reflex, causing him to push down on the accelerator and crash the patrol car into a row of parked cars. By the time Sergeant Scollan could respond, he found himself pinned by the driver's side airbag and unable to reach for his gun, but he did manage to put out a frantic ten-thirteen over division radio.

Back at quarters, where the SOD radio was cranked up at full volume, Scollan's ten-thirteen was relayed to the ESU at 5:15 A.M. Cops never run faster than when there is a confirmed ten-thirteen and cop shot, and before the dispatcher's message was read, both the truck and the Adam car were out of the pen and heading uptown on Broadway toward Amsterdam and 157th. Shotguns were removed from their racks, and pulsating waves of adrenaline and fear began to overtake emotion and calm. For Barlow and Rosato, veterans of the mean streets of Harlem, this was the worst kind of call to respond to—a veteran officer struck in the head by a mutt's gunfire. For Martinez, who had been shot at, and Bauman, who had been shot, this was déjà vu all over again, a living reincarnation of the nightmare that is sometimes police work.

By the time Two-Truck units reached the crime scene, Officer Lattimer had been rushed in a precinct car to Columbia-Presbyterian Hospital, where he was raced into surgery. The patrol car he was driving was a mess. Blood and brain matter were splashed on the windshield and on the dash; coagulated blood was in a puddle near the brakes and accelerator. Sergeant Scollan, Lattimer's blood all over him, was at first thought to be hit, but he was also extricated from the RMP and rushed to Columbia-Presbyterian for trauma treatment. Soon the dozens of cops who had responded turned into hundreds. Each passsed by the bullet-riddled police car and stood silent for a second. It was a daunting and frightening sight, one that angered the patrol officers as much as it fevered their determination to catch the shooter. As happens in all cop shootings, officers from all over the city raced to Columbia-Presbyterian to donate blood and stand vigil. The mayor was immediately notified following the shooting, as was Police Commissioner Howard Safir, Chief of Department Louis Anemone, and Chief of Patrol Wilbur Chapman. Washington Heights had been on the minds of the top brass for months. To curtail the rampant drug dealing that fueled much of the crime and murder in the area, the NYPD was preparing to flood Washington Heights with more than 600 new police officers from the Manhattan North Task Force, as well as backup from various state and federal agencies. Washington Heights was expected to be in the news soon, but not because of a cop getting ambushed and shot in the head.

For the ESU cops responding from 126th and Old Broadway, the immediate concern was setting up a perimeter and looking for the gunman. Perhaps he hadn't run very far? Perhaps he had been hit by police fire as well? Perhaps he was holed up in some apartment, barricaded, holding a family hostage? Quickly, and in the well-choreographed manner of doing something by instinct, the Two-Truck officers suited up, removed MP5s and Mini-14s from the truck, and awaited further instructions. Midnight crews from the Bronx had also come in from Four- and Three-Trucks, as well as Ten-Truck in Queens North.

The patrol captains and detectives working the scene immediately began to canvass the area for witnesses and possible clues; hundreds of other officers searched every bit of garbage and behind every sewer drain and parked car for the smallest sign of a clue or evidence, that "convictable needle in the haystack" that could help bring the shooter to justice—and soon. A few witnesses described the perp as a male black, approximately twenty-five years old, five-foot-nine, and wearing light-colored T-shirt, jeans, and an Oakland Raiders baseball cap. Some witnesses had him still on the block, while others had the perp escaping, fleeing on foot through a small garden across the street, heading toward 158th Street and Broadway. NYPD Aviation Unit helicopters hovered overhead, showering the area with light and overhead reconnaissance; K-9 units from throughout the city converged on the scene, with German shepherds and bloodhounds; and every available piece of equipment that could enhance the search for the perp or some evidence was rushed to Washington Heights. Nothing mobilizes the NYPD more than the shooting of one of its own.

For the next twelve hours, ESU owned Washington Heights. ESU commanding officer Inspector John Harkins came up from the field to direct personally the search for the shooter, and there were more chiefs, inspectors, deputy inspectors, and bosses than the cops working the case knew what to do with.

At 6:00 A.M., Sgt. Chris Farrell, the city north supervisor on midnights, reached the besieged street along with additional ESU personnel and a CAT car from Three-Truck; they were joined by Lt. Owen McCaffrey and other sergeants and supervisors who all realized what ESU would be doing for the next morning. ESU's plan was clear: await some inkling from the detectives about the possible whereabouts of the shooter, and then go in, hot and heavy, and attempt to apprehend him. There was a wealth of information gathered on 157th Street, as passersby, perp look-alikes, and perps were all grilled by detectives. Whenever a lead panned out and it appeared as if the shooter was identified, Sergeant Farrell would assemble his officers, get them inside the CAT car, and have them race toward the location where the midnight crew would perform a dynamic entry. Going after a perp who shoots a cop is one of the most dangerous tactical entries a police officer can make. Unlike a hit on a drug location or against a man wanted for a homicide, where the bad guys tend not to expect any police intrusion, cop shooters know that the boys in blue do not tolerate one of their own getting killed. Tempers and trigger fingers are tense.

By the time daylight shined its reassuring bright glow on the bloodstained pavement of 157th Street, news crews from throughout the city had swarmed behind police yellow lines. Long-range news cameras from the local TV station New York One followed the ESU effort, even carrying one entry into a walkup tenement live on TV. The scenario became almost comical and could have had tragic repercussions. When the ESU team gained entry to the targeted apartment, a Spanish lady, flabbergasted by the police presence, began yelling, "What is this all about?" Officer Vinny Martinez, glancing over at the television in the living room and tuned in to New York One and the hit being carried live, said, "Lady, cut the bullshit, you know exactly what's going on." There is a brief time delay when TV or radio broadcasts are carried live, and just as Martinez was arguing with the apartment dweller concerning what was going on, footage of ESU entering the building came on. "Hey, Ronnie," Vinny said in a burst of pride. "Look, we are on TV!"

In all, four apartments were hit that morning, a damn busy morning even by ESU standards, but the shooter was long gone. Yet, as one detective working the case would comment, "There is a God, and God must have a brother on the job, because perps are all stupid and victims of their own recidivism." Searching the crime scene, detectives soon found a Glock Model 23 .40 semiautomatic tossed in a garbage can, as well as knapsack discarded by the shooter. With a gun and other bits of physical evidence, detectives would have a solid foundation on which to begin an investigation. To encourage witnesses to come forward, the Police Benevolent Association, better known as PBA, drove a van around Washington Heights making announcements on a loudspeaker offering as much as ten thousand dollars for any information leading to an arrest.

Initially, cops were sure that the shooter was from the neighborhood; after all, he had escaped with such ease into the labyrinth of alleyways and side streets. But after investigating the gun and checking ballistics, as well as other crimes in the city committed with a .40-caliber gun, police in Brooklyn, in the 8-1 Precinct, arrested twenty-eight-year-old John Bynum, a career felon and known stickup man who specialized in livery cab robberies. Bynum's rap sheet dated back to 1985, when he was but seventeen years old, and contained various charges, indictments, and convictions ranging from gun possession to first-degree robbery.

News of Bynum's arrest satisfied the entire department, but details of his lengthy record outraged many top cops. "I will tell you that I am outraged at the fact that we have a fine young police officer in the hospital who was shot by a felon who should have been incarcerated," an angry Commissioner Howard Safir expressed at a news conference, and this fueled debate from City Hall to the Governor's Mansion in Albany requiring that violent felons serve the full terms of their sentences before being released.

Officer Francis Lattimer was from a family of individuals who had dedicated their lives to serving the city of New York. Both his father and uncle were retired New York City cops (his uncle, in fact, was a former E-man), and many of his cousins were cops and firemen. The initial prognosis of a near fatal and debilitating head wound would soon change as Officer Lattimer earned the affectionate nickname of "Miracle Cop." Perhaps it was the work of his surgeons, perhaps his will to survive and return to the job, or perhaps the prayers of more than 38,000 men and women in blue who willed the thirty-three-year-old officer to a miraculous recovery. But Officer Lattimer refused to succumb to his wounds, and he refused to allow massive head trauma and the loss of sight in one eye to compete with his dreams of being a cop. Three weeks after being shot in the head, Francis Lattimer left Columbia-Presbyterian Hospital for rehabilitation at a Westchester County clinic. He hopes one day to return to the job he loves so much.

The best types of emergency jobs are always those where there is no violence, no bloodshed, and no members of the service harmed. Unfortunately, part of the job description of a cop is not being able to pick and choose which jobs happen. That is a matter of fate and the criminal viciousness of the city's most desperate and dangerous perps. But not all midnights are like that. Some are slow and quiet—very slow, sometimes painfully slow and quiet. Some are painfully funny.

On one November night, when it appeared as if even the SOD radio dispatcher was fast asleep, the four officers working midnight decided that this was a good time to catch a bite and watch a meal hour's worth of the movie *Independence Day* on video—after all, "it fits with police work," one of the cops argued. "Martians and Manhattan North?"

As the tape was rewinding and some jokes were tossed around, a visiting city north supervisor was treated to two of the officers doing the "Harlem Macarena," a parody of the popular dance that has the dancer slowly, and to the beat, assume the position taken against the wall just before he or she is frisked by the police. The laughter was contagious, as was the biting truth behind the joke.

Thirty minutes into the movie, the SOD radio remained quiet. Division radios were silent as well, and even the FD radio, routinely monitored for pin jobs, was dead. The only job ongoing was in Brooklyn, in Eight-Truck territory, involving a raccoon in a tree.

In *Independence Day,* when the Martian space ships began to hover over New York City, four pairs of eyes perked up. "Imagine what a job that would be," one of the cops said.

"U-4 to Central, K," one of the cops began to utter in a distinctive accent, mimicking a certain ESU supervisor. "A Martian space ship is hovering over the Empire State Building. Please activate the Apprehension Team and please advise what the traffic is like on the Gawanus Expressway."

"U-4 to Central, K. There are little green men walking around Rockefeller Center. Can you please have EMS respond?"

The ad lib sparks a roar of laughter that causes one

of the cops to fall off his chair, and another to spill his coffee.

"U-4 to Central, K!" another cop begins to scream. "There are little green men with ray guns on the Cross-Bronx Expressway. Please have the Two-Truck RMI start out."

More laughter. In fact, the movie becomes a vehicle by which all of the ESU personnel, from the newest cop in the field to the most experienced man in the Bronx, is lampooned. When the Martian space ships begin to destroy the Empire State Building, the laughter is virtually deafening.

"U-4 to Central, K," a cop sputters, barely able to contain the laughter leaking out both sides of his mouth. "Be aware that the Empire State Building has been destroyed by alien space ships, and Central . . . please have authorized tow respond to a stranded motorist on Fifth Avenue."

Had a senior ESU boss rung downstairs and walked into the gathering, he certainly would have conducted a sanity test on the cops. But laughter is a tool that soothes eyes that have seen far too much tragedy for one tour, let alone a lifetime. It is the most effective means of therapy a cop can treat himself to, and also one of the most inexpensive.

Before the film was over and the tape was back in its box, the SOD radio awakened with a clatter of jobs.

"Emergency Adam-Nine. Report of an EDP in the confines of the 1-02."

"Emergency Truck-Three. Unconfirmed reports of a signal ten-thirteen on the corner of southern Avenue in the confines of the 4-1 Precinct."

"Emergency Service Adam-Two, Truck-Two." The call came, followed by a ten-second pause. "Respond over in the confines of the north precinct for a possible pin and vehicle fire."

Seconds later, with the trepidatious gnawing of hearts swelling with adrenaline and dread, the REP and "Big Blue" were racing out from 126th Street, straight for the

West Side Highway. The trip, at 4:21 A.M., to 54th Street took all of three minutes.

Ostensibly, this was a One-Truck job, but the midnight crew from uptown was handling it. Actually, there wasn't much to handle. A minor two-car collision had resulted in one brand-new Ford Taurus being hurled atop a divider and a gray Ford van being thrown against the outer roadway fence. The van had erupted into a ball of flames, but there was little for ESU to do. As FD units crowded the scene, attempting to put out the smoky fire, the silhouette of a man still sitting behind the wheel became visible through the fiery inferno. The van's driver, perhaps dead on impact, was still clutching the steering wheel, still by outside appearance driving the van as if all were fine and dandy. But he was dead, charred to the bones in a grotesque blackened state. It was a morbid sight, one that cops and rescue personnel must get used to. The scent off the Hudson River was no match for the stench of burning flesh and plastic. With little to do other than stare, the E-cops loaded their gear and returned to their REP.

There were still three hours left on patrol, and the SOD radio was getting busier. There were reports of an EDP in Queens, a fifty-three possible pin in the Bronx, and a perp search going on in Seven-Truck area in the confines of the notorious 7-5 Precinct.

Neither Martinez nor Bauman, as vocal a pair as can be found in the truck, made any comments or jokes after witnessing the burnt remains of the van driver. Silence meant something, though if ever a cop's psyche had needed a bit of comic relief, the humorous escape of watching *Independence Day* was paying generous dividends. As Martinez and Bauman departed the accident scene and headed back northbound on the West Side Highway toward a patrol of the Upper West Side, the SOD radio, static and all, gave over the job of unconfirmed shots fired in the 3-4 Precinct at 178th Street and Broadway.

"Let's start heading up there," Bauman told his partner. "The night is still young."

11

TWA Flight 800, July 17, 1996

●

"Hey, Sarge, you wanna eat now or you wanna get Chinese a bit later?"

"Let's eat early. I've gotta feeling we'll be busy later on."

It had been a quiet August, but something was eating at Sergeant Garcia's insides. Something was causing him to feel uneasy. He wanted his cops ready. He wanted them prepared and trained for whatever type of disaster might befall the city.

Roosevelt Island is one of those New York anomalies that sane minds have a hard time figuring out. Situated smack dab in the center of the East River, underneath the 59th Street Bridge, between Manhattan's ultra-chic Upper East Side and the working-class drab of Long Island City and Astoria in Queens, Roosevelt Island was designed as a miracle in urban planning, a residential refuge from the hustle and bustle of the city, all within eyeshot of one of the most breathtaking skylines in the world. Roosevelt Island sports a small population quartered in drab prefabricated apartment blocks, a little greenery, a few stores, and little else. It is one of those places that fit the infamous New York directional philosophy of "you can't get there from here." Roosevelt Island is accessible from Queens via a small narrow bridge, and access from Manhattan is courtesy of the Roosevelt Island tramway. "In a city where everyone lives atop one another crammed together like sardines," claims one veteran cop, "this place is truly in the middle of nowhere."

From an NYPD point of view, Roosevelt Island is also "contested territory." First, basic law and order on the island isn't even the responsibility of the NYPD—the island has its own public safety department, sanctioned by the State of New York to carry firearms and provide day-to-day protection and service to the island's residents. In cases where the shit hits the fan, the NYPD is called in to do everything from the investigation to the search for the perpetrators. Although, according to territorial maps of the city, Roosevelt Island belongs to Manhattan, its land access through Queens makes it the responsibility of the 1-14 Precinct in Astoria. There are, though, very few calls to jobs on Roosevelt Island. It is a quiet and gray dot on the river with one of the most spectacular man-made views known to man. But Roosevelt Island is also a target. Not because there are government offices on the island or a major air or rail terminal but because of a double-lined tramway that connects First Avenue and 60th Street in Manhattan, at the foot of the 59th Street Bridge, with the island. More a tourist attraction than an invaluable element of the New York City commuter network, it is a large, red, dangling box that moves across the East River in both directions on the half hour all day long.

To ESU, especially in the wake of the World Trade Center bombing, the tramway has more ominous tones. The tramway was the scene of a major Hollywood terrorist outrage. In the movie *Nighthawks,* a wily Carlos-like terrorist played by Rutger Hauer and his almond-eyed Middle Eastern beauty of an accomplice took the tramway and a bunch of innocent people hostage. A wily New York City cop, played by Sylvester Stallone, had to be hoisted up and down the tramway as it hovered over the island. Life is known to imitate art, and the possibility that a Hollywood scenario would inspire an organized terrorist faction or a loony with an arsenal was not lost on the Emergency Service Unit.

Theoretically, Roosevelt Island is the responsibility of Ten-Truck, and the squad in northern Queens is considered among the finest in the entire division. Some of its officers, like Sgt. Paul Hargrove, Police Officers Tommy Langone, Brian Gregory, Glen Klein, Ray Denninger, and Mike McKenna, are considered exemplary E-men of unflinching courage and unrivaled skill. But because Two-Truck, being a hop, skip, and a jump away in Manhattan courtesy of the Triborough Bridge and a race through the avenues of Astoria, is also nearby, the two trucks share responsibility for rescue and tactical work that needs to be handled on the small blip of land between Manhattan's East Side and the industrial sights of northwestern Queens. The system works. Both trucks are made up of workers, and both have an excellent working relationship.

For the training endeavor, to mimic and go through the motions of a rescue on board the tramway, the third squads from the two trucks assembled at the Roosevelt Island entrance to the tramway, carrying with them enough rope and climbing gear to scale Mt. Everest and enough goodwill to last through the most arduous mishaps that might follow along the way. The objective of the exercise was to take the tramway out mid-span, approximately 250 feet over the East River, and then have the officers rappel down the dangling box on a rope and land on a police launch that would wait below. The purpose wasn't to see if the cops could rappel; each E-man was a certified rope man. The idea was, first to get the officers used to the notion of going down, courtesy of a nylon rope, with nothing below their feet other than the polluted gray waters of the East River, and, second, to test the feasibility of cops lowering stranded or wounded travelers down to an awaiting police or rescue vessel. Could it be done? Sure! How it could be done with any reliable chance of speed or effectiveness was another story.

If you are afraid of heights, being in the emergency service is a very poor career choice. It sucks to be scared of heights when grabbing a jumper and when one needs to rappel out of a helicopter either upstate at Camp Smith or downtown atop the observation deck of the World Trade Center. And if you are afraid of water, ESU isn't a wise job choice, either. For underneath the dangling tramway was nothing but the murky depths of the East River. One false move, and instant inspector's funeral.

In the real world, if the tram were in trouble or under the control of terrorists or armed perps, ESU would reach the scene courtesy of Aviation Unit helicopters. But the unit does enough rappelling training at Camp Smith. The focus of this afternoon's fun was what happens after the cops are already on the damn thing. In all, the exercise went well. It proved to the unit, the department, and the bean counters in City Hall that not only could ESU handle virtually any problem on the tramway, from a bomb to a terrorist takeover, but even in the benign case of a simple malfunction, the E-men could safely, quickly, and with little fuss evacuate everyone from the perch 300 feet over the East River.

Garcia had good reason to feel as if the unit needed to be ready for the extraordinary, the bizarre, and the despicable. He had been there, on the scene on countless occasions, to help return normalcy from chaos, to help bring closure and resolution to calamities caused by both man and nature. In terms of a unit's tactical readiness, Garcia wasn't the kind of ESU boss who read *SWAT* magazine, had discussions with other cops about the difference in trigger pull between a Glock Model 19 and a Beretta M9. What is truly important to Sgt. Juan Garcia is the love of his family and the lives of his men. His specialty, in fact, is saving lives and turning disasters into tales of miraculous rescue. Garcia is emergency service of the old school—the one that could and would do just about anything if it would result in the salvation of an innocent life, and he has done so throughout the city, in places as diverse and in scenarios as striking as the devastation left by the forces of nature in Hurricane Hugo and the devastation left by man's hatred in Oklahoma City. Brought up as a beat cop in the Bronx, the former Marine would go on to service in Harlem and then with the then-notorious Three-Truck in the South Bronx. Breaking one's teeth at Three-Truck at the time was like learning to swim in a tidal wave. If you survived, you were damn good. It meant you had seen it all.

A month earlier, he had seen fire and no survivors.

July 17, 1996, was a lovely evening in New York City—it was one of those summer nights in the Big Apple that dreams, as well as settings for novels, are made of. The temperature barely hovered around the eighty-degree mark, the skies were crisp and blue all day, and twilight sprayed the city with a charming glow of crimson. Along Times Square, along Broadway and 145th Street, from the Harlem River Drive to the Midtown Tunnel, New York was a town innocent in the joys of summer.

Sgt. Juan Garcia was in a happy mood as well, for the beginning of a four-to-twelve. "Big Blue," the truck, was out of commission with one of its weekly ailments, and all of its equipment had been stowed on an REP that would serve as the truck. This was a reason to be happy. Garcia and the chauffeur, John Politoski, weren't relegated to sitting in quarters waiting for jobs to come over the air. They could get out and patrol. "It's nice outside," Garcia told Politoski as he attended to some paperwork. "Let's see what's happening in this fair city."

If there is anything that gets Garcia angry, it's getting to a fifty-three pin late. To try to catch the slack and pick up a few minutes, Garcia and many of the officers in his squad often will monitor the FD frequencies, a bit more advanced than the civilian-run system the NYPD has, so that they could get to a job faster. There were no pins this picturesque summer's evening, not even a ten-thirteen or a stuck occupied elevator. But the truck was out on patrol, and it was a pretty night. To both Garcia and Politoski, that was fine.

Garcia decided to focus the REPs patrol on the Upper West Side. Perhaps it was the Chinese food they would eventually bring back to quarters from the Broadway Cottage on Broadway and 103rd. Perhaps it was those Upper West Side women and their revealing summer clothing; there is no police regulation against sightseeing, after all. The streets of the West Side were filled that night with shoppers, diners, tourists, and the local psychos milling about. It was Thursday, payday. "Don't worry," Politoski told Garcia. "It'll pick up once the checks are cashed and everyone gets all liquored up."

The banter inside an REP can be bizarre or bewitching—discussions have ranged from office gossip to the personal hygiene habits of cab drivers. The conversation that night, though, focused on the upcoming Olympics and terrorism. Most cops in ESU had a gut feeling that some knuckleheads, either from overseas or from the American heartland, were going to try to make a political statement courtesy of the blood of a good many innocent people. Capt. Dan Connolly and several ESU cops, including Two-Truck's Seth Gahr, were in Atlanta as part of a FEMA deployment. The ESU personnel were sent to the Peachtree State specifically to be on call should a terrorist attack occur and the authorities find themselves in desperate need of having building debris removed from trapped victims, both survivors and corpses. No matter how many federal agents were in Atlanta and no matter how many military forces were on standby, there was a feeling that something big was going to happen. The ESU cops in Georgia, in fact, were there specifically in fear of a terrorist attack involving either chemical or biological agents.

Yet there was the foreboding sense of doom in New York City, as well. Inside the kitchen at Two-Truck, and in the kitchen of just about every ESU truck in the city, there was the real sense, almost a sixth sense, that if terrorists were going to strike, it wasn't going to be in Georgia but in New York City. This wasn't Munich twenty-five years earlier, after all. The Olympics didn't turn Atlanta into the media capital of the world—New York was, and remained, the epicenter of international communications, and it was in New York that many feared terrorists would be doing their evil bidding. There were so many places to strike in the city that NYPD officials and FBI personnel had a tough time figuring out where to apply additional layers of security. The NYPD-FBI Joint Terrorism Task Force had been readying itself for something big for months, but now that the Olympics were forty-eight hours from starting, nervousness became a staple of everyone's diet. "Where would the disaster come from?" everyone wondered. Cops throughout the city were nervous.

Sergeant Garcia has a God-given sixth sense about predicting disasters and the "big job." When in quarters he tells his men that there is going to be "something big" tonight, few cops will ever argue with him. His track record speaks for itself. The sixth sense must have been working this night, for Garcia had a feeling about something to do with a plane crash, and the discussion inside the REP, at the corner of Broadway and 72nd Street was about the last USAir jet that ESU had to pull out of the icy waters of Flushing Bay. "Remember that last plane job we had, John?" Garcia asked, thinking about some obnoxious chief, now retired, who was busting ESU's balls the morning after twelve hours of back- and heartbreaking work. "Remember the chief who yelled at us because he wanted us to move our trucks so that he could pull out without having to reverse?"

"Yeah," replied Politoski, remembering how removing the wounded and recovering the dead from those frigid waters was a rough job on both a mental and a physical level. "He was a real dick. Here we were working like mad to get anyone alive out, and here we come out of the water, tired, hungry, and wet, and we had to get back in our trucks and rearrange the parking line. What a dick. What was his name?"

Before Sergeant Garcia could recall that chief's name, a call came over the SOD citywide frequency.

"Truck-Nine to Central, K."

"Proceed, Truck-Nine," the dispatcher said in her high-pitched twang.

"Are you getting any word concerning a passenger jet that crashed off of Long Island?" the Truck-Nine supervisor asked, readying his mind and body for what could truly be the big job.

"Where are you getting this job from?" the dispatcher asked, getting testy that someone would have the nerve to summon her with a job not appearing on her screen.

"It's coming over on TV, Central. It's on Channel Four TV!"

It was exactly 9:37 P.M.

Seconds later, both Scuba and Aviation informed the harried dispatcher that they, too, had seen reports of a plane crash on the news. Truck-Ten and Truck-Seven personnel also called in the jobs. This was not a bullshit call or a prank. Something real was happening.

Inside the REP on Broadway, past the shimmering waterfalls of Lincoln Center, Politoski slowed to a crawl as both he and Garcia sat stone-faced, their jaws dropping to their chests, not believing that talk of a past plane crash could have precipitated a major catastrophe.

"We gotta go," Garcia told Politoski, still not knowing what had happened or where the aircraft had come down. In fact, they weren't sure what type of plane had gone down. It could have a helicopter, or it could have been a Cessna cub with two passengers. It also could have been a corporate jet or a DC-10 with 300 people on board. "Do we have a map of Long Island in this thing?" Garcia asked as he searched the glove compartment and behind the seat for any clues to how to get to the crash.

Slowly, as the sound of two hearts beating in fast cadence was all that was heard inside the cramped quarters of the REP, Politoski turned the vehicle around at 59th Street and headed back uptown, in the direction of quarters, through Central Park. He was hardly pushing his gas pedal, almost willing the REP on as he awaited further news about the job. "I hope it wasn't a large jet that went down," Politoski quietly told his sergeant. "I hope that this is all bullshit." Seconds later, the job was confirmed by the man whose word is God to all NYPD officers.

"Car-Three to Central, K." Chief of Department Louis R. Anemone came over the air. "Be advised that the Port Authority and Kennedy Airport are confirming a 747 down in the waters off of East Moriches, Long Island. Have ESU, Scuba, and Air-Sea Rescue respond, and call Harbor units as well. Contact Floyd Bennet Field, and have all available ESU personnel eighty-five me at Randall's Island for further instructions." It was a dynamic response to the first moments of a confirmed tragedy. Although East Moriches in the eastern reaches of Suffolk County was outside the boundaries of New York City, the NYPD was the one department in the area with the resources and trained manpower to get there and get there fast. When he was the XO of the Special Operations Division during the bombing of the World Trade Center in February 1993, Chief Anemone had taken dynamic command of a chaotic and desperate situation, and he had turned it into one of the NYPD's, and especially ESU's, finest moments. "We would walk through fire for the man," an ESU officer once proudly boasted. "He has all the confidence in us to do the job, and we have all the faith and trust in him to do whatever he says."

When Anemone came on the air, Garcia sat in silence, coiled like a spring waiting to pop, in the passenger's seat of the REP, holding his breath as the chief spoke. Garcia knew that this was a job ESU would be responding to, even though Two-Truck was more than a hundred miles from the site of the crash. As Anemone completed his transmission, Garcia grabbed the microphone and said simply, "Central, please inform Car-Three that Truck-Two is responding to Randall's Island."

Less than three minutes later, the truck was back on

126th Street, and both Garcia and Politoski were furiously assembling material and equipment to load onto a flatbed truck parked outside quarters that would ferry the gear to Randall's Island. Garcia had the right people working for him that night to respond to a plane down in the ocean. The newest cop in the squad, Police Officer Ray Nalpant, was low-key, enthusiastic, soft-spoken, and polite, "everything," as one Third Squad cop would comment, "that we weren't!" Nalpant was also a U.S. Marine Corps Force Recon veteran and an eight-year veteran of the NYPD Scuba Unit. Joining Naplant was Garcia's trusted squad cop, Steve Vales, an expert with a world of rescue experience notched on his belt. Throughout the city, the rescue-minded cops of ESU were calling their families, gathering equipment and supplies of gum and candy bars, and readying their trucks' spare vehicles for the rendezvous point at Randall's Island.

Although the crash was as far from the five boroughs as one could get, ESU mobilized itself as if the plane had come down in the East River. The SOD radio became a static-razzed chatterbox of REPs transmitting messages over to their trucks and citywide supervisors attempting to coordinate this massive rescue bid from the four corners of the city. When a job like the crash comes over the air, there is a natural tendency for a cop, especially an emergency cop, to want to drop whatever he or she is doing and race to the scene where lives might be hanging in the balance. Such tendencies are why ESU has endeared itself to the city for so long, but they do not jive well with the bureaucracy and operational requirements of maintaining ten trucks of E-men on patrol on a citywide basis. After all, not every emergency cop could race to the waters off Suffolk—someone had to stay in Harlem, in Bed-Stuy, and in Jamaica, to keep the city safe and on alert in case any other mountains of shit decided to hit the fan.

The phone lines at ESU HQ at Floyd Bennet Field were on fire. Most of those working the Third Squad knew who would be en route to the crash site and who would be staying behind in the city. Bosses called supervisors, supervisors summoned cops, cops called spouses, and spouses called baby-sitters.

By 10:00 P.M., the ESU contingent was on Randall's Island loading lifesaving material, scuba gear, oxygen tanks, sodas and bottled water, and other miscellaneous material that would assist in the search-and-rescue efforts. The work was carried about at a feverish pace. To the E-men, every second counted, even though the ride in the harbor launch that would ferry them out to East Moriches would take more than four hours. It was work fueled by high-octane adrenaline. As Chief Anemone supervised the preparations and issued orders through a myriad of radios and cell phones, Garcia even lost his head for a second and, thinking Chief Anemone to be a lieutenant on the scene, responded to an order by saying, "Sure, Loo, I'll take care of it!"

"Whaaaaat?" Chief Anemone replied, quite shocked and getting angrier by the second that a sergeant (albeit one in emergency) would call him by his first name, Lou.

"No, sir," Garcia said humbly as he carefully and slowly looked for the right words. "I thought you were a lieutenant for a second, and that's why I called you Loo."

Anemone was amused by the answer and pleased by it. He had seen Garcia on many jobs, from his time as CO of the 3-2 Precinct in Harlem to his stint as Special Operations Division executive officer at the time of the World Trade Center bombing. He knew how his men responded and that no matter how enthusiastic the cops got on the big job, no matter how pulsating the surges of adrenaline were in their veins, the E-men always maintained their composure. Under the chaos of the night and the desperate attempts to get an accurate update on the situation, Chief Anemone watched as the E-men, already toward the latter end of their shift, were working with unbridled enthusiasm and vigor to load the craft with aboveboard speed. If ever there was time to cut slack and smile, this was it. After all, as Harbor Launch Four left the murky waters off Randall's Island down the East River toward the waters off Brooklyn and the lengthy push east, past the Rockaways in Queens into the waters off Long Beach and then straight toward the crash site, no one yet had a clue about the magnitude of the disaster. The ten E-men were hoping to save lives. They prayed that this wasn't a bad one and that most of the passengers would be saved. They relied on hope and on their inner strengths. Most were already exhausted and somewhat fearful of what lay ahead.

Back at Two-Truck and at the other nine trucks in the city, cops were glued to the television set. Former Deputy Commissioner for Public Information and NBC reporter John Miller was one of the first to report live from the scene, from a boat heading out to the crash site. The images of a darkened sea supporting pockets of fire were daunting and humbling. In every truck in the city, the words "nobody could have survived that" were heard. E-cops, taken off stride by very little this world has to offer, were taken aback by the scenes of fiery destruction.

NYPD Harbor Launch Four with the E-men reached the waters of Moriches sometime after 2:00 A.M., and the sight that lay before them as they neared the crash scene was like nothing they had ever seen before and unlike anything they could have imagined. The darkened waters looked more like Dante's Inferno than the Atlantic Ocean, and it was as close to a glimpse of hell as any of the cops would want to get. Dozens of rescue helicopters milled about at low altitudes in the skies over the crash sight. There were UH-60 Blackhawks from a nearby Army reserve unit, Aerospatiale Dolphins from the Coast Guard Station in Brooklyn, and several NYPD Aviation Unit helicopters scanning the waters for signs of victims. The waves were covered by a sheet of debris and flaming jet fuel that was as wide as several footballs fields and three times as long. The flames turned the area into a blistering perimeter of death and chaos. No one could have survived that crash—there was too much debris, and the waters were far too deep. The heat began to affect the cops. They began to wipe sweat from their brows. Some wiped tears from their eyes. The closer they got to the epicenter of the crash, the more their hearts began to beat and their minds began to race. The cops wanted nothing more than to find life rafts with people floating about and to hear the words "Thank God you found us!" All they saw were bits and pieces of wreckage, suitcases, and empty hopes of finding survivors.

The Boeing 747 jumbo had shattered upon impact, they assumed, though they knew nothing of its altitude when it went down or how many people were on board. As bits of luggage floated by, a very powerful human aspect of the search-and-rescue job came into play. There were people in these waters. Fathers and sons, mothers and daughters, kids. This wasn't an accident on the FDR Drive where a drunk slammed into a divider and had to have his remains scraped off the roadway. These waters could hold the bodies of possibly 300 or 400 innocent people. Thoughts of what had brought down the plane had yet to be considered. All that the E-cops could think about was being extremely lucky and finding a survivor or two.

There would be no survivors, however, from the disastrous crash of TWA Flight 800. As the rescue boats slowly discovered that the waters were filled with bodies, thoughts of lifesaving were replaced by hopes of recovering as many of the dead as could be found as soon as possible so that at least the victims' families could have a sense of closure to the tragedy. Tragic it was. The blast and plummet to earth had not played kindly with many of the bodies. Clothes had been torn off by the blast and the impact with the water, and the sight of naked victims bobbing up and down in the water was emotionally challenging for the cops. For veterans of previous plane crashes, from USAir flights that fell short in Flushing Bay off the runway at LaGuardia Airport to the crash of the Avianca jet in Glen Cove, Long Island, this was a worse tragedy of untold horror. This was different from the destruction witnessed at both the World Trade Center, where six died, and Oklahoma City, where ESU cops worked feverishly searching for possible survivors and recovering bodies. This tragedy off the shore of East Moriches seemed unique.

If the NYPD's response to the crash of TWA Flight 800 between Kennedy Airport and Paris was a dynamic and resolute show of force and compassion, then the local response of Suffolk County Police vessels and local fishermen and yachtsmen was a rousing testament of the human spirit. Hundreds of boats, some as big as a million-dollar yacht and others as small as a two-man rowboat, raced toward the fiery crash site, hoping to come across a survivor floating in the water. Most of those who responded hadn't a clue about first aid and how to administer emergency care, but they had boats and they had the desire, and that was all that mattered.

The search for bodies in the waters was difficult and, in those first hours, uncoordinated. It was hard work for hardened emotions and the ESU cops, the cops from the NYPD's Harbor Unit, the Scuba Unit, and of course the tireless helicopter pilots from the Aviation Unit who flew close cover and air support, illuminating the area with powerful searchlights. The NYPD, the New York State Police, and the Nassau County and Suffolk County police departments all raced to the scene and worked endlessly to find at least one survivor; even the FDNY had sent its divers. After the ESU cops had been in the water for more than twelve hours, they received orders to head back home. For many of the cops, it was the longest twelve hours of their lives.

The NYPD pulled out all its assets from the crash site in the first few days after the crash, leaving behind only its finest scuba personnel; divers from the other local law enforcement agencies also had remained behind to join in the search for bodies and plane wreckage. The Fire

Department, as is often the case, attempted to get its divers in the middle of the recovery effort, but after a few near-fatal accidents, U.S. Navy personnel took over. "They told us that they wouldn't leave here until each and every piece of the plane was brought up," claims a diver who worked on the recovery effort, "but these guys, untrained for this work, hampered more than they helped."

For the next ninety-seven days, U.S. Navy divers, supported by NYPD scuba officers (and Officer Ray Nalpant back, for a while, in scuba), and divers from the Nassau and Suffolk County police departments and the New York State Police, worked difficult and hazardous shifts to retrieve the secrets and the victims of the tragedy from the ocean floor 120 feet below. The experience left all involved changed forever. Days after the mysterious midair explosion that sent TWA 800 plummeting 13,000 feet to the harsh waters of the Atlantic, federal officials and NTSB investigators realized that the only way to recover evidence, as well as retrieve bodies, was going to be from the ocean floor. As far as dives went, this was going to be a gut-wrenching one. With limited visibility and the dangers of being sliced by the miles of razor-sharp bits of twisted metal and dangling wires strewn about the wreckage, the divers carried body bags for the inevitable discoveries of death they were bound to uncover under the sea. They found bodies still buckled into their seats, and teddy bears and toys belonging to the younger victims. Many of these cops, veterans of the mean streets of New York, were overcome by the work. Only the determination to help the many families grieving over lives cut tragically short fueled their psyches and their hearts to persevere, often without a day off.

The underwater recovery effort was miraculously successful. By April 1997, more than 100,000 pieces of wreckage were brought up from the ocean depths and reconstructed, inside a massive hangar, in Calverton, Long Island. To this day, at the time of this book's writing, however, the cause behind the crash of TWA Flight 800 remains a mystery.

People who have never hung around cops can sometimes be put off by their self-imposed veil of being on guard, their desensitized exterior, and their police lingo. Yet there is a spirit of sacrifice and of willingness to help, no matter what, where, or when, that is simply beyond description. There is no money on earth that can adequately reward most of the cops who participate in rescue and recovery work, when lives are on the line and that race is on against the clock to retrieve life from the clutches of death. For the E-cops, their reward is not momentary. They receive spiritual payment, a warmth in the heart for having done above and beyond the call of duty for people who are total strangers.

Back at Roosevelt Island, staring into the murky waters of the East River was a stark reminder to Juan Garcia, Steve Vales, and Tommy Langone of what they had witnessed a month earlier. The training went well. The officers, roped in and secure, began the slow procession down to the East River, where an NYPD Harbor launch would follow in and pick up the officers. The exercise took more than two hours and was, even to the most cynical cops, good training. By the time the entire cast of characters had made its way down the line, the bright sunlight that had showered the 59th Street Bridge and the tramway was now dimmed to the dark crimson glow of twilight. Back on the island, as the officers assembled their gear and returned to their REPs, Garcia was happy. After TWA 800, after witnessing the wreckage, preparedness was an absolute necessity for Garcia's squad. The next time the big job comes over, that proverbial disaster requiring immediate emergency attention, his men will be ready.

12

Things That Go Boom: ESU and Bomb Jobs

•

"Hey, officer, what's going on up there? Why isn't this traffic moving?"

"Just hang loose, pal. There is a suspicious package on the corner of 42nd and Second. Hey! Are you deaf? Didn't you hear me? I'll write you a summons if you don't stop honking your horn."

"So, let the whole city blow to hell. Who gives a fuck? If I don't deliver these packages in time and I lose my job, I'll blow up the city myself!"

Ask any E-cop where he was when the Mets won the Series, and he'll respond, "I don't know." Ask a good many of them where they were when they found out they were going to be fathers, and the response will be, "Gee, really couldn't tell you." Ask any E-cop where he was when he heard about the bombing of the World Trade Center, and the answer includes the time, the place, and even what he had for lunch that day. Bombings engrave images and memories into the soul of an E-cop. Over the course of the last several years, from Lower Manhattan to Oklahoma City, there has been a lot of engraving going on.

There was a time when the thought of a terrorist of the hard-core variety blowing up anything in New York City was too far-fetched, even for the most anxious predictors of gloom. New York just wasn't that type of city. It could have blackouts, George Steinbrenner, and the

Son of Sam, but who had time for terrorism? "Who would want to strike in New York?" one retired ESU cop said. "Traffic sucked, so you'd be late for the flight you'd want to hijack. Take over a school? Sure, though better bring 100 of the meanest SOBs the Libyans could train, because many of those innocent kiddies keep 9mms in their Power Ranger lunch boxes. Leave a bomb on a subway? Sure! How many packages left on a subway train in New York City would remain there for more than fifteen seconds before some street person took them into the tunnel?"

New York just wasn't that type of city? Sure it was.

Federal, state, and city planners had long ignored the volatile nature of New York as a hub of terrorist activity. There had been bombings in New York before, but they were committed by fringe groups—the Weathermen, the Puerto Rican FALN, and some Yugoslavian psychos. Even the Jewish Defense League was linked to a few bombs in the city, mainly targeting Soviet diplomats and facilities, although the organization denied any involvement in the bombings. New York, though, policymakers at One Police Plaza had thought for years, would never become another Belfast, Berlin, Paris, or Jerusalem. Even during the Golf War, when mysterious Arabs right out of central casting were seen lurking behind every corner, New York came away intact, even though its nerves had been severely tested. It just wouldn't happen here.

Mohammed Salameh and his cast of merry bombers changed New York City forever. The World Trade Center blast, underneath the Vista Hotel directly below tower number one, on February 26, 1993, at 12:18 P.M., was a one-ton explosive wake-up call that the Big Apple, and the NYPD, still looks at as a turning point.

In Brooklyn, at some five-star restaurant, much of the ESU and Special Operations Division brass had assembled to treat one of their own, retiring after twenty-plus years on the job, to a meal to remember. As the dessert tray was brought out and sugar added to the last round of coffees, the feast was interrupted by a cascade of beeping sounds, the calls of a dozen pagers going off simultaneously, summoning the captains, lieutenants, and sergeants to the explosion in Lower Manhattan. The E-cops, racing out of the restaurant in a trail of smoke, left the retiring boss behind, rushing to what promised to be the "big job."

At the other end of the city, Sgt. Juan Garcia, the city north supervisor that snowy Friday afternoon, was in the northernmost stretch of the Bronx when the first calls of the explosion made it over the SOD airwaves, in the midst of talking a jumper off an overpass. "Come down now," said Garcia, his tone impatient after the job was confirmed, realizing that a landmark under the gun was far more important that a psycho wanting some attention. "We haven't got all day." Police Officers Steve Vales and Don "Rescue Ready" Costleigh had raced at lightning speed from Harlem to the world financial district in Lower Manhattan. They were among the first ESU units on the scene and, amid the smoke, confusion, and chaos, were instrumental in the calm and orderly evacuation of scores of smoke-suffering civilians, and they also had saved the life of a fireman from Rescue One who had fallen into a smoldering pit.

In the twelve hours following the blast, ESU raced, rescued, and rappelled off helicopters in their back-breaking efforts to save anyone trapped in the towers. For the next few months, ESU crews worked around the clock along with federal agents to sift through the damage and the debris. The response to the blast was, until the 1995 visit of the pope and the UN 50, ESU's shining moment.

New York City was lucky that snowy February afternoon, however. Quite literally, thousands could have been killed by the ton of explosives that detonated in the parking garage, perhaps tens of thousands had the terrorists opted to blow up the van outside the buildings, on West Street and Trinity Place, as the multitudes of workers and tourists took lunch-hour strolls. If the terrorists were really smart, instead of a ragtag group of holy warriors, they could have scored an act of murderous rage so wide-scale that this country would still be reeling from its sheer horror and loss of life. "Murphy's law works against terrorist scumbags, too," claimed a member of the Bomb Squad. "After all, Murphy's an Irishman!"

Yet where New York City was lucky, Oklahoma City was destined for tragedy. Even though the bombing of the Murrah Building in Oklahoma City would be far from the confines of the five boroughs, it brought back eerie reminders of the World Trade Center blast to just about every E-cop. In fact, when news of the bombing reached many of the ESU officers in the Third Squad on patrol in Queens, the Bronx, Brooklyn, and Manhattan, there were genuine fears that New York City, the true center of global communications, would be hit as well. In Manhattan North, where an element of Sgt. Juan Garcia's men was providing security for a visit by Vice President Al Gore, the bombing in the Southwest would be brought home in a flurry of terrifying activity. "As coincidence would have it, we were sweeping the parking garage of the Waldorf Astoria for explosives when we heard over the air that there had been a bombing in Oklahoma City," recalls a Two-Truck officer. "Less than a half hour later, the Secret Service hightailed the vice president the hell out of there in the fastest exit I've ever seen a motorcade do!"

For the crews back at quarters, checking their gear and simultaneously listening to the radio and watching New York One News on cable, the first reports that an explosion had ripped through the federal building in Oklahoma City brought them back to that fateful noontime, more than two years earlier, when news of an explosion turned into what would be, until 10:04 A.M. this morning, the largest bombing ever in American law enforcement history. Bombs weren't supposed to happen in the heartland. "This must be followers of the same crew that blew up the Twin Towers," a cop in Ten-Truck commented. "Why the hell would they hit the sticks?" While many cops feared that the destruction of the federal building would be but an opening salvo in a major terrorist bombing offensive, there were several E-cops who knew that this would involve them somehow. These cops called Floyd Bennet Field, they called the ESU executive officer, and they called home to suggest that their spouses begin packing their bags. When it came to emergency rescue and urban extraction, few units in the world could match the skills and experience of ESU.

For years, as a result of a remarkably tenacious ESU cop named Detective Mike Corr, ESU has been leading a FEMA (Federal Emergency Management Agency) umbrella called the Urban Search and Rescue Program, which mobilized ESU officers, firefighters, and EMS medical technicians into an on-call rescue entity that could be transported anywhere in the United States or the world. Following Hurricane Hugo, which ripped apart the island of Puerto Rico like a baseball bat slicing across a porcelain vase, ESU officers were sent to the island to provide emergency medical care and safe drinking water and to help repair some of the damage left behind by nature's fury. The localized FEMA programs were so successful that similar regional FEMA teams flourished throughout the United States. Yet the ESU contingent was the only such task force expert in the search and recovery of victims and evidence. Two hours after the Oklahoma City blast, ESU executive officer Capt. Curt Wargo, the assistant commander of the New York task force, known as NYTF One, learned that they had been activated. Officers assigned on the task force were notified and mobilized to a staging area at Floyd Bennet Field, where they would assemble and convoy to Kennedy Airport in Queens, where a U.S. Air Force C-141 from McGuire AFB in New Jersey would transport them and their containerized gear to Tinker AFB in Oklahoma City for what promised to be a most desperate and precarious search-and-rescue operation. In all, the NYTF One consisted of more than sixty men—including more than twenty ESU officers.

There are many in Two-Truck who like to joke that Sergeant Garcia, having been born and raised in the Bronx, has seen just about all there is to see of urban destruction, but the destruction in Oklahoma City was unlike anything he, or anyone else on the team, had ever seen before. "The destruction was awesome," claimed Officer Manny Hernandez of Three-Truck in the Bronx, one of the most experienced men in the division. "Had the perpetrators of the bombing wanted to make a statement, they could have set the device off in the middle of the night, destroyed the building, and let their agenda be known, but this was a crime against humanity!" In February 1993, most of the cops in ESU were sure that they had seen the absolute damage that a bomb could inflict, as they worked the endless hours inside the six-story-tall crater digging out evidence for the FBI, but the World Trade Center bombing paled in comparison to what was encountered out west.

Inside the devastated skeleton of a building, the NYTF One worked twelve-hour shifts in search of survivors. As dedicated rescue men, the officers realized the importance of pulling a survivor out of the destruction. Driven by adrenaline, anger, and the burning demand to help and pull a survivor out of the mangled steel trap, the E-cops worked without respite, using their heavy tools and the tips of their fingers in search of anyone still alive.

Tragically, there would be no more survivors found in the wreckage by the time ESU arrived a thousand miles from NYC, only corpses.

For many of the ESU rescuers, the most poignant recovery was the body of a U.S. Marine located on Monday, April 24, 1995, in the early morning hours. Of the ESU officers, Manny Hernandez and Juan Garcia were former Marines, and Mike Curtain is a sergeant in the Marine Corps reserves. Together with EMS paramedic Ray Boomer, also a former Marine, they meticulously searched for the body, recovered it, and preserved the Corps' colors in a somber and stoic salute to a fallen comrade. The Marine's body was removed from the rubble on a Stokes basket, draped with the American flag, and turned over to a Marine Corps honor guard. A moment of silence was observed and a few tears shed. The small ceremony was so touching and so appreciated by the Marines on the scene that word of the ESU retrieval made it all the way to the Marine Corps commandant's office in Washington, D.C. To this day, the widow of the Marine officer remains in close contact with the men who so gallantly and respectfully retrieved her husband's body.

ESU worked around the clock in Oklahoma City for one week. FEMA officials were careful to monitor the emotional well-being of the rescuers. There were men and women killed in the blast, and toddlers and infants, too. No matter how hardened a cop is, no matter how much a cop has seen, walking into the epicenter of the damage left by a 4,000-pound bomb reverberates through the psyche of the rescuer with ballistic backlash. On Thursday, April 26, 1995, the ESU cops were sent home, though several, including Two-Truck's Detective Henry Medina, stayed behind for special tasks. During the search-and-recovery operation at the World Trade Center, these officers had so impressed the FBI in their skills at cutting up cars and mangled debris that now federal agents not only demanded ESU assistance in the evidence recovery operation but requested E-cops by name and reputation.

Every time ESU cops hear a bomb job over the air, no matter how small or potentially trivial, the images of the World Trade Center and Oklahoma City immediately shoot into their minds. They are images engraved into the psyche of the unit forever.

Bomb jobs, through sheer volume, have become an ESU specialty. A suspicious package, what appears to be a device or a hand grenade or mortar shell, might be found by a precinct unit, and then ESU is summoned. ESU will first give the device, or suspicious package, a quick hands-off look-see. If a building super claims to have found a hand grenade, but it turns out to be a Taiwanese-produced love toy instead, the responding ESU cops will not summon Bomb Squad detectives—not unless they want to be ridiculed for the rest of their natural days in the division. Years ago, ESU called the Bomb Squad on rare occasions. Now, a day doesn't go by without at least one ESU squad looking at a box with wires or a duffel bag with Arabic writing and getting on the radio, saying, "Central K, better notify the Bomb Squad."

ESU's role in bomb jobs is to ICE off the area, (isolate, contain, and evacuate). They will cordon off a perimeter where the device has been located, contain the situation as is until Bomb Squad personnel reach the scene, and evacuate all civilian and nonessential personnel from within range of whatever might go off. There are a lot of people who, when they hear the word *bomb,* decide that they must go see the package or try to stand near it. Cops—regular cops, that is—suffer from the same ailment. And it drives ESU officers nuts. Once the Bomb Squad arrives, from bases in the Bronx or in Greenwich Village in Manhattan, ESU cops will assist the detectives in suiting up and setting up their equipment and anything else the EOD cops would need. If a suspicious package is deemed to be nothing more than a forgotten attaché case, then ESU will update the SOD dispatcher: "Proper ID by the Bomb Squad." If the device turns out to be the real McCoy, then there is usually a long silence from the job and its supervisors, until the words "Central, have Boy-Two respond with the TCV" are heard over the airwaves. Then, anyone listening to the SOD frequency knows that the "oh shit" has happened. A real bomb has been discovered.

Each ESU truck has a special piece of equipment parked in its garage that is to be summoned and brought to a job, anywhere in the city, at any time. Three-Truck in the Bronx and Nine-Truck in Queens have Peacekeeper armored cars, Four-Truck in the Bronx and Eight- and Six-Trucks in Brooklyn have an air bag for jumpers, Three-Truck and Eight-Truck have a CARV truck for large-scale highway mishaps and collapses, and Two-Truck has the RMI and the TCV. The TCV, or total containment vehicle, is a bomb-proof round container that sits on a trailer and can be towed to a location on the rear hitch of an REP. The TCV is ideal for hand grenades, letter bombs, and pipe bombs. If it'll explode and is bigger than a bread box and smaller than a lounge chair, it'll end up inside the TCV. "It's the luck of the draw," claims one Two-Truck cop who always has a hard time backing up the REP with the TCV attachment into the garage on the 126th Street near quarters. "Some trucks get armored cars, and some get air bags. We get to drive around with bombs by our ass!"

There isn't a cop in the NYPD, in any of the five boroughs and in any unit, who would not agree that the Bomb Squad is not the easiest unit in the world to work with! Many of the detectives (the unit is part of the Detective Bureau), though, are former E-men who worked hard and long in ESU before being appointed to the bureau and the Bomb Squad. On the whole, the NYPD's Bomb Squad is among the finest in the nation. It has certainly become one of the world's busiest. Like ESU, the unit is likened to a pressure cooker, although in the Bomb Squad, if you fuck up on a job, you usually end up in some cemetery on Long Island, stone cold in the ground following an inspector's funeral.

There are two types of bomb jobs in the ESU vernacular: potential ordeals and "Oh shit, the device is real!" Under its operations mandate, ESU responds to every significant report of a suspicious object or package—*significant* meaning that ESU does not get called if a half-eaten ham sandwich is discovered in the elevator of a major office building. A suspicious package can be anything from an abandoned briefcase left near a token booth at a subway station to a piece of mail delivered to an executive with gun grease stains, excessive postage, and no return address. And, depending on the season or what's happening in Israel, the Gaza Strip, Northern Ireland, Colombia, or half a million other places around the world from Damascus to a courthouse in Denver, ESU could get anywhere from a handful of calls a week to a dozen in one day. Because Two-Truck's piece of the Manhattan pie covers dozens of sensitive locations, including the world's largest synagogue and the homes of many consulate-generals and ambassadors, the E-cops of Harlem are called to their fair share of suspicious packages and genuine devices. In the past, these have ranged from a kit bag full of diapers left behind at the Plaza Hotel to an improvised incendiary device left near a church.

Many bomb jobs involving Two-Truck center on suspicious packages at sensitive locations that just don't feel right—an attaché case with several locks abandoned on a subway train, a bag of groceries left in front of a diplomatic mission, a package with a third-class label and first-class stamps addressed to a title rather than an individual. Mostly, however, the ID-ing of a suspicious package is routine business. The precinct cops on the scene will summon ESU at the first notice of the package, and the patrol cops will wait until the ESU officers have had a chance to look at the item and determine if it's harmless or if, a few seconds later, the call for the Bomb Squad will go out over the SOD frequency. When it is determined that the Bomb Squad is indeed needed, the dispatcher will also summon EMS and the Fire Department to stand by at a mobilization point either a block away for an outdoor device or a floor below for a suspicious package inside a building. Many of the precinct cops are not happy in dealing with bombs—they've become used to regular patrol work, issuing summonses, answering radio jobs, and interacting with the people in their sectors. Something with the potential to blow up an apartment building daunts them. "All my life," claims a cop in Midtown Manhattan, "I knew that there were two types of people in this world: those who saw the Bomb Squad in operation and stood around to watch and those who got the hell away!"

Not all ESU bomb jobs involve terrorist devices. In one job in the Upper West Side's trendy 2-0 Precinct, Two-Truck was summoned to a swanky apartment building on West 73rd Street between Columbus and Amsterdam Avenue in regard to a most unusual find. The tenant, a World War II veteran and collector of military memorabilia, had passed away, and when his relatives had come to empty out his spacious three-bedroom apartment, they came across some items that warranted a telephone call to the police. Besides several rare bayonets, two musket rifles, and some .50-caliber machine gun ammunition, three 81mm mortar rounds were discovered thrown in a closet, next to a pair of slippers and loafers. "Oh shit," was the only response that one of the 2-0 cops could give when he saw the 81mm High Explosive rounds. "Better get ESU!"

Sgt. Juan Garcia and Police Officer Steve Vales arrived at the location not knowing what to expect, though the sight of the truck and the EMS and Fire Department personnel standing by on the corner of 73rd and Amsterdam did not make many local residents too happy. "What's going on here?" one seventy-year-old woman commented, walking six terriers and smoking a long brown More cigarette, "I demanded to know what's going on," she continued, "you can arrest all my neighbors for all I care, nothing but a bunch of weirdos and freaks in my building. They can all go and fuck themselves!"

"Yes, Ma'am, you have a nice day!"

Upstairs, Garcia and Vales examined the apartment, checked out the .50-caliber and 7.92mm ammunition strewn about the bedroom floor, and, after looking at the shells, determined that it would be very prudent to alert the Bomb Squad "forthwith."

As the cops closed off the apartment, an EMS supervisor walked upstairs and wanted to know where his medics should position themselves, "just in case." A fire lieutenant also came upstairs and wanted to check out the apartment for himself. "Stay downstairs until we need you," one of the precinct cops said.

What do cops talk about at bomb jobs? Bombs, naturally. One of the sergeants, a son of Ireland, began to sing an IRA ditty about blowing up a British patrol in the Armagh, while another cop began talking about an Arnold Schwarzenegger movie in which half of Florida was incinerated. A few jokes about the Polish bomb squad, a few jokes about flying limbs, and a few comments concerning what parts of the city should actually be blown up, and the conversation was deteriorating from bad to worse. Two very attractive females emerged from one of the adjacent apartments, passionately kissing each other good-bye, completely oblivious to the twenty cops gathered in the hallway.

"Oh my God," one of them commented, finally noticing the cops and emergency personnel at her doorstep. "Are we in danger?"

"Don't worry, ma'am," one of the cops volunteered, beaming at the opportunity to be helpful in this situation. "You are in good hands with New York's finest!"

The job came over just as Israeli Prime Minister Benjamin Netanyahu was making one of his pilgrimages to Manhattan, and the Bomb Squad was fifteen blocks away, on alert outside the Essex House Hotel on Central Park South, so the two Bomb Squad detectives were over in a flash. Inside the apartment, the detectives examined the shells and X-rayed them. Determining that they were inert, the detectives quickly left the apartment for the Netanyahu detail, where threats of devices more powerful than three World War II souvenirs were possible.

Not all genuine bomb jobs deal specifically with terrorism—some have equally sinister though more domesticated motives behind the explosive punch. Some drug dealers, operating in northern Manhattan, have threatened or attacked rivals and competitors with explosive devices, ranging from Molotov cocktails, or pipe bombs fitted to gasoline canisters, to indigenously produced hand grenades. In fact, for a while Two-Truck units were plagued by a Dominican drug gang working in Washington Heights that was employing the services of a former Israeli special forces officer to build bombs and grenades so that rival dealers could be taken out with a bang. On many warrants in the 3-3 and 3-4 Two-Truck units would carefully gain access to apartments for narcotics and street crimes, only to find the improvised grenades stored next to the drugs, guns, and cash in safes and wall closets. The devices, some meant to the booby-traps, were good—they showed a sense of mechanical proficiency and ballistic expertise.

Sometimes bomb work has nothing to do with actual devices but rather the potential for routine substances used for criminal purposes, exploding in a massive fireball of death and destruction. One winter afternoon in Harlem, in a dilapidated tenement on Amsterdam Avenue and 138th Street, city marshals were busy evicting a group of tenants who were using a third-floor apartment for the production and distribution of crack cocaine. As the marshals sifted through the debris, the urine-soaked sofas, and the shards of broken glass, they came across a drum containing twelve gallons of ether—unstable ether. Drug dealers use the ether in cooking the cocaine, and when the material is stable, it is relatively safe. When it becomes unstable, a twelve-gallon supply could literally blow an apartment building off its foundation.

The city marshals were awake that brisk afternoon in Harlem. They paid attention to what they were doing and to what they were tossing out of the apartment. When they came across the ether, they contacted the NYPD, the NYPD contacted ESU, and ESU contacted the Department of Environmental Protection, who rushed one of their top chemists to Harlem.

The building in which the ether was found was home

to several families; indeed, the sight of kids playing in front daunted Capt. Ralph Pascullo as he pulled up on the scene to supervise the situation. First and foremost, Pascullo ordered the building with the ether and the two on either side evacuated; the street was cordoned off and the LaGuardia truck summoned from Eight-Truck in Brooklyn. The LaGuardia truck is a large maroon-steel mesh that resembles an indoor tennis tent carried on a flatbed truck; the wire mesh is made of the same steel cables found on the Verrazano Narrows Bridge connecting Brooklyn and Staten Island. The truck is designed to be a safe transport for a device until it can be safely disposed of in the Bronx. "If it's too big for the LaGuardia truck," according to one ESU sergeant, "then New York City is truly in deep shit."

Unstable ether, once it has crystallized, is one of the most explosive and volatile chemicals around. Anything could cause it to erupt—static electricity, a charge coming from a police radio, possibly even the heat from a police officer's hands. As Two-Truck units helped the Bomb Squad detectives suit up, nervous eyes watched the drum, hoping that the next thing they would see would not be part of Harlem flying a hundred feet into the air. The Bomb Squad detectives were true pros, however. They packaged the material inside the truck and secured it. Police Officers Dave Kayen and Dave Kayo of Eight-Truck were given the awesome task of driving the hulking vehicle slowly across the Cross-Bronx Expressway. With a Highway Unit escort and Captain Pascullo following close behind, the LaGuardia truck made it to the Bronx without incident or explosions.

When the Bomb Squad is called in for a genuine device, materials that really can explode, disposal takes place at the NYPD Range at Rodman's Neck in the Bronx, just off the coast of the Eastchester Bay and the Long Island Sound. Getting to Rodman's Neck, however, especially on highways with New York traffic and New York drivers, is not always a sure thing. The motorcade moves slowly and carefully, often ending up as the target of honking horns and curses from passing motorists.

An influx of one type of job or another, like steady EDPs or pin jobs, usually commences with one big, nasty, bizarre, and often frightening job. Perp jobs and hits always follow a cop shooting. EDPs tend to come out in the spring. And summer, when the sun shines free and the air is warm and innocent, is usually a good time for people to floor their gas pedals and end up wrapped around a highway divider. Bomb jobs are one of the most seasonal aspects of ESU work. If something happens in the Middle East, for example, some bus blows up or someone gets whacked inside a refugee camp, then calls to 911 concerning suspicious packages increase tenfold. When the Unabomber was driving everyone insane with his postal campaign of package paranoia, each time one of his devices exploded in one part of the country or another, New Yorkers were sure that the package they had just received from Sears or from nutty Uncle Leo was destined to explode. And when abortion clinics are bombed, sensitive locations throughout the city become increasingly nervous, aware of any and all possible threats.

Still, to most New Yorkers, the very notion of a bomb exploding in the city is a foreign concept too bizarre to truly believe. The notion that "it can't happen here" was extinguished somewhat following the series of bus and suicide bombings in Israel—especially since a Hamas commander, Musa Abu Marzuk, was sitting pretty watching cable TV and eating baloney sandwiches at the Manhattan Corrections Center awaiting deportation.

On January 13, 1997, however, there would be no mishandling of bomb jobs. Suspicious devices were deadly business. Winter is that special time for explosives, as well.

Eleven days earlier, on January 2, 1997, the Washington, D.C., office of *Al-Hayat,* an Arabic-language newspaper based in London and owned by Saudi Prince Khalid bin Sultan, received five packages, all with an Alexandria, Egypt, postmark and all with a computer-generated label and a number written on the envelope. Each letter was five and a half inches by six and a half inches and was neither bulky nor too tightly wrapped. Yet each contained an amply supply of Grade A Czechoslovak-produced Semtex plastic explosives, needles, wiring, and electrical contacts—the telltale signs of a professionally produced letter bomb meant to maim or kill anyone who opened it. An alert clerk in the *Al-Hayat* mailroom thought something about the packages was suspicious, and he contacted security. Hours later, FBI agents and Washington, D.C., Metropolitan Police bomb technicians in heavy Kevlar suits were removing the packets for disposal.

That same day, two similar packages were received at the federal penitentiary in Fort Leavenworth, Kansas, and a third intercepted at the Fort Leavenworth Post Office.

All the envelopes were mailed on December 21, 1996, and miraculously none of the devices exploded.

Because of the Alexandria postmark, federal officials were sure that the letter bombs were the handiwork of supporters of jailed Egyptian radical cleric Sheikh Omar Abdel-Rahman. Because *Al-Hayat* had been critical of the Egyptian fundamentalist movement, it seemed likely that an Egyptian-based terrorist group would wish to exact some revenge against one of the few voices of secular moderation in the Arab world. The fact that several of the World trade Center conspirators were serving their life-without-parole sentences in Leavenworth caused red flags to wave wildly at FBI headquarters in Washington. Counterterrorisim experts believed it wouldn't be long until these devices began to show up in New York City. They would have more than a week to wait.

At 11:00 A.M. on January 13, mail was being sorted at the ultra-busy, ultra-chaotic United Nations mailroom. More than 30,000 pieces of mail are received at the international organization's world headquarters every day, and keeping the flow of letters moving is almost as monumental a task as achieving world peace. As the mail was sorted, directed, and placed on delivery carts, two letters, both five and a half inches by six and a half inches, both addressed to *Al-Hayat,* and both bearing Egyptian postmarks, were noticed by a clerk. Something about them looked suspicious, and the floor's security chief dialed 911. Police were summoned, and ESU responded with units from One-Truck and the TCV from Two-Truck. Capt. Ralph Pascullo, the citywide patrol captain, raced to 45th Street and First Avenue to supervise what now promised to be a very busy day.

The United Nations is one of those odd footnotes to the American jurisdiction equation—an international organization with its own armed security contingent that is considered sovereign international territory on the eastern shores of Manhattan Island. The NYPD's jurisdiction on the premises is subject to a gentleman's agreement and letters of understanding and memos on file at One Police Plaza. The UN security contingent is under the direct command of the UN, and, as a result, the organization's best interests are often the dominant factor in how law enforcement is handled on the premises. Whether it responds to tactical security for UN 50 or to handle a confirmed letter bomb, the NYPD is always on its best behavior inside the confines of "international territory." From the UN's point of view, cooperation with the NYPD depends on discretion and in not making the UN look bad. Yet having to evacuate a thirty-story office building with thousands of employees, many of them temperamental diplomats, is never a public relations plus.

The sight of ESU personnel and Bomb Squad officers, their radios chattering away and their blue fatigues a far cry from the three-piece suits worn by many diplomats, was not the type of image that UN officials promote, and the obvious need for cooperation began to slip away in the bullshit of the moment. At first, the head of security had decided generously to "permit" the Bomb

Squad commanding officer to go upstairs to where the devices were isolated, but he didn't want the ESU cops on the premises. When there is a possibility of a real device, it is ESU's job help Bomb Squad detectives suit up, to help in the containment of the device, and because of their medical training, to provide immediate emergency care to the technician should the device detonate prematurely. The Bomb Squad CO, known as a cantankerous soul in his own right who did not always see eye-to-eye with ESU officers, refused to go upstairs and examine the package unless ESU personnel came along. "These guys are essential in us doing our job," he explained to the head of UN security. "They help us suit up, they help us with tools and equipment, and in case something blows up, namely us, they provide us with emergency trauma care. If they don't go up, neither do we!"

Faced with a battle of wills and a live explosive device, the head of UN security relented and allowed both ESU and the Bomb Squad to go upstairs and do their job. By all outside appearances, and by material read off the Teletype from the FBI concerning the devices examined in Washington, D.C., and in Leavenworth, the envelope addressed to *Al-Hayat* was the genuine article. This was not a forgotten briefcase on the E train, and it wasn't an inert mortar shell. This was disfigurement and death in a package the size of a greeting card.

Slowly and very gingerly, the letter bomb was carried downstairs to the underground parking garage at its northern entrance. As the Two-Truck officers looked on, all SWAT-ed out and ready to drive the TCV to the range, the Bomb Squad opted to dispose of the device in the basement of the United Nations. UN security personnel had prestored scores of sandbags in the basement of the parking garage for just such an eventuality. ESU cops grabbed the sandbags and quickly built a secured U-shaped protective wall. A Bomb Squad detective, looking as if he were moving in slow-motion, placed the letter against the sandbags and then positioned a small pipelike apparatus hooked up to a water canister. The device, a Bomb Squad technician's best friend, shot a shotgun-shell-like burst of high-pressure water into the central electronic mechanism of the bomb and destroyed its ability to explode. It also preserved much of the device for the investigation to follow. Before the water burst was launched, all those in the parking garage bit their nails and watched with anxious impatience. Would it explode anyway? Which way would the nails inside fly? The only definite about bomb work was that each job, each device, was very deadly. In fact, the deadly stakes involved in handling such devices were hammered home several thousand miles away. That same day, at nearly the same time, a letter bomb addressed to *Al-Hayat* exploded in the paper's London bureau, critically injuring two people.

That day, New Yorkers became bomb-sensitive or, to be more accurate, bomb-terrified. There were reports of a suspicious package in the Israeli mission at 42nd Street and Second Avenue (it turned out to be a computer motherboard), a suspicious package at the Tudor Hotel near 42nd Street and First Avenue (it turned out to be a gift-wrapped box of Godiva chocolates), and a suspicious package at the Colgate Building (it turned out to be a hoax sent in by some nut). Add to the mix the scared, the copycats, the psychos, and the sadistic, and a bomb scare engulfing the city can have the NYPD running around rampant. For ESU, bomb jobs mean units are taken off patrol and assets, already stretched thin, are spread even more so. On January 13, One-Truck units were busy assisting the Bomb Squad at the United Nations, Boy-Two was occupied with the TCV Two-Truck units were patrolling One-Truck's area. Three-Truck came into Harlem to help out Two-Truck, and Four-Truck and Ten-Truck assisted in covering Three-Truck's area. Adding to the bureaucratic mix of shifting units, patrol schedules knocked off their mark, and overtime slips, when one takes into consideration the number of streets, avenues, and access roads blocked off when a bomb scare is in place, the city that never sleeps becomes a city that barely moves. Even under the gridlocked thoroughfares, in what is considered the fastest and most efficient means of getting around in New York City, the subways were not immune from bomb hoaxes and scares. A report of a suspicious package at the IND line subway station at Queens Plaza shut down trains moving in and out of the city for nearly two hours.

For Capt. Ralph Pascullo and the men of One-Truck and Two-Truck, the eight-to-four tour had been an exhausting one. They had raced about, without letup, chasing imaginary bombs and the genuine article. As the Second Squad returned to home bases in Lower Manhattan at 21st Street and up in Harlem at 126th Street, the Third Squad working in Manhattan would have little time to grab a relaxing cup of coffee or engage in some in-quarters chitchat. Following the morning's first bomb, the United Nations was slowly and methodically examining more than 80,000 pieces of undelivered mail in its facility. Many of the letters and packages were fluoroscoped. Much of the mail, including correspondence to ambassadors from Bosnia and Victoria's Secret catalogs, was routine. The work was tedious, dangerous, and successful. A second letter bomb was found in the UN's mail-room at 4:15 P.M., a third at 9:00 P.M., and the fourth and final device at midnight. Sgt. Juan Garcia, the city north supervisor when the last three devices were discovered, did not like bomb jobs. Having witnessed the destruction and devastation in both Lower Manhattan and Oklahoma City, this was one aspect of the job he could do without.

Still, there is a certain mystery about bombs, a certain sense that "this package cannot be an explosive device," that still survives in the minds of many of New York's finest, even E-men. Some ESU cops, especially those working in slower trucks, have been known to move and open suspicious packages, not willing to wait for the Bomb Squad to examine their interiors. "It boggles my mind," claims an ESU sergeant who has witnessed this lackadaisical attitude and has ripped many a new asshole for cops not taking every bomb job seriously. "When these cops touch the wrong package, and their eyes and limbs fly across the East River, then they'll finally learn."

There is justice in some bomb jobs—sometimes what's good for the goose ends up being good for the gander.

On a unseasonably warm March afternoon, a day when Fifth Avenue was aglow in bright orange courtesy of a merciful sun, pedestrians on New York's great avenue of luxury and opulence allowed their minds to drift with thoughts of the coming spring. Even the postal workers delivering mail to the many doctors, lawyers, debutantes, and diplomats who live on Manhattan's Gold Coast were enjoying the carefree day. Yet at 14 East 79th Street on the corner of Fifth Avenue, thoughts were less whimsical. At the Iraqi mission, of all places, the U.S. Postal Service had delivered two bulky packages, addressed in a clear though somewhat eye-catching handwriting. The return address was local but unknown. Adding to the confusion and heart-pumping concern was the fact that there were postmarks on the packages from New York, as well as several other states. Iraqi security officials called 911. The 19th Precinct called ESU. Sgt. Kenny Bowen and the officers from Two-Truck's First Squad were rolling moments later.

The NYPD considers mosques, synagogues, missions, and other such locations to be "sensitive." The Iraqi mission to the United Nations is considered ultra-sensitive. Not only were these people, thanks to Saddam Hussein and the Gulf War, the enemy, but, because of that fact, keeping them safe from a terrorist bomb was a matter of great political sensitivity. Even if ESU and the Bomb Squad performed above and beyond the call of duty, and something happened, around the world and in the eyes of many Arabs it might look as if the NYPD just didn't give a damn about this one.

For the cops Two-Truck, it is a constant tugging at the psyche to have to balance political sensitivities, the ranting and raving of a Third World diplomat, the political worries of a duty captain, and with their desire to secure a device, isolate it, and make it back home to the suburbs at the end of the eight-to-four. Who cares about Iraq or some nut with an agenda? Just make it home in one piece, and in time to beat traffic on the Hutchinson River Parkway.

Sometimes packages are deemed suspicious just because of the crazy handwriting the mailer scribbled on the package. When the words "To: His Excellency, Ambassador . . ." are written in a manner that would embarrass a kindergarten dropout, the package might be suspicious. Added to that, the bulkiness of a package, an overabundance of postage, and even gun grease or visible wires are all signs for the "Oh shits." This package, however, just didn't seem right. Sergeant Bowen, not known to overreact, calmly and methodically examined the two packages without touching them, made an instantaneous conclusion, and requested the immediate presence of the Bomb Squad. The city north supervisor for the tour, en route to an EDP at a school in Lower Manhattan, quickly swung his Caprice around back uptown toward the bomb job.

Bowen instructed the SOD dispatcher to clear off the corner of 79th Street and Madison Avenue as a mobilization point for EMS and the Fire Department. If anything was going to blow, this was not the neighborhood to let a building burn or let the wounded lie unattended.

Bomb jobs with foreign missions and consulates are not always the smoothest of operations. Some diplomats are truly friendly and concerned not only with the ongoing job transpiring in their mail room but also with the welfare of the cops. Some diplomats, from some countries, view the cops walking about their premises as an annoyance and an intrusion. Nasty stares and rude comments in languages that require spitting face the ESU cops—along with the job at hand of anxiously waiting while whatever might be inside the package gets ready to explode. It's a sensitive business, too. If inside the mission of some Middle Eastern nation, for example, the diplomats begin to assault the cops with anti-American slogans or other nonsense, the cops are not at liberty to yell back and give them a piece of their mind. By the same token, on a job at a British installation, for example, Irish-American cops cannot begin humming tunes from the Provisional IRA's hit parade or a neat little ditty about how twenty-six plus six equals one (a reference to the counties in the Irish isles).

The Bomb Squad also treats job at missions or consulates with greater seriousness—after all, someone with an agenda is far likelier to send an improvised device to a consulate than to a little old lady in Canarsie whose sole transgression in life is occasionally jaywalking.

The initial Bomb Squad treatment of any suspicious package is to X-ray it. If the bulky package is seen to be nothing more than a sweatshirt and a note, then the job is over. If, however, the bulk is a cover for a small strip of pipe and a detonating mechanism, then the "Oh shits" are sounded loud for all to hear.

Luckily, the Iraqi mission job turned out to be nothing more than newspapers sent in by some psycho. The packages weren't expected by anyone on the staff, but they weren't going to explode, and that meant that the NYPD was no longer needed and, as indicated by the quick show of the door, no longer welcome, either.

"I hate bomb jobs, Sarge," one of the emergency cops told his boss as they assembled their gear and hightailed it out of the high-rent district back to the more comfortable confines of Harlem.

"Don't we all?" was the reply. "Don't we all!"

Days later, Sergeant Bowen's First Squad would be summoned again to a call on a suspicious package. This time it wasn't at the United Nations or at a consulate but at a drug location, in the 3-2 Precinct, on St. Nicholas Avenue between 145th and 146th streets. There was nothing out of the ordinary about this job, other than the possibility that a large explosion could kill dozens. Luckily, nothing detonated, and it is business as usual for the cops of Two-Truck and the ESU, just business as usual.

13

(A)mido Black, (B)ullets, (C)orpses, (D)rugs, (E)vidence . . . : The Two-Truck Alphabet of Evidence Recovery

"The FBI said that this was impossible, but I told 'em that whatever the feds can't recover with million-dollar gizmos, Emergency Service can get for us with their eyes closed!"—A 3-2 Precinct homicide detective on an evidence recovery

In the film *Dirty Harry,* Clint Eastwood's new partner, a wide-eyed rookie to homicide, wonders aloud why rogue loner Inspector Harry Callahan is called "Dirty Harry." "Well," Harry tells his partner after a jumper job, "because I get every dirty job in the book." ESU in many ways is just like Clint Eastwood in that title role. Every dirty, unstomachable, and unfathomable job that comes along in the department, from toxic waste removal to searching a Harlem sidewalk caked with someone's brain for bullet fragments, ends up involving ESU. After all, they have the specialized tools, and they have the training. "ESU cops," according to one precinct captain, "are also perfectionists and hate to leave a job until it is done and done right. Which is why we call them so often."

Anytime, Anywhere!

One of ESU's mandated tasks is evidence recovery, and whenever a precinct, a detective squad, or even the federal government requires the special talents of ESU to pull out bullets, bomb fragments, and human remains from a crime scene, they are called to action. It is one of the most delicate of ESU tasks, since the successful removal or recovery of a valuable piece of evidence buried in a lot or embedded in a wall can be the needle in a haystack that makes the difference in the conviction of a heartless perp. Evidence recovery is backbreaking work, and it is tedious. One of the largest ESU evidence salvation operations was in the wake of the February 26, 1993, bombing of the World Trade Center, when cops, sometimes working twelve-hour shifts in a six-story-high crater underneath one of man's great architectural achievements, spearheaded the federal government's investigation that recovered evidence, including the van axle that led to Mohammed Salameh.

In the movies or on TV, the search for evidence always appears to be dramatic, glamorous, and gratifying. That's why there is a Hollywood, of course. On the streets, evidence searches are among the most tedious, dirty, and despicable tasks an E-man can be called upon to perform. Realistically, routine evidence searches are the domain of the patrol cops. They search the initial crime scene area with their eyes and high-powdered flashlights, and then the detectives, usually hours later, come back to the scene with their high-powered beacons and eagle eyes for secondary searches. The detectives in the Crime Scene Unit are next in line to search for clues at a crime scene, to find blood prints, pieces of fiber that might be linked to a perpetrator or the victim, and any telltale signs of physical evidence that can be helpful in the investigation and prosecution of a criminal case. More often than not, however, the call comes out on the SOD radio for ESU to "assist" (it really means "please come and do all the gut-wrenching work") in a crime scene or evidence search.

"Emergency Service Adam-Two," the dispatcher will

summon. "In the confines of the 2-6 Precinct, you are being requested by the 2-6 Squad to search for a weapon in a sewer."

"Adam-Two," is the response, with a foreboding cadence to the voice. "That's a ten-four."

Evidence recovery throughout the city is quite similar—after all, a ten-week-old corpse in Brooklyn smells no different from a ten-week-old corpse in Harlem. Yet the higher the crime rate in an area, the more calls for evidence recovery ESU gets. And sometimes the more rampant the crime rate, the more bizarre the crimes.

During patrol on eight-to-four in Harlem, Police Officers Dan Donnelly and Eddie Torres were driving by some of the more colorful parts of the Upper West Side when they were summoned to the confines for the 3-2 Precinct on West 135th Street to help homicide detectives and crime scene technicians gather some rather tricky evidence. Over the air, the call came in with a request that the responding unit bring with it a "torch." "Either this is some nasty crime scene," Eddie Torres commented, "or we are gonna have a barbecue!"

Inside the building, a private though federally funded housing project with its own small and very active police force, NYPD detectives were sifting through the remnants of an apartment in search of evidence in a fresh though highly vicious homicide. Inside a fourth-floor apartment, a male in his mid-forties had been brutally slashed and stabbed and a beer bottle shoved violently, bottom side up, straight up his behind. "I guess this puts a new spin on the words bottoms up?" one of the detectives joked, laughing out the right side of his mouth as he gulped a stale cup of 7-Eleven coffee and smoked his tenth cigarette of the hour. The windows of the apartment were cracked wide open, and for good reason. The victim had been lying about, bottoms up, for nearly a week before tenants noticed that the stench in the hallway was worse than usual. When precinct cops finally made their way inside the apartment, it was overwhelming. The heat, as in most project buildings, was on full blast, and all the windows were closed. Maggots were already busy at work on the bloated corpse. One of the 3-2 Precinct cops barfed on the scene. Detectives did not have an easier go of it, either.

The killer, or killers, had made a mess of things. This wasn't a neat shot to the head on a street corner. It was a violent struggle accentuated by broken furniture, damaged walls, and blood and human tissue sprayed throughout the apartment. Blood was on the walls, on the floors, and on the ceilings. Yet detectives also found bloody footprints, sneaker prints that must have belonged to the murderer. The prints were found on the kitchen floor tiling, and here lay the problem. The detectives could produce top-grade photographs of the prints for possible use in a trial, but photos alone might not hold up in court. If they could pull up the tiles themselves, then they would have an irrefutable piece of evidence that could seal a conviction. The homicide detectives and crime scene detectives working the apartment sprinkled the floor with a chemical compound called Amido Black that picks up blood prints and makes them indelible. The problem was that as they attempted to peel the tiles back from the floor, the tiles began to crack and disintegrate. They were even thinking of sawing off a section of the floor, but the blade slicing through the ceramic tile and wood most certainly would have destroyed more than it would have salvaged. Perplexed and faced with a challenge, the detectives did what all cops do when they need help: they summoned ESU.

When cops volunteer into ESU, the captains, lieutenants, and sergeants who review each application always check the résumés for skills unrelated to police work. Can the cop drive a truck, operate heavy machinery, handle electrical work, cook? Most cops have a second skill or profession before coming into the unit. Many have worked in construction and plumbing. All E-cops can work wonders with their hands.

As Officers Donnelly and Torres came to the apartment and immediately began to breathe differently as the wretched stench bit their nostrils, they were introduced to the problem at hand. "No problem," Donnelly said as he assessed the job and conferred with his partner. "Emergency Adam-Two." Donnelly went over the air. "Have Truck-Two respond over here to 135th Street with the torch."

Ten minutes later, Sergeant Garcia wheeled in a heavy gas cylinder along with the welder's torch that ESU uses on various jobs from rescues to searches. "What do we have here?" Garcia asked, though after hearing the spiel from the detectives, his sole comment was, "If anyone can do it, my guys can!"

The work was laborious and incredibly delicate. The white-hot flame, not handled carefully, could seriously maim anyone nearby. Too much of the flame, and the evidence would be destroyed, Amido Blue or not. One swing in the right direction with the flaming rod, and an apartment in Harlem would begin to smolder.

Detectives, according to one detective working the Rockaways, are uncontrollable yentas—the Yiddish term for *busybody*—and the chance to bullshit with cops in a different unit is always attended to with zealous abandon. They talk about overtime, politics, the Yankees, and romantic or marital difficulties. "I've been in love with the same woman for thirty years," one detective boasts as he wipes cigarette ashes from his jovial middle-age spread, "and if my wife ever finds out, I'm a dead man!"

"Don't start a fire," a detective yelled now as he watched the flame move about in the kitchen. "I don't want to have to worry about some of the evidence here suddenly disappearing."

"You guys have problems with them?" one of the Emergency cops asked, referring to the firemen.

"We had this robbery arson once in a bodega near the Harlem River projects, and as FD left, the owner came up to one of the precinct lieutenants, crying and saying, 'They took my money, fifteen hundred dollars, my life savings, and now I'll lose the business!' Not knowing what he was talking about, the lieutenant was taken to the back, where he was shown a fire safe, cracked to pieces by an ax. The perps, of course, had guns and gasoline. Well, this lieutenant was an old school Irishman who took shit from no one. He went into his sector car, drove to the fire house, and gave them fifteen minutes, no questions asked, to return the money or else he'd lock up everyone there. Lo and behold, fifteen minutes later, a fire truck pulls up in front of the bodega, and two firemen walk in slowly and nervously. Seconds later, they leave, and there's fifteen hundred dollars on the counter. No fucking questions asked!"

"Unbelievable," one of the cops said. "I would have locked them up."

The talking and the work continued. After an hour of hard though truly delicate labor, the E-men managed to pull off two tiles in pristine condition. The evidence was placed in an envelope, cataloged, and prepared for processing. "We called the feds, and they said that this couldn't be done," one of the detectives boasted, proud that the NYPD had proved the FBI wrong, "but I knew if anyone in the world could do it, it was ESU!"

The job on 135th Street was a good one but not an uncommon occurrence. ESU is often called upon to search cars floating in the river for bodies and drugs and often summoned to search sewers, street gratings, and bushes for ditched weapons and narcotics. There isn't a crack house in Harlem that hasn't had its floorboards ripped up by ESU in search of drugs and cash. Sometimes entire buildings have been literally gutted by ESU squads searching for hidden compartments under floorboards, through brick walls, and over steel girders.

If there is an aspect of evidence recovery that the ESU cops enjoy, it is narcotics recovery. After drilling, pounding, sawing, cutting, and prying, being able to play a role in taking drugs off the streets is incredibly rewarding. Perps may not be the smartest souls when it comes to staying out of jail, but they are masters at camouflaging their drug stashes. In apartments, they have built-in wall safes with booby-trap gauntlets and trap door hazards. Perps have hidden guns inside bed frames and underneath stoves. They have stored ammunition in baby cribs. Yet the perps of today have made the greatest strides in narcotics hiding in the automotive field. They now send their BMWs, Lexus sedans, and Cadillacs to ghetto workshops where secret compartments are fitted into tire supports, steering columns, floorboards, and even retractable roofs. A traffic stop by a precinct unit or narcotics can yield five million dollars in coke stored in the trunk or a kilo of heroin inside the gearbox of a Mercedes sports car.

When it comes to using tools and sweat for evidence recovery, ESU's specialty is getting into safes—from the always fun fire safes, to heavy-duty security safes designed for the defense industry. There are some in ESU, like Six-Truck's legendary safecracker Police Officer Carl Russo, who could have enjoyed a lucrative second career as a cat burglar, and there are others who are so handy at picking locks that they should have taken the exam for service in the CIA.

For narcotics cops, Hamilton Place is one of those streets in Harlem where virtually every block, every building, and in some cases every apartment are known as "bad." A rough stretch of brownstones and grayish-brown apartment buildings is marked for suffering by hordes of drug gangs and homicidal narcotics pushers who have turned this piece of northern Harlem, only two blocks from the fenced-in walls of the City University of New York, into a dot on the map that is worked by virtually every local, state, and federal law enforcement agency. "We are summoned to Hamilton Place so often," claims one Two-Truck veteran, "that the city might just save on fuel by moving our quarters there."

On one frigid winter's night, during the four-to-twelve, Officers John D'Allara and Dan Donnelly were patrolling the stretches of Washington Heights in the Boy car, driving past the throngs of Christmas shoppers on Broadway and 181st Street by the 3-4 Precinct. There are livery cabs double- and triple-parked, peddlers operating out of stalls and the trunks of their cars selling designer jeans, jackets, and handbags, and Latin women wearing fur coats and tight jeans, walking up and down the boulevard on shopping sprees. By 3-4 Precinct standards, it's a quiet night. It was nearly mealtime, and nobody had been shot yet.

As the Boy car began to head south, back into the confines of Harlem, Boy Two was summoned to the 3-0 Precinct, to an apartment building right off the split with Broadway and 137th Street, for "evidence recovery." Hamilton Place and evidence can mean only one thing: drugs.

Back in September 1996, Police Commissioner Howard Safir spearheaded a large-scale drug sweep of northern Manhattan, from Columbia University to the water border with the Bronx, involving the NYPD, the State Police, the DEA, the U.S. Marshals Service, the FBI, ATF, Customs, Immigration and Naturalization, even, it was proposed, the U.S. Border Patrol. Known as the Northern Manhattan Initiative, the operation was a joint NYPD-federal effort to break the backs of the more than 150 known drug gangs that have turned Hamilton Place and the northern corridor of Manhattan between Harlem and Washington Heights into an American narcotics epicenter, responsible for much of the illegal narcotics sold on the northern seaboard. It was hard work, and it was extremely dangerous. Those who work the drug trade are ruthless and desperate guns for hire, who will kill, torture, and maim anyone who interferes with their million-dollar-a-week enterprises. They employ lookouts, enforcers, and shooters. Their headquarters are protected by surveillance cameras, pit bulls, and weapons. There isn't a drug location hit that doesn't turn up a mini-arsenal.

The Northern Manhattan Initiative was a busy time

for law enforcement agencies assigned to the drug sweep, and it was a busy time for ESU and Two-Truck. Besides the countless warrants served with local precinct squads and with FBI SWAT teams, there were apartments to be searched and ripped apart and safes to be opened. On this wintry night, narcotics detectives had hit an apartment in which perps, drugs, cash, and guns were found. The plainclothes officers, some masquerading as local drug sellers and consumers, fit into the surroundings like pieces in a puzzle; others were so big, so unmistakably NYPD-Irish, and so blue-eyed and blue-hearted that they simply did their best not to stick out too much. As the Boy-Two pulled up at the location, they encountered a six-foot-nine cop with blue eyes and a blue NYPD windbreaker watching a van full of prisoners. "It's on the fifth floor, apartment Five-C," the cop advised. "A safe was found in a wall inside a very busy bad location."

Breaking into a safe is not an easy task—each one is different, and sometimes the most flimsy-looking devices are a bitch to open, and sometimes a cast-iron relic that could have been used at Fort Knox can be cracked open with the ease of slicing through an eggshell. When called to open a safe, ESU cops take with them their rabbit tool, the Haligan tool, two sets of sledgehammers, and each officer's own personal toolbox. In apartment 5-C, narcotics cops had done a good job in a cop's version of urban renewal. The door had been popped off its hinges, floors ripped up, sofas sliced open and tossed about, plumbing ripped out, and a bedroom reduced to wooden splinters and paint chips. "Here's the safe," a narcotics lieutenant instructed D'Allara and Donnelly. "So far, we've found a lot of shit here, some hundred thousand dollars in cash and a lot of guns, so we think that whatever is inside the safe must be good!"

"No problem, Loo," Officer Donnelly replied as he and D'Allara stood back for a minute to size up the safe and what they'd do to get into it. "How about the Hurst tool and then the sledge, John?"

"Sounds good to me!"

The safe was a fire safe, ostensibly meant to protect valuables from the high-heat effects of an apartment blaze. Weighing about 200 pounds, the safe was a bulky black box that had been secured in a wall closet by wooden planks and heavy-duty screws. The two cops attempted to get through the back panels of the safe for about five minutes, though all the device managed to do was bend the metal and distort the mechanism. After about ten minutes of backbreaking work, it was decided to try the halogen and the sledge. The cops began banging away with the long metal tools for the better part of a half hour, each strike of the sledge onto the halogen causing a bang that sounded like a howitzer going off. The E-cops wiped the sweat from their brows and tried once again. The narcotics officers wanted to get out of the apartment quickly, as they had a score of suspects waiting to be interviewed at the precinct—this had been a good bust, and perhaps some of the mutts would be willing to give up their bosses in exchange for a deal. "Any idea how much longer this is going to take?" the lieutenant asked. "I retire in about six years."

"No problem, Loo, we are just about there."

One final smash with the sledge, and the safe's rear steel panel popped loose, allowing the E-cops to chip away at the asbestos back frame that was the fire safe's protective antiflame barrier. "If you don't want to die of lung cancer in a few years," one of the officers suggested, "you might want to wait in the next room." The asbestos was hardened like a slab of concrete, but chipping away at it was a lot easier than breaking through steel. After a few more minutes of sledging and hammering away, Donnelly finally saw a gap that was large enough for the detectives to place their hands inside and remove any additional evidence. "The mother lode must be in there," one of the narcotics cops commented, barely able to contain his anticipation. "Anyone want to wager what we'll find inside?"

Like everything in police work, the unexpected always

lands in your lap, and what you hope to seize or gain always turns out to be a big zero. Inside the safe that had taken nearly an hour of muscle-aching effort to open, the NYPD recovered two hundred dollars in cash and a pack of cigarettes. The E-cops were surprised; the narcotics officers were mad. "What kind of stupid, fucking, retarded bunch of mentally challenged perps leave hundreds of thousands of dollars in cash, not to mention coke and guns, in an apartment and out in the open but leave only a few hundred in twenties inside a wall safe? What is this world coming to?"

The E-cops left before one of the narcotics supervisors popped a blood vessel from aggravation, happy that they had gained access to the safe but somewhat disappointed that the haul wasn't larger. Before they could head back to quarters, Boy-Two received another call for evidence stemming from the Northern Manhattan Initiative. Narcotics units working the 3-3 Precinct on 161st Street between Broadway and Amsterdam had summoned ESU to secure a firearm. As a drug location, 161st Street makes Hamilton Place look peaceful and picturesque. Nestled near the border of Harlem and Washington Heights, 161st between Amsterdam and Broadway is a notorious block of shot-out streetlights, brownstones covered in graffiti, and heavily armed drug gangs protecting their turf with 9mms and .50-caliber Desert Eagle handguns. Inside an apartment hit by the Initiative, detectives came across a few kilos of cocaine, cash, and an arsenal including a Streetsweeper shotgun and what looked like the gun that killed Lincoln.

The narcotics cops, eager to book the antique weapon into evidence, knew that a round was in the chamber, but the weapon was far too old to be handled safely by any of the cops bringing the crates of evidence down to their van. D'Allara, a weapons expert and always eager to crack a joke, looked at the weapons, slid back a bolt, opened the cylinder containing the rounds, and removed the one bullet in the chamber. "This is a really old .45," Officer D'Allara pointed out. "It dates back a hundred years or so, and in fact we have officers in this unit who are so old that this might have been their service revolver."

Body recovery, or body part recovery, is not a glamorous aspect of evidence searches, and no job was a bigger excavation, in the true sense of the word, than a remarkable job well done by ESU in one of Harlem's most dangerous confines—from a drug den's basement to the murky depths of the Hudson River. Even from veteran Harlem cops, whether a ten-year veteran of Two-Truck or a sergeant in the 3-2 Precinct, if you mention the words *Bradhurst Avenue,* the response is usually, "What a fucking shithole." Splitting off from Edgecome Avenue at 141 Street, Bradhurst is a small street that runs north to 155th Street and the entrance to the Polo Ground Houses, a squalor-ridden project built atop the memories of the old Polo Grounds at Coogan's Bluff where a young Willie Mays, then playing with the New York Giants, amazed a generation of baseball fans. Bradhurst Avenue looks more like Beirut at the height of the Lebanese civil war than it does a street in New York City at a time when crime in the Big Apple is nearing its lowest rates since the days when Ozzie and Harriet were on TV and a subway ride cost a dime.

Bradhurst Avenue is urban decay and destruction at its worst—a Swiss Alps of bombed-out building, squatters, drug infestation, and despair. If a building isn't condemned, burned out, wrecked, or inhabited by squatters or crack whores, then it's in the minority. "Even by Harlem standards, this is shitty," claims one veteran cop who has seen the best and the worst of Manhattan North. "This place is a scene out of Armageddon with an NYC zip code.

Yet Bradhurst Avenue, for all its destructive charm, was a million-dollar business center for a drug gang known as the "Preacher Crew," a group that worked the streets of the Bronx and Upper Manhattan for nearly fifteen years with untold cruelty and remarkable viciousness. Police sources attributed nearly eighty homicides to the group that was allegedly headed by Clarence Hartley and John Cuff, a former housing cop. The gang routinely extorted money from drug dealers, sold drugs, and punished without mercy anyone not falling in line with torture, savage beatings, and murders. One building, a burnt-out shell of a tenement on Bradhurst and 148th Street, was, federal officials believed, used by the gang as a dumping house for the bodies of its victims.

In January 1996, the U.S. Attorney's office was busy working on its federal indictment and prosecution of the Preacher Crew, and they needed evidence linking the kingpins to their murderous trail. The Bradhurst Avenue building was believed to be the final resting place of one of the crew's victims, former gang lieutenant Anthony Boatwright, whose head and charred arms were believed to have been dumped in the building. But because a fire had destroyed much of the inner structure, it was not safe for federal investigators to go inside and engage in the laborious work of sifting though the debris for bones and teeth. Luckily for the FBI, ESU was more than happy to pitch in.

Under the command of Lt. John McArdle and the Second Squad's Sgt. Jimmy Spratt, teams of ESU personnel proved to the federal authorities just why ESU was so different from every other unit in American law enforcement. ESU officers were lowered into the burned-out crater courtesy of a heavy-duty crane in steel cages normally used for construction work. With porta-lights providing illumination, the crew worked amid the splinters, broken glass, hypodermic needles, and other debris to search every inch of the building's inner skeleton for evidence that could be used in the forthcoming trial. Because the building's roof was destroyed in the fire that initially gutted and destroyed the structure, ESU officers constructed a wooden platform large enough to be lowered atop the roof of the building when the search wasn't under way to maintain the evidence. Called the "dance floor" by the cops, it was constructed in a matter of hours and amazed federal officials who joined the E-cops in the exhaustive search. New York City had been fortunate in the winter of 1996–97, with few days ever dipping below the freezing mark, but the week the excavations began, New York City was facing the coldest week in perhaps a hundred years. Temperatures hovered at five degrees, and wind chill hit the minus-twenty mark every day. Yet, wearing their helmets, respirators, and heavy-duty gloves, the ESU cops worked at a hurried pace until some bones and other bits of evidence were recovered. During the entire search, Red Cross trucks serving coffee, hot chocolate, and cookies stood by ready to replenish the frozen bodies with refreshments and doses of caffeine.

On a Sunday morning, when the temperature straddled zero, the feds called off the search. Sgt. Juan Garcia and Police Officer Ray Nalpant returned to quarters, frozen stiff, their overalls coated with frozen dust and debris. Their faces were beet red from the cold, and they looked like some of the city's more colorful street people. One of the cops in the Third Squad patted his sergeant on the back, smiled, and said, "I can't give you a handout, Mr. Hobo, but if you'd like I can drive you to a shelter."

"Be happy my old bones are frozen," one of the hobos replied, "but if you saw the good work we did, you'd be bowing to us instead of ragging us!"

When police commanders want evidence removed from a building, they bust the balls of the detectives in their squad. When detectives want the evidence removed with integrity, efficiently, and cleanly, they summon ESU. There is a lot of evidence to be removed from crime scenes in Harlem and Washington Heights, and Truck-Two stays busy digging, picking, cracking, burning, cutting, dissecting, hammering, illuminating, and removing evidence. ESU cops like to boast that there isn't an aspect of evidence recovery that they cannot handle—whether it is digging a spent round out of a wall or removing ten-year-old bones from the well-manicured lawn of a park. Often, as at the diggings on Bradhurst Avenue, ESU assists in evidence searches because it is truly the only unit in the city (including city, state, and federal agencies) with the tools, the knowledge, and the experience to turn the skeletal remains of a burned-out building inside out, and do so safely, so a detective can get a small sliver of evidence crucial in the assembling of a case. Other times, it seems as though ESU is called out simply so the investigating officers can file in their report the statement "ESU called in for an evidence search, and the results were negative." One such case, in the winter of 1997, involved an attempted murder on Broadway and 204th Street in Washington Heights. A male Hispanic in his mid-thirties was the target of a 9mm barrage as he left a travel agency specializing in travel to the Dominican Republic. The sidewalk was caked with large splats of blood from where the bullets went flying to where the victim eventually collapsed and was attended to by EMS. Yet the neighborhood didn't come to a stop at the sight of the shooting, nor did the store owners in front of whose establishments the bullets went flying. In fact, at a hair salon right next to where neat 9mm holes had punctured and shattered a glass storefront, beauticians wearing small tank tops and tight jeans were busy shaping the coif of a woman even though a large spraying of blood and tissue had dirtied their window.

Police Officers Seth Gahr and Kevin Flanagan, riding in the Adam-Two car that night, had returned to Two-Truck's quarters for a quick cup of coffee and to replace a blade on one of the REP's saws (damaged when cutting up a tree knocked down in the middle of 66th Street by a cab). No sooner had they sat down and prepared themselves for some shop talk around the kitchen table than the call came over SOD that the 3-4 lieutenant was requesting ESU to search for a weapon. Usually, evidence searches are not considered emergencies—meaning that the cops are not warranted to race to the scene with lights and sirens as if there were lives on the line or as if they were responding to a confirmed ten-thirteen. Nevertheless, every three or four minutes, as the Adam car made its way up the West Side Highway toward the 204th Street exit, Central was coming on the air requesting at ETA. "What's the emergency there?" Gahr asked a puzzled Flanagan in his unique half-Southern, half-Brooklyn brogue. "What they got up there?"

"Emergency Adam-Two to Central, K," Seth returned to the dispatcher. "Is there an emergency at 204 and B-way?"

"Negative, K," was the dispatcher's response. "The lieutenant is just asking for an ETA."

"We'll be there in three minutes, K," Seth replied, hoping to end the communication, but ninety seconds later he was again hit up for an ETA. "We are pulling up now, Central!"

Upon arriving at the scene, Gahr and Flanagan must have thought the person shot was some celebrity for all the ETA's the precinct lieutenant was requesting, but when they emerged from their REP, they noticed nothing out of the ordinary—just the typical Washington Heights scenery of cars honking, blaring Dominican rap songs, and local residents pushing baby strollers down the boulevard. The yellow crime scene tape was still up, and cops were standing around, trying to keep warm while awaiting the arrival of ESU and CSU detectives. After less than two minutes, the lieutenant looked at Gahr and Flanagan, smiled, and then said, "OK, guys, that's it. You can go. 'Bye!" Gahr and Flanagan, attempting to make sense of the confusing set of circumstances, simply shrugged their shoulders, returned to their REP, and said to each other, "What the fuck was that all about? I guess this wasn't the 'Big Job'?"

The cops in Two-Truck have seen just about every sight in the northern half of Manhattan, from every which angle, and sometimes evidence searches take them away from the island and to other boroughs to assist in the recovery of evidence and weapons. From such mundane tasks as pulling a spent round out of a wall to being lowered by crane into the rickety caverns of a burned-out tenement, ESU cops like to claim that there isn't piece of evidence that they cannot recover—no matter how small and no matter how routine.

On a day when an NYPD captain, a narcotics unit commander, was shot on the Grand Concourse in the Bronx and every Boy car in the city was in search of the shooter, Truck-Two was summoned back to the Bronx on an eight-to-four to assist the 4-1 Precinct in searching for shell casings after a shooting. The gunplay, senseless and bloody, was waged from the window of one apartment to that of a rival drug dealer across the street, on Lafayette near Bryant Avenue. The Bronx was a ballistic bastion that day, and shots were ringing out everywhere. Flesh and bone were being sprayed on street corners and inside tenement hallways. It reminded borough commanders of the good old days when the Bronx was burning, when the 4-1 Precinct, one of the smallest in the city, boasted a whopping sixty-plus homicides in a year, and when the borough was known more for being the embattled Fort Apache than for its zoo and the "house that Ruth built."

Following the 4-1 sergeant to what cops believed was the source of the gunfire, the two E-cops found themselves looking up at a window over a courtyard filled with water, debris, condoms, hypodermic needles, crack vials, rubber hoses, human teeth, diapers, Styrofoam containers from McDonald's, tossed-out betting slips from OTB, and scores of dead rats. "The shooter must have stuck his hand out that window over there," the sergeant rationalized, "and aimed the 9mm downward, so that he could hit the guys standing in front of the bodega. Of course, the genius hit some mother of two watching Spanish soap operas, but witnesses say the gunfire came from here." With their high-powered flashlights on and attempting to wade through the filth and the stench, Garcia and Donnelly walked slowly through the water, looking for anything that was shiny. "There's a round," Garcia pointed out. "Here's another one."

"Hey, Sarge," Officer Donnelly yelled as he came across three more spent shells. "This guy must have emptied his clip."

The building's landlord, a Yiddish-speaking Hasidic gentleman in his early twenties whose command of the English language was as good as that of the Spanish-only inhabitants of the building he charged four hundred dollars a month for rent, came to the rear of the building, more nervous that his slum would be hit with building code violations than that one of his tenants was playing Wild West on his property. "Who lives in that apartment?" one of the precinct cops asked the landlord, who was making as if he didn't speak a word of English. "Amazing, nobody speaks English in this motherfucking city anymore," the cop replied, exasperated and exhausted.

In all, seven 9mm shells casings were recovered from the disease-riddled pool of water behind the South Bronx tenement. Precinct could have handled the job, but why get dirty, why get wet, and why catch the plague?

As Sergeant Garcia and Officer Donnelly removed the film of rat guts and used condoms off their boots and contemplated what horrid diseases they might have contracted while searching for a few lousy 9mm shells casings, the precinct sergeant looked at the two E-men, smiled, and said, "Ain't police work glamorous?"

Back at quarters, half the officers of Sergeant Spratt's Second Squad attended to some overdue paperwork, while others readied their gear for patrolling the streets of Harlem and Washington Heights on the four-by. The change of tours had been uneventful, and the sugar rush left by a box of fresh doughnuts and high-octane coffee had yet to reach its maximum level of overdrive. The cops were looking for a good job to start their tour. A pin job? A rescue of some kind? Perhaps a gun run with Street Crime?

"Emergency Adam-Two on the air?"

"Ten-four, K" was the anticipatory reply.

"You are being requested by the 3-3 Squad to search for a weapon tossed down the toilet and clogging up the pipes at 177th Street. Do you copy, K?"

A pause of nearly a minute by everyone in house, followed by a very loud, "damn it!"

"Ten-four, Central. Show Adam-Two responding."

14

Barricaded EDPs: Psychos with an Agenda

•

"Come out of there," the cop yells through the door at the 400-pound woman inside her barricaded room at a single occupancy hotel on Broadway. "All we want to do is talk to you."

"Are you earthlings or Martians?" the woman demands to know.

"I'm not playing Star Trek *with this one," the lieutenant orders. "Break down the door, and get her out!"*

It had been a hectic four-to-twelve for Sgt. Juan Garcia's Third Squad the previous night—there was that pin job of a car crashing into a wall (and the wall subsequently collapsing only inches from the E-men), and there were two hours of waiting and doing nothing inside a CAT car for a hit and a warrant on a known drug headquarters in the 2-6, located right around the corner from quarters on Old Broadway. It was a new day, however, though there was a feeling inside quarters that this Sunday would be a slow one. The snow of the previous day had ended just as abruptly as it had started, and a brilliant glow of sunshine blanketed much of New York City, casting a bright shine over the buildings and street corners of Harlem. It actually looked pretty and peaceful.

As is the case on many Sundays, the SOD radio was quiet. Earlier in the day, in Brooklyn, it had been chaotic for Eight-Truck units and most of the ESU squads in the Borough of Kings who were busy on a job involving a kidnapping, a rape, the Russian Mafia, a suspect with a bad sense of personal hygiene and one large furry eyebrow, and a cache of weapons in a disco. Queens, the Bronx, and Lower Manhattan, though, had been quiet. Perhaps too quiet. In Upper Manhattan, for the first few hours of the tour, in fact, there had been only one job—a pit bull had taken a chunk of flesh out of a pedestrian on Riverside Drive.

At 6:00 P.M., as darkness engulfed the city, the beauty of the winter's night became apparent. It was crisp, with a nip in the air, and the clear skies gave the lights in the distance a sharp, crystal horizon. As the Adam and Boy cars returned to quarters following the dog job, the call came over the division that in the 2-6 Precinct, sector cars had given chase to an individual who had tossed a yellow plastic bag into the Hudson River at 125th Street—right up the block from Two-Truck's quarters. Usually, when cops in the 2-6 chase a drug suspect along the Hudson River and evidence is tossed into the water, it is either a gun, a bag of drugs or cash, or body parts. After all, in the American justice system, you can't be arrested, let alone convicted, for a selling drugs if the vials of crack are sinking to the bottom of the Hudson River; you can't be locked up for a shooting if the Taurus 9mm you used to blow a gaping hole in the head of one of your rival dealers is now a bottom-of-the-river ornament. Come to think of it, there hadn't been a good evidence recovery job in a while for Two-Truck. When they noticed a yellow plastic bag floating in the river, they hoped it contained something major—$100,000 in cash, perhaps? Maybe a few kilos of heroin or cocaine. It would be nice to be interviewed on TV, along with precinct cops, detectives, and the Manhattan District Attorney, and tell how they'd fished out a bag of evidence that was the missing piece of the puzzle in a ten-year-old major criminal investigation.

Officer Joe Ocasio, a former Transit Police rescue man, lurched over the fence along the dilapidated wooden piers and attempted to fish out the bag with an elongated pole, usually used for animal control. Although in his days in the subway, while breathing in the metal dust and the aromas of the other garbage that litters the city's subway tunnels, Ocasio had had few opportunities to go near the water, the rest of the squad, holding him upright and out of the water, were impressed by his fishing abilities. The bag, a filled-to-capacity yellow plastic one of the supermarket variety, was placed on the wooden planks of the pier and as three sets of flashlights were shined on it, Officer Eddie Torres removed a sharp blade from his utility belt and made a small gash in its bottom.

"Holy shit," one the officers claimed as the contents began to drain out. "It's blood."

When cops see blood in a bag that was just tossed into the river, they immediately expect to find either a head or a two-day-old infant. A head is nothing new, and neither is a dead infant, but the cops hoped it wasn't a newborn. They took in a chestful of the night's chilly air and expected the worst. Yet when Torres cut the bag again, a steady stream of blood and dirt emerged from the bottom, as did feathers. "Feathers?" Soon, two fish, two geese, crucifixes, and rice and beans emerged from the wet sack.

"Hey, this is some Santeria voodoo bullshit," claimed one of the precinct cops.

"I think we are all cursed now and the evil spirits are about to be unleashed," offered one of the Two-Truck officers.

Cops tend to be very superstitious about their daily routines, but the practices of Santeria do not bother most of them. Yet the discovery of the yellow plastic bag was definitely an omen. A harbinger of evil and of madness and of a night the cops of ESU Truck-Two will never forget.

No sooner had the REPs departed the waterfront than a job came over the SOD citywide frequency. Just before 6:30 P.M., a call came over division for ESU to respond to an unconfirmed EDP at 875 Amsterdam Avenue, at the Frederick Douglass Houses on the corner of 102nd Street in apartment 12-G.

"That's the 2-4," Dan Donnelly said to Joe Ocasio in the Boy car as he recalled his days as a precinct cop before coming to Emergency. "That apartment sounds familiar. I think I've been there before. Let's see what division has on the job." But the radio was quiet, and like many of the countless EDP jobs that come over the system, both cops thought it would end up being a "cancellation by division." The Boy-Two crew, who had taken the meal requests, ventured toward the Floridita for a Sunday night's fare of Puerto Rican "stick to your ribs" food. The Santeria offering a few moments earlier had triggered the craving for Hispanic food, and for some reason the cold snap in the air had driven appetites into overdrive. The cops were hungry. It was another omen.

Usually, the big job comes over the radio the moment the fork hits the plate. It's known as the mealtime curse. This time, however, the curse (probably Santeria-inspired) came as the food was just placed inside one of the storage bins as the REP responded to the job.

"Emergency Adam-Two, Boy-Two, Truck-Two, K. Division confirming that they have a barricaded EDP with a history of mental illness at 875 Amsterdam, apartment 12-G. The EDP has his parents inside there with him. The duty captain requesting an ETA."

The Adam and Boy cars, the truck, and the RMI raced out at top ESU speed down Broadway. They were eighty-four three minutes later.

Coming to a barricaded EDP job, the ESU cops never really know what to expect. They can encounter a psycho inside an apartment who simply refuses to come out, or they can be up against a door covered in shit and blood and hear the sounds of insanity barking from inside an apartment turned killing zone. For all EDP jobs, especially barricades, ESU cops suit up in their SWAT regalia—heavy vests, helmet, and specialized equipment ranging from heavy-duty pepper spray cans to water cannons to netted restraining devices, more commonly known in the unit vernacular as the "nut bag." Usually, EDP jobs aren't pure tactical assignments, and even barricaded nuts don't warrant an MP-5 and Ruger Mini-14 response. If an EDP is armed with a gun, the job changes. It becomes a "gun job" and is handled accordingly—like a barricaded perp. Usually, in fact, EDP work is routine. This time, though, even for the "we've seen it all and done it all" men of Truck-Two, the barricaded EDP would be like nothing any one of these cops had ever been through before.

By the time Sergeant Garcia, Joe Ocasio, and Dan Donnelly reached the twelfth floor, Steve Vales and Ray Nalpant had tied off the door in order to make sure the nut didn't suddenly open his door and challenge the cops to a final showdown, and they were shielding themselves with a body bunker. They were also staring in disbelief at what was in front of them.

"Sarge, you ain't never gonna believe this," Vales said with an amazed expression as Garcia walked gingerly toward 12-G. Steve Vales was one of the more experienced cops in the truck. He was a worker and a highly respected E-man. He wasn't known to exaggerate very often, nor did many things take him aback or by surprise. Garcia had seen "Steve-O," as Vales is known in the division, on many big jobs, from the World Trade Center bombing to plane crashes, and he knew just by looking at his trusted cop's face that something here was very wrong. Moments later, another jaw was heard dropping to the floor. It would be Garcia. "Holy shit!" was all Garcia could utter. "Holy shit!"

Although each apartment in each housing project has the same metal door, a Housing Authority issue lock, and a peep hole, the door on apartment 12-G looked more as if it had been used in medieval times as the mighty entrance to a castle. One of the precinct cops, in fact, one of the first officers at the scene, called the place "The Dungeon." A heavy gray steel door, something the likes of which are seen sometimes in front of banks or embassies, was secured by four dead-bolt and three cylinder locks. E-men are challenged by such fortifications. Immediately their minds begin to ponder the type of tool that'll be needed to remove the mighty steel obstacle from its frame and what is the quickest and least destructive means for breaching the fortified frame.

"Looks like Fort Knox," Capt. Philip Von Gostein, the 2-4 Precinct duty captain commented to Sergeant Garcia. "This is unbelievable. I've never seen anything like this in my life."

But there was an added piece to the psychotic-inspired door that made entry the last of everyone's concerns. A series of weblike wires were coming out the door, apparently attached to something on the other side of the door. Fearing some kind of diabolical explosive device on the other side of the monster door, Garcia immediately told his cops to stop knocking on the door and to cease and desist giving the steel frame the old ESU door knock (a massive blow by the sole of a boot). The wires were indeed ominous. From the outside, with Vales and Nalpant securing the door and lurching behind the body bunker, it was impossible to tell what type of gauntlet was waiting for them on the other side. Had the EDP wired the door to electrocute anyone who touched it, or did he have a few sticks of dynamite attached to a detonator? Garcia did what all E-men are trained to do in such scenarios: he immediately called the Bomb Squad. As a precaution, the entire floor was evacuated. If this was a bomb, Von Gostein did not want any of the casualties to be civilian. Even EMS crews, standing by the ready, were sent to safety on the floor below. Somehow there was a feeling on the twelfth floor that a long night lay ahead of them.

When precinct cops respond to a 911 call about an EDP (people calling in an emergency usually refer to the subjects as "stark raving fucking psychos"), the dispatcher sends a sector car over to respond and attempt to find out what is going on; at the same time, ESU gets the call over their SOD radio concerning an "unconfirmed" EDP, and usually the patrolling Adam or Boy car will begin heading in the direction of the job, "just in case." Many times, what the 911 operator received as an EDP is nothing more than a crank call or a misdiagnosis by a concerned citizen (some who call 911 are more mentally disturbed than the subjects they are trying to report), and sometimes the EDPs are real but benign in their insanity and quirky behavior (this description fits a good majority of the city's inhabitants).

Paul Miller, the resident in apartment 12-G, was different. In the ESU dictionary, under the word *EDP,* was his picture. A thirty-nine-year-old white male, Miller was a veteran of the New York City mental health system and had been locked up on numerous occasions for all sorts of psychotic behavior. Throughout the Frederick Douglass Houses, Miller was known as a "fucking nut." He hated minorities (which meant he was living in the wrong zip code) and was known to walk around the hallways in his underwear and knock on doors, threatening people, walking across the hallway in his bare feet and waving an American flag, ranting and raving incoherently. Neighbors had complained about him drilling peepholes into other apartments, and he was often seen entering his apartment carrying armfuls of electronic and mechanical gear. He often stood by the window, completely naked, taunting neighbors.

But the fact that he had barricaded himself inside his apartment with his seventy-five-year-old Alzheimer's-afflicted father, Leo, and his eighty-year-old mother, Margaret, made this job a precarious one. This was no longer a simple barricade of a lunatic out for attention. This was now a hostage job, an EDP job, and a bomb job all rolled into one clusterfuck. More assets would be needed, and fast. Sergeant Garcia summoned additional ESU personnel from Three-Truck in the South Bronx to come in and provide support, and he requested that all on-duty members of the countersniper team be summoned as well and dispatched to 865 Amsterdam Avenue, the building across the courtyard, where they could set up observation posts peering into Paul Miller's apartment. Captain Von Gostein summoned the NYPD's legendary Hostage Negotiation Team and the department's technical unit, known as TARU (Technical Assistance Response Unit), to respond forthwith to the location. Officer Donnelly listened in as Garcia called in the Bomb Squad. Using his best "Irish" slang, Donnelly looked at fellow Irishmen, 2-4 Precinct Sgt. Michael O'Riordan, and simply said, "This is going to turn into a big fucking megillah."

As Police Officers Ed Lutz and Jim Malley arrived from Three-Truck, Lieutenant Chris Ellison, the ESU supervisor working citywide north, made it to the twelfth floor. In some jobs, too many bosses create confusion. On other jobs, however, where the sense of impending doom permeates a crowded housing project hallway, you cannot have enough bosses, supervisors, and white shirts on hand. This was one such job.

ESU works hostage jobs with great finesse and patience. The objective is always to wait the situation out and to exhaust all possible means before making a dynamic entry. The policy of "We'd rather bore you to death than shoot you" is sacrosanct. Yet dealing with an EDP is not as controlled a situation as dealing with a barricaded perp, and control is an element in all hostage jobs that is all-important. Part of that control is knowing what the parties on the other side of the barricade are doing and what surprises they might possess. In Two-Truck's repertoire is the RMI truck, the vehicle that carries the robot and the remote tactics equipment that come in most useful in hostage and barricaded jobs. There are lots of high-tech gadgets on board the truck, some of which are classified by the NYPD, and there are some bits and pieces of gear that are indispensable when, on the other side of a door, hostages are held at gunpoint. One such piece of equipment is known as the pole camera. Mounted on an extendable metal pole, the video camera attaches to a Sony Watchman TV. This enables the ESU cops to lower or raise the camera into the window of the targeted apartment and to view what's going on inside, "real time." The perp or EDP can say that everyone inside the apartment is fine, but if the pole camera indicates that there are three dead corpses inside, then it signals to ESU and to the gathering of bosses, duty captains, and deputy inspectors that the time for a forceful entry is *now.*

Sergeant Garcia dispatched Officer Eddie Torres to the roof at 875 Amsterdam, to position himself over apartment 12-G right below and provide up-to-date intelligence on what was going on inside. Initially, the view was crystal-clear. The apartment was clean, orderly. But there was no sight of the parents or, more importantly, Paul Miller. Torres manipulated the camera to encompass as much of the scene as it could, but he was still unable to locate either Miller or his parents. Finally, moments later, a heavyset male wearing nothing but white decorated boxer shorts approached the window and lowered the shade. It was the only view ESU would have of the EDP. It was Paul Miller.

"Was he carrying a gun? A bomb? A remote control device of some sort? What was he holding in his hands?" Torres couldn't tell. He only saw the subject for a blink of an eye.

Whenever the Bomb Squad is called to a job, both the Fire Department and EMS deploy, as well. It is prudent to have people who can put fires out on hand to extinguish whatever might blow up, and it is smart to have at least two ambulances ready and waiting. When bomb jobs are indoors, especially in apartment buildings, both FD and EMS wait on the floor below, just in case the device goes off prematurely.

The Bomb Squad arrived shortly after summoned, much to Captain Von Gostein and Sergeant Garcia's relief. Both Bomb Squad technicians, detectives who had been seasoned veterans of Eight-Truck in Brooklyn North, were used to the clusterfuck that surrounded barricade jobs. They had responded to hundreds of jobs of psychos refusing to come out of their apartments in projects during their long careers in emergency, and they recalled the dozens of tense nights they had stood all SWAT-ed out in a project hallway in the notorious Williamsburg Houses, trying to convince a psycho that it would be a smart thing to release his family unharmed. This time, without knowing what was on the other side of the door, it was difficult for the two specialists to come to a quick determination about the nature of the wires leading out of the door. But, according to many in this country, the NYPD's Bomb Squad is among the nation's finest, and both detectives earned the accolades this wintry Sunday evening. After checking the wires for live currents and X-raying the door, the determination was certain: there was no bomb or other incendiary device waiting to go off on the other side of the steel obstacle.

The Bomb Squad's finding was supposed to be good news. It was supposed to mean that an end to the job was in sight. The emergency cops would gain entry, subdue the EDP, and free the parents. It was textbook Emergency Service. Captain Von Gostein, who maintained cell-phone communications with the boroughwide duty inspector, predicted a quick resolution to the job.

The usual ESU entry tools, sledgehammers and halogens and hydraulic rabbit tools, work on most doors in New York City—even heavy fire doors with four-way Multi-locks. But this door was different, and something heavier would be needed. The sixty-inch ram from the Hurst tool seemed appropriate and, with its thousands of pounds spreading power, the only tool in the ESU arsenal capable of making a scratch on the door. Officers Lutz and Malley of Three-Truck fired up the Hurst tool's generator twenty feet away in the building's stairwell, while Vales and Donnelly protected by body-bunker-wielding cops, engaged the Hurst tool into the openings in the hope of prying the door loose. According to ESU experience, the Hurst tool should have cracked that door open like a can of sardines in less than a minute. Nearly ten minutes of manipulating the eighty-pound device all along the door frame and the steel gate was still preventing entry into the apartment. It took several more minutes of backbreaking, sweat-dripping work to get inside. Entry should have meant an end to the job. This job, however, was only beginning.

"Captain, you gotta see this," was all that Sergeant Garcia managed to utter in a low and trepidatious voice as he emerged from the apartment now covered in a cloud of smoke and dust. "You just gotta see this."

Captain Von Gostein and several of his officers looked on anxiously as the Two-Truck officers lifted the separated door off its frame and entered apartment 12-G. The job was now nearly two hours old, and there was a lot of work to be done in the precinct confines. Von Gostein had hoped to hear a loud "all's clear" bellowing from the apartment once the ESU entry team was inside, but instead he was back on his cell phone to the borough patrol inspector, forced to tell him that the job had gone from bad to worse.

Inside the apartment, directly to the right of the main door, the emergency cops found themselves up against yet another fortified door, this one making the front door seem like a wire-screen porch door, that was secured by deadbolts, three cylinder locks, and seven hinges. Miller was holding his parents behind yet another door, inside a cramped six-foot by eight-foot bedroom, crammed with garbage and debris. Yet another series of fortifications wasn't all that troubling—the ram would see to that. What cops found on the floor, though, indicated ominously how the job would culminate. The hardwood floor was littered with open boxes of plastic aircraft and battleship model kits and empty shell casings from a .22 rim-fire rifle. Paul Miller was no longer just a barricaded loony. He was an armed loony holding hostages.

The NYPD's Hostage Negotiation Team is considered one of the finest such units in the world. It is the unit that has written the book on how municipal police agencies deal with, contain, negotiate with, and eventually resolve hostage-taking incidents. HNT detectives are as patient as a nun glued to a church bench and as insightful as the craftiest jailhouse con. Since their inception in the mid-1970s, they have negotiated with terrorists, and they have negotiated with heroin-addicted bank robbers. They have turned potential massacres into resolved jobs, they have saved lives with a cheeseburger and a sympathetic ear, and they have talked suicidal cops, trembling fingers caressing the trigger of off-duty revolvers, out of killing themselves. They are trained to defuse potentially lethal situations, but they are, above anything else, negotiators. Police departments around the state, the country, and indeed the world have ventured to New York to watch HNT in action. They aren't magicians, though. They require human response and dialogue.

Lt. Huey McGowan, the HNT commander, arrived at 875 Amsterdam hoping to engage Paul Miller's trust and to talk him out of the apartment, alive, with his parents. A former E-man, McGowan had been on too many EDP jobs to remember, and he knew the routine like the back of his hand. Assisting McGowan with his efforts were the high-tech wizards of TARU, the Technical Assistance Response Unit. Employing eavesdropping devices and fiber-optic cameras, they were at least able to hear much of the lunatic ranting and raving transpiring inside 12-G. It wasn't good. There were a few attempts to appeal to Miller's evaporating hold on reality and persuade him to release his aging parents, but McGowan's sincere attempts were answered by shouting, screaming, and then silence. According to one ESU cop, "If McGowan feels there is hope, he'll negotiate until his vocal cords are sore and hoarse. Yet he's savvy enough to know when there is no hope and when to call in the boys with the tools."

At 875 Amsterdam, across the courtyard, snipers from the countersniper team were attempting to observe what was going on inside the apartment and to communicate the intelligence back to the cops inside the apartment.

Peering through the scopes of their M-24 rifles, the snipers were in place just in case Miller began shooting his parents or at the cops. Their vantage point was poor, and with the shades down, their precision ballistic equipment had limited use. Using a secure frequency, just in case Miller was listening in on a Radio Shack scanner, the snipers relayed updates and received feedback, but the marksmen were all experienced E-men, and they understood the situation, realized where it was heading, and knew it was but a matter of time.

Sergeant Garcia's primary concern, now assuming that Miller was armed, was that he would begin to shoot through the walls and possibly hurt one of his men. With their bunkers nestled up against the door and the Hurst tool and the hydraulic battering ram ready to go, Garcia had little choice but to wait until Miller surrendered or precipitated an ESU tactical response. Miller made his move at 9:45 P.M.

The emergency cops were getting a bit tired standing around up against the door, their heavy tools in hand, but the monotony of the job was suddenly interrupted by what sounded like a "thomp," similar to the noise made by the machine that is used to launch tennis balls at novice students, followed by a high-pitched scream. "Shit, he's killing them!" yelled one of the cops. "Crank up the Hurst tool!" While several officers maneuvered the Hurst tool around the door frame, Donnelly began pounding the wall with his sledgehammer, hoping to create a hole large enough through which to reach into and grab a hostage. The cops didn't know if Miller had shot at them or at his parents. A sense of desperation set in. Gnawing feelings began to creep from the stomachs of the E-men up toward their chests and throats. This was the essence of their work, hours of boredom interrupted by seconds of sheer, heart-stopping terror.

Attempts to get into Miller's room with the Hurst tool were meeting with Murphy's law. The door was heavy steel, fastened to its hinges by a series of cast-iron pins and rivets and secured by scores of cylinder locks. The work to get in through the obstacle was backbreaking; freeing a trapped motorist from the twisted metal cobwebs of what was once a car on the Henry Hudson Parkway never proved to be so difficult. Each second seemed like minutes. The cops didn't know what they'd face on the other side of the door. Would they find everyone dead? Would Paul Miller be waiting for them, rifle in hand, ready to go down in a blaze of gunfire.

Once the door was literally lifted off its mark, the job became a tactical entry—just like a warrant. Vales and Nalpant, followed by Donnelly and Ocasio and Sergeant Garcia, moved through the hallway slowly, secure, and gingerly, their guns and body bunkers ready for any contingency. Inside the hallway to Paul Miller's room, littered with garbage and model airplane and battleship kits, they encountered militarylike fortifications. Walls had been reinforced by additional bricks and covered by wooden blocks supported by metal hinges. As they turned the corner down the hall, doing that ultra-dangerous twist and turn to see what was waiting for them, they encountered the beginnings of what appeared to be a mini-bunker within a bunker under construction. They also encountered the bodies of Leo Miller, shot twice in the chest, and Paul Miller, shot once through the mouth, lying on the floor. Margaret Miller, shocked and bewildered, was standing over them, not knowing what to do. She had watched as her son took his .22 rifle and shot her husband in the chest. She then looked on as her son placed the barrel of his rifle into his own mouth and pulled the trigger. By the time EMS raced into the apartment, the ordeal was over. EMS crews, who had waited patiently throughout the entire job one floor below, worked valiantly on both father and son, but there was nothing left to do. Margaret Miller was removed in complete shock, having been forced to watch her world disintegrate before her eyes in the muzzle flash of a rifle.

For the men of Two-Truck and the responding personnel from Three-Truck and One-Truck, their three hours at 875 Amsterdam Avenue left them saddened and resigned to the fact that they had done all that could have been done to bring a peaceful resolution to the barricaded episode. No E-man wants to lose a hostage. No E-man wants to leave a job knowing that a life that could have been saved wasn't. Yet the cops on the scene were still amazed by the doors, by the insane ingenuity that had guided the twisted mind and the determined hands. They were also shocked to see a window, overlooking Amsterdam Avenue, that had been bricked up and fortified, like a sniper pit, camouflaged by a custom-made window shade. There were targets inside the room, as well, indicating that Paul Miller was practicing for the signal—his own silent calling to begin a war in Upper Manhattan. From his perch, and the manner in which it was fortified, he could have rained bullets down all along Amsterdam Avenue until stopped by ESU.

No one knows exactly what it was that set Miller off that night. It was clear to the investigators sifting through the evidence in the apartment that Miller had been preparing for something and that his preparations were incomplete. Perhaps it was a family argument that set him off. Perhaps voices inside his head. No one will ever know. Miller had been preparing for his final showdown with the world, and reality, for quite some time. On this frigid night, his final showdown destroyed his family.

Back at the 2-4 Precinct, the cops who were first in the apartment sat around for a few hours and wound themselves down as they awaited an interview by the homicide detectives who had caught the case. They were covered by a heavy coat of dust and dirt from the shattered walls inside the apartment, and under their heavy Kevlar body armor, they were covered by thick sweat that refused to dry. As they reloaded their trucks on Amsterdam Avenue, their damp uniforms had clashed with the subfreezing winds of a wintry night and sent chills up their spines. Even though they see chaos and insanity on a daily basis, watching dementia materialize into a murder-suicide takes cops back a few steps and causes moments of introspection. Back at the precinct, the down time was therapeutic. Sodas were guzzled down, phone calls made, and the men of Two-Truck had the chance to talk over the job, review it, and critique themselves. Sergeant Garcia's crew had managed a stellar performance through an impossible situation. Garcia was proud of his men. He was happy that none of them had been hurt.

The following day, only the *Daily News* printed a small article about the ordeal, barely mentioning ESU's impassable gauntlet and the skill and determination required to break through the fortified barrier and rescue the mother. Some of the cops were bitter at the media's apathy and the disregard that the department's public information apparatus had for a job that should be textbook emergency service curriculum, but the E-men were used to the routine.

There is always a lot of second-guessing following a job where the EDP and some of his hostages end up "paws up," and cops in other squads and other trucks, people who hadn't seen the door and the fortifications, were quick to play Monday-morning quarterback with comments and critical analysis. But, as Sergeant Garcia pointed out to his men in the postjob debrief over coffee and bagels at quarters the next evening, "We did everything that was in our power, and we used all the tools and equipment at our disposal." The cops in the Third Squad knew that their sergeant was right. A job like Paul Miller's bunker was impossible to second-guess and impossible to believe. In their hearts, though, the Two-Truck cops knew what they had done, and the 2-4 Precinct cops knew what they had done.

In the world of emergency service, that was really all that mattered.

15

Arresting Moments with the A Team: Stories from the A Files

•

"Hey, what's that?" the 8-8 Precinct anticrime sergeant asked the ESU officer.

"It's called a rabbit tool. It's a battery-powered spreader that is good on any New York City door," the officer replied. "Or on the legs of a young Irish virgin!"

There was no reply from the anticrime sergeant, not used to the tools or to the wickedly wild and sarcastic sense of humor in the E-cop arsenal, other than an expression of mild resignation.

If life inside a squad can be described as a pressure cooker, a dysfunctional family where for the good of all some attempt to get along and "play nice" must be made, then service on the ESU Apprehension Tactical Team, the A Team, can be looked upon as a summer's vacation away from the chaos. For the emergency cops, service with the A Team is a chance for a renewal, a refresher, and a place for spiritual awareness. It is the place where officers from different squads and different trucks are tossed together into a temporary ten-man force and tasked solely with serving tactical warrants for precincts, anticrime units, detective squads, the Special Operations Division's elite Street Crimes Unit, and even various state and federal agencies, from the ASPCA to the DEA. A team can be comprised of officers from

...ten Island and Queens mixed together with a Bronx unit sergeant, with several Manhattan cops thrown in for the mix. The A Team is a place where personalities, work habits, and "the way we do things on the street" are all thrown out the window. It is where tactics are rethought, where weapons skills are reconsidered and reviewed, and where a cop's proficiency in that very dangerous life-and-death work of entering a hostile location, be it a crack house or the home of a serial murderer, is honed into second nature.

Every ESU officer must go through at lest one stint on the A Team. It is a tactical refresher course and a break from the day-to-day routine of patrol and the focus of rescue work. There are emergency cops who, for various reasons of attachment to various aspects of the job, hate to leave their trucks, their squads, and the areas they patrol. There are officers who become such integral facets of the sections of the city they usually work in that serving on temporary assignment to the A Team really bothers them. There are others, though, who cherish the chance to get away from the truck for a few months. After the harried pace of patrol and responding to pin jobs, perps, and stuck occupied elevators, a schedule of kicking through doors and cuffing bad guys sounds like fun.

Because teams are rotated with different personnel, no two teams are ever the same; each assumes the personality of the eight officers assigned to the force and the sergeant selected as its commander. Yet, even though in the beginning the team consists of a group of officers who have probably never worked with one another before, an espirit de corps slowly develops from taking those eight separate (and sometimes bizarre) personalities into a single-minded tactical sword that works like clockwork, where the bunker man will know without a word being spoken exactly what the tool man will be thinking, and the tool man will know exactly what's on the mind of the sergeant.

Although most E-cops will hate to admit it, the A Team is where the officers can really have some fun.

The fun and the "staying alive" aspects of the A Team are in many ways the responsibility of A Team commander Lt. Richard Greene, A Team One CO Sgt. Tommy Urban, and especially two of the unit's training officers, Jack Griffith and Derek Dunston, usually assigned to A Team Two, with officers rotating in from throughout the unit. The training officers provide the unit with its spirit and its motivation, and, at well over six feet, Griffith has little trouble getting people's attention or getting them motivated. "All my life I was a buff," the six-foot-plus officer proudly proclaims, beaming with pride as he talks about his unit, "and being able to work here is the greatest thing in the world. I love what I do, and how many people can actually say that and mean it as well?"

Griffith is more than a buff—he is a catalyst who makes people move and things happen. He also incorporates a certain element of fun in what he does—enjoyment keeps the officers fresh, it keeps them cohesive, and it makes them happy. Griffith is also a rock of reliability to the unit—especially when in tandem with his steady partner, Derek Dunston. They have been partners for about fourteen of their fifteen years on the job. Just how much fun is enjoyed while serving on the A Team is ideally illustrated by the officers serving on Sgt. Jimmy Spratt's squad. Although the team includes Officer Roger Mack, a former housing ERU cop from One-Truck, it is a Two-Truck A Team: Sergeant Spratt is Two-Truck's Second Squad supervisor; Officers John D'Allara and Jerome "Kaz" Kazlauskus are from the Third Herd; Officers Vinny Martinez and Ronnie Bauman are Harlem midnight men; and Officer Paddy McGee, who serenades the team with melodies from his bagpipes, is from Spratt's squad back at Two-Truck.

Initially, the atmosphere in the team wasn't one of great positive energy. Some called it the A Team from Hell, since it was made up of officers from the truck who had yet to do the team once and who, for reasons varying from school schedules to personal preferences, had not been on previous squads. Yet, after a week of refresher training at Floyd Bennet Field and some morale boosting by Sergeant Spratt and Officer Griffith, the A Team from Hell was proving to the division not only that they were more than capable but that they were damn good. They also proved just how much fun one could have while on tactical assignment.

The following, however, is from the files of "you can't make this shit up!"

The A Team primary deployment vehicle is a square fiberglass GMC bread truck that looks as innocent as a UPS van making its rounds. The A Team possesses two such trucks—a white one used by A Team One and a gray one deployed by A Team Two. To the untrained eye, all that identifies it as an NYPD vehicle is a small (and removable) red flashing light located near the steering wheel and several police radios monitoring division and citywide frequencies. Inside, however, the truck is right out of the pages of *Motor Trend.* The cabin is a roomy rectangular box consisting of two upholstered benches facing each other. Underneath the benches are a small support cache of hand tools, animal control equipment, plastic Flex-cuffs, and other assorted tactical gear. Behind the benches, on the walls of the truck, local tinkerers built support shelves where each officer stows his Kevlar Fritz helmet and Kevlar tactical assault vest. "Not only is this a neat and manageable place for each of us to store our gear," boasts Vinny Martinez, proud of the innovative thought behind the process, "but the vests also provide us with an added measure of protection should one of the 'Recalcitrants from Retardville' decide to take a shot at the truck." A secured cabinet at the front end of the truck serves as the unit armory, holding its MP-5s, Glocks with flashlights, and Ruger Mini-14s, and a case at its base holds a DM50 saw and a battering ram. An electronic rabbit tool is stored in a bin across the armory, as is the motor and generator for the Hurst tool. A video player and a monitor sit atop the armory, allowing the officers to affix a video camera somewhere and, on stakeouts, to have the officers watch ongoing surveillance from the bulletproof safety of their revamped bread truck. Police mechanics at CRS also made it livable—a vent, fan, and air-conditioning system was installed to make the inside bearable during the meltdown days of summer, along with a heater so that on long stakeouts in the middle of a subzero New York winter, the officers can manage to do more than get frostbitten fingers while waiting for perps to arrive at a targeted location.

Perhaps the most important aspect of the SWAT truck, as Vinny Martinez likes to point out to just about anyone who'll listen, is that "it looks cool and the chicks dig it!"

Before the team embarks on a hit, the truck's chauffeur will shut off the regular lights, switch to the red internal "combat" lighting, and then cue up a very special piece of musical fanfare: the Isaac Hayes-ish sounds from the short-lived yet always memorable 1970s television show *SWAT*. Sure, the show was campy; sure, each episode had more shootings than a department usually goes through in a year. But it was the first time that national TV had portrayed this new type of police work. Previously, cops had been shown as bumbling patrolmen (*Car 54, Where Are You?*), sexy detectives (*Starsky and Hutch*), and maverick, if unbelievable, lone wolf investigators (*Beretta*). While most of those shows, by today's standards, were terrible, *SWAT,* even though it was inaccurate as hell, was the first of its kind, and, as Vinny Martinez would comment, "it had cool trucks, cool guns, and the chicks loved it!"

Most important, when *SWAT* was on TV, most of the cops currently serving in the A Team were ten-year-old kids, sitting in front of their old sets, drinking Yoo-hoos and eating Ring Dings while watching Hondo Harrelson kick in a barricaded door with little difficulty and the team sniper pick off bad guys with the ease (and freedom) of a guy shooting targets in a boardwalk arcade. It was the kind of Hollywood fantasy that turned kids on and made them aspire to a profession in law enforcement.

So, naturally with an audio tape of "TV Theme Songs from the '70s" purchased at a record store, the theme from *SWAT* is played full-blast inside the truck as the team goes to a hit. The officers, sitting on their benches facing one another, sing along with vigor and joy. It is a surreal scene and a unique sound—especially from the outside, to the residents of the neighborhood targeted for a warrant, as the muffled bad 1970s music and bad voices mix to blanket a stretch of East New York or South Jamaica with unidentifiable noises. After the theme from *SWAT* ends, the next song is from another campy show of explosions and misguided ammo, *The A Team,* with Mr. T and his cast of rifle-wielding madmen. Again, the bad tune is joined by eight bad voices, humming and singing in a motley choir of off-key and sour notes.

Of course, every great performance deserves a fitting finale. After successful hits, precision-run dynamic entries yielding the proper suspects and whatever drugs, weapons, and cash the detectives and investigators were after, the team returns to the trucks where they de-SWAT. Heavy tactical load-bearing vests are removed, weapons are stored back in their bins, and the pulsating rhythms of reggae and the song "Bad Boys," the theme from the TV show *Cops,* is blasted at full volume. It is almost a comical sight, a gray bread truck moving slowly about the vacated streets of Bed-Stuy, East New York in Brooklyn, the Rockaways in Queens, or the University Heights section of the Bronx being the source of an ear-drum-popping serenade of reggae. "Bad boys, bad boys, what ya gonna do, what you gonna do when they come for you . . ."

Hits, though, are deadly serious business, and no matter how much fun Sergeant Spratt's A Team actually has while working warrants, they realize that laughter can turn into terror in the flash of a muzzle blast. Back at their headquarters in Queens, a four-to-twelve begins under the frigid winds from the Long Island Sound and the bone-chilling drops of rain that make elbows ache and knee joints twinge. It's a quiet evening, and no warrants are scheduled. Several officers sit with their mouths wide open as they watch the TV news and hear the 911 tapes of the hellacious shoot-out in North Hollywood between two AK-47-wielding bank robbers and the LAPD. "Shit," one officer comments. "Listen how the cops are calling in a ten-thirteen. They're giving their location, their situation, and the locations of the perps. Here, whenever we heard ten-thirteen, there is screaming, cursing, and never a proper location. Listen to these dispatches. They speak English! Do you think our dispatchers would be that cool and collected?"

The tape of the shoot-out, the close-quarter melee, and the perps' unimaginable firepower daunts the cops at the A Team. As does the conclusion to the bloodletting, a self-inflicted round to the head of one perp and the SWAT officers pulling up, Wild West style, to shoot it out with the second perp in a flurry of 5.56mm and 7.62mm full-auto chaos.

Several of the cops attend to some gun repair. Others are cleaning their Glocks. Perhaps in no other profession on the planet are the words "you never know" more apropos.

The discussion around the table at base is typical NYPD bullshit, the reading material a cross-section between *Hot Rod* and some unique examples of adult reading. Some of the cops are in the gym next door, working out with weights or playing basketball. Other are digging into heaping plates of pasta adorned with marinara sauce and parmesan cheese. By themselves, they are all individuals—each with different interests, goals, and agendas. Once the phone rings or the fax comes up with an agenda, they bond into one cohesive element. "Time to crank up the SWAT tape, Jack!"

The A Team proceeds toward the precinct or task

force headquarters executing the warrant an hour or so before the intended warrant for the TAC meeting. While TAC meetings for hits with regular ESU personnel are sometimes attended to quickly and haphazardly because the cops need to be back on the streets on patrol, A Team briefings are detailed and lengthy. This is the only work they do, and they want to make sure that no one has to be rushed to an emergency room with the unthinkable.

Although Sergeant Spratt's team is pretty much a Two-Truck dominated squad, they deploy citywide anywhere and anytime there is a warrant—from the bowels of the Bronx to the heroin markets of Lower Manhattan.

One Friday in March was a busy day. There were three warrants scheduled for the apprehension team, with several more pending. The team was called in to base in northern Queens early to prepare for the busy schedule at hand and to ready their minds and bodies for the three dynamic entries they'd need to perform. Sometimes the cops on the team prefer not to know about upcoming warrants so far ahead of time, so that their minds can't think about possible dangers and threats. They prefer to get to work, use any down time to check their weapons, run around the nearby track or use the adjacent weight room, and then suit up and just wait for the phone or fax to ring with news of an immediate assignment. "What's worse," a cop in Two-Truck once asked, "getting hit in the face or thinking about getting hit in the face?"

The three hits scheduled for Friday are at three separate corners of the city. The first takes the team to very familiar territory—the confines of Manhattan North and Harlem's notorious 2-8 Precinct. As is always the case, A Team training officers take the SWAT truck and all the equipment to the precinct while the remaining officers follow in the van. SOD radios are monitored just in case. If there is a ten-thirteen that comes over the air, who better to respond than the A Team?

The ride into Harlem, across the Bronx into Manhattan, is uneventful, though a warming of the weather has turned 125th Street into a gridlocked impasse of human waves. "The shit's gonna fly here today," one of the Two-Truck officers on the team comments. "Once the weather gets warm, it's crazy here."

The 2-8 Precinct is a congested and busy house—among the busiest in the city. Landlocked by Central Park, Fifth Avenue, 127th Street, and Morningside Avenue, the 2-8 was once known as the worst precinct in New York City. It is still bad, and today's warrant is for what most crimes are about in Harlem: guns and drugs. The targeted location is on the same block, almost at the identical address, where years earlier the Black Liberation Army had run its campaign of terror against the cops of the 2-8.

Before the briefing commences, the A Team officers race to the vending machines to load up on sweets (each precinct is judged not by the officers in the command but by the goodies in the vending machine), but the cops are having a hard time finding new crisp dollar bills that the machine will accept, and nerves are beginning to fray. "More soda and candy machines are shot up in precincts," one of the cops comments, "than anywhere else in the world." Finally, after jiggling, jostling, and searching the detectives squad for that new dollar bill, several fruit pies and Ring Dings are retrieved and quickly consumed. "Now we can proceed with the hit," one of the officer says as a mustache of powdered sugar covers his own hairy lip.

The sergeant, whose warrant this is, is well known to the men of the team, especially since most worked Manhattan North in Two-Truck. He is known as a fun guy and a worker, someone who makes a mission out of taking guns and drugs off the streets. As Officer Jack Griffith jots down the details of the warrant for the unavoidable tree stump of paperwork needed for the PD bureaucracy, scores of plainclothes officers enter the squad room. These cops are beefy, wearing sweatshirts, jeans, and shamrock tattoos, and look as though there is little that scared or intimidated them. Dozens of uniformed officers are present as well, all making mental notations and preparing for the dangerous work at hand.

"There are two apartments to be hit in the targeted location on Seventh Avenue and 119th Street," the sergeant explains to the assembly as the duty captain looks on. "The first apartment is where the drugs are sold, and the second apartment where they store the shit." Diagrams are quickly handed out, but the emergency cops know from experience that trusting a diagram is dangerous. They'll rely on the instinct and fast-moving wit they have relied on for years.

"Any puppies in the apartment?" Sergeant Spratt asks. "Any kids?"

"None, Sarge," the warrant officer replies. "Or at least none that we've seen."

"Any guns?" one of the A Team officers asks.

"We need to assume that there are guns there, though what type we can't tell you for sure."

One of the dangers in a hit involves miscommunication and one side not knowing how the other operates. "If the apartment door is open, do not go inside," Sergeant Spratt tells the assembled cops, hoping to avoid the unpleasant and possibly lethal scenario of having plainclothes officers, the color of the day not visible, walking around an apartment with their guns out as ESU bursts in. "Also, we will not follow the perps outside the apartment. If they run out the windows, they are yours. We handle everything inside the location. You guys handle everything outside."

After the briefing, which is truly brief, the A Team assembles in the rear of the SWAT truck to suit up. So that outsiders cannot see what they are doing, the doors are shut, and body bunkers conveniently cover window portals that could allow a passerby a brief glimpse of the type of gear and equipment carried inside the truck. As a result of several unpleasant occurrences on past warrants when the unit sergeants serving the warrants (narcotics, street crime, or SNEU) have given out a wrong address or apartment number, resulting in the cops bursting through the front door of a little old lady eating her cereal, the team makes a point of always having an officer, preferably a supervisor, come in the SWAT truck for the ride-along. The ride-along isn't for companionship or to add another voice to the choir; it is for the officer in charge of the warrant personally to finger the location to be hit. Some of the precinct duty captains, lieutenants, or sergeants are not too excited by the tactical aspect of the work, though others get, in the vernacular, "a big hard-on" just getting to ride in the truck. One sergeant in the 4-6 Precinct in the Bronx has even managed to obtain his own Fritz helmet. Why shouldn't he? Hits are almost a daily occurrence in the notorious 4-6. On this day, to keep their record clean, the 2-8 anticrime sergeant lead assumes his rightful seat next to Jack Griffith in the front of the truck. This way, in case the wrong door or building is hit, it isn't the ESU supervisor who ends up being called on the carpet for the mistake. The one thing that the unit tries to avoid at all costs is entering an apartment with guns at the ready only to find that it's the wrong location.

The ride from the stationhouse to the targeted location takes all of three minutes. It is a convoy led by the SWAT truck, consisting of several marked cars, a few unmarked Chevy Caprices, and the duty captain's car. It takes a lot of police cars to serve such a warrant. Plainclothes officers need to be deployed outside to arrest lookouts, uniformed cops provide security (so that residents, angry that the pharmacy has been closed, don't take matters into their own hands), and additional cops secure escape routes in rear alleyways. A hit is, in the ESU vernacular, a big megillah.

The 2-8 sergeant is immediately amused by the sounds of the TV show *SWAT* being played at high decibels, as he is amused by the fist-pounding prehit choreography going on in the back of the truck. The officers pound the clenched fists of the cops sitting next to them in a sign of moral support and tactical cohesiveness. Sergeant Spratt, in what is now tradition, removes his heavy-duty flashlight and whacks Officer Vinny Martinez over the head for good luck.

"Sarge," one officer comments. "You know that hitting the retarded is not nice!"

"Hey, Sarge," Martinez replies. "I'm not retarded, I'm special!"

Humor before a hit, even at someone's expense, is healthy. When the truck cops perform a hit, there is usually little time to enjoy a few seconds of tension-relieving laughter. The cops are usually standing, very uncomfortably, in the back of the big truck, and they are thinking just as much about getting back to patrol and possibly picking up a pin job as they are about the location they are about to tactically enter.

The officers sit in the order by which they'll exit the truck. Roger Mack and Ronnie Bauman, the bunker men, armed with Glocks with flashlight attachments, exit first. Derek Dunston and Vinny Martinez, with the MP-5s, exit second. Sergeant Spratt and Jerome Kazlauskus, the commander and the tool man, exit third. And John D'Allara, the rabbit tool entry man, and Jack Griffith, rear security, exit last. Before the truck pulls up at the targeted corner, before the tires stop rolling, the door will swing open, and the officers will head out in a high-speed race toward the unknown.

This hit is no different. Plainclothes anticrime officers have already arrested lookouts and buyers standing outside the building. Uniformed officers are keeping curious crowds at bay, and ESU's A Team is busy surrounding the first-floor apartment's fortified door. As the team lines up, ready for whatever might be behind the door, Officer D'Allara slides the rabbit tool's metal teeth through a small crack separating the door from its frame and then allows the battery-operated machine to spread a slot between the two so that Kaz, the tool man, can use his large size and heavy tools to smash his way through. Once the door is opened, the officers race across each room, shouting, "Police, don't move, stay down!" as they search for perps. Anyone discovered is put down and cuffed. ESU doesn't care about the evidence inside the apartment, only that the bad guys are cuffed and secured and will be in no position to reach for a weapon and harm any of the officers. Each officer will shout out that the room he has entered and searched is secure. Closets are checked, as are the insides of sofas, the bottoms of beds, and any other conceivable and inconceivable nook and cranny that a human being can fit into.

Outside, with his Ruger Mini-14 5.56mm assault rifle in hand, Jack Griffith covers the adjacent stairwell through the sights of his weapon. His job is to secure the E-men inside, and he does so with the determination of a man whose path should not, and most definitely will not, be crossed.

The hallway of the building is a darkened display of paint chips, graffiti, and crack vials, with the nauseating stench of urine (dog or human?) and shit (dog or human?). Inside the apartment, the stench is equally vile. One male suspect has been seized in the living room, and a female has been taken inside the bedroom. A third male, however, was in the midst of, in NYPD terms, "pinching a loaf."

"Hey," one of the officers asks. "Is Shit Boy secured?"

"Yeah, I got him," John D'Allara shouts back, "though someone light a match."

A perp getting the shits is common on hits. Sometimes they'll toss the narcotics down the toilet and then shit on them for good measure. Other times, the bowel movement is genuine. Whatever the situation, it makes for a messy evidence recovery that many detectives would just rather not do.

After the perps are secure and the apartment crowded with detectives, cops, and supervisors, the third-floor apartment is attended to. This time, though, the location is empty.

Less than ten minutes after jumping out of the truck, the A Team cops grab their tools and return to the vehicle to change. As the cops enter their van, an officer raises his MP-5 to a shoulder firing position and covers the windows of the building they are quickly departing. "Sometimes the neighbors get stupid," one of the cop reflects, "and nobody here wants to take a bullet after the hit is done!" After the precinct cops and the duty captain thank them, the cops head back to the 2-8 Precinct to handle some of nature's pressing issues and then to grab their van for the ride to the next hit of the day—a narcotics warrant in Brooklyn. As the officers head down 125th Street toward the Triborough Bridge, one of them says, "Wouldn't it be funny if Adam-Two gets a call for an evidence search to search Shit Boy's load?" Laughter permeates the vehicle, as does a call over the SOD frequency: "Emergency Service Adam-Two, K. In the confines of the 2-8 Precinct, you are requested for an evidence search at 118th Street and Seventh Avenue."

There isn't a dry eye in the van as it heads into Queens for the cross-borough ride into one of the nastier areas of Brooklyn.

The 7-3 and 7-5 precincts are to Brooklyn what Beirut is to Lebanon—a symbol of violence gone mad. Covering neighborhoods that have long since gone to top the FBI's top ten lists, with names like East New York, Bedford-Stuyvesant, and Brownsville, the two precincts have for years been among New York's deadliest. For the A Teams, both Sergeant Urban's steady A Team One and the rotating A Team Two, these two precincts are visited very often. Tonight's warrant for Sergeant Spratt's crew is a narcotics warrant in a housing location. On this A Team, four members are former housing cops, so hitting a project is like strolling down the urine-soaked floors of memory lane. You couldn't be a docile cop working in the projects, one cop once remarked; you had to be a wild man. A look inside the PSA Two stationhouse, and one can see why. Heavily decorated officers, some as burly as an iron girder, walk about joking with one another as they head out on patrol. These cops encounter a dichotomy of Brooklyn's most despotic and their most beleaguered. Housing cops need to have guts of steel and hearts of gold. It is a most difficult beat to master.

PSA Two is located on Sutter Avenue, the main artery of Brooklyn North and the prime narcotics conduit. As the former housing cops search for former partners and old friends, Sergeant Spratt and Jack Griffith discuss business with the Housing Bureau sergeant from the warrant squad that will be leading today's warrant. "It's a drug location, on Sutter Avenue in the Brownsville Houses," the sergeant offers as he checks his paperwork in a small office adorned by dilapidated holding cells, peeling paint, and flickering fluorescent lights.

Just as in the 2-8, Sergeant Spratt goes through his spiel about what everyone's job should be. The duty captain at PSA Two, a tall Irish cop with a chestful of medals, adds some important information. "ESU sometimes uses diversionary devices. If you hear one go off, do not race into the apartment. Also, if you hear gunshots coming from inside the apartment, do not, under any circumstances, race toward the apartment with your weapons at the ready. ESU can handle everything, and if they can't, they will surely let you know."

Inside the SWAT truck, Vinny Martinez and Spratt remove ballpoint pens from their pockets and write, in clear large letters on their left wrists, the address and apartment number of the location they are about to hit. "Just in case the shit hits the fan and I need to call in a ten-thirteen on the radio," Martinez explains. "At least I won't have to fumble around and look for a piece of paper or try and remember it when my mind is concentrating on more desperate thoughts. This way, the hand where I am holding the radio serves as a billboard with all the information I need. And, of course, if I need to call in a ten-thirteen, it means that I've run out of bullets and we are all in deep shit!"

The team continues to suit up and ready themselves

for their two-minute ride east on Sutter Avenue toward the Brownsville Houses. Unbeknownst to most Americans, the Brownsville Houses owns a special place in the history of American sports legends. For it was in those brick-walled towers of poverty that a young Mike Tyson honed his "Eye of the Tiger" instincts by beating the shit out of little old ladies so that he could steal their welfare and social security checks. It is one of the worst projects in the city, situated in one of the worst precincts in the five boroughs.

The targeted location, a first-floor apartment in one of the four buildings that make up the projects, is a suspected narcotics location where crack cocaine is cooked and sold. It is unknown if there are any guns at the apartment, but, as one narcotics officer claims, "drugs and guns go together like hemorrhoids and assholes." The A Team will be especially careful because there are kids known to be in the apartment. Kids are always a dangerous factor in executing a warrant, because they could get hurt, stepped on, or, if their drug-selling parents decide to get stupid, caught in the middle of a shoot-out. Kids make tactical work much more volatile and increase the danger quotient tenfold.

"This is it," the warrant squad sergeant shouts as Griffith grinds the SWAT truck to a stop. As the officers race out of the back of the truck, they glance, if only for a second, at a small photocopied sign purposely taped to the inner walls of the truck. It says, simply, "Through these portals pass the finest men and women of the NYPD!"

There are dozens of people, mainly drug lookouts, hanging around outside the project, and the race to the front door is a precarious one. Inside, a small flight of stairs is negotiated and the apartment reached. For a drug location, the door is poorly fortified, and Officer D'Allara faces little difficulty in having his rabbit tool get the job done. Inside, the shouts of the police are met with the cries of children and the screams of older women. "Why don't you people leave us alone?" a grandmother pleads with one of the cops as she holds a toddler. "Why do you sell drugs?" the cop replies.

Outside the apartment, Griffith peers to his right, up the stairs, aiming his Mini-14 where he thought he heard a suspicious sound, but danger looms from an adjacent apartment. Two possible perps, a male and a female, decide that the middle of an ESU warrant is the ideal time to go shopping. As they open their door, the male clutching something in his pocket, Griffith swings around, raises his Mini-14 into firing position, and politely warns the two to get back inside the apartment and to stay inside until allowed out.

"Shit, motherfucker," the male says with anger in his voice. "I am going outside, and I don't give a shit what anyone says."

Jack Griffith is well over six feet tall and a mighty icon of power—even without the Mini-14. As he moves closer toward the two, finger now caressing the trigger, he says, "Get in your apartment *now* or *else!*" Ronnie Bauman is called in to hoist his body bunker over the door just in case the two decide to aim a shot through the door. People sometimes get stupid when the police come calling. Stupidity can sometimes lead to gunfire, and nobody wants a tragedy to stem out of someone being stupid.

The housing duty captain enters the apartment, and at the sight of the adults in cuffs and the children in the care of some female officers, he searches to see what evidence has been gathered and then thanks ESU for "another job well done." As the team exits the houses, their withdrawal resembles a military departure, something akin to a British patrol in Northern Ireland, more than cops heading back to their truck. Housing projects are notorious for "airmail," the NYPD term for junk tossed off project roofs at cops, and nobody is in the mood to take a brick or a steel plate or a door in the head. As one officer aims his MP-5 at the windows above, the officers quickly depart. Griffith provides cover with his Mini-14 raised at onlookers who are cursing at the cops from the fourth and fifth floors. "Go back in your apartments and shut the windows!" Vinny Martinez yells, his MP-5 hoisted at shoulder level and his eyes focused on the bar inside his MP-5's sights. "Do it now!"

As the officers move toward Sutter Avenue, more housing cops are brought in, as are several FDNY ambulances—just in case. "Let's get out of here," one of the cops says. "This might get ugly."

The unseasonably warm March Friday has made the A Team's trek through the city's largest and most diverse borough an uncomfortable one. "Hey, Sarge," Roger Mack, driving the van, tells Sergeant Spratt. "We need to get some gas. I think I'll stop by the 9-0, they're always pumping."

"Yeah," one of the other cops says. "We also need the song 'No Sleep Till Brooklyn' by the Beastie Boys if we are gonna continually come here for hits."

"Sure," another cop says. "It sounds good, and the chicks dig it!"

Williamsburg is another one of those unique New York neighborhoods. Near Broadway, under the elevated train line, right where the 9-0 Precinct and ESU's Eight-Truck are located, are some of the poorest Hispanic neighborhoods in the city. Mini-sport-utilities, with darkened windows and the pulsating vibrations of rap music played at eardrum-shattering decibels, blanket the neighborhood, as do packs of teenagers out to rob and sell drugs. One or two blocks over, though, and the streets are quiet, though crowded with people from another world and another mindset. Hasidic Jews, the ultra of the ultra-Orthodox, return home from synagogue wearing their black coats, white stockings, and furry *shtreimels* atop their heads.

There is another "hit" a few hours later and not having to hurry takes some tension out of the cops usually "all-business" mindset. The jokes begin to flow freely and with that now-trademark ESU cruel affection. As they drive past a local hospital one of the cops looks at the daunting sight of a major city hospital and comments, "If someone ever tries to take you here, shoot 'em! This hospital kills people like it was going out of style. All the nurses are nasty cows who'll rob you blind, and the stench of pot coming out of the hallways is so strong, you'll never really need anesthesia." Hospitals are important to the E-cops. If they are shot on a hit, they need to know, for their own peace of mind, that the trauma center they'll be rushed to can actually save a life rather than prolong the suffering and the inevitable.

"We once saved a guy who fell on train tracks right across the street from the hospital," one of the cops adds. "And before we managed to get back to base and clean up, we got a phone call from the administrator that the poor bastard was dead. I don't know how or why, but he was a stiff!"

"Maybe they threw him back on the subway tracks," one of the cops adds, his observations getting more than a few chuckles.

At the 8-8 Precinct, inside a stationhouse that looks as if it was built when Teddy Roosevelt was the NYPD's police commissioner, the officers brace themselves for what they hope will be the last hit of the night. Inside the squad room, an anticrime sergeant, wearing heavy-impact rubber gloves, is vouchering a large supply of hypodermic needles confiscated from a hit on a heroin den in Fort Greene. "Don't sit on the needles, guys," the sergeant warns. "It would be a shame to get a virus from a needle when you can get it from a hooker instead."

ESU was early at the 8-8, and that meant that the vending machine, offering such delicacies as Pop-Tarts and Drake coffee cakes, was suddenly bombarded by dozens of crumpled-up dollar bills. As sugar levels were restored and cans of Coke guzzled, a mountain of a man, introducing himself to Sergeant Spratt as the 8-8 anticrime boss in charge of the warrant, came into the room. Although he was ostensibly in plainclothes so as not to be identifiable as a New York City police officer, you'd need to be blind not to recognize this rock of a man as a cop—six feet and change, muscular, a Marine Cops buzz cut, a Long Island smile, and wearing a Notre Dame "Fighting Irish" sweatshirt. How many white men with crew cuts and leprechauns on their shirts walk the ghetto?

Like most warrants these days, the A Team's last hit for the week involves drugs—a first-floor apartment on Grand Avenue used by the occupants, a family of four, as a narcotics supermarket. Nothing really revolutionary in the Fort Greene section, of course, but again the element of kids in the location is a matter of concern to the cops. None of the A Team officers wants to discharge his weapon if it can be avoided, and that apprehension is twice as strong when there are children present. Apprehension isn't a productive emotion when performing a hit. A cop hesitating for even a milli-second, because a kid's toy in the room has him thinking when he should be returning fire, could end up being rushed to the ER "or worse."

Each of the anticrime officers assembled in the squad room wears a blue NYPD windbreaker with the words "NYPD: POLICE" stenciled on the back in big white letters. Each plainclothes officer also wears the color of the day, an article of clothing or band meant to distinguish the cop from a civilian in the hope of avoiding friendly-fire incidents. The color of the day in Brooklyn is red, and many of the cops wear red armbands.

The targeted location on Grand Avenue is an aging, deteriorating, mildew-smelling building held together by iron bars and chipping paint. The apartment, at the far end of a long corridor of black-and-white tile barley illuminated by a twenty-five-watt bulb, is in a precarious spot. Exposed to a stairwell and a boarded-up window, probably where drugs are stored or sold from, the cops going in could end up caught in an ambush of sorts, and great care is taken. One of the officers with the MP-5 shines his weapon-mounted flashlight toward the rear, in possible cover fire position, while Jack Griffith, his Mini-14 at the ready, stands prepared to counter any possible threat to the officers inside.

The door is breached with a little finesse and a lot of strength, and the apartment is entered in typical ESU fashion: "This is the police, get down now, stay down, keep your hands where I can see them!" Some of the adults in the apartment show varying signs of resistance, and a few are grabbed and tossed over pieces of furniture so that they can be cuffed and secured. The kids seem oblivious to the chaos. Obviously, 8-8 anticrime has been there before.

A cracked mirror with cocaine residue is found in the apartment, as is a small bag filled with crack. The hit has been a success. Anticrime, narcotics, and detectives who will sift through the rubble will undoubtedly uncover more drugs, wads of cash, and possibly some weapons.

"It's been a good day," Sergeant Spratt says. "Now let's head back to Queens."

Famished by the multiple hits that have taken up half of their eight-and-a-half-hour tour, the team decides on Spanish food—the kind that sticks to one's ribs. On Broadway, the stores on one side of the street are all adorned by Spanish-language signs, while on the other side one would need a Yiddish-English dictionary to know what's what. As he inhales a bag containing his roast pork, rice and beans, and fried plantains, one of the officers looks across the street, at a matzo factory and its Yiddish sign and says, "Only in New York."

While many hits are relatively small affairs, some are very big deals involving state and federal agencies from the FBI to the DEA. Sometimes the hits are so big that one A Team isn't enough, nor are two or even three. On this night, ESU would need its two A Teams and then some for the take-down of a very dangerous crew.

While Hollywood's depictions of how different police agencies interact always show an open hostility between local and federal authorities, ESU maintains a very good working relationship with the various federal law enforcement agencies working in the city. Perhaps it is because of the close cooperation in the wake of the World Trade Center bombing, or perhaps it is because of the rapport developed in those incredible days of tired eyes and frayed nerves during the papal visit and UN 50. Whatever the reason, the FBI, the Marshals Service, U.S. Customs, and the DEA all enjoy deploying together with the NYPD's Emergency Service Unit. "On this night, the DEA would be in shit's creek if they didn't get along with us," claimed one NYPD officer. "Because we were their heavy-weapons backup against a very mean and dangerous crew."

The U.S. Attorney's office and agents and local cops from the joint DEA-NYPD task force were after a crew nicknamed the "Blue Meanies." The gang of five made a living ripping off drug dealers. Making matters worse, the five posed as cops when they ripped off drugs and cash from local pushers and dealers; the theft of narcotics by violent felons posing as cops was, in the words of Assistant U.S. Attorney Eric Friedberg, chief of the Narcotics Bureau, "an alarming trend not only for the crimes which are committed but because of the collateral damage it does in the public's confidence in law enforcement."

To snare the Blue Meanies, the DEA had set up a dummy warehouse in the Fort Greene section of Brooklyn, where drugs and cash were stored. The warehouse was wired with video cameras and other recording instruments. The moment the crew would enter the warehouse and move in on the narcotics and money, the DEA agents and ESU would move in for the apprehension. The crew favored firearms and was known throughout the Bronx and Brooklyn for its propensity for firepower. Nothing would be taken for granted with this lot.

For the sting and the snare, nearly fifty ESU officers, NYPD detectives assigned to the DEA task force, DEA agents, and their bosses, as well as a small command staff of captains and deputy inspectors, had gathered at a nondescript location in Brooklyn for the TAC meeting. The overall ESU commander was Capt. Ralph Pascullo, and Lt. Richard Greene was in charge of the tactical aspects. Sgt. Tommy Urban's A Team One was responsible for moving in on the drug gang inside the warehouse. Once the DEA signaled them in, the team of veteran officers would leap out of its van and gain entry into the location. Sergeant Spratt's A Team Two would wait outside and handle the lookouts, as well as hinder any attempts by the crew to escape should shooting begin. The shoot-out and chaos from the Bronx Terminal Market was still fresh in everyone's mind—especially Lieutenant Greene's. For him, this was déjà vu all over again, and there would not be any wild car chases or shootouts this time. Sergeant Spratt's team was well equipped to make sure that if the "oh shits" happened, the "oh shits" would not travel farther than an enclosed area around the warehouse. A truck carrying a cargo container (and a Trojan horse with cops inside) was strategically parked at one end of the street, while a flatbed truck driven by ESU was parked at the other end of the block. ESU personnel were on rooftops surrounding the warehouse entrance, equipped with powerful beacon lights and Mini-14 5.56mm assault rifles. DEA agents were ready to block the road with Stinger roadblock spikes. Officers Roger Mack and Derek Dunston were tasked with taking the getaway cars on the street, along with Officers Vinny Martinez and Ronnie Bauman, who were in a Nissan minivan along with several task force detectives. Captain Pascullo, shotgun in hand, was ready to provide backup. "Captains are not supposed to carry shotguns," claimed one of the ESU cops proud to call Pascullo a boss, "but he's a real fucking cop and not a desk jockey. Real cops lead from the front and know when to play boss and when to play cop!"

As the stakeout continued and adrenaline and bile entered the throats of many of the cops, three vehicles slowly turned a corner and pulled up to the warehouse entrance. There was one Mustang, a Lincoln, and a Nissan, and as the crew talked and discussed their plan, Officer Joe Zogby from A Team One observed the group through a small opening in the door of the SWAT truck, fitted with a special commercial door panel for the evening's activities. Zogby noticed the group talking over the heist, and he observed as they removed a weapon from the trunk of one of the vehicles. He also observed as one of the crew unzipped his trousers and urinated on the A Team One truck. One of the Blue Meanies was having bladder troubles. The evening was getting off to an odd start.

Three members of the crew went inside the warehouse, and two stayed outside for perimeter security. The ESU cops were silent though nervous. At any second in the ordeal, wild bursts of gunfire could erupt. Nobody wanted to pull the trigger, and nobody wanted triggers pulled at him. Inside the warehouse, the three robbers quickly and methodically sought out the stash of cocaine and cash. The moment their hands touched the drugs, Lieutenant Greene and A Team One deployed inside. Tossing two diversionary devices for effect, the long line of heavily armed E-cops proved too daunting a gauntlet for even this crew to try to challenge. They surrendered without a fight. Outside, Captain Pascullo led the takedown of the two lookouts, one of whom, it was observed, was armed with a .380 automatic. There were no injuries.

It had been a remarkably good job. Once again, the A Team had come through.

It was a warm April evening in New York City, and Sergeant Spratt's A Team was once again out pursuing its favorite pastime—hits. Anticrime officers in Brooklyn's 6-7 Precinct were waiting for the A Team to arrive in order to execute a warrant on a known drug location, situated only a few hundred feet from the stationhouse. The bad guys, known to sell their dope in front of a two-family residence, were so brazen that they didn't even care that every radio car in the precinct routinely passed their selling spot en route to other jobs. "Thank God the perps aren't smarter than us," an anticrime sergeant once said out loud in Harlem as he listened to a drug seller explain why the fifty vials of crack inside his pants pocket did not belong to him. In Brooklyn, some bad guys were about to find out that overconfidence and stupidity usually meant a nice cold cell at Riker's Island.

In order for the A Team to do the hit, several factors needed to be in place—most importantly, finding the precinct. There are seventy-seven precincts in New York. Cops can find some of them with their eyes closed; others are nameless buildings on nameless streets in boroughs rarely ventured to. For Sergeant Spratt's team, the 6-7 was the latter kind of precinct. Located as far from Harlem as one could imagine, the 6-7 was a real shlep from Queens, and with rush-hour traffic at its usual horror, the trip took nearly an hour. "Are we late?" one of the officers asked his partner. "Naaaah," was the reply. "We're here, aren't we?"

A retired ESU lieutenant once commented that coming to do hits in a precinct is like going to your high school reunion—you see a lot of people you don't know and then suddenly a score of familiar faces. The visit to the 6-7 was no different. An anticrime officer who used to work in Harlem's 2-8 Precinct immediately recognized the men of Two-Truck who often backed up his squad on hairy situations, one officer found a former sergeant, and Officer Paddy McGee found an old lieutenant friend of his from the Emerald Society. It was like a giant get-together, but this was in the holding room of a pretty busy house, next to a vending machine emptied of all its goodies and three street whores handcuffed to folding chairs. As Jack Griffith found the anticrime sergeant whose hit this was and the two began to exchange information, a cry of disgust suddenly gained everyone's attention. "Who farted?" Turtleneck blouses were raised over suffering noses, and suspicious eyes gazed across the room, lit by a powerful fluorescent bulb. The suspicious eyes eventually turned to one of the whores, a large lady who looked amused and relieved. "Let's take the TAC meeting upstairs," one of the anticrime sergeants pleaded, "before we are all overcome by the stench."

The drive to the hit took all of thirty seconds. "Location on the driver's side," the anticrime sergeant told Paddy McGee as he carefully swung a right on the poorly lit side street houses away from the location. A convoy of unmarked vehicles and RMPs followed the SWAT truck closely. As the officers clutched their entry tools, MP-5s, and Mini-14s, the squeaking of the brakes and the shouts of "Police, get down!" resonated through the thick Brooklyn air. By the time the rear doors of the truck swung open and the team leaped out, about ten youths, all in the latest perpetrator fashions, were lying on the pavement, arms spread, some with a Glock aimed right behind the ear. "Officer, sir, I am not with these guys, they just asked me for a cigarette," one of the men on the ground pleaded. "I'm innocent." As the tall Irish cop standing over him searched his pockets and uncovered some rolling papers, wads of ten-dollar bills, a beeper, and crack residue, his only response was, "Keep quiet. I talk, and you listen. Think you can handle that?"

The moment the arrests went down, a middle-aged woman in the neatly kept apartment immediately locked her door, hoping that the cops wouldn't be coming in. As McGee peered through the sights of his Mini-14, aiming his weapon at the windows directly above the targeted location in order to cover his team, D'Allara did his magic with the rabbit tool. The door was breached and eventually kicked in. Once inside the apartment, the A Team split up into its well-choreographed sweep of the location. "Kitchen secure!" one E-cop yelled. "Bedroom secure!" The entire place was secured in less than a minute. With all suspects cuffed and anticrime and narcotics detectives readying their gear for a top-to-bottom search of the place, the A Team made like the Lone Ranger and departed with the wind and in a cloud of exhaust smoke.

For the ride back to the 6-7 and the de-SWAT-ing phase of the hit, Paddy McGee decided to entertain the troops with a tape of bagpipe "oldies but goodies."

When gear was returned to its bins and vests returned to their stalls a cop noted, "You could land a space ship here, and nobody would pay attention. Not unless they were out to steal the car stereo!"

"Let's head back to Queens," Sergeant Spratt ordered. "There might be a few more hits down the pike."

Back at their base, the team watched an episode of *Law and Order* (to see how "real" cops solve crimes) and munched pints of Chinese food. As the ensemble began to critique the TV show for inaccuracies and impossible plot twists, Officer Dunston got off the phone with the 6-7 anticrime sergeant with the results of the hit. "They got pot, crack, cash, and some guns," he told the crew. "Plus they got a whole crew locked up." It had been a good night.

16

From the West Bank to West 34th Street: The Empire State Building Massacre

"I've never seen so much blood in my life."
—An EMS rescue worker atop the 86th-floor observatory

It was another Sunday in New York, and in the ten ESU trucks throughout the city and at the field, the talk was of the upcoming visits of President Clinton and Palestinian President Yasir Arafat. Politics mattered little to the emergency cops, but two heads of state visiting the Big Apple would mean overtime, and that was always a popular subject around quarters. Otherwise, the city was quiet.

The SOD radio was *very* quiet on Sunday, February 23, 1997, as the tours changed throughout ESU and yet another four-to-twelve began. There hadn't been too many pin jobs to speak of, not too many gun runs, and the EDPs had been behaving themselves. The weather was chilly yet comfortable, especially with a bright yellow sun showering the city with a warming light. In Ten-Truck in Flushing, Queens, in Six-Truck in Brooklyn South, and in Two-Truck thoughts shifted back to four years earlier and the big job, the World Trade Center bombing. February does that to E-men. It ignites their memories and causes muscles, still aching from the back-breaking work, to flash back.

At 5:15 P.M. the silence of the SOD radio was interrupted by several ear-splitting beeps and the job: "Emergency Adam-One, Boy-One, and Truck-One. Gunshots reported on the eighty-sixth floor at 350 Fifth Avenue. Unconfirmed at this time. U-4, redirect?"

Sgt. Juan Garcia's ears perked up. "Eighty-sixth floor? What building on Fifth Avenue has eighty-six floors?"

Before the old memory banks could be jump-started, instinct told him to get his ass in gear. Gun and utility belts were fastened around his waist, and the Two-Truck chauffeur, Dan Donnelly, raced toward "Big Blue" to fire up the often unreliable engine. By the time both Garcia and Donnelly were sitting inside the truck ready to pull out of quarters, the job came in as confirmed; 350 Fifth Avenue was the Empire State Building, and there had been a bloodbath on the observation deck. February was unlucky for ESU with big-city landmarks.

The ride to West 34th Street from West 126th Street was more like a missile path. Sensing the urgency of the job and monitoring the SOD radio, Garcia and Donnelly could tell that this was not going to be a pretty one. Reports filtered in first as "multiple gunshot victims," then "fatalities," and finally scores of ambulances were ordered. By the time "Big Blue" reached the entrance to the Empire State Building, ten minutes after the job came over, the entire world and his mother was on Fifth Avenue. Officers from One-Truck were already upstairs, shotguns in hand, clearing out the building to look for additional shooters, and aiding the victims, all shot at close range in the head or upper torso; U-4, the city north supervisor, Lieutenant Chris Ellison, formerly of Transit Rescue, was also on scene. Adam-Two, with Steve Vales and Eddie Torres, was eighty-four, as was the Boy-Two car with Joe Ocasio. Manhattan South Precinct officers had quickly roped off the area, Manhattan Task Force cops were cordoning off traffic and creating free access lanes for ambulances racing to Bellevue Hospital with the wounded, and camera and news crews from just about every news organization in the city were broadcasting live. Amid the police lights, flashing cameras, news lights, and pandemonium, it was the true picture of "fucking chaos."

For the cops on the scene, keeping order at ground level was an impossible job. News crews, scuttling amid the chaos like cockroaches underneath a kitchen sink, sought out anyone for an interview or a photo op. Survivors of the shooting scrambled out of the building like refugees fleeing the red hordes. Japanese tourists, some white as ghosts from witnessing a point-blank New York bloodletting, still managed to grasp their Nikons and Minoltas and snap their holiday pictures. "Hey!" a precinct cop yelled at some tourists posing for a group shot amid the madness. "What do you think this is, Tokyo Disney? Get on the sidewalk across the street!"

"It's unbelievable," one of the Midtown South detectives would say when looking at the crowds of tourists assembled on Fifth Avenue gawking, taking pictures, and shooting video. "Haven't they ever seen a multiple homicide before?"

Upstairs, the emergency cops from One- and Two-Trucks saw nothing but a sea of blood. The 86th-floor observation deck, a panoramic temple to the greatest city in the world, was a battlefield. Eyeglasses, cameras, and shopping bags from Macy's were floating in the never-ending sea of red ooze pouring from the dead and dying. One of the emergency cops saw a child's shoe. Another cop gazed, frozen in horror, at a teddy bear soaking up the blood of a victim. EMS crews and emergency cops worked feverishly to save the lives of those shot and those injured in the melee. The body of one young man lay near a viewing stand; he was dead at the scene. A man in his sixties also lay mortally wounded. His gunshot wound appeared to be self-inflicted. A .380 Beretta lay near his hands. He was the shooter.

As cops moved upstairs, and rescuers headed down the eighty-six floors, one question was asked anytime two cops crossed paths: "Did you see the shooter?" It was, after all, the first thing that goes through a cop's head. Who was the perp? Was he white? Black? Hispanic? Asian? Was it a she? Was it a random act? Was it a mugging gone bad? What the hell happened?

First reports indicated the shooter was Hispanic. He had olive skin and a non-Anglo face. There was no reason to suspect anything else.

Once the wounded and the dead were removed from the observation deck, most of the ESU personnel summoned to the shooting decided it was prudent to leave. When the bodies were out and the cameras set up on tripods, it was time for the bosses to mill about, and bosses, on a hairy job like this one, can sometimes lead to a long and painful evening. The mayor was bound to make an appearance, along with the PC and various chiefs and deputy commissioners.

Capt. Pascullo responded from Brooklyn, as did ESU Commander Inspector Harkins. On the 86th floor observatory, Chief Anemone summoned the two ESU and his instructions were clear. Once again, Pascullo was to lead a Manhattan Archangel Package.

Several One-Truck units remained behind, but the cops from Harlem headed back to quarters and, they hoped, a meal back at 126th Street. An act of madness, even in Midtown, could spark copycats throughout the city. "This is might be a wild night," Officer Donnelly told Sergeant Garcia. "Mark my words." As the truck pulled around Amsterdam up 126th Street, the familiar voice of Capt. Ralph Pascullo came over the air. "U-3 to Central, K. Have the following units meet me at 59th and Fifth: Truck-Two, Boy-Four, Boy-Three and the Peacekeeper, Boy-Ten, Boy-Nine, and Boy-Six. Also, have an MLG eighty-five us there along with all available Manhattan North Task Force and Highway units."

"Holy shit!" was all Sergeant Garcia could utter. "What the hell is going on?" Calling all the Boy cars throughout the city to one location in Manhattan meant an Archangel package. It meant preparing for disaster, and it meant that the shooting atop the Empire State Building was not just a routine act of bloodshed 1,250 feet above the island of Manhattan.

"The guy must have been a fucking terrorist," Steve Vales thought as the truck made a brief pitstop back at quarters and Vales and Torres, in the Adam car, prepared to assume patrol responsibilities for One-Truck's half of Lower Manhattan. Even for the Two-Truck cops who made it to the observation deck and walked through the film of blood, the thought of this being a terrorist attack never crossed anyone's mind. "Imagine if this fuck had been a terrorist and strapped a dynamite vest onto his chest. You'd have bodies flying off the roof into the street. Imagine if the fuck had tried to bring down the antenna. Shit. Hey, aren't Clinton and Arafat due in this week?"

"Truck-Two, Central," Sergeant Garcia replied as he attempted to wolf down some of the Colonel's finest drumsticks in a matter of thirty seconds. "Show us responding."

"This is gonna be a big megillah," Officer Donnelly quipped to Garcia as the truck pulled out of its perch and headed toward the West Side Highway. "It's gonna be a big fucking Megillah Gorilla type of evening!"

No matter how hard its detractors might try to knock it, the NYPD is the only municipal police department in the country and perhaps the world that could respond to seven shots fired atop a landmark with the show of force that makes up an Archangel package. Few other departments have the mighty assets. Most other departments don't have the will to display that much force and firepower—most other departments don't have the firepower to display. The rationale behind the Archangel was clear. If this guy was indeed a terrorist, was he acting alone? Would another target be hit later in the evening? Where were his supporters? Where did he come from? After the World Trade Center bombing, there wasn't an NYPD boss worthy of his white shirt willing to downplay the very dire potential of terrorism—even an amateur stupid enough to try to get a deposit back on a truck used as a bomb managed to kill six, wound more than 1,000, and grind a city to a halt.

Fifth Avenue and 59th Street was as far removed from the chaos outside the Empire State Building as could be. It was Sunday night, there was a nip in the air, and the traffic was slow outside the Plaza Hotel. A few horse-drawn carriages galloped by, taxis searched for fares, and tourists emerged from the southeast corner of Central Park eating pretzels and absorbing the view. Sergeant Garcia arrived first at the rendezvous, followed by Boy-Three and Officers Steve Stefanakos and Richie Winwood bringing in the Peacekeeper, Officers Pat Fazio and Tony Favarro from Six-Truck in Brooklyn South, Officers Jimmy Grogan and Ray Butkowitz Jr. from Brooklyn's Seven-Truck, and Officers Phil Isaacson and Billy Fischer from Nine-Truck in the southern half of Queens. None of the cops knew what was going on, and all were more mystified than worried. Captain Pascullo's arrival did little to answer the major questions of who and why.

"Listen, guys," Pascullo told the ensemble of blue uniforms and tired faces. "The mayor, the PC, Chief Anemone, and a lot of other chiefs are still at the Empire State Building, and the squad is still trying to run a make on this guy. All we know is that he had a .380 Beretta, but they are running his prints and trying to come up with a name. We don't know if this was a psycho, a domestic situation gone sour, or somebody with an agenda, but there may be a Middle Eastern connection involved, so here we are. Inspector Harkins was on the scene, and he wants a strong presence in Manhattan ready to fly at a moment's notice. We'll find a spot to gather at the entrance of the park, before the Plaza Hotel management complains, and we'll just sit and wait tight."

For two of the officers that night, it was *indeed* déjà vu all over again. The Boy-Four REP from the Bronx was actually two Queens cops, fly men that night, Officers Glen Klein and Ray Denninger of Ten-Truck in northern Queens. Klein and Denninger were regular partners. They were highly regarded E-men noted for their skills and courage, and they were veterans of a similar night a few years back when someone with a mysterious agenda decided to unload as many gunshots as he could. On Sunday night, December 18, 1994, Wen Ping Hsu, age forty-six, a deranged immigrant from Taiwan, shot and killed his landlord, Chang Ming Lee, in Elmhurst, Queens, and then ventured to the Tung Shing House Chinese restaurant on Queens Boulevard in the confines of the 112th Precinct, where he shot and killed Mr. Lee's wife, Shirley Yim, who was working behind the cash register. Hsu, eager to flee, headed west on Queens Boulevard toward the Long Island Expressway, but he was followed by the restaurant manager David Yuksham. Yuksham was shot in the leg and seriously wounded. Across the street from the restaurant, an officer from the 1-12 was manning a post outside a strip club called Wiggles, scene of neighborhood protests, when he witnessed the shooting. Calling in a "ten-thirteen shots fired" and radioing for backup as he raced across the eight lanes of Queens Boulevard with his service revolver cocked and ready, he followed the suspect into a parking garage, where Hsu was attempting to steal a car. Patrol cars from the 1-12 soon flooded the area, and Hsu took a hostage, Lakhraj Dalipram, firing wildly at the approaching cops as he shielded his body behind his hostage's frame. Police fired back, and Dalipram was killed. Hsu raced deep into the darkened cavern of the garage, lying in wait with a 9mm pistol and a briefcase full of ammunition.

Inside the ground-level garage, Hsu loaded a fresh clip into his Taurus 9mm semiautomatic and fired as precinct cops moved in; 1-12 Precinct Officer Thomas Kohler was hit in the leg and nearly died when a round pierced his femoral artery. Adam-Ten, with Officers Klein and Denninger, was the first ESU unit on the scene. With the explosive fury of a firefight serving as a backdrop, the officers grabbed their shotgun and their ballistic bunker and ventured into the garage, where shell casings and blood littered the floor and the cordite smoke was choking the air. The gunfight inside the garage was hellacious, and unlike anything that had ever befallen that quiet and middle-class section of Queens. "Bullets were hitting everything," Klein told reporters. "It was like being in a tin can. It was an endless gun battle. He just kept shooting." Hsu was cut down by a barrage of police fire as he began firing wild bursts from behind a parked car. In all, an astounding 300 rounds of ammunition had been exchanged; Hsu had brought ten loaded clips with him for his murderous rampage and had been hit nearly fifty times by a combined fusillade of 9mm and 12-gauge ordnance.

To say that numerous rounds were fired by the responding cops that night would be like saying there are a lot of psychos in Bellevue. It would be a gross understatement. Both Klein and Denninger had taken a lot of ribbing because of the number of rounds fired that evening, and both had taken it in stride. Yet the memories were there, and this new act of indiscriminate violence brought their thoughts back to that Queens Boulevard garage in 1994. "It was like a bad Hong Kong martial arts movie, the kind you see on cable," said a Queens homicide detective surveying the scene the following morning as he searched nearby stores for stray bullets. "It was nuts."

"Nuts" is what New York has in abundance. It is a resource it should export (at discount rates), but for some unexplained reason, it seems to import much of its insanity from abroad—especially the violent variety. A deranged psycho who went on a killing spree with a machete on the Staten Island ferry was an import from the Mariel boat lift in Cuba, Hsu was Chinese, and the gunman responsible for the .380 barrage atop the Empire State Building was also from overseas. As the ESU cops assigned to the Archangel package milled about, talked, joked, and waited for the opportunity to sit tight and wait some more, Sgt. Vic Politi, M.D., returned to the staging area to brief Captain Pascullo and the assembled units and to confirm a Middle Eastern connection.

Sergeant Politi, or "Doc" (he is both a cop and a trauma surgeon!) as he is referred to, had just come from the Empire State Building and was happy to be far removed from the chaos and, to use an Italian cop's medical terminology, *"Mishegas!"*

"OK, guys," Politi told the gathering of blue. "The shooter is identified as one Ali Hassan Abu Kamal, a Palestinian male in his sixties. No one knows who this guy is, what he is all about, or if he is part of some other shit that is supposed to come down."

"Hey, sixty years old? What, don't those terrorists get a pension?" one of the officers quipped. "Talk about moonlighting." Hey, he wasn't Santa Claus [a reference to the popular nickname for Sheikh Abdel Rahman of World Trade Center bombing fame]?"

"Naaah," one of cops from Six-truck replied, "Santa is in some federal facility flying his carpet."

"Well, the bosses want us to remain here until they figure this thing out," Politi added. "So I guess we sit and wait."

When cops, especially E-men, hurry up and wait, the assembly looks more like a high school reunion than a gathering of ready-to-go SWAT cops. On a day-to-day basis, most of the cops in a squad never get to see one another unless it's the big job. After all, one group of cops is patrolling and working in the Bronx, another in Queens, another in Brooklyn. The "big ones" are when the cops can shake hands, talk shop, and, most of all, joke around like schoolkids. There wasn't a lot of intellectual banter being exchanged, and very few of the E-men were talking about geopolitical strategy or the latest writings of Professor Stephen Hawking. Instead, they did what cops do better than any other race of people on the planet—they bullshitted. They joked about one another ("his head is so big, he looks like the kid in the movie *Mask*"), about their surroundings (two men holding hands elicited much more than just raised eyebrows), about the love and tenderness existing among cops in the unit ("he is a scumbag and a bastard, and if I see him, I am going to rip him a new asshole"). Just another night in the park.

To keep everyone sharp, Sergeant Garcia sprang for doughnuts and coffee. Standing around doing nothing reduces an E-man's readiness, and Garcia wanted everyone ready to roll, at least with a caffeine and sugar blitz, should the SOD radio summon them to a job worthy of an Archangel response. The fact that the shooter was a Palestinian sparked some concern, and, just for good measure, out of instinct, the cops checked the equipment bins in their vehicles, fired up their REP engines (just in case), and raised the volume on their radios. Should the big job, the second big job of the night, come over, the convoy of REPs, trucks, MLG, and Peacekeeper would be able to respond at a moment's notice, with lights and sirens wailing.

But until that call came, the order of the day was to sit tight and bullshit, the mindless, senseless, unimportant, irrelevant, and jovial bullshit of cops.

By 1:00 A.M., with the shooting now a breaking story on every local station, on the national networks, and on CNN, RAI Italian TV, and the BBC, the order came down for the Archangel package to stand down. Ali Hassan Abu Kamal, the sixty-nine-year-old shooter, was apparently not linked to any organized terrorist groups, not part of any larger plot, and not out to do anything else but commit homicide, suicide, and chaos. New York had once again imported the rejected, dejected, and explosive. Welcome to the Big Apple.

The following day, Mayor Rudy Giuliani and the PC, Howard Safir, elaborated in great detail about the man who had killed and shot eighty-six stories above Fifth Avenue. According to his family, mourning in the Gaza Strip, Ali Hassan Abu Kamal was a schoolteacher, an English professor, no less, who had been despondent over losing more than $300,000, his family's entire life savings, in some back-door investment scheme. He had arrived in the United States on December 24, 1996, and even though allegedly swindled out of the money he had been saving after fifty years of work, he found enough cash to buy a .380 Beretta semiautomatic from a Florida gun shop; he also allegedly had enough twenty-dollar bills on him to become quite the man about town with the local crack whores. Mayor Giuliani was livid about Abu Kamal being able to purchase a gun using only a residency card obtained from the local cockroach-infested motel as proof of his residency in Florida. "That Abu Kamal, who had been in the country only two months, was able to buy a Beretta semiautomatic handgun from a Florida gun shop is totally insane," Giuliani told a City Hall news conference. It was later revealed that three out of every five handguns used in a crime in New York City originate from one of the Southern states, where it is easier to buy a Glock than a Chevy.

Later, the NYPD would reveal contents of a note written by Abu Kamal in which his motives appeared to be less of personal revenge over a lost fortune (evidence of the alleged swindle have never surfaced) and more a bullet-ridden statement of political hate and radical Palestinian nationalism. His note, written in a methodically flowing mix of English and Arabic, accused the United States of using Israel as an instrument against Palestinians, and he expressed bitterness toward France and England.

"England and France," an E-cop would comment while watching the news conference from City Hall at quarters. "What the fuck was his problem? If he wanted revenge, why didn't he just get a hack license, not shower for a month, and drive a cab in the city? He could have killed a greater number of people that way."

Police sources also revealed that the shooting was not the spontaneous act of a madman. Abu Kamal had reconnoitered the observation deck the day before, apparently checking the installation for its security detail and any signs of metal detectors.

The following morning, all visitors heading up to the observation deck had to walk through a metal detector barrier. Hindsight is always twenty-twenty.

The Empire State Building is visible from every borough in the city; its majestic needle can be seen by every truck in every part of the city. When Sgt. Paul Hargrove and the crew at Ten-Truck in northern Queens respond to a pin along the Triborough Bridge, the Empire State is a landmark often gazed upon with awe. When Sgt. John Boesch in Nine-Truck responds to a man in the water near Kennedy Airport, it can be seen from the shimmering waters off the Rockaways. It is visible from the Greenpoint in Brooklyn when Sgt. Marty Garvey responds with Eight-Truck units to a barricaded EDP who speaks only Polish, and it can be seen in all its glory at Fifth Avenue and 116th Street, in Two-Truck territory, when Sgt. Ken Bowen and squad respond to a gun run.

Still, even though the landmark can be seen from just about every corner of the city, its luster has forever been tarnished by the trigger pull of a madman. ESU personnel were never able to look at the World Trade Center in the same way after the bombing. It was a cauldron of destruction and death, not a marvel of architecture and a fixture of the New York skyline. The Empire State Building has joined the twin towers as an icon remembered not by its majesty but by the reflections of lives lost and bodies shattered forever.

Postscript

Tolerant, Tough, and Tenacious: Heroes Like No One Else

•

"You never know when the big job is going to come and bite you in the ass, or where the teeth marks will be from!"

—*Officer Anonymous*

Over the last several years, cops from ESU and Two-Truck have responded to jobs in all corners of the city, and they have been deployed to outer counties, as in the case of a barricaded perpetrator in upstate Orange County; to different states, as in the search-and-rescue effort in Oklahoma City; and even to Puerto Rico, as in setting up emergency assistance following several hurricanes and a natural gas explosion.

On Thursday, March 21, 1996, ESU was summoned to the Westchester Country suburb of Eastchester to respond to a sniper who had ambushed and assassinated a local cop, Michael Frey, who was shot and killed in his patrol car. The gunman, Richard Sacchi, described as a loner and known EDP, had called in a complaint to 911 and then waited for the patrol car to pull up in front of his house. Frey was hit as he was about to get out of his car, cut down by a shot to the chest and several for good measure at his arms and torso. Frey's partner, forty-five-year-old Richard Morrissey, was grazed by a bullet and pinned down by Sacchi's fire near the police car. As Eastchester cops raced to the scene, responding to a job they had never thought could happen in their picturesque community, Sacchi barricaded himself inside the house with his grandmother, taunting responding cops with fusillades of gunfire from his high-powered rifle. A force of about fifty cops, the Eastchester Police Department was ill equipped and ill trained to cope with a barricaded psycho with a scope. The sleepy town had nice homes and manicured lawns—not firefights. Chief James Maher, the Eastchester police commander, sent out the ten-thirteen to nearby departments in a desperate plea for help. ESU got the first call.

Soon after the shots were fired, SWAT cops from the nearby towns of New Rochelle and Greenburgh flooded the area, establishing a perimeter and awaiting the call to action, and within a short time after the assassination of Officer Frey, E-cops from Three-Truck in the Bronx and Ten-Truck in Queens North were in position in the suburb, their MP-5s and Mini-14s locked, loaded, and peering onto the targeted location. The Peacekeeper armored car was brought up to Eastchester, as was the Ten-Truck RMI and even the "tank," the M75 ERV. Senior ESU tactical commanders, like Lt. Richard Greene, were helicoptered up to Westchester County, as were the eagle-eye marksmen of the ESU countersniper team, including Two-Truck's own Officer Ed D'Allasandro. Former E-cop and the commander of the NYPD Hostage Negotiations Team, Lt. Hugh McGowan, also deployed with his unit.

From the moment of gunfire launched at the Eastchester cops, it was clear that Sacchi had access to lethal firepower and a generous cache of ammunition. It was also clear that he had a murderous intent and suicidal rage. The question was, how many more cops was he willing to take down? At Eastchester, overall tactical command was handed to the E-cops from the city.

ESU's first priority was to evacuate the pinned-down officer and to retrieve the lifeless body of Officer Frey. Up until ESU's arrival, Sacchi had, according to witnesses, fired in excess of 100 shots at the cops. The gunfire was deafening, fired in rapid succession, and it lasted nearly two full hours. As the ESU cops readied their recovery plan, in which the Peacekeeper would provide ballistic cover to the evacuation of the two wounded cops, Sacchi's gunfire ceased. Not leaving anything to chance, the E-cops proceeded cautiously in the Peacekeeper, while other cops, moving the large-size ballistic shields carried in the Ten-Truck RMI, rolled the large bullet-resistant bunker between the house and the pinned-down officer. While nearly fifty tactical officers trained their Ruger Mini-14 assault rifles and MP-5 submachine guns on the Sacchi home, covering every window and ready to blow away anything that moved, the officers were removed to safety. Frey was rushed to nearby Lawrence Hospital, where he was announced dead moments later. He was the first Eastchester cop to die in the line of duty. The E-cops also removed the keys from Frey's patrol car, just in case Sacchi had any wild plans about emerging from the house with his weapons ablaze and attempting an escape in the abandoned and shot-up vehicle.

For the next fourteen hours, ESU and Lieutenant McGowan attempted in vain to negotiate with Sacchi. Using bullhorns, they pleaded with him to talk to them. "Pick up the phone and talk to us!" Lieutenant McGowan begged, but after a brief talk at about 9:30 P.M., all the cops heard was loud rock music played at an earsplitting volume. At around 3:30 A.M., after all reasonable attempts to reach Sacchi came up fruitless, ESU went in. First, Ten-Truck's robot, the Andros, went in. Equipped with a mounted video camera, the robot allowed the E-cops to gain a bird's-eye view of the house, called by cops on the scene "the Killing Field." After the robot, NYPD K-9 units went in, followed by a cautious advance of ESU cops. At 5:00 A.M., after fourteen hours of terror, the siege at Eastchester ended.

Inside the house on quiet Morgan Street, cops found Catherine Sacchi, the gunman's eighty-eight-year-old grandmother, dead at the base of the first-floor staircase; she had been ravaged by a 12-gauge shotgun blast to the chest. Upstairs, cops found a .22-caliber rifle and a 12-gauge shotgun in a second-story sunroom, along with a World War II vintage 30.06 Garand rifle. In the rear bedroom, cops found the gunman, dressed in his Sunday best, dead from two self-inflicted gunshot wounds to the stomach. In his room, they found three additional rifles. It had been a long job, far from ESU's usual confines, and one where their skills, tools, and courage helped to save the lives of four local cops.

Four days later, in a small church in Tuckahoe, also in Westchester County, a large contingent of ESU cops joined nearly 10,000 brother and sister officers, some of whom had traveled from as far away as New Hampshire and Washington, D.C., to pay their final respects to Officer Frey. The ceremony was tear-filled and heart-breaking. Frey had been a New York City cop for the Transit Authority, but he had left the dangers of the big city for the peace and quiet of the suburbs.

At the funeral, many of the ESU cops who had helped recover his body wore their dress blues, their white shields, and their chestfuls of medals. They also had tears in their eyes and holes in their hearts. They did all that they could do, but still a cop was dead. Officers from nearby municipalities looked at the E-cops with respect and thanks, grateful that NYPD's finest had traveled far from home to lend a hand.

Eastchester was an anomaly, a big job within immediate response time of ESU's assets in which the unit could make a difference. Sometimes, though, even the biggest jobs come over very close to home.

Spring was coming. It was still cold but getting warmer. A certain scent of future warmth was in the air, and the sun had been shining brilliantly. The second squad was working in Two-Truck, and they were hoping for an easy, uneventful night. There had been hits, perp searches, pin jobs, and some stuck occupied elevators that had been handled. It was the fourth turn of a five-day swing, and bones were getting tired. The warming winds had brought an air of optimism to the streets of Harlem, and the squad, enjoying the temporary peace and quiet of quarters, stood outside greeting officers from the task force next door and just doing what cops do best—bullshitting.

As the sun began to set and hit the elevated train lines over Broadway, an orange glow descended over the Manhattanville Housing Project right across the street overlooking Old Broadway. As the SOD radio began to kick up and jobs came over the air, the REPs and the truck responded to jobs from the northernmost stretch of the island of Manhattan to 59th Street. They were running about like mad. It turned out to be a busy night in Harlem.

Working on Sundays, ESU patrol Capt. Ralph Pascullo often enjoys the quiet of the day of rest to catch up on some paperwork and visit a few of the trucks in the unit. Sundays can be slow, and when there are no meetings to attend, supervisory boards to chair, or other bits and pieces of what a boss does, Pascullo enjoys patrolling the city, being ready for any eventuality, and getting on the SOD radio with the words, "Emergency Service U-3 to central. Show me responding to the job!"

Sundays, however, can also be busy. Not the regular busy of job coming in after job, but busy to the point where even if there were twenty ESU trucks in the city, it wouldn't be enough. Sunday, March 23, 1997, was one such day. At around 8:00 P.M., the Second Squad had made its way back to quarters for a takeout meal and a brief viewing of *The Simpsons.* The SOD radio was quiet, and divisional frequencies weren't summoning the squad to anything at all. Suddenly, without warning, a large explosion blasted the cops off their chairs, causing the table to rock and windows to shudder. "What the fuck was that?" one of the cops commented, racing to put his jacket on and get outside. That blast was no ordinary gunfire and no act of nature. The cops were sure it was a bomb—from the sound and aftershock, they were sure it was the same size as the device that had ripped apart the federal building in Oklahoma City nearly two years earlier. As the cops opened the garage door at quarters, still awaiting the job over the SOD frequency, they saw smoke billowing out of the Manhattanville Housing Project up the block on Old Broadway, and they heard the cries and screams of people who were hurt. There was no need for the dispatcher to tell them where the job was. The big one had happened right across the street.

Racing toward the entrance to the building at Old Broadway and 133rd Street, the E-cops immediately put on their emergency Scott packs. As people were racing out of the building into the rainy street below, the cops raced up the stairs to the fifteenth floor in a mad dash to rescue victims. "The blast wasn't big," one cop commented, "it was enormous. It completely blew out apartment Sixteen-G, the flat decimated by the fireball and subsequent concussion, and the force of the explosion blew the heavy metal door of apartment across the hall inward, propelling them like matchsticks flying at supersonic speeds."

For Detective Medina and crew, the job was simple: assist and aid in the evacuation and emergency medical care of the wounded. The smoke was black and acrid, and the confusion in the hallway immense. For nearly ten minutes, before firefighters arrived, all that stood in the way of calamity and massive loss of life were the six cops working Two-Truck. When FD arrived, the situation wasn't any easier. Many of the firemen, angry that ESU had beaten them to the job, and some even hampered the rescue efforts of the E-cops; one fireman, a notorious supervisor known throughout both departments, even shoved several of the cops. One of the cops went over the SOD radio and informed his supervisors, exasperated and soon to be overcome by smoke, that FD bosses were obstructing the emergency rescue efforts. An ESU boss was needed. Luckily for the residents of the Manhattanville Houses, one was en route.

Capt. Ralph Pascullo was heading toward Manhattan, halfway over the Triborough Bridge, when the job came over as a confirmed explosion. Pushing his unmarked car to its envelope, Captain Pascullo raced toward Old Broadway and 133rd Street, not knowing what to expect—the frantic calls over the air by his cops in Two-Truck were a sobering indication that this job was bad. Having lived through countless emergencies at projects in his twenty-plus years as a housing cop, Pascullo thought he had seen it all, but this was different. Without hesitation, Pascullo launched himself upstairs to help in the rescue effort. The fire was still raging, the smoke had become a lethal cloud of black and gray, and no one was sure if this was a simple gas line explosion or something far more sinister. The *why* would be something for detectives to figure out. The *what* at least for the moment, was to save lives.

No one is sure how many lives ESU saved that night. The blast was too hellacious, the tumult too chaotic. It took the FDNY almost two full hours to extinguish the blaze. At the job, as rescue crews were hard at work, Fire Commissioner Thomas Von Essen made a beeline for Captain Pascullo and the E-cops, offered his hand, and thanked them for a job well done. The E-cops were happy that they could play a small part in saving the lives of hundreds of people rocked out of their Sunday routine. And, the E-cops knew, it could have been much worse. It looks as if the explosion in apartment 16-G was not an accident but rather an orchestrated act of arson-inspired revenge. The perpetrator, one Gary Renelique, had apparently decided to settle a long-standing dispute with his neighbors by disconnecting his stove from the gas line and lighting a candle in the hallway (he claimed it was an accident). The gas fumes filled the air, exploded with the flame, and results could have been catastrophic. It was a miracle that only twenty were seriously hurt.

After the job, an exhausted Captain Pascullo went

over the airwaves and said, "Please thank all units involved for a job well done!" The E-cops knew that they wouldn't be getting their picture in the paper (that honor went to a fireman), nor did they expect their problems with the other city agency to go any further. All they had was the fact that they had done the job, done it quickly, and done it proudly. To an E-cop, that's really all that matters.

For Truck-Two and the entire Emergency Service Unit, as well as the men and women who suit up every day to protect and serve the city of New York, a job well done is what happens day in and day out. They don't just succeed at being the city's force of last resort, they shine in the face of impossible tasks and death-defying circumstances. In the days following the crash of TWA Flight 800, Deputy Inspector Robert Giannelli, the executive officer of the NYPD's Special Operations Division and the city's top cop overseeing much of the rescue effort, told a reporter that the NYPD would be at the scene of the crash until the job was done. That tenacious dedication to the mission of emergency work is the very hallmark of ESU. Today, as the CO of the NYPD's Emergency Service Unit, Inspector Giannelli commands a force of dedicated top cops who are always the first on the scene utilizing their knowledge, their tools, and their guts to get the job done. That dedication was illustrated months earlier, at the funeral of Eastchester Police Officer Michael Frey, by Police Officer Jim Ludwig of Ten-Truck in Queens North, who said of the ESU race against time to aid the shot cop, "I just couldn't leave him there alone."

That dedication, no matter what or where the emergency and no matter how dangerous the circumstances, is what defines the E-cop. In Harlem's Two-Truck and the other nine ESU trucks in the confines of the five boroughs, whenever someone needs assistance, whether it be the victim of a car crash or a cop pinned down by gunfire, ESU will be there. Anytime, anywhere!

The Extremely Unofficial and Completely Off-the-Record NYPD/ESU Truck-Two Glossary

•

Disclaimer to all those in high office or of the politically correct mindset: While some of these police terms, such as radio codes and titles, are accurate and authorized, some of the police slang included here and commonly used by the NYPD and cops in ESU is absolutely unofficial, completely unauthorized, and used solely by Officer Anonymous.

Achnard. A derivative of "Ahmed"; taxi or livery cab driver.

Airmail. Items, ranging in size from a mouthful of spit to a refrigerator, that are hurled off the roofs of housing projects at police officers.

BDF. Big dumb F##!@.

"Big Blue." Affectionate name for the big truck.

Boss. Anyone in command.

BPS. Brain-picking stick; a small wooden stick used to search through a deceased victim's brain or other bodily parts in search of a slug or any other evidence.

Bus. Ambulance.

Camel stop. A livery cab stand.

Car One. The radio designation for Police Commissioner Howard Safir.

Car Two. The radio designation for Deputy Police Commissioner Thomas Kelleher.

Car Three. The radio designation for Chief of Department Louis Anemone.

Carpet stop. When cops stop a livery cab driver for operating a flying carpet without a license.

Cecill B. DeMille. A huge job that turns into a giant clusterfuck.

CO. Commanding officer.

Coney Island whitefish. Used condoms floating in the city's waterways.

CPR. Courtesy, professionalism, respect; a new departmental bumper-sticker campaign to promote goodwill among citizens. In light of how underpaid the cops are, CPR now means "Can't Pay Rent."

Crane. A very large hook in the department (*see* Hook). As in, "Where you gonna try and get transferred to?" "I think I'll go to Harbor." "Harbor? You must have a heavy-duty crane working for you."

DEA. Drug Enforcement Administraiton, and it also stands for Detective Endowment Association.

De-SWAT. That cooling-off period when ESU cops remove their heavy vests and return their heavy weapons to the truck.

Ducks. New York City firemen (*see* Quacks).

DWI. Driving while intoxicated.

DWO. Driving while Oriental.

E-man. An Emergency Service Unit cop. Usually an affectionate or respectful term, as in "He's a good E-man!"

EMS. New York City Emergency Medical Service (now part of FDNY), though it also stands for "Every

Minute Sucks" as a result of their low pay, problems with FDNY hierarchy, and other miscellaneous bullshit.

FDNY. Fire Department New York.

Feds. Federal agent, from ATF, FBI, U.S. Marshals Service, DEA, Customs Service, Secret Service, or INS.

FEMA. Federal Emergency Management Agency.

The Field. ESU HQ at Floyd Bennet Field in Brooklyn.

Five-by-five. When radio transmissions are coming in clear. As in, "Central, K, how ya reading me?" "Five-by-five, K." Poor radio reception is known as "one-by-one."

Flying. When an ESU officer is "flown" from his permanent truck to temporary assignment with another truck in the city. The mode of transportation that brings said officer to and from his assignment is known as the "fly car."

Flying carpet. A livery cab.

Frequent-flyer mileage. Racked up by an officer who, for whatever reasons, does more time flying to other squads than he does on patrol in his parent truck.

Good people. An NYPD term to describe those who are trustworthy, hard-working, and reliable.

Harlem heater. A pot of water placed on a stove's top burner, used to heat an apartment (or the stove in the kitchen at Two-Truck) where the heating isn't working (also good for abandoned tenements), or leaving the oven door open at 700 degrees.

Hasidic cowboys. Hatzolah Volunteer Ambulance drivers.

Hasidic missile. Hatzolah ambulance.

Hemorrhoid. A boss who's being a real pain in the ass.

HH. Hispanic hysteria, an affliction that seems to strike

Hispanic women around crime scenes, accidents, and high-pressure situations. Symptoms include flailing of the arms, gyrations of the neck, rambling in Spanish, and the occasional urge to pass out on a city street.

Hole in the doughnut. The enclave around Columbia University, from Riverside Drive and 111th Street to LaSalle and Morningside Heights, separating the white liberals from the remainder of Uptown and Harlem.

Hook. One's connection and protection in the department. As in, "How'd *he* get into ESU?" "He had a strong hook, one with heavy balls."

Housing enema. Taking a hit of heroin on the roof of a project and the resulting loss of sphincter control.

HNT. The department's elite Hostage Negotiations Team.

IBF. Itty bitty F##!@@.

Ice Station Zebra. The "affectionate" name for Four-Truck in the northwest Bronx.

In the hole. When ESU personnel descend into the depths of a subway station or tunnel while on a job.

Jamaican assault vehicle. A sport-utility vehicle commonly driven by perps.

Launching pad. The roadway leading to the West Side Highway from the George Washington Bridge that seems to launch cars into a spin and a fifty-three pin.

Lieutenant Death. The "affectionate" nickname for a certain Highway lieutenant who, every time he comes on the air, is reporting one roadway calamity or another in which bodies are strewn about like fallen leaves.

Mojo. The Two-Truck mascot, known to sleep most of the day, to snore with the rumblings of a jet engine, and to be capable of eating (as well as vomiting and shitting) until he drops. Also known as "Mojowitz," "Pukawitz," "Ballbagowitz," "Stinkowitz," "Humpowitz," "Vomitowitz," and "The Creature."

Mope. A perp, criminal.

MOS. Member of service.

Mutt. A perp, criminal.

Nut bag. The politically incorrect term for the mesh-net EDP restraining bag used to contain EDPs and nut jobs high on narcotics. Also known as a "burrito bag."

NYMSOG. New York Metropolitan Special Operations Group.

One PP. NYPD HQ at One Police Plaza in Lower Manhattan.

Packin'. When a perp is carrying a weapon.

Paws up. When a perp or a barricaded EDP is found deader than a doornail.

PC. The police commissioner.

PDU. Precinct Detective Unit.

Police Boy. The term in ESU for a young cop in the unit for twenty minutes, who then spends the rest of his career behind a desk somewhere, talking about the terror of being involved in a "barricade" to anyone who will listen.

Puppy. Pit bull.

Quacks. FDNY (*see* Ducks).

REP. Radio Emergency Patrol, the small trucks that ESU units use to patrol their sectors.

Riker's Island syndrome. When a woman, being held hostage by her boyfriend or husband, does not want "her man" arrested, so that she won't have to take the three buses from Harlem to Queens to visit him on Riker's Island.

RMI. Remote Mobile Investigator.

RMP. Radio Mobile Patrol, a blue-and-white patrol car.

Santa Claus. The "affectionate" name for World Trade Center bombing mastermind Sheikh Omar Abdel-Rahman. As in, "We got a detail tomorrow!" "What detail?" "You know, that blind bastard who looks like Santa Claus."

SCU. Street Crimes Unit.

Shabootha. A mythical and anatomically endearing female figure in Manhattan North.

SNAG. Street Narcotics and Gun Unit.

SNEU. Street Narcotics Enforcement Unit.

Soboisms. A derivative of the English language spoken by a now-retired ESU lieutenant.

TARU. Technical Assistance Response Unit.

TCV. Total Containment Vehicle.

10-1. Call command.

10-2. Return to Command.

10-3. Call dispatcher.

10-4. Acknowledgment.

10-5. Repeat.

10-6. Stand by.

10-7. Verify address.

10-30. Robbery in progress.

10-31. Burglary in progress.

10-33. Bomb threat (explosion).

10-52. Dispute.

10-53. Vehicular accident.

10-59. Fire.

10-61. Precinct assignment.

10-62. Out of service—administrative.

10-84. Arrived on scene.

10-90 Nora. Situation normal, false alarm.

10-90 Union. Situation normal, unable to gain entry.

10-90 X-ray. Situation normal, unfounded.

10-90 Yellow. Situation normal, unnecessary.

10-90 Zebra. Situation normal, gone on arrival.

10-91. Condition corrected.

10-98. In service and available for patrol.

That other city agency. FDNY.

Tunnel rat. A police officer working for the Transit Bureau.

U-1. ESU commander.

U-2. ESU executive officer.

U-3. ESU patrol captains.

U-4. ESU city north supervisor (Bronx and Manhattan).

U-5. ESU city south supervisor (Queens, Brooklyn, and Staten Island.)

U-6. ESU city wide supervisor.

Unmarked car. A Chevy Caprice or Ford Crown Victoria used by patrol supervisors (including ESU), street crime units, and detectives.

Urine express. An elevator in a public housing project.

Vest out. Retire after fifteen years.

Welfare mommas. Fifteen-year-old females strolling through the "ghetto" with big gold earrings and a baby carriage.

WFW. Coast is clear. . . .

Whaaaaaa? What ESU cops say when they receive an unintelligible message from the citywide dispatcher.

White man's welfare. A civil service job.

XO. Executive officer.

Yahoo. The "affectionate" name for Israeli Prime Minister Benjamin "Bibi" Netanyahu. As in, "Yahoo, I am finally gonna get some overtime."

Zipperhead. A common name for New York City motorists who decide that a police car in their rearview mirror racing with its lights and sirens on is not cause enough to move out of the way. As in, "Get out of the way, Zipperhead, can't you see my truck says 'Police' and your car says 'Asshole'????"